Clinical Topics in Psychotherapy

Edited by
DIGBY TANTAM

Clinical Topics
in Psychotherapy

GASKELL

Gaskell is an imprint of the Royal College of Psychiatrists,
17 Belgrave Square, London SW1X 8PG

British Library Cataloguing-in-Publication Data
A catalogue record for this book is available from the British Library.
ISBN 1-901242-22-6

Distributed in North America
by American Psychiatric Press, Inc.
ISBN 0-88048-592-2

Typeset by Dobbie Typesetting Limited, Tavistock, Devon
Printed in Great Britain by Bell & Bain Limited, Thornliebank, Glasgow

Contents

Contributors

Dinesh Bhugra, Senior Lecturer in Psychiatry, Institute of Psychiatry, De Crespigny Park, London SE5 8AF

Max Birchwood, Service Director and Consultant Clinical Psychologist, Early Intervention Service, Northern Birmingham Mental Health Trust, 97 Church Lane, Aston, Birmingham B6 5UG

Tom Burns, Professor of Community Psychiatry, St George's Hospital Medical School, Jenner Wing, Cranmer Terrace, Tooting, London SW17 0RE

Jose Catalan, Reader in Psychiatry, Chelsea and Westminster Hospital, 369 Fulham Road, London SW10

Christopher Cordess, Professor of Forensic Psychiatry, The University of Sheffield, Regent Court, 30 Regent Street, Sheffield S1 4DA

Rick Driscoll, Consultant General Adult Psychiatrist, Severn NHS Trust, Park House Community Mental Health Resource Centre, Park Road, Stroud, Gloucestershire GL5 2JG

Paul Garfield, Senior Registrar, Brookside Family Consultation Clinic, Douglas House, 18d Trumpington Road, Cambridge CB2 2AH

Dennis Gath, University of Oxford, Department of Psychiatry, Warneford Hospital, Oxford OX3 7JX

Elspeth Guthrie, Department of Psychiatry, University of Manchester and Rawnsley Building, Manchester Royal Infirmary, Oxford Road, Manchester M13 9BX

Keith Hawton, Professor, University Department of Psychiatry, Warneford Hospital, Oxford OX3 7JX

M. R. Hilton, Consultant Clinical Psychologist, Henderson Outreach Team, Henderson Hospital, 2 Homeland Drive, Sutton, Surrey SM2 5LT

Sheila Hollins, Professor of Psychiatry of Disability, St George's Hospital Medical School, Cranmer Terrace, London SW17 0RE

Chris Jackson, Clinical Psychologist and Honorary Research Fellow Birmingham University, Early Intervention Service, Northern Birmingham Mental Health Trust, 97 Church Lane, Aston, Birmingham B6 5UG

Peter Maguire, Cancer Research Campaign Psychological Medicine Group, Stanley House, Christie Hospital, Wilmslow Road, Manchester M20 4BX

G. C. Mezey, Senior Lecturer and Consultant Forensic Psychiatrist, Section of Forensic Psychiatry, St George's Hospital Medical School, London SW17 0RE

L. M. Mynors-Wallis, St Ann's Hospital, 69 Haven Road, Canford Cliffs, Poole, Dorset BH13 7LN

Rory Nicol, Children and Adolescents' Department, Maudsley Hospital, Denmark Hill, London SE5 8AZ

Anthony Ryle, Senior Research Fellow and Honorary Consultant Psychotherapist, UMDS Guy's and St Thomas's, London

Jan Scott, Professor, University Department of Psychiatry, Royal Victoria Infirmary, Newcastle upon Tyne NE1 4LP

Valerie Sinason, Research Psychotherapist, St George's Hospital Medical School, Cranmer Terrace, London SW17 0RE

Digby Tantam, Clinical Professor of Psychotherapy, Centre for Psychotherapeutic Studies, University of Sheffield, 16 Claremont Crescent, Sheffield S10 2TA

Janet Treasure, Co-Director, Eating Disorders Unit, Bethlem and Maudsley Trust, Denmark Hill, London SE5 8AF

Stuart Turner, Traumatic Stress Clinic, Camden & Islington Community Trust, 73 Charlotte Street, London W1P 1LB and Vice-Dean, University College London Medical School

Preface

Several years ago, while I was an assistant editor of the *British Journal of Psychiatry*, I thought that it would be a good idea for the journal to publish a series of articles about psychotherapy which would be clinically relevant but also evidence-based. These articles are now published together in this volume, supplemented by additional articles on topics which would not otherwise have been covered.

The book has been a long time in its gestation, and the perceived importance of basing clinical practice in evidence has increased greatly during that time. So much so that, for the moment, possible drawbacks of the evidence-based approach as it applies to psychotherapy are discussed by psychotherapists among themselves, but there is still a reticence to sharing these misgivings with other practitioners. With ancestors who sold snake oil in the American West, mesmerised Parisian ladies, and orchestrated colourful and dramatic healing rituals in almost every part of the world, psychotherapists are only too aware of the opprobrium that can surround their work. It is tempting to write that every family has one or two eccentric members, and to remind psychiatrists of insulin-coma therapy or psychologists of the hey-day of Rorschach tests as events in their family history that they may care not to dwell on. However all these interventions met a practical demand, and had practical consequences which were sought after. The fact is that doing nothing if it does not have proven effectiveness is not an option in practice. By the time that a person comes to a mental health practitioner, something usually needs to be done.

The authors of the following chapters were asked to be as practicable as possible, and to anticipate actual clinical situations before considering the applicability of research evidence. The book could be taken simply as a guide to evidence-based practice for the commoner or more challenging clinical conditions in which psychotherapy is clearly indicated. If that is all this book contained, it would add little to the review of the literature recently commissioned by the Department of Health. What the authors of this book do, which the editors of that book were prohibited from doing, is to behave like people do in practice i.e. to consider what constitutes evidence and how evidence can be brought to bear on the individual case, as well as considering what the evidence is. Consider two case examples:

Natalie had Asperger syndrome, a type of autism associated with marked social impairment. Over a period of years, after the birth of a son, she became increasingly socially withdrawn and neglectful of her son, who had to be taken into care. She was admitted to hospital, reported hearing voices, and a diagnosis of schizophrenia was made. She was begun on depot neuroleptics, but her social withdrawal, lack of initiative and inexpressiveness persisted and were attributed to schizophrenia. The evidence in the literature is that: hearing voices is not characteristic of schizophrenia (Ellason & Ross, 1995), social withdrawal is characteristic of depression, schizophrenia is not common in Asperger syndrome but depression is, neuroleptics make the social impairment of Asperger syndrome worse, but anti-depressants are effective in depression comorbid with Asperger syndrome. Given these findings, it was not difficult to think of other evidence that might be looked for, such as the presence of a depressive syndrome, or to decide what treatment to give, since selective serotonin reuptake inhibitors (SSRIs) have been shown to be particularly effective in autistic disorders.

Fred heard a knock on his door one afternoon. He answered to find a distraught neighbour who did not speak, just beckoned. He followed the neighbour across the road and into the neighbour's house where he encountered a scene of horror: the neighbour's husband lying on the floor in a growing pool of blood. Fred did what he could, but it was not enough, and the man died under his hands. Fred became unremittingly anxious. The security of his home was gone, and he expected attack there at any time. He could not work because of intrusive images of the dead man, and because he constantly argued with himself whether he could have saved the man's life if he had done more. Later it emerged that he was also unable to shake off the worry that he might have contracted HIV infection. His general practitioner gave him benzodiazepines and this secured some improvement in his sleep but Fred worried that the tablets might be doing him some other harm.

Fred and Natalie both had a disorder which could be found in ICD–10, both were in altered brain states, and both gained symptomatic relief from medication. Knowing this was enough to help Natalie, but not enough to help Fred. Fred's experience was insufferable because it was so personal. His personal safety was jeopardised, and with it the assumptions about himself and his security which rested on it. The studies which provided the evidence to help Natalie are designed to minimise the effect of individual variation in favour of main effects. For Fred, the relevant study would do exactly the opposite: it would be designed to put how most people behave in this situation into the background, and to consider how Fred is unique and in what unique way his safety has been threatened.

It would, I think, be generally agreed that reproducibility is a key criterion for the former type of study, the sort that would lead to evidence to help Natalie. But there may be less consensus that this type of evidence will not help Fred. Possible arguments in favour of confining evidence to that gained from reproducible studies are that 'at least it is objective'; that the personal is merely a special case of the general; and that the only reliable evidence is the sort that is reproducible.

The 'at least it is objective' approach is often described as pragmatic, making reference to a school of philosophy whose central tenet is that the meaning of something expresses itself in its practical consequences[1]. Its moral justification is based on the consequences of action ('consequentialism'), not on the compatibility of the actions with the rights of the individuals affected (Nagel, 1979). A pragmatic approach to Fred might have included the following elements: asking him to come back in two weeks time (or giving him an appointment for the counsellor in two weeks), knowing that many personal crises have resolved in that time; starting him on an SSRI on the assumption that it may possibly do some good, and would not do any harm; and if Fred has not responded to that after three weeks, changing him to another one, on the assumption that although the mode of action is the same, you never know, some people just respond to the colour of the tablets. Each of these interventions has practical consequences which may be successful – people do respond to placebos or to changes of medication which give hope – but at the cost of misleading patients about what is effective in their treatment. If I believe that I have responded to an antidepressant because it has given me hope, my future strategy for combating depression will be to try to maximise hopefulness in my life. If I believe that I have responded to it because I have an illness for which it has been a specific treatment, I am likely to take a very different view of myself and my future. The 'at least it is objective' approach cannot easily account for these subjective responses, even if they have practical consequences. Following the approach with Fred would not only have reduced his autonomy, which may be a sufficient objection to it for many medical ethicists (Gillon, 1994), but would have in the long run been maleficent, to which consequentialists would also have objected.

Another counter-argument may be that the personal is merely a special case of the general, that Fred is not typical of people who find murder victims, or of people who try to save another person's life, or of neighbours of a person who has been murdered, but that the findings from studies of each of these groups can be put together to make a composite which can be used to typify him. However this argument fails

---

[1]According to the *Oxford English Dictionary*, an older meaning of pragmatic is "2. Busy, active; *esp.* officiously busy in other people's affairs; interfering, meddling, intrusive".

if there is something in the personal attitude that can never be captured in the objective attitude. Natalie did not reflect on herself, and her condition. She did not consider herself the agent responsible for her situation. For her there was no personal attitude to speak of, and therefore the objective attitude was not ill-fitting. Fred was preoccupied with what he did, and whether it was good enough.

Nagel (1979, p. 199), in an essay on the subjective and the objective, writes "Even if an action is described in terms of motives, reasons, abilities, absence of impediments, or coercion, this does not capture the agent's own ideas of himself as its source. His actions appear to him different from other things that happen in the world . . . They seem in some indescribable way not to happen at all . . . though things happen when he does them. And if he sees others as agents too, their actions will appear to have the same quality". Nagel indicates that agents are concerned with whether their actions are right or wrong, not what caused them. Fred's distress was about himself as an agent. It pointed to the central concern that he had – did I do right? Treating his distress impersonally, considering the chain of events which led from over-arousal to hypervigilance to sleep deprivation to an anxiety state, would have been to make it impossible to get to his concern. Considering his personal experience – the sudden nature of the call, the horror of an apparently unstaunchable wound, the sense that behind every door there might lurk the potential for sudden violence – did uncover these concerns.

Medicine and psychotherapy have been dogged by charlatanism and prejudice. The tradition of the study leading to a reproducible finding has been an effective corrective against both these ills but, as with other correctives, the treatment may suppress other, innate, protectives. Without drawing attention to it, the contributors to this book make regular reference to knowledge which is not based on epidemiologically sound surveys or double-blind trials. However I am convinced – and the reader too, I hope – that this knowledge is not based on either artifice or prejudice. Other criteria are available to separate true knowledge from false belief. These evidential criteria include logical criteria such as internal consistency and consistency with other things that I know about the world (validity), but they also include personal judgements. I am biased against accounts which seem to fit in with a person's emotional need to construct the world in some way or another – whether that it is a paranoid or a euhemeristic world view. I am biased against bombast, and what I take to be ignorance. To make these judgements I use the same kind of evidence that I would use when weighing up a new acquaintance. None of these judgements is itself beyond judgement, and I may have to defend them to others, but not my right to make them.

If I am careful I do not accept another person's judgement about a new acquaintance without asking them the evidence on which their judgement is based, and adding some of my own. It is a commonplace that this evidence may turn out to be misleading, and my judgement must therefore be open to revision. However by dismissing this kind of evidence as unreliable, we make two mistakes. The first is that we assume that we can do without it, and the second is that we miss the possibility of improving our use of it. Elsewhere I have argued that the evidence can be made sufficiently reliable for a particular kind of knowledge, which I called practical knowledge, to come out of it. An example that I gave of the practical knowledge of the psychotherapist is that the past can be changed more easily than the future. Fred's experience illustrates this: he came to see that, far from letting his neighbour down, he had done far more than most other people would have been able to. He also had the opportunity to talk to the pathologist who had examined the body and discovered that the wounds that he had tried to staunch were not lethal: there had been an aortic puncture which had bled, invisibly, into the chest.

I believe that the strength of this book lies less in its contributors' constant references to evaluative research but in that other, overlooked, corrective against error, their practical knowledge. I am very grateful to them for their excellent contributions, and for their patience during the many delays in bringing the book to fruition. I am also grateful to Emmy van Deurzen for her comments and encouragement.

Digby Tantam
Sheffield
May 1997

References

ELLASON, J. W. & ROSS, C. A. (1995) Positive and negative symptoms in dissociative identity disorder and schizophrenia: a comparative analysis. *Journal of Nervous and Mental Disorders*, **183**, 236–341.

GILLON, R. (1994) Medical ethics: four principles plus attention to scope. *British Medical Journal*, **309**, 184–188.

NAGEL, T. (1979) *Mortal Questions*. Cambridge: Cambridge University Press.

1 Anxiety and anxiety-related disorders

RICK DRISCOLL and DIGBY TANTAM

Bowlby began an article on anxiety with the statement "Anxiety is protean". That could be modified to read: "Anxiety is ubiquitous, disabling, and protean". Anxiety-related disorders are the most common psychiatric disorders. Epidemiological Catchment Area data found a population prevalence of 7% (Regier *et al*, 1990). Anxiety-related disorders significantly impair quality of life (Markowitz *et al*, 1989) and sufferers from severe anxiety disorders have a risk of suicide as great as for major depressive disorder (Allebeck *et al*, 1988).

Anxiety is common to most mental abnormalities. Even restricting consideration to ICD–10 categories F40–F48 (World Health Organization, 1992), as we shall do, comorbidity is the rule rather than the exception. Over 60% of panic disorder sufferers meet criteria for another concurrent DSM–III–R (American Psychiatric Association, 1987) Axis I diagnosis (Sanderson *et al*, 1989), with a lifetime risk for another Axis I diagnosis of 80% (Andrews, 1990). The most common other lifetime disorders in people with generalised anxiety disorder are major depressive disorder (70%), other anxiety disorders (70%), panic disorder with or without agoraphobia (49%), alcohol abuse (28%) and drug abuse (16%) (Van Ameringen *et al*, 1991). Many anxiety disorder sufferers also meet diagnostic criteria for personality disorder, particularly dependent, avoidant and anankastic personality disorders (Reich *et al*, 1987).

Terminology and classification of anxiety disorders

Fear and anxiety

The Oxford English Dictionary defines fear as "the emotion of pain or uneasiness caused by the sense of impending danger, or by the prospect of some possible evil". Pain and fear are in some sense 'primitive'

1

emotions. Even philosophers are sure that other animals feel them (DeGrazia & Rowan, 1991).

Fear is usually *of* something and anxiety *about* something, while pathological anxiety is often apparently about nothing at all (Kirkegaard, 1960), but these differences are more about how people perceive their anxiety rather than reflecting clinical differences. Intensity and quality do not distinguish normal fear from clinical anxiety and they share many of the same characteristics, including neurobiology.

Worry is driven by the intention to ward off some possible undesirable future consequence, and it becomes chronic when this intention cannot be translated into effective action; fear is associated with the need to escape from some immediate threat or danger. 'Stress' is the term used in both ICD–10 and DSM–IV (American Psychiatric Association, 1994) to denote a state of mind associated with intense fear in which dissociation predominates. This use should be distinguished from the everyday use of the term 'stress' to cover various states of dysphoria.

Physical and cognitive symptoms are used in DSM–IV to distinguish panic disorder, defined as being particularly associated with physical symptoms of autonomic excitation, and generalised anxiety disorder, defined as being particularly associated with cognitive symptoms of hypervigilance. Phobias and obsessive–compulsive disorder, included as anxiety disorders in DSM–IV and with anxiety in 'neurotic, stress-related, and somatoform disorders' in ICD–10, are characterised by avoidance, checking, or other behaviours.

Causes of anxiety and anxiety disorders

Psychodynamic approaches

This approach continues to be dominated by the work of Freud who wrote numerous papers on anxiety, and indeed first recognised generalised anxiety disorder as a distinct syndrome, giving it the name of 'anxiety neurosis'. Freud grafted the theory of thinking worked out in the *Interpretation of Dreams* onto a theory of anxiety. As soon as anxiety was felt, Freud speculated, defence mechanisms dealt with the wishes or impulses that had triggered the anxiety. Freud used the Hobbesian metaphor of the mind as a city (Freud, 1926). In the city-state, social ferment (anxiety) occurs when the government (the ego) does not know what action to take in response to some threat to social order (an id impulse). When the authorities crack down (repression), there is further social ferment (anxiety), and if the revolt is a determined one, indirect ways are found to express dissent e.g. by mounting allegorical plays (i.e. symptoms).

The theory that symptoms are messages which have become systematically disguised – or more technically, that symptoms are signifiers transformed according to the operations of displacement and condensation which leave significance unchanged – is arguably Freud's most influential contribution to psychotherapy suggesting, as it does, worlds of meaning in everyday events and emotional struggles in ordinary lapses of behaviour. It is in agreement with later behavioural ideas that anxious people use strategies to escape from or to avoid uncomfortable thoughts, an idea for which there is also experimental evidence (Freeston *et al*, 1991). Other entailments of the theory are less well substantiated. In particular, there is little empirical evidence that the content of the symptom, decoded along psychoanalytic lines, does give a clue to the exciting stimulus. The content of obsessions is, for example, often of a magical or child-like nature, with nursery fears of catching something, hurting someone, or being found out, well to the fore.

Learning theory

Unlearning has been the mainstay of behavioural approaches to fear management. Arguably the most naturalistic method, habituation, is the basis for the most used clinical method, exposure. Exposure is the "most studied and helpful psychological treatment for PD [panic disorder] with or without agoraphobia . . ." (O'Sullivan & Marks, 1991). Its very success may have extinguished interest in other behavioural methods. However, some, like modelling, continue to be occasionally used, and others remain to be investigated.

Behavioural treatments target unconscious learning processes, in which cognitive factors are also important. Conscious learning plays a large part, too. Fearful beliefs may be triggered by sensations, thoughts, or images. The beliefs then trigger further anxiety producing a spiral of rising fear. The beliefs are often that some catastrophe will occur unless the situation is avoided. They are linked to behavioural avoidance, and thus diminish the likelihood of habituation.

Cognitive processes

Cognitive processes are involved in (1) registration of, and attention to, a fear or anxiety-producing stimulus; (2) determining the degree of danger; (3) initiating a response, or 'coping'. All three processes may be unconscious or conscious (using this word in the sense common to psychoanalysts and cognitive psychologists to refer to learning that can be brought into awareness even though it may normally remain outside it).

Normal thinking may be propositional ('I could die'), but imagery and other processes may also play a part. Cognitive therapy has tended to concentrate, although not exclusively, on propositional beliefs. Other interventions, for example some used in hypnosis and integrative therapies, make more use of non-linguistic imagery.

The components of the anxiety response

It has been one of the great achievements of 20th-century psychology and psychiatry to lay bare the principles of 'conditioning' which determine how anxiety comes to be attached to, or removed from, stimuli of various kinds. However, the universality of anxiety-related behavioural syndromes – obsessions and compulsions, for example, or dissociation – suggests that learning plays a relatively small part, and biology a larger one, in the aetiology of anxiety, and there are many similarities with the behaviours associated with fear in animals. For example, 'paralysis' is a conversion symptom associated with acute traumatic stress in people, and with the freeze response in threatened mammals.

Not all behavioural syndromes associated with anxiety are universal. Some are culture bound, and others are highly individual. Some syndromes are obsolescent, for example, frequent fainting, and 'grand hysteria'. Others are developing; a fear of vomiting is an example.

Anxiety may be associated with bodily changes, cognitive changes, behavioural changes, changes in appetite and sleep, and altered feelings. Thus a particular individual's anxiety response may be a diverse and unique expression of these variables. There is evidence that some are more likely to have cardiovascular responses to anxiety, and others to have gut responses, etc.

The course of anxiety

Infection can be used as a metaphor for anxiety, and we turn to it to illustrate some of the principles by which anxiety may become a chronic disorder. Infection may remain confined, often the case in acute disorders, but it may spread to infect a whole organ or body. Spread takes place along preferred pathways, and is influenced by the risk status of the organism. The original source of infection may heal as the infection takes hold elsewhere, or it may continue to be a source of infection although the metastatic infection may cause the presenting symptoms and may be more dangerous. We argue that each of these phenomena may occur in anxiety, as in infection. Accordingly, chronic anxiety has often spread to involve relationships, self-appraisal, behavioural expectancies, and other aspects of life which may become more important in treatment than the original anxiety. The tendency for anxiety to 'generalise' has to be addressed in treatment, as does the likelihood of the spread of anxiety leading to the anxiety becoming embedded in a person's life – 'consolidation' – leading to a difficulty in relinquishing anxiety which may be interpreted as a 'resistance' to treatment.

Generalisation

Fear pervasively spreads to involve previously neutral objects, situations, or thoughts (Pavlov termed this process 'higher conditioning'). Our understanding of this is that clinical disorders of any duration are not confined to any one aspect of emotional psychopathology. Some of the most difficult patients to treat are those in whom panics may rarely or never occur, because the patient has made avoidance of panic their major concern and developed collusive relationships with people to do so.

Consolidation

The longer that a person has an anxiety disorder, the more likely it is that it will be associated with supplementary, characteristic behaviours or actions. Often there will be a specific concern, or 'phobia', associated with the behaviour. Coping with the phobia also becomes restricted, even stereotyped with any deviation from the coping strategy adopted being itself a potent source of anxiety.

Case example

A racing driver had always had a passion for cars. There was a family history of anxiety, but the racing driver never allowed himself to feel fear: he drove himself as fast and as furiously as his cars. Three years before referral he had a bad crash, and had a number of broken bones. Almost exactly a year after, he had another accident, and although this was much less severe, he experienced an attack of anxiety. Having been someone who always thrived on confrontation, he began to avoid it and worry about it after it had happened. His family, who were used to his dare-devil ways, began to tell him that he had lost his bottle. He became beset by nervous neurotic symptoms and dealt with this by following a ritual when he got up after resting for a certain length of time, taking a tablet, going out to do trivial duties in the garage, and then coming back inside to lie down.

Having once enjoyed parties, he now liked to go to bed at 8 pm, and hated meeting people. He felt constantly frightened and apprehensive of impending disaster. Everything in his life seemed to have reversed.

Other types of consolidation are social, or biological. People alter their lives, and expect others to alter theirs, to accommodate their anxieties. Such social adjustments may, like the neuroses themselves, be anxiety-reducing in the short term but anxiety-maintaining in the longer term. Reassurance seeking is a case in point.

People with anxiety disorders may resort to increased alcohol or substance misuse (Blanchard *et al*, 1993) or may become depressed as a result of exhaustion of their coping strategies. These secondary conditions must be treated before anxiety treatment can be successful.

Resistance to treatment

People with anxiety and anxiety-related disorders do not always respond to treatment as rapidly as their doctors or therapists would like. There are various possible explanations for this 'treatment resistance'. The first is that the patient does not agree with the doctor's explanation of their difficulties, and the type of approach taken. Over-facile explanation, or too symptomatic an approach, can make patients feel dismissed, rather than helped. Many patients do not take anxiolytic medication for this reason. A second reason may be that the treatment is either wrong, or inadequate, or both. A third reason is that the anxiety has some undisclosed maintaining factor, such as sleep deprivation, pending litigation, relationship conflict, threatening circumstance, or substance misuse. A fourth reason might be that a person is unsure whether to give the anxiety up. This reason is usually the one meant when the term 'resistance' is used *tout court*. It is not an explanation that should be used lightly. It stops the search for any other explanation for a failure of treatment response and patients may, rightly, see it as blaming. However, there is no denying that anxiety can, however aversive it is, be better than its alternative.

Immunity

Anxiety-proneness, or conversely immunity or resilience, has a number of determinants. Anxiety-proneness is strongly familial, with contributions from both biology and upbringing. Bowlby has made the greatest contribution to the understanding of early upbringing and anxiety. He emphasised the importance of the maternal relationship in protecting against anxiety. It has been well established that failures of mother–child 'attachment' lead to difficulties for the child, and subsequent adult, in intimate relationships later. Anxious mothers fail to soothe, and are over-protective of their offspring, and so inculcate anxiety in them.

Trauma in childhood

Trauma in childhood affects anxiety-proneness in later years. Clinical experience indicates that trauma which undermines a person's belief that the world, or their place in it, is safe is particularly likely to lead to anxiety.

Immunity to anxiety is variously called 'defence style', 'attachment style', or 'coping style', depending on theoretical background. Interference experiments, in which delay starting on an independent cognitive task following exposure to a fear-inducing word is measured, show the same delay relative to controls in people with anxiety disorders and people without clinical disorder but high in trait anxiety. Macleod (1991) suggested that unconscious appraisal processes influence anxiety-proneness, and that conscious coping mechanisms then determine whether people with high tonic anxiety go on to develop a disorder.

Both attachment styles and psychodynamic formulations of defence styles are descriptions of factors tending to anxiety responses. However, expectations that there would be particular psychological 'organisations' leading to specific anxiety-related disorders have not been realised: there is not an anal personality type which leads to obsessive–compulsive disorder. Most research indicated that there are two 'types': we might label them, as the attachment theorists do, 'secure' and 'insecure' (Vaillant *et al*, 1986; Andrews, 1991). Other dimensions of social behaviour may also influence anxiety-proneness: those that have received some experimental support include blaming others for one's difficulties or blaming oneself, and avoiding others or making social approaches.

Anxiety-proneness is enduring and cannot be expected to be abolished by psychotherapy or otherwise. However, the likelihood of becoming anxious in response to a specific happening can be influenced by training, sometimes termed 'stress inoculation' (Jay & Elliott, 1990). Susceptibility to anxiety disorder is not only determined by trait anxiety, but by other factors, such as coping strategies, in which conscious processes play an important part (Freeston *et al*, 1991).

Implications for psychotherapy are that some degree of persistent anxiety-proneness is likely even in successfully treated individuals. Cognitive or other treatment leading to a change in conscious coping strategies is unlikely to reduce anxiety-proneness, although it may reduce the risk that high levels of anxiety will lead to disorder.

Managing confusion

The complex, overlapping nature of many disorders may make it difficult to plan management and it may be tempting to adopt a blunderbuss approach such as prescribing an anxiolytic antidepressant, or using a non-specific anxiety management programme. It is our view that it is better to break treatment down into stages, particularly as that is often the first step in the reduction of the patient's own sense of 'confusion'. We often say to patients that anxiety is a signal which tells someone that something is wrong, but that this signal value is lost when anxiety becomes intrusive or persistent. We say that there are two main approaches to anxiety-related problems: to find out what has caused the anxiety in the first place, or to concentrate on reducing distress or disability. We stress that these approaches, the exploratory and the symptomatic respectively, can be combined albeit sequentially. Aiming to do both simultaneously muddles the situation. We explain that when anxiety is very great it is not possible to think effectively or to open oneself up to new possibilities and that a symptomatic approach may therefore be an essential first step in a treatment.

In planning treatment we consider whether or not simple treatment of the anxiety itself may be enough. It has the edge on most other treatments (exposure treatment is an exception) in being so simple. Since the least invasive effective treatment is the one that is usually to be preferred, it is sometimes useful to try simple anxiety management first in every patient who is to receive symptomatic treatment, whatever the degree of consolidation of their anxiety.

Simple management of anxiety

The first treatment element is having a clear and meaningful explanation to the patient of their disorder. A very simple intervention at assessment may be enough to help some anxiety disorder sufferers. Similarly self-help has been found to be efficacious (Tyrer *et al*, 1988).

Anxiety management often consists of instructions about breathing, ostensibly to reduce hyperventilation; relaxation training; time management and assertiveness training; and psychological hygiene, including attention to adequate sleep, regular meals, identification of caffeine toxicity, and exercise. Current practice for many anxiety disorder sufferers is to join an anxiety management group which involves a psycho-education component, and training in the simple anxiety reduction measures, such as those mentioned above. Powell & Enright (1990) and Cadbury *et al* (1990) have reported uncontrolled evaluations of anxiety management groups for mixed groups of anxiety disorder sufferers. Both studies found that psycho-education was the highest rated specific factor and universality the highest rated non-specific factor. Relaxation was rated as more effective than cognitive techniques.

Relaxation

Like anxiety management groups, relaxation therapy is a widely applied treatment for anxiety disorders. However, its efficacy and its place in the management of anxiety disorder is less than certain. There are different levels of relaxation therapy ranging from progressive muscular relaxation, muscular relaxation, cued relaxation, applied relaxation and differential relaxation. For a patient to be able to relax rapidly in an anxiety-provoking situation, which is the goal in applied relaxation, they must have developed good relaxation skills. Applied relaxation is thought by some to be a treatment in itself for anxiety disorders. However, it is unclear whether relaxation has any specific effect (Hunt & Singh, 1991). It does have the virtue of requiring a person to make time for themselves. Some patients may experience an increase in anxiety during relaxation.

Breathing control

Hibbert & Pilsbury (1988) found that panic disorder sufferers could be divided into hyperventilators and non-hyperventilators. Hyperventilators tend to have more spontaneous panic attacks, whereas non-hyperventilators have more situational panic attacks. Most hyperventilators reproduce the symptoms of panic disorder on hyperventilation. Both groups responded better to controlled breathing than to psycho-education (Hibbert & Chan, 1989). Salkovskis *et al* (1991) found hyperventilators benefited more from controlled breathing.

The core of all breathing control is distraction, and carbon dioxide enrichment. Breathing needs to be made more inefficient which it can be by slowing respiration, by pausing at full inspiration before breathing out, or by introducing a physiological dead-space, for example by breathing through the nose.

Specific symptomatic treatments

The best validated symptomatic treatments for anxiety are behavioural and cognitive–behavioural psychotherapy. Psychodynamic therapies should also be considered. Hypnotherapy and meditation are sometimes recommended, but there is little evidence of their efficacy.

Panic disorder

Both behavioural and cognitive–behavioural treatment for panic are based on the premise that anxiety diminishes with prolonged exposure to the feared stimulus. The treatment strategy is to reduce avoidance. Swinson *et al* (1992) saw patients for one hour only after presenting to an emergency room with a panic attack. The treatment group in this study were instructed to face fear and specifically the situation they were in when they had their panic attack, while the control group only received reassurance that there was nothing physically wrong with them.

The group receiving exposure instructions did significantly better than the control groups at follow-up. Slightly more structured exposure treatment, using a self-help book, has also been found to be effective for phobias (Gosh *et al*, 1988).

The cognitive element of cognitive–behavioural treatment additionally identifies and challenges the thoughts that anxiety provokes. 'Catastrophic thinking' is an example. One of our patients would have episodes of chest pain associated with dyspnoea when more than a certain distance away from home. These gradually became worse, and began to occur at home, too. He was rarely able to identify the stimulus to his attacks at home, although sometimes he would note that it followed a row with his wife. He was a fit man, but with parents who had died before he was 20 from heart disease. As soon as the chest pain began, he saw himself, in his mind's eye, collapsing with a heart attack and the fruitless attempts of others to resuscitate him. At this point he would begin to panic. Cognitive treatment concentrated on challenging his evidence for thinking that his chest pain was an indication of heart disease, so that he could interrupt the images that intensified his anxiety.

Cognitive–behavioural groups are often used for treatment. Evaluations have however concentrated on individual treatment. In study conditions between 86% and 90% of panic disorder sufferers are panic attack-free at the end of cognitive–behavioural therapy (Klosko *et al*, 1990). Walkowitz *et al* (1991) found that psychopharmacologically oriented clinicians could obtain good results with cognitive–behavioural therapy. Michelson *et al* (1990) found cognitive therapy alone, without the exposure or breathing retraining, to be effective in uncontrolled trials. Psychodynamic psychotherapy may sometimes be useful, often as an adjuvant approach. A man who panicked when his parents were away, and therefore uncontactable, panicked when he was in traffic jams. Much of his life had, in fact, been organised by the need to avoid this and other situations in which he might panic. This man also had a problem with rage – he was very much like his father in this respect – and spent much of his time discussing his anger, usually in connection with his father. This improved his ability to manage his symptoms, and reduced his anger, but did little to change his behaviour.

Generalised anxiety disorder

Hunt & Singh (1991) reviewed five controlled trials of cognitive–behavioural therapy and found it to be both efficacious and the treatment of choice for generalised anxiety disorder, with an effect size of over 2. They emphasised the fact that cognitive–behavioural therapy focused on both the cognitive and somatic components of anxiety in generalised anxiety disorder sufferers. Butler *et al* (1991) carried out a further study where cognitive–behavioural therapy was found to be more efficacious than behavioural therapy. Cognitive factors which perpetuate anxiety include worry and alarm. Since there are rarely situational precipitants to generalised anxiety disorder, behavioural treatments have a less obvious place although exposure, without psychological or 'covert' avoidance, to alarming thoughts is important.

Simple measures such as distraction may be helpful, as may identifying and sharing worries. Worries and alarms gain their force because a person feels that they cannot ignore them. However, they can be discounted if there is evidence to do so. A nurse, a single parent, worried over her ability to bring up her five-year-old son, particularly because she often had to leave him in the care of others when she went to work. She would become so anxious that she would lose her temper, and then would feel that she could not cope. Careful discussion of the sequence of her thoughts showed that she would first feel anxious that she could not deal with him in time to go to work, or would feel irritated with him because he was too demanding. This would make her flustered, but still able to cope. She would then think that he would grow up copying her, and become as anxious as she was. She presented this idea to herself as 'I'm ruining his life because I'm giving him an anxiety problem', and she would then become considerably more anxious. Socratic questioning successfully challenged her negative thought patterns and emotional responses.

Agoraphobia and social phobia

Exposure, and the prevention of avoidance, are the cornerstones of the treatment of phobia. This will usually be sufficient in the case of simple phobias. Agoraphobia and social phobia, however, are consolidated by a system of beliefs and habits, for which the best treatment is currently a cognitive approach coupled with more systematic graded exposure although the latter may produce lasting improvement on its own. When panic disorder coexists with agoraphobia, as it very often does, the cognitive approach used should be similar to that in panic disorder.

Social phobia is often less easy to treat, and more likely to be associated with life-long patterns of anxiety avoidance. Much of the anxiety of social phobia is associated with the mental rehearsal of social situations, and simple exposure to actual situations is therefore usually insufficient. Cognitive changes are usually thought to be necessary for maximal improvement. Cognition and behaviour often interact. A person may, for example, avoid joining other acquaintances during a break at work, and then use the fact that they were not approached as evidence that others find their company distasteful. Social phobia is often sustained by a person's belief that they are manifestly abnormal, or socially unattractive, or both. People may be preoccupied with physical symptoms of anxiety, such as blushing or tremor; with their appearance or body odour; or with their inability to manage social interactions, for example because they are not capable of making small talk. It is often necessary to deal with these beliefs at the same time as a graded exposure programme is being followed. Video-feedback and social skills training may both be useful. Mattick (1990) found between 33% and 37% of patients had improved substantially after such treatment. Public speaking social phobia has a better prognosis as it is less pervasive.

Obsessive–compulsive disorder

Obsessive–compulsive disorder (OCD) is almost as complex, and as protean, as anxiety itself. The presenting symptom is a repeated thought or action which is maintained because it seems to guard against anxiety. Repetitive or ritualistic behaviour appears to be inherently soothing, and is shown by many other groups of anxious people: for example, people with autism, schizophrenia, learning disability, people in institutions, and mammals in cages. The most successful psychological emphasis has been on rituals as a type of avoidance. As is usual with avoidance, the consequence of OCD is that anxiety is heightened and this tends to sustain or even increase the ritualising. Even more importantly a person with OCD develops an idiosyncratic set of anxiety triggers which become invested with immense potential for alarm and which are customarily dealt with by ritualising. It seems likely that these triggers do have some psychodynamic significance, but exploring it is rarely of any value in treatment.

Case report

A radiographer had a serious road traffic accident. She remained anxious and lacking in confidence after her complete physical recovery. She felt that she was treated unsympathetically by her colleagues, especially by her supervisor. She began to worry about picking up an infection in her debilitated state, and took an increasingly scrupulous interest in washing. Her psychological state deteriorated and she went onto the long-term sick. At the time of presentation she was washing her hands about 20 times a day, sometimes in bleach, was changing her clothes and having them washed at least twice a day, and was avoiding any stimuli to immediate hand-washing. By then, these included seeing a nurse, a hospital, a person who had just been to see a doctor, a policeman, an ambulance, or reading the name of an illness in a magazine. Each of these triggers could, she thought, transmit disease to her.

Treatment consists in identifying the triggers and requiring that the patient expose themselves to them, in graded steps, until their anxiety habituates. The trigger may be a happening, or it may be a thought. There is some evidence that people with OCD are particularly intolerant of anxiety, and these triggers are immediately followed by the need to act, without pausing to reflect how serious or how likely the concerns associated with the triggers are. The possibility of harm is usually unacceptable. The second step in treatment is therefore response prevention. The radiographer was, for example, asked to reduce the frequency of her hand washing, and not to take a paper wipe with her when she went out.

When the symptoms are obsessional ruminations, avoidance is 'covert' because it is expressed in a person not thinking or not saying certain things, and there is a more distant relationship with the compulsive thoughts which are often designed to neutralise the trigger. However, the principles of treatment – exposure and prevention of the neutralising thoughts or words – are the same.

Somatoform disorders

Somatoform disorders are discussed in chapter 7.

Conversion and dissociation

These are responses to stress that most if not all people may make, but are the preferred response only in a proportion of people who may be predisposed by upbringing or heredity. Acute onset dissociation or conversion is more common after psychological shock, for example a threat to physical survival or to personal identity. The symptom may sometimes be a dramatisation of an idea: one of our patients developed hysterical blindness rather than open his eyes to his wife's infidelity. Like the other disorders in which anxiety is consolidated, it may not be clear on presentation that anxiety is a cause of either conversion or dissociation. Since both conversion and dissociation are a form of avoidance of subjective anxiety, their persistence also militates against effective treatment.

There do not currently exist any simple measures for blocking these responses. Dramatic cures, which themselves partake of some of the superficiality of hysterical symptoms, are unreliable and often contain an element of coercion. They include catharsis, which may be induced by intravenous medication; social disinhibition which may occur in a religious ceremony, or as a complex startle response to a sudden aversive stimulus; a command by an authoritative person which may be explicit or implicit, the latter sometimes disguised as a comment or interpretation; and hypnotic instruction. None of these treatments is to be recommended.

The most important treatment is to avoid further consolidation of the symptoms which might otherwise occur if the patient's sick or invalid status is increased. Incapacity should be respected, but attributed to stress or psychological factors. The patient's emotions should be carefully monitored, and much greater interest shown in these than in physical symptoms. The links between worsening or improvement of the hysterical symptoms and the patient's personally significant happenings should be noted and discussed with the patient. The therapist should pay constant attention to his or her own attitude to the patient. Trying to outsmart the patient; to trick them into recovery; or to remind patients of their inconsistencies should be particularly avoided. Having a mind that cannot be relied upon or a body that does not work is likely to lead to feelings of inadequacy. Increasing these can only worsen the symptoms. The psychotherapist who has had a personal therapy experience may find these reactions easier to avoid.

It is important to remember that conversion or dissociation may be a way of coping and that their removal without an alternative means of dealing with the underlying stress may result in a worse psychological outcome. Patients may become depressed or acutely suicidal: a further reason for choosing a treatment involving carefully negotiated progress according to an agreed therapeutic contract rather than dramatic symptom removal.

Exploratory treatment

The results of symptomatic treatments are impressive in study populations, but in clinical practice matters are often more complicated. Patients may be distrustful of the therapist, reluctant to trust themselves to a new treatment, or pessimistically convinced that they will never get better. All the therapist's interpersonal skills may be called on to establish a therapeutic relationship.

For some patients, the focus on the relationship with the therapist may lead on to a wish to explore the causes of anxiety, rather than to concentrate on symptom relief. This is particularly likely to be true of patients whose anxiety is not consolidated, whose symptoms are not severe, and who have experienced a recent life event or who are preoccupied by a long-standing concern.

Anxiety that is a consequence of failure in close relationships may be an indication for longer-term psychodynamic, group analytic, or psychoanalytic psychotherapy, but exploratory therapy for anxiety disorders does not necessarily have to be long-term. In many people with recent-onset anxiety there is focus for it – usually a situation which provokes conflicting, and irresolvable, feelings. 'Predicaments' like this can be successfully treated within eight sessions, indeed sometimes much less. Catalan *et al* (1991) used a problem-solving approach and were able to show significant improvement in anxiety in primary care patients treated for 12 weeks when compared with controls.

Coda

Anxiety disorders are highly individual and call for a highly individual response by the psychotherapist. They are debilitating, result in chronic attendance, and often do not respond well to medication. They are the bug-bear of the general practitioner who rarely has the time or training to handcraft a treatment, even for the most expensive repeat attender. It is likely that, in the future, many counsellors will have the responsibility of treating anxiety, and that they will use a mixed approach with elements from cognitive–behavioural and psychody-namic traditions. We support this approach so long as the methods used are carefully integrated with each other, and that the treatment package is developed to fit the needs and wishes of the individual patient. We call this approach 'practical psychotherapy' and have shown that it can be effective even for long-term disorder (Mangold, 1993). Anxiety is about insecurity as well as avoidance, about catastrophising as well as interpersonal conflict. Whatever treatment approach is used, patients will ask how they can cope with their anxiety as well as why they have it. Clinicians must be prepared to answer both of these sorts of questions whether they are analysts, psychopharmacologists, or cognitive therapists.

Acknowledgements

We are grateful to the many patients who have taught us about anxiety. We are also grateful to Emmy van Deurzen who read and commented on earlier drafts of this chapter. The cases referred to are amalgamated and do not correspond to particular individuals.

References

ALLEBECK, P., ALGULANDER, C. & FISHER, L. (1988) Predictors of completed suicide in a cohort of 50 465. *British Medical Journal,* **297,** 176–177.

AMERICAN PSYCHIATRIC ASSOCIATION (1987) *Diagnostic and Statistical Manual of Mental Disorders* (3rd edn, revised) (DSM–III–R). Washington, DC: APA.

—— (1994) *Diagnostic and Statistical Manual of Mental Disorders* (4th edn) (DSM–IV). Washington, DC: APA.

ANDREWS, G. (1990) The diagnosis and management of pathological anxiety. *Medical Journal of Australia,* **152,** 656–659.

—— (1991) Anxiety, personality, and personality disorders. *International Review of Psychiatry,* **3,** 293–302.

BLANCHARD, R. J., MAGEE, L., VENIEGAS, R., *et al* (1993) Alcohol and anxiety: ethopharmacological approaches [Review]. *Progress in Neuro-Psychopharmacology and Biological Psychiatry,* **17,** 171–182.

BUTLER, G., FENNELL, M., ROBSON, P., *et al* (1991) Comparison of behavior therapy and cognitive behavior therapy in the treatment of generalized anxiety disorder. *Journal of Consulting and Clinical Psychology,* **59,** 167–175.

CADBURY, S., CHILDS-CLARK, A. & SANDHU, S. (1990) Group anxiety management: Effectiveness, perceived helpfulness and follow-up. *British Journal of Clinical Psychology,* **29,** 245–247.

CATALAN, J., GATH, D. H., ANASTASIADES, P., *et al* (1991) Evaluation of a brief psychological treatment for emotional disorders in primary care. *Psychological Medicine,* **21,** 1013–1018.

DEGRAZIA, D. & ROWAN, A. (1991) Pain, suffering, and anxiety in animals and humans. *Theoretical Medicine,* **12,** 193–211.

FREESTON, M. H., LADOUCEUR, R., THIBODEAU, N., *et al* (1991) Cognitive intrusions in a non-clinical population. I. Response style, subjective experience, and appraisal. *Behaviour Research and Therapy,* **29,** 585–597.

FREUD, S. (1977) *Inhibitions, Symptoms, and Anxiety* (Original edition 1926). New York: W. W. Norton.

GOSH, A., MARKS, I. & CARR, A. (1988) Therapist contact and outcome of self exposure treatment for phobias. *British Journal of Psychiatry*, **152**, 234–238.

HIBBERT, G. & PILSBURY, D. (1988) Hyperventilation in panic attacks. Ambulant monitoring of transcutaneous carbon dioxide. *British Journal of Psychiatry*, **153**, 76–80.

—— & CHAN, M. (1989) Respiratory control: its contribution to the treatment of panic attacks. A controlled study. *British Journal of Psychiatry*, **154**, 232–236.

HUNT, C. & SINGH, G. (1991) Generalized anxiety disorder. *International Review of Psychiatry*, **3**, 215–230.

JAY, S. M. & ELLIOTT, C. H. (1990) A stress inoculation program for parents whose children are undergoing painful medical procedures. *Journal of Consulting and Clinical Psychology*, **58**, 799–804.

KIRKEGAARD, S. (1960) *The Concept of Anxiety*. Princeton, New Jersey: Princeton University Press.

KLOSKO, J., BARLOW, D., TASINARI, R., *et al* (1990) A comparison of alprazolam and behaviour therapy in treatment of panic disorder. *Journal of Consulting and Clinical Psychology*, **58**, 77–84.

MACLEOD, I. (1991) Clinical anxiety and the selective encoding of threatening information. *International Review of Psychiatry*, **3**, 279–292.

MANGOLD, M. (1993) *Placebo factors as determinants of the efficacy of brief cognitive behavioural therapy. A pilot study.* Unpublished MSc Thesis, University of Warwick, Coventry.

MARKOWITZ, J. S., WEISSMAN, M. M., OUELETTE, R., *et al* (1989) Quality of life in panic disorder. *Archives of General Psychiatry*, **46**, 984–992.

MATTICK, R. (1990) Treatment of panic and agoraphobia: an integration review. *Journal of Nervous and Mental Diseases*, **31**, 163–173.

MICHELSON, L., MARCHIONE, K., GREENWALD, M., *et al* (1990) Panic disorder: cognitive–behavioural treatment. *Behaviour Research and Therapy*, **28**, 141–151.

O'SULLIVAN, G. & MARKS, I. (1991) Follow-up studies of behavioral treatment of phobic and obsessive compulsive neuroses. *Psychiatric Annals*, **21**, 368–373.

POWELL, T. & ENRIGHT, S. (1990) *Anxiety and Stress Management*. London: Routledge.

REGIER, D., NARROW, W. & RAE, D. (1990) The epidemiology of anxiety disorders: the Epidemiological Catchment Area (ECA) experience. *Journal of Psychiatric Research*, **24** (suppl. 2), 3–14.

REICH, J., NOYES, R. & TROUGHTON, E. (1987) Dependent personality disorder associated with phobic avoidance in patients with panic disorder. *American Journal of Psychiatry*, **144**, 323–326.

SALKOVSKIS, P., ATHA, C. & STORER, D. (1991) Treatment of panic attacks using CT without exposure of breathing retraining. *Behavioural Research and Therapy*, **26**, 431–434.

SANDERSON, W. C., RAPEE, R. M. & BARLOW, D. H. (1989) The influence of an illusion of control of panic attacks induced via inhalation of 5.5% carbon-dioxide-enriched air. *Archives of General Psychiatry*, **46**, 157–162.

SWINSON, R., SOULIOS, C., COX, B., *et al* (1992) Brief treatment of emergency room patients with panic attacks. *American Journal of Psychiatry*, **149**, 330–336.

TYRER, P., SEIVEWRIGHT, N., MURPHY, S., *et al* (1988) The Nottingham study of neurotic disorder: comparison of drug and psychological treatments. *Lancet*, **2**, 235–240.

VAILLANT, G. E., BOND, M. & VAILLANT, C. O. (1986) An empirically validated hierarchy of defense mechanisms. *Archives of General Psychiatry*, **43**, 786–794.

VAN AMERINGEN, M., MANCINI, C., STYAN, G., *et al* (1991) Relationship of social phobia with other psychiatric illness. *Journal of Affective Disorders*, **21**, 93–99.

WALKOWITZ, L., DAPP, L. & CLOITRE, M. (1991) Cognitive–behavior therapy for panic disorder delivered by psychopharmacologically oriented clinicians. *Journal of Nervous and Mental Diseases*, **179**, 473–477.

WORLD HEALTH ORGANIZATION (1992) *The Tenth Revision of the International Classification of Diseases and Related Health Problems (ICD–10)*. Geneva: WHO.

2 Psychological treatments for depression

JAN SCOTT

There is robust evidence for the efficacy of pharmacotherapy in the treatment of depressive disorders (Paykel & Priest, 1992). However, patient preferences for non-drug therapies, contraindications to pharmacotherapy, the nature of the presentation (particularly Axis II comorbidity), failure to respond to medication and non-adherence with antidepressants have all contributed to the increased interest in psychological treatments for depression. As well as the need for these alternatives to be cost-effective, Howard *et al* (1986, 1989) identify clinical and pragmatic reasons for promoting short-term (about 20 sessions) interventions. Firstly, at least 66% of the therapeutic gain accrues in the first 20–25 sessions. Secondly, the median number of sessions attended by individuals receiving out-patient psychotherapy in the USA is 14. The need to improve on the 'dose-effect' curve and to work within the limitations of the average length of a course of therapy has focused attention on the so-called 'manualised' therapies for depression, namely behaviour therapy (BT), cognitive therapy (CT), interpersonal therapy (IPT) and brief dynamic psychotherapy (BDP). These are time-limited, 'here and now' therapies that primarily target symptom or problem resolution rather than personality change (United States Department of Health & Human Sciences (US DHHS), 1993). This paper gives a brief update on these treatment models, identifies therapy characteristics that may contribute to efficacy and highlights some questions that still need to be answered.

This paper was first published in the *British Journal of Psychiatry* (1995), **167**, 289–292.

Psychological approaches to depression

Behaviour therapy

The most frequently practised models of BT are self-control therapy (Rehm, 1979) and social skills training (Bellack *et al*, 1983). Most BT packages are derived from social learning theory (Bandura, 1977) which assumes that depression and reinforcement are related phenomena and also that social skills deficits may contribute to the inability to obtain available positive reinforcers and/or cope with adversity (Lewinsohn *et al*, 1982). There are four core elements in BT for depression: functional analysis, daily monitoring and then planning of activities, managing aversive experiences and developing social skills.

Cognitive therapy

At least eight models of cognitive therapy (CT) are described (Scott, 1994), but the most widely researched is Beck's approach (1976, 1983). Most depressed people express 'negative automatic thoughts' about themselves, their world and their future. Beck noted that these negative cognitions are sustained through faulty information processing and so a vicious cycle is set up in which low mood increases the intensity of negative thinking which increases affective, cognitive and behavioural disturbance. These negative cognitions may arise from the re-activation of dysfunctional underlying beliefs. The essential characteristic of CT is its use of a collaborative, 'hypothesis-testing' approach (Beck *et al*, 1979). The acute symptoms of depression are tackled through the use of behavioural and verbal techniques (identifying and challenging negative cognitions). Later interventions are targeted at challenging dysfunctional beliefs to try to reduce vulnerability to future episodes.

Interpersonal therapy

Klerman *et al* (1984) hypothesise that interpersonal problems may be a cause or consequence of depression. Interpersonal therapy aims to reduce the acute symptoms of depression and recognise and resolve associated role impairment in one or more of four problem areas: prolonged grief reactions, role disputes, role transitions and interpersonal deficits. The approach targets current problems and feelings and also aims to reduce relapse. It draws on familiar techniques such as education and clarification plus interventions aimed at improving interpersonal communication and social skills (Cornes, 1990). Given the appeal and efficacy of IPT it is surprising that it is not more widely available in Britain.

Brief dynamic psychotherapy

These therapies are firmly grounded in psychoanalytic principles and the disorder is viewed in terms of adaptive failure resulting from inner conflicts (Strupp *et al*, 1982). Rather than targeting depressive symptoms *per se*, the goal of BDP is to use the therapeutic relationship to clarify and explore neurotic conflicts (such as problems of intimacy or relatedness). Several different brief therapy models have been published (Luborsky, 1984; Strupp & Binder, 1984; Ryle, 1990). The approaches share one or more of the following characteristics (Strupp *et al*, 1982; Worchel, 1990): therapy is focused on a central theme such as loss or separation, early sessions are used to assess and select highly motivated individuals, extensive use is made of transference interpretations, and grief and anger about therapy termination are worked through.

Outcome studies

The majority of psychotherapy outcome studies in depression focus on CT, a smaller number investigate BT and IPT and relatively few examine BDP (Hollon *et al*, 1993; Karasu, 1993; Scott, 1994; Weissman, 1994). Methodological problems such as inadequate sample size are common, but the major flaw in most studies is the lack of a pill–placebo control. The only acute study to rectify this (Elkin *et al*, 1989) was incorporated into the most recent 'intent-to-treat' meta-analysis (US DHHS, 1993). Outcome data from 28 carefully selected randomised controlled trials of group and individual therapy for major depressive disorder were defined in categorical (recovered; not recovered) terms. It was found that the efficacy of individual CT (response rate=50%), BT (55%) and IPT (52%) in the treatment of the acute episode were not significantly different and compared favourably with pharmacotherapy (58%). Brief dynamic psychotherapy was less potent (35%). Whether the lack of a specific depression treatment model or the preponderance of group rather than individual BDP studies had an adverse effect on outcome is unclear. Cognitive therapy is less effective in a group format (39%), BT is equally effective, while IPT may be more beneficial if a 'significant other' takes part.

Data on whether the use of a combination of psychotherapy and pharmacotherapy is advantageous are inconclusive. No studies are available on BDP, and meta-analytic data from eight outcome studies (CT=5) suggest that neither CT, BT nor IPT plus antidepressants are any more effective than pharmacotherapy alone (US DHHS, 1993). However, Hollon *et al* (1993) found a non-significant trend for greater symptomatic improvement (an increment of 15% in absolute terms) in those with more severe disorders receiving a combination of pharmacotherapy and CT as opposed to either treatment alone. There are few adequately designed follow-up or maintenance treatment studies examining the role of psychotherapy in the prevention of relapse of depression. None are available on BDP and there are no maintenance treatment studies of BT. Follow-up studies of BT (Hersen *et al*, 1984; McLean & Hakstian, 1990) and IPT (Weissman *et al*, 1981) do not demonstrate any significant differences in outcome between these interventions and the other psychological or drug treatments with which they were compared. However, there is evidence from a well-designed three year study of maintenance IPT (undertaken at monthly intervals) that IPT alone may significantly delay the onset of relapse in those individuals not receiving antidepressant medication (Frank *et al*, 1990). Blackburn *et al* (1986) undertook a study of maintenance CT (about five sessions in the six months following acute treatment). At two year follow-up, the relapse rate in people who had received pharmacotherapy (72%) was significantly higher than that in people who had received CT either alone or in combination with drugs (22%). Other publications suggest a possible role for CT in preventing relapse (*n*=7), but interpretation is hampered because they consist of naturalistic follow-ups of treatment responders from acute depression studies. An exception is Evans *et al*'s study (1992) which comprises a follow-up of a cohort of people treated in a randomised control trial of CT and pharmacotherapy (Hollon *et al*, 1992). The relapse rate in the CT group (20%) was non-significantly lower than that in the drug continuation treatment group (27%) but was less than half that of the group whose drug treatment was withdrawn when their depressions remitted (50%).

Common factors in effective therapies

Reviewing the IPT, BT and CT models of treatment for depression (BDP manuals are not disorder specific), it is possible to identify certain features that may help explain why they are effective (Zeiss *et al*, 1977; Kornblith *et al*, 1983; Teasdale, 1985; Scott, 1994): the individual is provided with an understandable model of depression; each therapy has a well-planned rationale and is highly structured; plans for producing change are made in logical sequences; therapy encourages independent use of skills to promote change; change is attributed to the individual's rather than the therapist's skilfulness and importantly, the individual develops a greater sense of self-efficacy.

It can be hypothesised that how the client and therapist relate to the model will play an important role. Research confirms that client attitudes and quality (rather than quantity) of therapy significantly influence outcome. The client's belief in the model of depression advocated and their expectation that they will benefit both predict treatment response (Sotsky *et al*, 1991; Scott, 1994). The therapist's level of skill and adherence to the treatment model are also significant factors accounting for up to 30% of the variance in outcome (Marziali, 1984; O'Malley *et al*, 1988; DeRubeis & Feeling, 1990; Hollon *et al*, 1993).

Conclusions

If the client or clinician wishes to pursue a psychological alternative, which therapy is to be recommended? The US DHHS (1993) report suggests that in the first instance clinicians should choose a 'manualised' therapy that has an established record for efficacy in randomised controlled clinical trials. While this is sound advice, the meta-analysis reported earlier suggested that BT, IPT and CT were equally effective. Unfortunately, we do not know whether individuals who respond to one approach will also respond to other interventions. Studies aimed at identifying specific predictors have failed to produce consistent findings (Sotsky *et al*, 1991; Scott, 1994). This is a crucial question for future research, as knowledge about which people respond to which treatment in which particular setting (Clark, 1989) will allow interventions to be targeted more systematically. In the interim, the four most pragmatic considerations are: the severity of the disorder, the individual's preference, the nature of any psychosocial difficulties and the availability of a trained therapist.

In mild to moderately severe unipolar depressions, a psychological or pharmacological approach may be effective and, provided a 'manualised' therapy is available, individual preference may largely dictate choice. If a person with a severe depressive episode (crudely defined by a Hamilton score >21) requests psychotherapy, it should generally be combined with antidepressant medication as the research evidence (although inconsistent) suggests that a 'manualised' therapy alone may not be sufficient (US DHHS, 1993). Specific indications for the use of psychotherapy as an adjunct to pharmacotherapy are under-researched although clinicians identify potential benefits from combined therapies in chronic disorders or in cases with co-existent Axis II or other long-term psychological problems (Manning & Frances, 1990).

The fact that psychological treatments can be as effective as antidepressants in alleviating acute depression is not in itself a reason to extend their use, particularly as time and cost considerations tend to favour the use of pharmacotherapy. Greater emphasis on health gain and relapse prevention may increase the use of psychological treatments and, in this context, the efficacy of IPT and CT as alternative maintenance treatments is noteworthy. However, for psychotherapy to be promoted more actively controlled larger scale research studies must replicate the findings of Evans *et al* (1992). At present, research support for the idea that psychotherapy has a more durable effect is inconclusive, but the potential importance of these results is highlighted by Hollon *et al* (1993). They noted that if the risk of depressive relapse after completing a course of CT is reduced to the same level as that of patients continuing to receive maintenance pharmacotherapy it will be the first time any form of antidepressant treatment has been shown to have an effect beyond the point of termination of the intervention. It would also provide a cogent clinical and economic argument for greater accessibility to 'manualised' treatment models.

References

BANDURA, A. (1977) Self-efficacy: Toward a unifying theory of behavioural change. *Psychological Review*, **84**, 191–215.

BECK A. T. (1976) *Cognitive Theory and the Emotional Disorders*, pp. 47–132. New York: International Universities Press.

—— (1983) Cognitive therapy of depression: New perspectives. In *Treatment of Depression: Old Controversies and New Approaches* (eds P. Clayton & J. Barrett), pp. 265–284. New York: Raven Press.

——, RUSH, A. J., SHAW, B. F., *et al* (1979) *Cognitive Therapy of Depression*. New York: Guilford Press.

BELLACK, A., HERSEN, M. & HARMONDSWORTH, J. (1983) Social skills training compared with pharmacotherapy and psychotherapy for depression. *Behaviour Research and Therapy*, **21**, 101–107.

BLACKBURN, I., EUSON, K. & BISHOP, S. (1986) A two year naturalistic follow-up of depressed patients treated with cognitive therapy, pharmacotherapy or both. *Journal of Affective Disorders*, **10**, 67–75.

CLARK, D. (1989) Cognitive therapy for depression and anxiety: Is it better than drug treatment in the long term? In *Dilemmas and Difficulties in the Management of Psychiatric Patients* (eds K. Hawton & P. Cowen), pp. 52–96. Oxford: Oxford University Press.

CORNES, C. (1990) Interpersonal psychotherapy of depression. In *Handbook of Brief Psychotherapies* (eds R. Wells & V. Giannetti), pp. 261–276. New York: Plenum Press.

DERUBEIS, R. & FEELING, M. (1990) Determinants of change in cognitive therapy of depression. *Cognitive Therapy and Research*, **14**, 469–482.

ELKIN, I., SHEA, M., WATKINS, J., *et al* (1989) National Institute of Mental Health Treatment of Depression Collaborative Treatment Programme. *Archives of General Psychiatry*, **46**, 971–982.

EVANS, M., HOLLON, S., DERUBEIS, R., *et al* (1992) Differential relapse following cognitive therapy and pharmacotherapy for depression. *Archives of General Psychiatry*, **49**, 802–808.

FRANK, E., KUPFER, D., PEREL, J., *et al* (1990) Three year outcomes for maintenance therapies in recurrent depressions. *Archives of General Psychiatry*, **47**, 1093–1099.

HERSEN, M., BELLACK, A., HIMMELHOCH, J., *et al* (1984) Effects of social skills training, amitryptyline and psychotherapy on unipolar depressed women. *Behaviour Therapy*, **15**, 21–40.

HOLLON, S., DERUBEIS, R., EVANS, M., *et al* (1992) Cognitive therapy and pharmacotherapy for depression: singly and in combination. *Archives of General Psychiatry*, **49**, 774–781.

———, SHELTON, R. & DAVIS, S. (1993) Cognitive therapy for depression: Conceptual issues and clinical efficacy. *Journal of Consulting and Clinical Psychology*, **2**, 270–275.

HOWARD, K., KOPTA, S., KRAUSE, M., *et al* (1986) The dose–effect relationship in psychotherapy. *American Psychologist*, **41**, 159–164.

———, DAVIDSON, C., O'MAHONEY, M., *et al* (1989) Patterns of psychotherapy utilization. *American Journal of Psychiatry*, **146**, 775–778.

KARASU, T. (1993) Depression: the relative merits of pharmacotherapy and psychotherapy. *Current Opinion in Psychiatry*, **6**, 184–190.

KLERMAN, G., WEISSMAN, M., ROUNSAVILLE, B., *et al* (1984) *Interpersonal Psychotherapy*. New York: Basic Books.

KORNBLITH, S., REHM, L., O'HARA, M., *et al* (1983) The contribution of self-reinforcement training and behavioural assignments to the efficacy of self-control therapy for depression. *Cognitive Therapy and Research*, **6**, 499–528.

LEWINSOHN, P., SULLIVAN, J. & GROSSCUP, S. (1982) Behaviour therapy: Clinical applications. In *Short-term Psychotherapies for Depression* (ed. A. J. Rush), pp. 50–87. Chichester: Wiley.

LUBORSKY, L. (1984) *Principles of Psychoanalytic Psychotherapy*. New York: Basic Books.

MANNING, D. & FRANCES, A. (1990) *Combined Pharmacotherapy and Psychotherapy for Depression*. Washington: American Psychiatric Association.

MARZIALI, E. (1984) Three viewpoints on the therapeutic alliance. *Journal of Nervous and Mental Disease*, **7**, 417–423.

MCLEAN, P. & HAKSTIAN, A. (1990) Relative endurance of unipolar depression treatment effects: Longitudinal follow-up. *Journal of Consulting and Clinical Psychology*, **58**, 482–488.

O'MALLEY, S., FOLEY, S. & ROUNSAVILLE, B. (1988) Therapist competence and patient outcome in interpersonal psychotherapy of depression. *Journal of Consulting and Clinical Psychology*, **56**, 496–501.

PAYKEL, E. S. & PRIEST, R. (1992) Recognition and management of depression in general practice: consensus statement. *British Medical Journal*, **305**, 1198–1202.

REHM, L. (1979) *Behaviour Therapy for Depression*. New York: Academic Press.

RYLE, A. (1990) *Cognitive–Analytic Therapy: Active Participation in Change*. Chichester: Wiley.

SCOTT, J. (1994) Cognitive therapy of depressive disorders. *Current Opinion in Psychiatry*, **7**, 233–236.

STRUPP, H., SANDELL, J., WATERHOUSE, G., *et al* (1982) Psychodynamic therapy: Theory and research. In *Short-term Psychotherapies for Depression* (ed A. J. Rush), pp. 215–250. Chichester: Wiley.

——— & BINDER, J. (1984) *Psychotherapy in a New Key*. New York: Basic Books.

SOTSKY, S., GLASS, D., SHEA, M., *et al* (1991) Patient predictors of response to psychotherapy: Findings in the NIMH treatment of depression collaborative research programme. *American Journal of Psychiatry*, **148**, 997–1008.

TEASDALE, J. (1985) Psychological treatments of depression: how do they work? *Behaviour Research and Therapy*, **23**, 157–165.

US DEPARTMENT OF HEALTH & HUMAN SCIENCES (US DHHS) (1993) *Depression in Primary Care: Treatment of Major Depression*, pp. 71–123. Depression Guideline Panel. Rockville: AHCPR Publications.

WEISSMAN, M. (1994) Psychotherapy in the maintenance of depression. *British Journal of Psychiatry*, **165** (suppl. 26), 42–50.

——, KLERMAN, G., PRUSOFF, B., *et al* (1981) Depressed out-patients: Results one year after treatment with drugs and/or interpersonal psychotherapy. *Archives of General Psychiatry*, **38**, 51–55.

WORCHEL, J. (1990) Short-term dynamic psychotherapy. In *Handbook of Brief Psychotherapies* (eds R. Wells & V. Giannetti), pp. 193–216. New York: Plenum Press.

ZEISS, A., LEWINSOHN, P. & MUNOZ, R. (1977) Non-specific improvement effects in depression using interpersonal skills training, pleasant activity schedules, or cognitive training. *Journal of Consulting and Clinical Psychology*, **47**, 427–439.

3 Psychotherapy for personality and relationship disorders

ANTHONY RYLE

There are very few psychiatric disorders which are not accompanied by some disruption of interpersonal and social relationships. Winnicott's (1960) statement that there is no such thing as a baby, emphasising that the mother–baby pair was the appropriate unit of observation, could be echoed by saying 'there is no such thing as a patient'. Personality is formed and sustained in a web of human relationships, and this web can both cause and be disrupted by psychiatric illness.

People seek help when they are in conflict with, or damaged or unsupported by, their network, most commonly when close emotionally central relationships are absent or strained. Psychotherapists will seek to help such people understand their own contribution to these difficulties, by working with the individual or with those involved in the troubled relationship jointly. When the individual's contribution seems to be substantial and when it is apparent in a range of relationships of different types, a diagnosis of personality disorder is often applied. In this chapter some of the various forms of therapy available will be discussed; to begin with, the process of referral for therapy and of assessment and diagnosis will be considered.

Referral for psychotherapy

Referral for therapy is a somewhat haphazard affair. The main routes and obstacles are described below.

Primary care settings

A shift in public attitudes to therapy and counselling in recent years has meant that many people who, in the past, might have presented their relationship and personality problems through vague somatic or psychological complaints and who might have been treated pharmacologically, today request or readily accept referral for psychological treatment. Parallel with this change has been an increasing provision of therapy and counselling in general practice settings, involving community psychiatric nurses, social workers, clinical psychologists and counsellors. Other agencies such as 'Relate' and community mental health centres also offer easy access to psychological treatments. However, both the provision of such resources and the referral of patients to specialist psychotherapy centres is very uneven. Morton & Staines (1993) found wide differences in the use made by general practitioners (GPs) of such resources and suggest that specialist centres need both to encourage appropriate referral and to become involved in the training and supervision of workers in primary care settings.

Referral by general psychiatrists

Common factors leading to the referral of people for psychotherapy by general psychiatrists are: (a) relapse in psychiatric disorders evidently related to interpersonal stress; (b) the person's non-compliance with the treatment; and (c) blatantly self-destructive behaviour.

In my experience, people who do not pose therapeutic difficulties (perhaps due to over-compliance) and who are not overtly self-destructive are less likely to be referred, although in many of them personality and interpersonal difficulties or self-provoked life stresses play a large part in their disability.

Psychotherapeutic approaches which address personality as well as symptoms can play a part in treatment and in preventing relapse (Robins, 1993). Psychodynamic assessment of people presenting with psychiatric problems, especially of those with depression, would improve case management and yield suitable cases for psychotherapy.

Liaison psychotherapy

There are many people who display a negative relationship with themselves or with their doctors through their failure to cooperate in the treatment of serious medical conditions. Personality factors and dysfunctional attitudes which, under different circumstances, might be regarded as relatively trivial, can in such cases lead to life-threatening consequences. For example, insulin-dependent diabetic individuals who are poorly controlled are in nearly every case non-compliant with aspects of self-care (Tattersall, 1985) and the reasons for this are usually the operation of disturbed personal or interpersonal attitudes and behaviours (Milton, 1989; Ryle *et al*, 1993). This suggests a role for liaison psychotherapy in a range of conditions in which individuals are required to cooperate with long-term treatments.

Obstacles to referral

Resources

National Health Service (NHS) provision of psychotherapy services is uneven and in virtually every part of the country inadequate, leading to long waiting lists or to low referral rates because of the absence of a responsive service. While increased resources are clearly desirable, existing services could extend their availability if responsibility was defined in terms of population needs rather than the demands of those people actually seen. Thus a service needs to be planned on the basis of a knowledge of the epidemiology of treatable personality problems and the pathways to referral and assessment should be clear. Wherever possible economic forms of treatment should be offered, such as short-term individual or group therapy. Eight people seen in individual short-term treatments or in a two year group need the same therapist input as a single case seen weekly for two and a half years.

Research in the field of effectiveness has largely ignored issues of effective delivery and costing (Parry, 1992). Current changes may put some pressure on services in this respect but seem unlikely to lead to a more equitable distribution of resources.

Referral bias

Proportionately fewer people from working class and ethnic minority backgrounds receive therapy. It is probable that the attitudes of practitioners contribute to this fact. The characteristics listed by Coltart (1988) as being necessary for dynamic therapy are 'intelligence, moral character and money' and even if the last is not an obstacle in NHS practice the other two are social judgements notoriously open to social class bias. Practitioners who are committed to NHS work, who are prepared to examine their own social and linguistic assumptions and who do not expect people to arrive with an informed understanding of the nature of psychotherapy or to be already, in their terms, 'psychologically minded', find that they can work with people from most backgrounds.

Prejudice

Many professionals, perhaps particularly psychiatrists, remain prejudiced against any form of psychotherapy.

Diagnosis, assessment and case formulation

The best current classification of personality disorders is provided by DSM–IV Axis 2 (American Psychiatric Association, 1994) but it remains problematic. Multiple diagnoses are frequent and the discrimination of some disorders from Axis 1 diagnoses and the borders between normal variability, eccentricity and disorder remain blurred, as Stone (1993) points out.

Assessment for personality as distinct from symptomatic disorders remains, however, important. Once psychiatric illness has been excluded, this requires a style of interviewing distinct from the structured, question-and-answer method of formal history taking. The interview should be carried out in an open, exploratory way, encouraging the individual to convey both fact and feelings. The interviewer will note not only the content of what is said, but also the style, the underlying assumptions conveyed, and the direct and indirect pressures exerted as the person evidently seeks or expects particular responses. These aspects will be central to the psychodynamic therapist; the cognitive–behavioural approach will attend less to historical data and to the emerging relationship, and more to tracing sequences of thought and behaviour associated with the person's disturbed relationships.

At the end of the interview most therapists will offer the patient a preliminary understanding of the nature of the problem, and unless further diagnostic interviews are necessary (and possible), the form, frequency and duration of therapy will be negotiated.

In making sense of this material psychodynamic therapists will be concerned with two linked systems. One, the intrapersonal, will be understood in terms of the biological, social and cultural factors which have served to shape the complex, self-contradictory and only partially self-observing individual. The subject's assumptions about themselves and others will be a component of this. The other, the interpersonal, will describe how individuals so constituted seek to mesh their needs and wishes with those of others. A psychodynamic assessment will aim to identify the early experiences which formed the person's personality and defensive structures and to link these with the present life circumstances in a description which will both rely upon and anticipate the relationship with the therapist.

A clear account of one such approach, seeking to link current, infantile and transference patterns of object relations and to identify centrally important distresses and defences, is provided by Hinshelwood (1991).

The resulting formulation, linking the individual's story and problems to the theoretical model, will form the basis on which therapy is planned and conducted. While psychoanalytic case formulations have tended to be rich in detail and speculation but low in reliability, a number of workers in the field of time-limited dynamic therapy have established ways of case formulation in terms of key disturbances which show satisfactory inter-rater agreement. The main examples are Luborsky's 'Core Conflict Relationship Themes' (Crits-Christoph *et al*, 1988), Horowitz's 'Role Relationship Models of Configuration' (Horowitz & Eells, 1993) and Strupp's 'Cyclical Maladaptive Pattern' (Binder & Strupp, 1991).

Integrated models of therapy have made case formulation a central aspect of their approach. Thus Safran & McMain (1992) draw on Sullivan's interpersonal theory and on cognitive therapy to identify 'dysfunctional interpersonal schemas', to the revision of which therapy is directed. In cognitive–analytic therapy (Ryle, 1990, 1995) the process of 'reformulation' is carried out jointly with the subject. Restrictive or harmful procedures which have defied revision are described in verbal and diagrammatic forms during the first few sessions and these descriptions determine the aims of therapy and are actively used by both subject and therapist through the course of therapy.

At a more general level it is helpful to consider relationships in terms of two main axes concerned with affection and need on the one hand and domination and submission on the other. A given relationship, unless mutual, will normally reflect a complementary pattern, as when one offers controlling care to a submissively dependent other; such patterns become unstable when the needs of one or other are no longer satisfied. Birtchnell (1993) has re-defined these axes in terms of the power differential (upperness and lowerness) and distance regulation (closeness and distance), arguing that none of the positions so defined are, in themselves, pathological. The appropriate pattern in a relationship will reflect its purpose, which may be intimate, familial or occupational, for example. Certain problem attitudes, notably those concerned with issues of control, are likely to be manifest in many different contexts.

Treatment methods for less severe problems

Many approaches to treatment are suitable over a wide range of severity, and many are suitable for use by workers in primary care settings. In the less severely disturbed individual in whom symptomatic disturbances are commonly linked with personal and interpersonal stresses, the exact therapeutic method used may not be of great importance. Research suggests that most are effective compared to control interventions (Orlinsky & Howard, 1986) but has not established clear indications of which conditions respond to which kinds of therapy. This may, in part, be due to the power of those factors common to all therapies, as Frank & Frank (1991) argue, but it can also reflect the fact that subjects are capable of making use of a wide range of different specific techniques. Researchers have paid relatively little attention to measuring changes in personality and interpersonal functioning. In recent years there is less concern with large-scale outcome studies modelled inappropriately on drug trial designs and more interest in combining process and outcome measures. The great variability in people classified together, and the unique evolution of each therapy even when carried out on the same theoretical basis, can be taken account of by designs which follow the small-scale processes of therapy in relation to clear definitions of the therapeutic method being applied.

The little hard evidence that exists on which to compare and evaluate the different approaches has been reviewed by Roth & Fonagy (1996).

Crisis counselling

People frequently consult in primary care settings because of a crisis in a key relationship. In such cases support can be linked with an attempt to help the person clarify his or her own contribution to the crisis. Often such crises are recurrent, as precarious adjustment 'decompensates'. It is helpful in such cases to carry out a full assessment leading to a case formulation which can be shared with the individual, so that the present and future problems can be linked specifically to the long-term personality or relationship issues underlying them.

Supportive therapy

People undergoing chronic life stresses or apparently lacking in personal resources may be offered, or may slip into, long-term dependency on professionals. There are considerable dangers in such a situation, which can be gratifying for the professional and undermining for the individual. Safe long-term support needs to be based on an awareness of the shifting psychodynamic implications of the relationship, and in most cases brief, possibly recurrent, problem-solving strategies are to be preferred. Social and human support is best provided by peers; the work of 'NEWPIN' with severely isolated and deprived young mothers is an example of the power and potential of such methods (Pound, 1990).

Individual counselling and psychodynamic psychotherapy

The distinction between counselling and psychotherapy is not an absolute one. In both approaches change depends on the development of a working relationship in which the subject's past and present life are reviewed and in which the therapist's acceptance serves to mitigate irrational guilt. Some counsellors and therapists will also understand the therapy relationship in terms of transference: the patterns of interaction, the omissions and the discrepancies between declared and indirectly expressed feelings all serve to allow the therapist to construct a model of the subject's unacknowledged or unconscious processes and of unresolved conflict and restrictive defences. Through interpretation of these in the 'here and now' of the therapy relationship, the subject becomes more aware of his or her feelings and wishes and more able to act from choice. The basic principles of psychoanalytic therapy are clearly spelled out in Brown & Pedder (1991) and the underlying concepts of psychoanalysis are described by Sandler *et al* (1979).

For common relatively mild relationship problems the outcome of dynamic therapy is usually satisfactory. However, the relative passivity of the therapist is frustrating for some people and drop-out rates are high; in a study by Pollak *et al* (1992) only 28% of people offered long-term therapy remained in therapy for over a year, the rates of unnegotiated terminations being highest in the early weeks. Of those people continuing in long-term therapy, many develop dependency of a type familiar to those for whom personal psychoanalysis was a part of training. The advantages of, and indications for, such long-term work as opposed to group or time-limited work are yet to be clearly defined.

Time-limited dynamic therapy

The power of time-limited therapy derives from the heightened involvement engendered from the clear identification of the focus of the work and from the emphasis on termination which is present from the earliest sessions. This emphasis may be of particular value to the more deprived individuals, whose fear of dependency and intense ambivalence makes open-ended therapy unacceptable or unmanageable. Time-limited work, as Mann observes (Mann, 1973; Mann & Goldman, 1982) can show such patients the possibility of using a limited offer and can provide a level of disappointment which is not based on idealised fantasies of perfect care and which is, therefore, tolerable.

Many therapists, however, apply very narrow criteria for time-limited work. This was true of Malan (1963, 1976, 1986) who was, for many years, the most influential figure in the field in Britain. Malan was also restricted in respect of the issues on which he was prepared to work, choosing a notionally 'Oedipal' issue (i.e. one supposedly derived from the third to fifth year of childhood) and confining interpretations to the linking of historical, current and transference issues to this issue. As regards outcome, DeWitt *et al* (1983) in seeking to replicate Malan's outcome studies, demonstrated very low inter-rater reliability for dynamic formulations and estimates of outcome. While the overall impression of the clinical reports is favourable to the approach, Malan is quoted (Demos & Prout, 1993) as saying that only 3% of subjects passed his selection criteria, and that of these only 25% showed major therapeutic change. Perhaps for this reason, Malan, in recent years, has espoused the methods of Davanloo (Davanloo, 1980; Malan, 1986). In this approach the therapist is highly active (and, some would say, highly aggressive). Rather than selecting a focus, the aim is to 'unlock the unconscious' and reveal the core neurotic conflicts. Davanloo is prepared to treat a wide range of people, including those with personality disorders.

In recent years a number of American writers have described dynamic, time-limited approaches which are relatively broad in their intake criteria and which have in common the identification and description of core processes which therapy aims to modify. These descriptions are shared with the subject (Mann, 1973; Mann & Goldman, 1982; Luborsky & Mark, 1991; Binder & Strupp, 1991); up to now, however, these approaches have had little influence on practice in Britain.

Cognitive–behavioural treatment

Traditionally, cognitive and behavioural therapists have focused on symptomatic or behavioural disorders and have shown little interest in personality disorders. However, people need to be cooperative for such treatments to be effective, and the more seriously disturbed personality-disordered individuals are prone to disrupt therapy in the same ways that they disrupt everyday relationships. To some degree this tendency may be contained by structured cognitive–behavioural approaches, and many interpersonal problems can be conceived of in terms of self-reinforcing behavioural sequences and negative assumptions about the self. In the past few years the limitations of these approaches have been faced and more complex models of development and structure have been evolved; examples include the work of Guidano (1987, 1991), the recent work of Beck (Beck & Freeman, 1990) and the model of 'early maladaptive schemas' proposed by Young & Lindemann (1992). Much of this work re-states ideas already developed in psychoanalysis and some directly acknowledges this derivation (e.g. Lockwood, 1992). The distinction between new cognitive developments and integrative models is therefore a blurred one.

Integrated therapies

In the past decade there has been a growing interest in integrating the techniques and, to a lesser extent, the theories of different therapies. This work is reviewed in Dryden (1992) and Stricker & Gold (1993).

The most developed model emerging from a primarily cognitive background is that of Safran (Safran & Segal, 1990) in which Sullivan's interpersonal theory is linked with cognitive ideas and with a developed model of emotion. Patients' difficulties are conceptualised in terms of 'dysfunctional interpersonal schemas' and the importance of the therapy relationship in modifying these is emphasised. Safran's work on ruptures in the therapeutic alliance (Safran, 1993) promises to be of particular value to psychotherapy researchers.

Cognitive–analytic therapy (CAT; Ryle, 1982, 1990) developed from a concern to define and measure the focus in brief dynamic therapy (Ryle, 1979) and, in this respect, resembles the focal time-limited approaches of the American workers referred to above. It differs, however, in that the attempt is also made to integrate, at the theoretical level, ideas from object relations theory with those of cognitive psychology, initially through the work of Kelly (1955) and latterly extending into the post-Vygotskian ideas of activity theory (Ryle, 1991; Leiman, 1992) in which the role of culture and of language in the formation of personality is emphasised.

The theoretical model (the Procedural Sequence Object Relations Model) describes personality and relationships in terms of the dominant 'reciprocal role procedures'. The concept of the procedure links, in sequence, mental processes (perception, emotion, appraisal, choice of action) with action or role playing and with the perceived consequences of the action, notably the response of others. Sequences are normally self-adjusting through processes of anticipation and feedback but 'neurotic' procedures are, for various reasons (classified as traps, dilemmas and snags), unrevised and the task of therapy is to find ways of identifying and modifying these. Subject and therapist collaborate in generating clear verbal and diagrammatic descriptions of these problem procedures and these are a central tool in the therapy, which aims to achieve change through the use of a range of techniques but centrally through the individual's enhanced self-reflective capacity and the therapist's avoidance, with the help of the reformulation, of collusion with negative procedures.

In a comparison with Mann's approach, CAT applied to an out-patient sample produced similar symptomatic but greater cognitive change (Brockman *et al*, 1987). The use of CAT in borderline personality disorder will be described below.

In a recent development, Shapiro *et al* (1992) describe a preliminary model of therapy based on the 'assimilation model'. This grew from a research comparison of two approaches, one 'prescriptive' (essentially cognitive–behavioural) and the other 'explanatory' (based on a psychoanalytic and interpersonal model). These two approaches are used in different sessions, the choice and order being negotiated with the subject. This model makes explicit, and keeps separate, the different elements which are combined in single integrated modes in the work of Safran and of Ryle described above, and does not create a joint description of the issues in the way characteristic of these approaches.

Group therapy

There are obvious advantages in using group therapy in treating people whose main problems are in their relationships with others (Yalom, 1985; Roberts & Pines, 1991). The interpersonal problems manifest in the relationship formed with a single therapist may emphasise the more childish and dependent aspects of the individual and may fail to mobilise both their problems and their strengths as evoked by peer relationships. Luborsky & Singer (1975) reported that the overall efficacy of group therapy was similar to that of individual therapy, and its cost over two years per person is similar to the cost of time-limited individual work. Not all people are suitable for group therapy, however: profoundly narcissistic individuals may have difficulty in joining or being tolerated by the group, and most therapists will restrict the number of borderline individuals in a group to two, because of their explosive potential. However, group work may be particularly valuable for borderline subjects, as may non-clinical group experiences such as are provided by self-help groups (Kretsch *et al*, 1987; Gunderson & Sabo, 1993).

Successful group therapy requires careful preparation. For more disturbed people, the combination of a short-term individual therapy of one of the sorts described above with longer-term group work may be an effective and humane approach.

Time-limited group therapy can offer the same advantages of focality and intensity as are found in individual brief work (Budman *et al*, 1980), but has been little used in Britain.

Duignan & Mitzman (1994) describe a group in which subjects received four individual sessions culminating in a CAT reformulation of their problems, followed by 12 group sessions in which these reformulations were shared with the group. The group contained three individuals with borderline personality disorder and one with narcissistic personality disorder. Seven of the eight completed the therapy, of whom only two requested further (group) therapy at follow-up, and psychometric changes were of the same order as those obtained in individual time-limited CAT. Further evaluation of this approach is clearly needed before its potential can be assessed.

Couple therapy

Couple therapy is appropriate where the couple request joint work on their relationship, or where the problems of a consulting individual are centrally based on one relationship and where the partner is willing. Where one or both have additional personality or symptomatic difficulties, individual therapy may also be indicated, the choice of which to do first depending on individual circumstances. If the problems complained of are evidently due to the psychiatric illness of one member, for example a depressive illness or paranoid personality, couple therapy is not appropriate.

The assumptions underlying joint work, which must be accepted by the couple, are that the problem is jointly created and maintained, so that blaming or defining as ill one partner is not acceptable, and that the aim is to help both to a clearer understanding of the self and of the other, on the basis of which each may be able to change and make choices about the future of the relationship.

Treatment depends upon the identification of the negative interactions which damage or dominate the relationship. These will be the focus of a systems theory therapy. They can be spelled out in behavioural terms as the reinforcement by each of the unwanted behaviours of the other; treatment will seek to encourage behaviours which reward desired behaviour. A cognitive approach will add to this the identification of individual and shared negative beliefs and assumptions; the way in which these generate negative interactions will be described and challenged. In a psychoanalytically-based approach, these interactions will be understood in terms of the pre-existing object relations of each partner, whereby both the selection of the other and the mode of interaction reflect intrapsychic, largely unconscious forces. Psychoanalytic ideas are particularly valuable in understanding highly disturbed couples in which both partners have a split personality structure. A typical example would be the relationship between two people with deprived or abused backgrounds, each of whom seeks, and initially seems to find, ideal care in the relationship with the other. Disappointment can lead to an abrupt switch to abuse and hate, which generates a like response from the other. States of fusion and fury can alternate in bewildering and exhausting ways, often with increasing intensity. Such sequences may be plotted diagrammatically in CAT (see Ryle, 1990); the inclusion of the interaction with others in the description of individual personality, embodied in the procedural sequence model, makes CAT a link between psychoanalytic and systems approaches.

Couple therapy is often successful on the basis of relatively infrequent meetings, for example every three or four weeks, and with a relatively small total number of sessions. Success need not imply the continuation of the relationship; where separation ensues, therapy may still play an important role in helping each deal without excessive bitterness with the loss involved and with the issues of children and money, which can become long-term vehicles for a continuing war (Toomin, 1972).

Transference is less central in couple therapy than in individual work, although couples may compete for, or unite against, the therapist. Countertransference awareness is, however, essential; treating a couple can easily mobilise unresolved feelings towards parents in the therapist, and, more generally, the temptation to be drawn into allying with one of the couple can be strong. For this reason many therapists prefer to work in a couple when treating a couple, an approach which greatly reduces the chance of unnoticed collusion and which offers the person a model of interaction. 'Parallel process', whereby the therapist couple come to repeat in their relationship some of the subjects' difficulties, can, like countertransference, be informative so long as it is recognised.

Categories of difficulty for more severely disturbed people

People whose personality and interpersonal difficulties present particular problems may be categorised as follows.

Disruptive and controlling symptomatic and behavioural disturbances

Some personality problems are accompanied by, or manifest in, symptoms and behaviours which serve to control the therapist or prevent the patient's cooperation in treatment. Examples would include anorexia nervosa, substance abuse, and severe obsessive–compulsive disorders. In such cases psychotherapy for personality and interpersonal problems may need to be preceded by, or to incorporate, management, medication, and the individual's agreeing to certain conditions (e.g. minimum weight maintenance, abstinence).

Dominant defensive patterns

Some people will be unable to engage in the tasks of therapy or the relationship with the therapist because of the very interpersonal patterns which are the cause of their distress. Thus the person with schizotypal disorder who consults either because of the despair of emotional distancing or the confusion of emotional closeness will face the same dilemma in engaging in therapy and be unable to make a useful therapeutic relationship. Other people may see any task or involvement as requiring their (resented) compliance and will in consequence demonstrate (usually passive and indirect) resistance to the therapy. Dependent people may form a powerful attachment to the therapist while resisting all suggestions that they might themselves participate in the process of change.

Dissociated personality disorders

Patient with traits of, or the full blown picture of, borderline personality disorder, histrionic personality disorder, narcissistic personality disorder and antisocial personality disorder are characterised by their propensity to destroy their relationships, and this is reflected in their frequent destruction of their therapy relationships also. The confusing variability of mood, of access to and control of emotion and of interpersonal behaviour characteristic of these people requires considerable skill and understanding from therapists of all persuasions.

People with narcissistic traits will frequently initiate 'special' relationships with their therapists, while denigrating all past helpers; when this fails they will become dismissive. Both these attitudes can be understood as ways of avoiding entering a state of vulnerable envious need. The aim of therapy must be to make entry into this state tolerable.

Treatment approaches for more difficult-to-treat people

Most approaches to therapy for the more difficult disorders described above are psychodynamic, and in many cases prolonged treatment two or more times weekly is recommended. While there is little doubt that understanding in these cases owes much to psychoanalysis, and while a clear conception of transference/counter-transference and the therapeutic use of the treatment relationship is essential, the evidence for the efficacy of dynamic approaches in severe disturbances is far from clear. In the case of borderline and narcissistic disorders Stone (1993), on the basis of large-scale follow-up studies, concludes that cognitive–behavioural approaches are to be preferred. This observation may reflect the possibly harmful effects of psychoanalysis, whether in the mode of Kohut (Kohut, 1971, 1977; Goldberg, 1988; Lee & Martin, 1991) or of Kernberg (Kernberg, 1975, 1984; Kernberg *et al*, 1989; Clarkin & Kernberg, 1993), as is suggested by Robbins (1989) and Ryle (1992, 1993). It may also demonstrate the power of well designed behavioural programmes to contain and transform these individuals. Linehan (Linehan & Koerner, 1993; Shearin & Linehan, 1993) has described a particularly well-articulated therapy combining individual behavioural work with group work and emphasising the need to support therapists in their work with these very difficult individuals.

Reviews of current practice are provided by Higgitt & Fonagy (1992), Paris (1993) and Tyrer & Stein (1993). The increasing attention paid to these conditions in the past two decades has been accompanied by a trend towards integrative or behavioural approaches, by the combination of psychological and pharmacological treatments and by a lesser use of in-patient care, although the availability of short-term admission remains important (Gordon & Beresin, 1983; Miller, 1989; Gunderson & Sabo, 1993). Although there is some evidence for the effectiveness of in-patient psychotherapeutic care (Rosser *et al*, 1987), Silver & Rosenbluth (1993) conclude that it should be regarded as 'heroic treatment reserved for a very small minority of patients'.

Cognitive–analytic therapy

The approaches to treatment considered above, whether psycho-dynamic or behavioural, are all relatively or very intense or prolonged, and demand a level of resource seldom available in NHS practice. Because of these resource limitations, time-limited cognitive–analytic therapy has been used as the main or only therapeutic intervention in borderline subjects, case examples being provided in Ryle (1997), Ryle *et al* (1992), Ryle & Beard (1993) and Ryle & Low (1993). In a current, accumulating research series, individuals are given up to 24 sessions, with follow-up at one, two, three and six months. The essential feature of CAT applied to borderline subjects is the identification and diagrammatic mapping of the individual's separate 'self-states', these being described, after Horowitz (1979), in terms of the pattern of reciprocal roles expressed in relationships and self-management, and in terms of the dominant affect and the degree of access to feeling. The Sequential Diagrammatic Reformulation, linking these self-states and identifying their characteristics, enables the therapist to avoid collusion and provides the individual with a means of recognising the states and switches between them, with a resultant rapid gain in the ability to monitor and control behaviour. Results of ongoing research show that the less severely disturbed half of the sample no longer meet borderline criteria six and 18 months after therapy.

As an integrated approach CAT can combine the understandings of splitting and of transference and counter-transference offered by psychoanalysis with the structure, attention to sequence and problem-solving approach of behavioural methods, while its collaborative approach and use of conceptual tools can recruit, more than either, the patient's hidden capacities. As Breuer & Freud (1893–5) observed, 'splitting of consciousness' can occur in people 'of the clearest will and highest critical power'.

Contemporary psychoanalytic approaches to the treatment of personality disorders, with their emphasis on regression and with their transfer of ideas of conflict and defence (which grew out of the study of symptoms) to the arena or personality seem to have lost sight of this understanding of dissociated patients. In doing so they may damage, and they certainly fail to recruit, these strengths.

Conclusion

For less severe personality and relationship problems individual group and couple therapies based on a range of theoretical models are effective. These treatments are likely to be increasingly offered in primary care and community resources. Research and audit may be able to identify which treatments are both effective and brief and may clarify the indications for the more prolonged approaches.

The treatment of the more severe personality disorders should be carried out in specialist settings where psychotherapy may be combined with medication and where in-patient and day hospital resources are available with suitably trained and supervised staff. It is argued that behavioural and integrated approaches may have more to offer than therapy carried out on purely psychoanalytic lines.

References

AMERICAN PSYCHIATRIC ASSOCIATION (1994) *Diagnostic and Statistical Manual of Mental Disorders* (4th edn) (DSM–IV). Washington, DC: APA.

BECK, A. T. & FREEMAN, A. (1990) *Cognitive Therapy of Personality Disorders*. New York: Guilford Press.

BINDER, J. L. & STRUPP, H. H. (1991) The Vanderbilt approach to time-limited dynamic psychotherapy. In *Handbook of Short Term Dynamic Psychotherapy* (eds P. Crits-Christoph & J. P. Barber), pp. 137–165. New York: Basic Books.

BIRTCHNELL, J. (1993) *How Humans Relate*. London: Praeger.

BREUER, J. & FREUD, S. (1893–5) *Studies in Hysteria*. (Standard Edition, Volume 3).

BROCKMAN, N., POYNTON, A., RYLE, A., *et al* (1987) Effectiveness of time-limited therapy carried out by trainees: comparison of two methods. *British Journal of Psychiatry*, **151**, 602–610.

BROWN, D. & PEDDER, J. (1991) *Introduction to Psychotherapy. An Outline of Psychodynamic Principles and Practice*. (2nd edition). London: Routledge.

BUDMAN, S. H., BENNETT, M. J. & WISNESKI, M. J. (1980) Short-term group psychotherapy: an adult developmental model. *International Journal of Group Psychotherapy*, **30**, 63–76.

CLARKIN, J. F. & KLERNBERG, O. F. (1993) Developmental factors in borderline personality disorder and borderline personality organisation. In *Borderline Personality Disorder: Etiology and Treatment* (ed. J. Paris), pp. 161–184. Washington, DC: American Psychiatric Association.

COLTART, N. (1988) Diagnosis and assessment for suitability for psychoanalytic psychotherapy. *British Journal of Psychotherapy*, **4**, 127–134.

CRITS-CHRISTOPH, P., LUBORSKY, L., DAHL, L., *et al* (1988) Clinicians can agree in assessing relationship patterns in psychotherapy; the core conflictual relationship theme method. *Archives of General Psychiatry*, **45**, 1001–1004.

DAVANLOO, H. (1980) *Short Term Dynamic Psychotherapy*. New York: Jason Aronson.

DEMOS, V. C. & PROUT, M. F. (1993) A comparison of seven approaches to brief therapy. *International Journal of Short Term Psychotherapy*, **8**, 3–23.

DEWITT, K. N., KALTREIDER, N. B., WEISS, D. S., *et al* (1983) Judging changes in psychotherapy. *Archives in General Psychiatry*, **40**, 1121–1128.

DRYDEN, W. A. (ed.) (1992) *Integrative and Eclectic Therapy: A Handbook*. Buckingham: Open University Press.

DUIGNAN, I. & MITZMAN, S. (1994) Change in patients receiving time-limited cognitive analytic group therapy. *International Journal of Short Term Psychotherapy*, **9**, 151–160.

FRANK, J. D. & FRANK, J. B. (1991) *Persuasion and Healing: A Comparative Study of Psychotherapy*. Baltimore: The Johns Hopkins University Press.

GOLDBERG, A. (1988) *A Fresh Look at Psychoanalysis: The New Self Psychology*. Hillsdale, NJ: The Analytic Press.

GORDON, C. & BERESIN, E. (1983) Conflicting treatment models for the inpatient management of borderline patients. *American Journal of Psychiatry*, **140**, 979–983.

GUIDANO, V. F. (1987) *Complexity of the Self: A Developmental Approach to Psychopathology and Therapy*. New York: Guilford Press.

GUIDANO, V. F. (1991) *The Self in Process*. New York: Guilford Press.

GUNDERSON, J. & SABO, A. N. (1993) Treatment of borderline personality disorder: a critical review. In *Borderline Personality Disorder: Etiology and Treatment* (ed. J. Paris), pp. 385–406. Washington, DC: American Psychiatric Association.

HIGGITT, A. & FONAGY, P. (1992) Psychotherapy in borderline personality disorder. *British Journal of Psychiatry*, **161**, 23–43.

HINSHELWOOD, R. D. (1991) Psychodynamic formulation in assessment for psychotherapy. *British Journal of Psychotherapy*, **8**, 166–174.

HOROWITZ, M. J. (1979) *States of Mind: Analysis of Change in Psychotherapy*. New York: Plenum Press.

—— & EELLS, T. D. (1993) Case formulation using role-relationship model configurations: a reliability study. *Psychotherapy Research*, **3**, 57–68.

KELLY, G. A. (1955) *The Psychology of Personal Constructs*. New York: Norton.

KERNBERG, O. F. (1975) *Borderline Conditions and Pathological Narcissism*. New York: Jacob Aronson.

—— (1984) *Severe Personality Disorders: Psychotherapeutic Strategies*. New Haven: Yale University Press.

——, KOENIGSBERG, H. W., CARR, A. C., *et al* (1989) *Psychodynamic Psychotherapy of Borderline Patients*. New York: Basic Books.

KOHUT, H. (1971) *The Analysis of the Self*. New York: International Universities Press.

———— (1977) *The Restoration of the Self.* New York: International Universities Press.

KRETSCH, R., GOREN, Y. & WASSERMAN, A. (1987) Change patterns of borderline patients in individual and group therapy. *International Journal of Group Psychotherapy,* **37,** 95–111.

LEE, R. D. & MARTIN, J. C. (1991) *Psychotherapy after Kohut.* Hillsdale, NJ: The Analytic Press.

LEIMAN, M. (1992) The concept of sign in the work of Vygotsky, Winnicott and Bahktin. Further integration of object relations theory and activity theory. *British Journal of Medical Psychology,* **65,** 209–221.

LINEHAN, M. M. & KOERNER, K. (1993) A behavioural theory of borderline personality disorder. In *Borderline Personality Disorder: Etiology and Treatment* (ed. J. Paris), pp. 103–122. Washington, DC: American Psychiatric Association.

LOCKWOOD, G. (1992) Psychoanalysis and the cognitive theory of personality disorders. *Journal of Cognitive Psychotherapy,* **6,** 25–42.

LUBORSKY, L. & SINGER, B. (1975) Comparative study of psychotherapies. *Archives of General Psychiatry,* **32,** 995–1008.

———— & MARK, D. (1991) Short term supportive–expressive psychoanalytic psychotherapy. In *Handbook of Short Term Dynamic Psychotherapy* (eds P. Crits-Christoph & P. Barber). New York: Basic Books.

MALAN, D. H. (1963) *A Study of Brief Psychotherapy.* London: Tavistock.

———— (1976) *Towards a Validation of Dynamic Psychotherapy.* New York: Plenum Press.

———— (1986) Beyond interpretation: initial evaluation and technique in short term psychotherapy. Part 1. *International Journal of Short Term Psychotherapy,* **1,** 83–106.

MANN, J. (1973) *Time-limited Psychotherapy.* Cambridge MA: Harvard University Press.

———— & GOLDMAN, R. (1982) *A Casebook of Time-limited Psychotherapy.* New York: McGraw-Hill.

MILLER, L. J. (1989) Inpatient management of borderline personality disorder: a review and update. *Journal of Personality Disorders,* **3,** 122–134.

MILTON, J. (1989) Brief psychotherapy with poorly controlled diabetics. *British Journal of Psychotherapy,* **5,** 532–543.

MORTON, A. J. & STAINES, J. (1993) GP use of psychotherapy services. *Psychiatric Bulletin,* **17,** 526–527.

ORLINSKY, D. E. & HOWARD, K. I. (1986) Process and outcome in psychotherapy. In *Handbook of Psychotherapy and Behaviour Change* (eds S. L. Garfield & A. E. Bergin), pp. 311–381. New York: Wiley.

PARIS, J. (1993) *Borderline Personality Disorder: Etiology and Treatment.* Washington, DC: American Psychiatric Press.

PARRY, G. (1992) Improving psychotherapy services; applications of research, audit and evaluation. *British Journal of Clinical Psychology,* **31,** 3–19.

POLLAK, J., MORDECAI, E. & GUMPERT, D. (1992) Discontinuation from long-term individual psychodynamic psychotherapy. *Psychotherapy Research,* **2,** 224–234.

POUND, A. (1990) The development of attachment in adult life: the NEWPIN experiment. *British Journal of Psychotherapy,* **7,** 77–85.

ROBBINS, M. (1989) Primitive personality organisation as an interpersonally adaptive malfunction of cognition and affect. *International Journal of Psychoanalysis,* **70,** 443–459.

ROBERTS, J. & PINES, M. (eds) (1991) *The Practice of Group Analysis.* London: Routledge.

ROBINS, C. J. (1993) Implications for research in the psychopathology of depression for psychotherapy integration. *Journal of Psychotherapy Integration,* **3,** 313–330.

ROSSER, R. M., BIRCH, S., BOND, H., *et al* (1987) Five year follow-up of patients treated with inpatient psychotherapy at the Cassel Hospital for Nervous Diseases. *Journal of the Royal Society of Medicine,* **80,** 549–555.

ROTH, A. & FONAGY, P. (1996) *What Works for Whom? A Critical Review of Psychotherapy Research.* New York: Guilford Press.

RYLE, A. (1979) The focus in brief interpretative psychotherapy; dilemmas, traps and snags as target problems. *British Journal of Psychiatry,* **137,** 475–488.

———— (1990) *Cognitive-Analytic Therapy: Active Participation in Change.* Chichester: Wiley.

———— (1991) Object relations theory and activity theory: a proposed link by way of the procedural sequence model. *British Journal of Medical Psychology*, **64**, 307–316.

———— (1992) Critique of a Kleinian case presentation. *British Journal of Medical Psychology*, **65**, 309–317.

———— (1993) Addiction to the death instinct? A critical review of Joseph's paper 'Addiction to near death'. *British Journal of Psychotherapy*, **10**, 88–92.

———— (ed.) (1995) *Cognitive Analytic Therapy: Developments in Theory and Practice.* Chichester: Wiley.

———— (1997) *Cognitive Analytic Therapy and Borderline Personality Disorder: The Model and The Method.* Chichester: Wiley.

————, SPENSER, J. & YAWETZ, C. (1992) When less is more or at least enough. *British Journal of Psychotherapy*, **8**, 401–412.

———— & BEARD, H. (1993) The integrative effect of reformulation: cognitive analytic therapy with a patient with borderline personality disorder. *British Journal of Medical Psychology*, **66**, 249–258.

————, BOA, C. & FOSBURY, J. (1993) Identifying the causes of poor self-management in insulin dependent diabetics: the use of cognitive analytic techniques. In *Psychological Treatment in Disease and Illness* (eds M. Hodes & S. Mooney). London: Gaskell and The Society for Psychological Research.

———— & LOW, J. (1993) Cognitive analytic therapy. In *Comprehensive Handbook of Psychotherapy Integration* (eds G. Stricker & S. G. Gold). New York: Plenum Press.

SAFRAN, J. D. (1993) The therapeutic alliance rupture as a transtheoretical phenomenon; definition and conceptual issues. *Journal of Psychotherapy Integration*, **3**, 33–50.

———— & SEGAL, Z. J. (1990) *Interpersonal Process in Cognitive Therapy.* New York: Basic Books.

———— & McMAIN, S. (1992) A cognitive–interpersonal approach to the treatment of personality disorders. *Journal of Cognitive Psychotherapy*, **6**, 59–68.

SANDLER, J., DARE, C. & HOLDER, C. (1979) *The Patient and the Analyst.* London: Karnac Books.

SHAPIRO, D. A., BARKHAM, M., REYNOLDS, S., *et al* (1992) Prescriptive and exploratory psychotherapies: toward an integration based on the assimilation model. *Journal of Psychotherapy Integration*, **2**, 253–272.

SHEARIN, E. N. & LINEHAN, M. M. (1993) Dialectical behaviour therapy for borderline personality disorder: treatment goals, strategies and empirical support. In *Borderline Personality Disorder: Etiology and Treatment* (ed. J. Paris), pp. 285–318. Washington, DC: American Psychiatric Association.

SILVER, D. & ROSENBLUTH, M. (1993) Inpatient treatment of borderline personality disorder. In *Borderline Personality Disorder: Etiology and Treatment* (ed. J. Paris), pp. 349–372. Washington, DC: American Psychiatric Press.

STONE, M. H. (1993) Long-term outcome in personality disorders. *British Journal of Psychiatry*, **162**, 299–313.

STRICKER, G. & GOLD, J. R. (1993) *Comprehensive Handbook of Psychotherapy Integration.* New York: Plenum Press.

TATTERSALL, R. B. (1985) Brittle diabetes. *British Medical Journal*, **291**, 55–56.

TOOMIN, M. K. (1972) Structured separation with counselling; a therapeutic approach to couples in conflict. *Family Process*, **11**, 299–310.

TYRER, P. & STEIN, G. (eds) (1993) *Personality Disorder Reviewed.* London: Gaskell.

WINNICOTT, D. W. (1960) *The Maturational Process and the Facilitating Environment.* London: Hogarth Press.

YALOM, I. D. (1985) *Theory and Practice of Group Psychotherapy (3rd Edition).* New York: Basic Books.

YOUNG, J. F. & LINDEMANN, M. D. (1992) The integrative schema-focussed model for personality disorder. *Journal of Cognitive Psychotherapy*, **6**, 11–24.

4 Management of the positive symptoms of psychosis

CHRIS JACKSON and MAX BIRCHWOOD

The application of psychological techniques to the management of psychotic symptoms is by no means a new phenomenon. Beck, now famous for his pioneering work in cognitive therapy for depression, reported 'success' in working with a person with persecutory delusions as far back as 1952 (Beck, 1952). More recently developments in cognitive therapy for other psychological disorders, most notably depression (see chapter 2), have been adapted for use with people experiencing hallucinations and delusions (Chadwick & Lowe, 1990). Early results of large-scale evaluations of a cognitive–behavioural approach to residual symptoms appear promising (Tarrier *et al*, 1993).

Cognitive–behavioural approaches to the management of hallucinations

Ever since the introduction of neuroleptic medication to treat positive symptoms, it has been known that a significant number of people still experience persisting symptoms, including auditory hallucinations (Curson *et al*, 1988).

Hallucinations can be extremely distressing for the individual (Chadwick & Birchwood, 1994) and in extreme cases prompt people into life-threatening behaviours whether directed towards themselves or others (Falloon & Talbot, 1981; Rogers *et al*, 1990). They may also play a role in the formation and maintenance of delusions (Maher, 1974).

Slade & Bentall (1988) reviewed 15 studies which considered the percentage breakdown of people with schizophrenia experiencing various types of hallucination. Auditory hallucinations were found in about 60% of the people with schizophrenia on average, and visual hallucinations in 29%. In all studies more people reported experiencing auditory hallucinations than visual hallucinations. Overall, it is generally thought that auditory hallucinations are more prevalent in schizophrenia but visual hallucinations are more often associated with organic brain syndromes (Goodwin, 1971). We will focus here on working with people with auditory hallucinations.

Assessment and measurement of hallucinations

Specific questionnaire and scales for the measurement and assessment of hallucinations are still, unfortunately, quite rare. Symptom rating scales known as the BPRS (Overall *et al*, 1962), the Manchester Scale (Krawieka *et al*, 1977) and the ComPRS (Åsberg *et al*, 1978), assessing overall symptomatology (including hallucinations), were initially designed for monitoring change in large group research designs (Garety, 1992). The analysis of individual symptom change has been less of a priority.

Aggernaes (1972) used a structured interview in an attempt to distinguish between 'true' hallucinations and other experiences. The scale is more useful as a research instrument than one which measures change after an individual therapeutic intervention (Slade & Bentall, 1988; Garety, 1992).

A more clinically useful scale is Slade's (1972*b*) Auditory Hallucinations Record Form. Its overall focus is on the precipitating factors of auditory hallucinations but also includes ratings of presence/ absence of 'voices', intensity and mood state. The scale also attempts to assess the 'quality' of 'voices' on 15 semantic differential scales. Lately, colleagues of Slade (Haddock *et al*, 1993; Bentall *et al*, 1994) have updated and added to this by including a modified version of the Personal Questionnaire Rapid Scaling Technique (PQRST) (Mulhall, 1978) assessing frequency of voices over the past week, the distress caused by the voices, the disruption to their life caused by the voices and the extent to which the subjects believed their voices to be their own thoughts (i.e. subject's attribution).

A similar approach has been taken by Hustig & Hafner (1990) who report the development of a self-report questionnaire that is used in the form of a diary, to be completed three times a day. Firstly subjects are asked to describe what their 'voices' are saying, and then on five-point Likert scales, rate the intensity of the 'voices' ('very loud–very quiet'), their clarity ('very clear to very mumbled'), degree of distress they cause ('very distressing to very comforting') and degree of distractability ('very easy to ignore to compelling me to obey them').

Chadwick & Birchwood (1994) have attempted to measure beliefs about hallucinations. Based on a cognitive model, they have argued that "behavioural and affective symptoms of voices (i.e. distress, anxiety) are not antecedents but consequences of particular negative beliefs" (Chadwick & Birchwood, 1994). Hence, measurement of the belief(s) is based on conviction ratings of four major components on a percentage scale (0–100%): Identity (who is talking to client?), meaning (why is client hearing voices?), compliance (what would or would not happen if he/she resists?), and control (can the client control (stop/start) the voices?).

Psychological treatment of auditory hallucinations

Psychological approaches to the treatment of auditory hallucinations originally drew heavily on behavioural theories of operant and classical conditioning. Systematic desensitisation was used successfully (Alumbaugh, 1971; Slade, 1972a), as was *in vivo* desensitisation (Slade, 1973), contingency management (Bucher & Fabricatore, 1970), faradic aversion (Alford & Turner, 1976), covert sensitisation (Moser, 1974) and time out (Haynes & Geddy, 1973). Unfortunately, most of these are single case studies and where controlled studies of behavioural approaches have been carried out equivocal results have been reported (Wiengaertner, 1971). More importantly, however, it is difficult to establish genuine change because of an over-reliance on verbal reports of hallucinating experiences and an incentive to change reports because of the contingencies of the operant programme (Birchwood *et al*, 1988). Furthermore, the single state theories upon which such interventions were based were often unsophisticated and simplistic (Heilbrun, 1993).

More elaborate theories such as Slade & Bentall's (1988) five factor theory of hallucinations (discussed later) and Birchwood *et al*'s (1988) four stage model have been consistent with a more varied approach to the management of auditory hallucinations. For instance, seeking to prevent voice occurrence by reducing stress and arousal, and encouraging tasks or activities which involve attention and engagement with the external environment (i.e. keeping busy when voices do occur etc.), promoting strategies which seek to interrupt the voices (i.e. thought stopping, singing, talking to others etc.); distraction from voice to meaningful stimuli which will hold the person's attention ('point and name') would all be consistent with such models. It is also of note that discouraging behaviours that reinforce the voice(s), i.e. laughing at their content, doing what they say etc. would also be predicted from such a model. Few of the above strategies have been properly evaluated in between-group designs but hallucinators in natural settings do frequently use these strategies to prevent and/or control their voices (Falloon & Talbot, 1981; Breier & Straus, 1983; Tarrier, 1987).

Chadwick & Birchwood (1994) have recently sought to use the principles of cognitive therapy to identify and challenge the central beliefs about the 'omnipotence of voices'. In order to reduce the powerful and distressing impact of hallucinations (Falloon & Talbot, 1981), it is argued that such a cognitive approach would seek to make "the individual aware of the potent way in which beliefs can influence behaviour and emotion, and to weaken this influence through a combination of verbal disputation and empirical testing" (Chadwick & Birchwood, 1994).

Once the client is engaged and rapport is established, the central beliefs about the hallucination and evidence used to support them are defined. Clients are given information about hallucinations and introduced to other hallucinators and/or videos of hallucinators in order to normalise their experiences. Beliefs are then disputed through the use of hypothetical contradiction (Brett-Jones *et al*, 1987), generating alternatives, verbal challenges (Chadwick & Lowe, 1990) and testing beliefs empirically. Such techniques are illustrated in the following case.

Case report

M.T. is a 59-year-old single woman who had experienced auditory and visual hallucinations since the age of 31. She had been known to psychiatric services since 1976 when she initially presented with disorientation, depression and hallucinations. Since then numerous suicide attempts and episodes of depression accompanied her auditory and visual hallucinations. There was no clear consistent diagnosis. She worked as a domestic in a hotel. M.T. was assessed for intervention during a protracted acute admission precipitated by a worsening of her hallucinations and her beginning to act on them with potential danger to herself and others. During admissions she had been treated with a combination of neuroleptics, antidepressants and electroconvulsive therapy with no effect. During assessment M.T. described hearing a voice through her ears that announced itself as God. The voice instructed her to kill herself, members of her family and a work colleague ("Do your work – kill her", "Go to the canal", "Kill yourself"). It also suggested that non-family members were evil and that she should not communicate with them ("Don't talk to him he's evil"). The voices occurred in short bursts approximately 10 times daily. These were linked to visual hallucinations of her deceased daughter and her dog that came to her and woke her up at night beckoning her to join them in heaven by following the commands of God. M.T. had attempted suicide in the past and had on occasions carried a knife with the intention of carrying out the mission demanded by the voice, although in retrospect she felt that both were acts of "appeasement" towards the voice.

Intervention, as pointed out previously, began with an opening phase used to engage the client and establish rapport with her. "Collaborative empiricism" was essentially gained after the following questions "Just suppose that this was not the voice of God, for example an impostor, what would the consequence be for you?" In other words were she to kill herself, then according to her faith she would have sinned and would not go to heaven (and join M and R). She was invited to discuss her beliefs in order to make sure she was making the right decision.

Although these beliefs about the voices (with supporting evidence) were agreed together, for the sake of space, therapeutic work with only two of the three beliefs will be described.

The first of these was the belief that if she resisted the commands of her voices they would punish her. Drawing on the evidence of voice content (they told her she would be punished) and the fact they nagged her if she resisted, she had held the belief over three years. This evidence was then challenged by the therapist by pointing out that she had resisted the commands for over three years but had not been punished.

Having undermined the omnipotence of the voice through a verbal challenge of the evidence supporting one of the beliefs, evidence for a second, more strongly held belief was challenged. M.T. believed with 100% conviction, that God was talking to her. She claimed (i.e. evidence) that the voice knew her thoughts and intentions and that it announced itself as God. Visual hallucinations of her deceased daughter and dog provided additional potent evidence for this belief.

Using cognitive techniques, inconsistencies in her evidence were challenged as follows: "If this is the voice of God why are you being instructed to kill, as it is a sin in the Catholic faith?" The plausibility of the plan was then challenged. The plan involved killing one person in a public place, then catching a bus for a 12 mile journey, to complete the mission. Not only did she realise that she would be caught but she also questioned how God could have given her such a flawed plan. After further verbal challenges of evidence supporting the belief, her conviction score fell to 5% after 10 weeks and 5% at 26 week follow-up (for further details see Chadwick & Birchwood, 1994, 1995). However empirical confirmation of this new approach to auditory hallucinations is still needed.

Tarrier (1987) has suggested that since coping methods are used spontaneously and naturally by many people, it is worthwhile encouraging them, in a structured and systematic way, to use such strategies more frequently and more effectively. Tarrier (1992) has argued that such an approach, which he names Coping Strategy Enhancement (CSE), has three distinguishing characteristics:

(1) Assessment of the coping strategies used by the person already.
(2) Encouragement of *in vivo* practice. That is, people are persuaded to practise their coping strategies by either entering situations where their hallucinations occur or by actively trying to stimulate or bring them about.
(3) Encouraging the use of an array or combination of individual coping strategies.

CSE, unlike most other psychological techniques to reduce residual hallucinations, has the advantage of having been evaluated in a controlled trial. Tarrier *et al* (1993) randomly allocated 49 people with a DSM–III–R diagnosis of schizophrenia into one of two conditions: CSE or problem solving (D'Zurilla & Goldfried, 1971). Half the subjects were then allocated to a high-expectancy positive demand condition and half to a counter-demand condition in order to evaluate whether expectation of improvement would affect the results. Findings indicated that subjects receiving either treatment showed significant reductions in symptoms compared with those on a waiting list. This was not due to expectancy effects. Although there was a trend towards CSE being more effective than problem solving, this was not statistically significant.

Unfortunately, since its conception in 1987, Tarrier has placed little emphasis upon the types of persistent symptoms for which CSE would be most effective. Findings from his most recent study suggest that greater improvements appear to occur with delusions than with hallucinations (Tarrier *et al*, 1993). Clearly further investigation, with perhaps more emphasis on different types of symptoms, is warranted.

Bentall and Slade have postulated that hallucinators have a propensity to engage in what they call 'sensory deception' whereby they fail to discriminate between self-generated and external sources of information. In addition they argue that people who hallucinate are more likely to be tolerant of ambiguous stimuli and have a tendency to 'jump to perceptions' (Slade & Bentall, 1988; Garety, 1991). The therapy is underpinned by their five factor model mentioned previously. This specifies that the following factors may lead to the onset of hallucinations:

(1) Stress-induced arousal.
(2) Predisposing factors (e.g. cognitive deficiencies such as suggestibility; Young *et al*, 1987).
(3) Environmental stimulation.
(4) Reinforcement (although not completely understood it is suggested that misperception may be strengthened through reinforcement).
(5) Expectancy (i.e. as a perceptual set in determining the person's ability to discriminate from reality).

Although not without its critics (Heilbrun, 1993), Slade and Bentall's model is one of the most comprehensive theories of hallucinations that has been subject to empirical investigation and which has formed the basis of a psychological therapeutic procedure. In essence, the aim of what they call 'focusing treatment' is to 'reduce the frequency of voices and/or the distress associated with them by means of the gradual reattribution of the voices to the self' (Bentall *et al*, 1994).

The treatment approach (Haddock *et al*, 1993; Bentall *et al*, 1994), involves a combination of the following: self-monitoring (i.e. completing a diary); completion of anxiety and depression ratings and a modified version of the PQRST to measure subject's attributions (Mulhall, 1978); techniques which encourage the subjects to reattribute their voices to themselves (i.e. getting subjects to focus and discuss physical characteristics of their 'voices' such as number, loudness, tone etc.) focusing on the content of voices and discussing with the subjects their beliefs and thoughts about the voices.

Although theoretical differences exist between Haddock, Bentall and Slade's therapy and Chadwick and Birchwood's there are some parallels. This is most in evidence in the emphasis given to the thoughts and beliefs the clients have about their voices.

In a recent paper Chadwick & Birchwood (1995) have demonstrated a correlation between self-perceived identity and meaning of voices, and depressive symptomatology. People who report that their voices are malevolent are significantly more likely to be depressed than those describing their voices as either benevolent or benign. In addition, those people who saw their voices as omnipotent or powerful, irrespective of benevolence, were also more likely to have high scores on the Beck Depression Inventory.

Cognitive–behavioural approaches to the management of delusions

Like hallucinations, delusions of persecution, reference and thought control are often resistant to pharmacological intervention and ultimately can be distressing for the individual. However, despite being among the most common psychotic symptoms (Birchwood & Tarrier, 1992), our understanding of the psychological factors involved in how they first develop and are maintained is poor (Garety, 1991).

Measurement and assessment of delusions

False beliefs have been traditionally viewed as either present or absent. A number of clinicians and researchers, however, have argued that delusions, like other beliefs, can be measured on a continuum of certainty (Straus, 1969; Chapman & Chapman, 1980; Garety, 1985). Garety & Hemsley (1987) using factor analysis of Kendler *et al*'s (1983) scale identified three other major dimensions along which delusions could be measured: distress, concern, strength and obtrusiveness, as well as certainty of belief.

Further support of a multidimensional continuum approach to the measurement of delusions comes from Brett-Jones *et al* (1987) who, in single case studies, attempted to measure variables that describe the relationship between the believer and the belief (i.e. 'those that would be expected to change if a subject recovers from a deluded state' (p. 257). They found that it was possible to evaluate certainty, preoccupation with and behavioural interference of the delusional belief. Furthermore, they reported lack of covariance between the measures, thus suggesting the true independence of different dimensions of a delusional experience.

Recent attempts to measure the behavioural correlates of delusions through self-report are also suggestive of a need for a more multidimensional approach to assessment of delusions (Wessely *et al,* 1993).

Psychological treatment of delusions

Delusions, like beliefs, differ widely and it is possible that some delusions will be more certain and therefore more resistant to change than others. Fundamental cognitive differences may exist between people with paranoid and non-paranoid schizophrenia (George & Neufeld, 1985). Broga & Neufeld (1981) found that people with paranoid schizophrenia may display information processing deficits which are accompanied by an overly liberal tendency to draw inferences while people with non-paranoid schizophrenia may be more conservative about drawing inferences and reaching decisions despite processing the information more efficiently. However, these results were not replicated by Garety *et al* (1991).

Techniques for behavioural treatment of delusions such as extinction, use of social reinforcement, tokens, privileges, feedback differentially to reinforce non-deluded talk (Wincze *et al,* 1972), verbal conditioning and assertiveness training (Nydeggar, 1972), satiation (Wolff, 1971) and time out (Davis *et al,* 1976) have mostly reported positive results in terms of reductions in verbal expressions of delusional beliefs. Such reductions may merely represent successful verbal modification as opposed to any true underlying change in belief content or conviction.

Cognitive approaches which have concentrated more on beliefs admitted to when questioned than on spontaneous talk have been less frequently utilised. An early exception of this is Watts *et al's* (1973) study of the delusional beliefs of three people with paranoid schizophrenia. Using a non-confrontational style, these authors first tackled those parts of the delusion which were most weakly held. Clients were then asked to consider an alternative view to the delusion as opposed to having one forced upon them. As much evidence as possible was used and the subjects were encouraged to acknowledge the arguments against the delusions. These were endorsed and discussed further by the therapist. After six sessions all three patients showed significant reductions in the strength of the delusional beliefs although none of the subjects completely abandoned them.

As pointed out above, Watts *et al* (1973) argue against the use of confrontation. Further evidence for such a stance comes from Milton *et al* (1978) who in an empirical test of this noted that belief modification (as adapted by Watts *et al*, 1973) had benefits over and above those of pure confrontation. These authors also found that confrontation was more likely to produce greater increases in disturbance (as measured by BPRS) than a non-confrontational approach. Building on the work of Watts *et al* (1973) and Beck's (1967) cognitive therapy for depression, Chadwick & Lowe (1990) attempted to modify the long held delusions of six clients using two defined interventions: (a) a structured verbal challenge and (b) a reality test in which the belief was subject to an empirical test. Verbal challenges were used to "encourage the patient to view a deluded belief as being only one possible interpretation of events" (p. 227). Like Watts *et al* (1973) Chadwick & Lowe (1990) only challenged the belief after questioning the evidence for the belief. By doing this through a verbal challenge they initially sought to expose, in the client's belief system, any inconsistency which would suggest that the belief did not make as much sense as the client first thought. Alternative explanations for client's experiences were then suggested (Maher, 1974) and then, in the light of new information on the individual's interpretation and therapist's alternative, were re-evaluated.

After the verbal challenge, where it was deemed suitable and necessary, some of the clients with Chadwick & Lowe worked together to test the reality of their belief. It has been a long-standing tradition of cognitive–behavioural therapies such as relational emotive therapy (Dryden, 1989) to encourage the use of behavioural techniques to back up and confirm initial cognitive disputing. As Beck *et al* (1979) commented when talking about cognitive therapy for depression:

> There is no easy way to "talk the patient out" of his conclusions that he is weak, inept or vacuous. . . . By helping the patient change certain behaviours, the therapist may demonstrate to the patient that his negative, overgeneralised conclusions were incorrect (p. 118)

Case report

D.D. is a 46-year-old single man who had his first episode of schizophrenia in 1971 and has a history of multiple hospital admissions. A devout Roman Catholic since childhood, D.D. believed with 100% conviction that he was the 'Son of Man' who had been given the task by God to 'redeem the souls in hell and the devil and his angels'. As a consequence of this, because he was the 'Son of Man' he intermittently believed that staff at the hospital and strangers were human robots sent to persecute him and eventually kill him which naturally was quite distressing. Far from being pleased with the responsibility of being the 'Son of Man' D.D. saw it as a burden, and talked about the relief he would feel if such responsibility was taken away from him. He had held this delusion since 1972. At the time of assessment there was no evidence that he was hallucinating and medication (chlorpromazine, Modecate depot and procyclidine) remained stable throughout baseline and intervention periods.

Baseline assessments over a 4-week period indicated that conviction in his belief that he was the 'Son of Man' remained absolute (i.e. 100%). He claimed to be preoccupied with it 2 or 3 times a day and denied that there was any evidence over the 4-week period that would make him want to alter his belief.

In an atmosphere of empirical collaboration, D.D. was asked for the evidence which supported the delusion. It fell into three main parts. Firstly, the onset of the delusion had followed a period of acute psychosis when he reported having experienced 'Jesus talking through him' saying 'love your enemies'. Confirmation that it was Jesus talking through him came from the fact that these words do actually appear in the Bible.

It was put to D.D. that 'love your enemies' is a fairly common phrase used not infrequently by a great number of people. He agreed. He was also asked whether there could be another possible explanation for his experiences. He suggested that he 'may have been unwell at the time'. The outcome of this was that, although he maintained his 100% conviction in his belief, he began to doubt the reliability of his evidence.

The second piece of evidence cited in favour of his delusion was that the Bible contained a description of the 'Son of Man' which D.D. felt was an accurate picture of himself. When challenged about this he readily admitted to a confirmation bias, in that he selected out those bits of the description which could relate to him and ignored those which did not. At this stage his confidence in his evidence was further undermined to the extent that he now had serious doubts about whether his belief was in fact true. This was reflected in his conviction score which fell to 55%.

His conviction score fell further after challenging inconsistencies in his evidence that he had been granted special powers by God (because he was the 'Son of Man') to cure people. Four years previously, while an in-patient, he had been convinced that he had stopped the 'confusion' of another patient by simply touching that person. Asked for alternative explanations of these events he admitted that he could not recall with 100% accuracy whether in fact he had cured her or whether she had merely reported it. Again, the main feature here had been to challenge his beliefs in the reliability of the evidence which supported the delusion.

In between sessions, over a period of a week, D.D. reported that he no longer believed that he was the 'Son of Man'. His conviction score of 3% reflected perhaps the last remnants of doubt about the belief. As D.D. put it: 'The evidence is still there but I am now convinced it is false'.

As a final test of the evidence that he had been granted special powers, a behavioural experiment was set up. Because it was felt that it would be unethical to attempt to 'cure' another person, D.D. agreed to test the belief on himself, to 'give Jesus the opportunity to improve his eyesight'. D.D. suffered from a congenital eye condition which meant he was extremely short-sighted and had to wear specially designed glasses. It was agreed that D.D. should have his eyes tested at his optician (which he did on a routine basis anyway) in order to provide a baseline against which to measure any improvement. If at any time, over an agreed specified period, he felt that he had been granted special powers to improve his own eyesight then he would go back to his optician to obtain independent validation. At the time of writing and drawing to an end of the agreed time period, no improvement had been reported. D.D.'s belief that he was the 'Son of Man' fell to 0%.

It should be noted that D.D.'s expectation that his eyesight would improve was very low and for such reasons it was felt that the behavioural experiment did not give him false hope for a dramatic improvement to his eyesight.

How such therapeutic techniques work is still not entirely clear. In a later paper, Chadwick & Lowe (1994) have argued that cognitive therapy may initially lessen specific confirmation bias towards a belief. Alternatively, there is some suggestion from research in social psychology that value-relevant involvement (where attitudes are linked to important values) may motivate recipients to defend their initial attitudes and underlying values in favour of arguments for those attitudes (Tesser & Shaffer, 1990). It could be hypothesised that without exploration of what are the underlying values linked to a patient's delusion, little therapeutic progress could hope to be made. We know that 'normal' beliefs are very slow to change, even when represented with counter evidence (Ross & Anderson, 1981).

Delusions, like other beliefs, can be about values rather than facts (Maher & Spitzer, 1992). It is, for such reasons, important that cognitive therapy for delusions is conducted in an atmosphere which allows such values to be discussed openly, and not used as a technique that gives people little option other than letting go of their original belief.

Another consideration is the role of unconscious mechanisms in hallucinations and delusions. Recent attempts to parallel and integrate cognitive approaches with more traditional psychodynamic views of the unconscious (Power & Brewin, 1991) have only just begun within the area of psychosis (Hingley, 1992). It is argued that major themes within psychodynamic theory such as the breakdown of normal defences (i.e. repression) and the 'emergence of primary process thinking regarding the boundary between conscious and unconscious mind' can be integrated with cognitive research into such things as delusional formation in the context of a stress vulnerability model. It is hypothesised that addressing the weakness that may give rise to reality distorting defences in the absence of the ability to repress traumatic cognitions through psychodynamic psychotherapy will significantly decrease the distressing positive symptoms of psychosis (Hingley, 1992). However, despite the presentation of data from one case this still remains an hypothesis or suggested mechanism rather than a model or theory to underpin psychological management of the positive residual symptoms.

For those seeking more information about psychodynamic psychotherapy for people with residual symptoms of psychosis the reader is referred to McGlashan (1983).

The role of the family

It has now been established in a number of controlled studies throughout the world that high levels of intrafamilial stress ('expression emotion') in the form of 'emotional over-involvement', 'criticism' or 'hostility' can increase the likelihood of a psychotic relapse (Leff *et al*, 1982; Vaughn *et al*, 1984; Barrelet *et al*, 1990). This has led to a proliferation of research whose principal aim has been the control of relapse through reduction in EE. Seven studies have now been completed and while the content of these interventions differs from study to study they have many features in common (Lam, 1991). These include:

(1) Increasing the understanding of the illness by the family. Here the therapist is concerned that the family should, through education and discussion with other families, construe the behaviour of the individual where appropriate in 'illness' rather than 'personality' terms to reduce criticism and improve empathy.

(2) Reducing family stress. Here the therapist tries to curb stressful interactions between subject and family by providing them with concrete suggestions for coping with the stressful behaviour of each other and to improve communication of relatives' emotions without resorting to criticism and coercion.

(3) Enhancing social networks. This is a further stress reduction measure where the individual and family are encouraged to develop personal, social, recreational and work contacts outside of the family.

(4) Reducing intra-familial conflict. Any long-standing relationship problems between family members are addressed using 'family therapy' techniques. (For more information on intervention techniques with families of people with schizophrenia see Barrowclough & Tarrier, 1993). Four of these studies demonstrated that family interventions significantly reduce relapse rates when compared to control groups (Falloon *et al*, 1982; Leff *et al*, 1982; Hogarty *et al*, 1986; Tarrier *et al*, 1988) and a common characteristic of these programmes was the inclusion of both the relative and the patient in the treatment strategies.

References

AGGERNAES, A. (1972) The experienced reality of hallucinations and other psychological phenomena: an empirical analysis. *Acta Psychiatrica Scandinavica*, **48**, 220–239.

ALFORD, G. S. & TURNER, S. M. (1976) Stimulus interference and conditions of inhibition of auditory hallucinations. *Journal of Behaviour Therapy and Experimental Psychiatry*, **7**, 155–160.

ALUMBAUGH, R. V. (1971) Use of behaviour modification techniques toward reduction of hallucinatory behaviour: a case study. *Psychological Record*, **21**, 415–417.

ÅSBERG, M., MONTGOMERY, S., PERIS, C., *et al* (1978) The comprehensive psychopathological rating scale. *Acta Psychiatrica Scandinavica*, **271**, 5–27.

BARRELET, L., FERRERO, F., SZIGETHGY, L., *et al* (1990) Expressed emotion and first admission schizophrenia: a replication of a French cultural environment. *British Journal of Psychiatry*, **153**, 532–542.

BARROWCLOUGH, C. & TARRIER, N. (1993) *Families of Schizophrenic Patients: Cognitive–Behavioural Intervention.* London: Chapman and Hall.

BECK, A. T. (1952) Successful outpatient psychotherapy of a chronic schizophrenic with a delusion based on borrowed guilt. *Psychiatry*, **15**, 305–312.

—— (1967) *Cognitive Therapy and Emotional Disorders.* New York: International Universities Press.

——, RUSH, A. J., SHAW, B. E., *et al* (1979) *Cognitive Therapy of Depression.* New York: Guilford Press.

BENTALL, R. P., HADDOCK, G. & SLADE, P. D. (1994) Cognitive–behaviour therapy for persistent auditory hallucinations: From theory to therapy. *Behaviour Therapy*, **25**, 51–66.

BIRCHWOOD, M., PRESTON, M. & HALLETT, S. (1988) *Schizophrenia: an Integrated Approach to Research and Treatment.* Harlow: Longman.

—— & TARRIER, N. (1992) Self control in psychotic disorders. *Archives of General Psychiatry*, **40**, 141–145.

BREIER, A. & STRAUS, J. S. (1983) Self control in psychotic disorders. *Archives of General Psychiatry*, **40**, 1141–1145.

BRETT-JONES, J., GARETY, P. A. & HEMSLEY, D. R. (1987) Measuring delusional experiences. A method and its application. *British Journal of Clinical Psychology*, **26**, 265.

BROGA, M. I. & NEUFELD, R. W. (1981) Multivariate cognitive performance levels and response styles among paranoid and non-paranoid schizophrenics. *Journal of Abnormal Psychology*, **90**, 495–509.

BUCHER, B. & FABRICATORE, J. (1970) Use of patient administered shock to administer hallucinations. *Behaviour Therapy*, **1**, 382–385.

CHADWICK, P. D. J. & LOWE, C. F. (1990) Measurement and modification of delusional beliefs. *Journal of Consulting and Clinical Psychology*, **58**, 225–232.

—— & BIRCHWOOD, M. (1994) Challenging the omnipotence of voices: A cognitive approach to auditory hallucinations. *British Journal of Psychiatry*, **165**, 190–201.

—— & LOWE, C. F. (1994) A cognitive approach to measuring and modifying delusions. *Behaviour Research and Therapy*, **32**, 355–367.

—— & BIRCHWOOD, M. (1995) The omnipotence of Voices II. The beliefs about voices questionnaire. *British Journal of Psychiatry*, **166**, 11–19.

CHAPMAN, L. J. & CHAPMAN, J. P. (1980) Scales for rating psychotic and psychotic like experiences as continua. *Schizophrenia Bulletin*, **6**, 476–489.

CURSON, D. A., PATEL, M., LIDDLE, P. F., *et al* (1988) Psychiatric morbidity of a long stay hospital population with chronic schizophrenia and implications for future community care. *British Medical Journal*, **297**, 819–822.

DAVIS, J. R., WALLACE, C. J., LIBERMAN, R. P., *et al* (1976) The use of brief isolation to suppress delusional and hallucinatory speech. *Journal of Behaviour Therapy and Experimental Psychiatry*, **7**, 269–275.

DRYDEN, W. (1989) *Relational Emotive Counselling in Action.* London: Sage.

D'ZURILLA, T. J. & GOLDFRIED, M. R. (1971) Problem solving and behaviour modification. *Journal of Abnormal Psychology*, **78**, 1067–1126.

FALLOON, I. R. H. & TALBOT, R. E. (1981) Persistent auditory hallucinations: Coping mechanisms and implications for management. *Psychological Medicine*, **11**, 329–339.

——, BOYD, J. L., McGILL, C. W., *et al* (1982) Family management in the prevention of exacerbations of schizophrenia. *New England Journal of Medicine*, **306**, 1437–1440.

GARETY, P. (1985) Delusions: Problems in definitions and measurement. *British Journal of Medical Psychology*, **58**, 24–34.

—— (1991) Reasoning and delusions. *British Journal of Psychiatry*, **159** (suppl. 14), 14–16.

—— (1992) The assessment of symptoms and behaviour. In *Innovations in the Psychological Management of Schizophrenia* (eds M. Birchwood & N. Tarrier). Chichester: Wiley.

—— & HEMSLEY, D. (1987) Characteristics of delusional experience. *European Archives of Psychiatry and Neurology Sciences*, **2346**, 294–298.

——, —— & WESSELY, S. (1991) Reasoning in deluded schizophrenic and paranoid subjects: biases in performance on a probabilistic inference task. *Journal of Nervous and Mental Diseases*, **179**, 194–201.

GEORGE, L. & NEUFELD, R. W. (1985) Cognition and symptomatology in schizophrenia. *Schizophrenia Bulletin*, **11**, 264–285.

GOODWIN, D. W., ALDERSON, P. & ROSENTHAL, R. (1971) Clinical significance of hallucinations in psychiatric disorders. *Archives of General Psychiatry*, **24**, 76–80.

HADDOCK, G., BENTALL, R. P. & SLADE, P. D. (1993) Psychological study of chronic auditory hallucinations: 2 case studies. *Behaviour and Cognitive Psychotherapy*, **21**, 335–347.

HAYNES, S. N. & GEDDY, P. (1973) Suppression of psychotic hallucinations through time out. *Behaviour Therapy*, **4**, 123–127.

HEILBRUN, A. B. (1993) Hallucinations. In *Symptoms of Schizophrenia* (ed. C. G. Costello). New York: Wiley.

HINGLEY, S. M. (1992) Psychological theories of delusional thinking: in search of integration. *British Journal of Medical Psychology*, **65**, 347–356.

HOGARTY, G., ANDERSON, C. M., REISS, D. J., *et al* (1986) Family psychoeducation, social skills training and maintenance chemotherapy in the aftercare treatment of schizophrenia 1: one year effects of a controlled study on relapse and expressed emotion. *Archives of General Psychiatry*, **43**, 633–642.

HUSTIG, H. H. & HAFNER, R. J. (1990) Persistent auditory hallucinations and their relationship to delusions of mood. *Journal of Nervous and Mental Diseases*, **178**, 264–267.

KENDLER, K. S., GLAZER, W. M. & MORGENSTERN, H. (1983) Dimensions of delusional experience. *American Journal of Psychiatry*, **140**, 466–469.

KRAWIEKA, M., GOLDBERG, D. & VAUGHAN, M. (1977) Standardised psychiatric assessment scale for chronic psychotic patients. *Acta Psychiatrica Scandinavica*, **36**, 25–31.

LAM, D. (1991) Psychosocial family intervention studies in schizophrenia: a review of empirical studies. *Psychological Medicine*, **21**, 423–441.

LEFF, J., KUIPERS, L. BERKOWITZ, R., *et al* (1982) A controlled trial of intervention in the families of schizophrenic families. *British Journal of Psychiatry*, **141**, 121–134.

MAHER, B. A. (1974) Delusional thinking and perceptual disorder. *Journal of Individual Psychology*, **30**, 98–113.

—— & SPITZER, M. (1993) Delusions. In *Symptoms of Schizophrenia* (ed. C. G. Costello), pp. 92–120. New York: Wiley.

McGLASHAN, T. H. (1983) Intensive individual psychotherapy of schizophrenia: Review of techniques. *Archives of General Psychiatry*, **40**, 909–920.

MILTON, F., PATWA, K. & HAFNER, R. J. (1978) Confrontation vs. belief modification in persistently deluded patients. *British Journal of Medical Psychology*, **51**, 127–130.

MOSER, A. J. (1974) Covert punishment of hallucinatory behaviour in a psychotic male. *Journal of Behaviour Therapy and Experimental Psychiatry*, **5**, 297–299.

MULHALL, D. (1978) Manual for Personal Questionnaire Rapid Scaling Technique. London: NFER-Nelson.

NYDEGGAR, R. N. (1972) The elimination of hallucinatory and delusional behaviour by verbal conditioning and assertive training: A case study. *Journal of Behaviour Therapy and Experimental Psychiatry*, **3**, 225–227.

POWER, M. & BREWIN, C. (1991) From Freud to cognitive science. *British Journal of Clinical Psychology*, **30**, 289–310.

ROGERS, R., GILLIS, J. R., TURNER, R. E., *et al* (1990) The clinical presentation of command hallucinations in a forensic population. *American Journal of Psychiatry*, **147**, 1304–1307.

ROSS, L. & ANDERSON, C. (1981) Shortcomings in the attribution process: On the origins and maintenance of erroneous social assessments. In *Judgement under Uncertainty: Heuristics and Biases* (eds D. Kahneman, P. Slovic & A. Tversky). New York: Cambridge University Press.

OVERALL, J. E., GORHAM, D. R. & SHAWYER, J. R. (1962) Basic dimensions of change in symptomatology of chronic schizophrenia. *Journal of Abnormal and Social Psychology*, **62**, 597–602.

SLADE, P. D. (1972*a*) The effects of systematic desensitisation on auditory hallucinations. *Behaviour Research and Therapy*, **10**, 85–91.

—— (1972*b*) The psychological investigation and treatment of auditory hallucinations. *British Journal of Medical Psychology*, **46**, 293–296.

—— (1973) The psychological investigation and treatment of auditory hallucinations: a second case report. *British Journal of Medical Psychology*, **46**, 293–296.

—— & BENTALL, R. P. (1988) *Sensory Deception: A Scientific Analysis of Auditory Hallucinations*. Chichester: Wiley.

STRAUS, J. S. (1969) Hallucinations and delusions as points on continua function. *Archives of General Psychiatry*, **21**, 581–586.

TARRIER, N. (1987) An investigation of residual positive symptoms in discharged schizophrenic patients. *British Journal of Clinical Psychology*, **26**, 141–143.

—— (1992) Management and modification of residual psychotic symptoms. In *Innovations in the Psychological Management of Schizophrenia* (eds M. Birchwood and N. Tarrier), pp. 147–170. Chichester: Wiley.

——, BARROWCLOUGH, C., VAUGHN, C., *et al* (1988) The community management of schizophrenia: a controlled trial of a behavioural intervention with families to reduce relapse. *British Journal of Psychiatry*, **153**, 532–542.

——, BECKETT, R., HARWOOD, S., *et al* (1993) A trial of two cognitive behavioural methods of treating drug resistant psychotic residual symptoms in schizophrenic patients: I. Outcome. *British Journal of Psychiatry*, **162**, 524–532.

TESSER, A. & SHAFFER, D. R. (1990) Attitudes and attitude change. *Annual Review of Psychology*, **41**, 479–523.

VAUGHN, C. E., SNYDER, K. S., FREEMAN, W., *et al* (1984) Family factors in schizophrenic relapse: a replication in California of British research on expressed emotion. *Archives of General Psychiatry*, **41**, 1169–1177.

WATTS, F. N., POWELL, E. G. & AUSTIN, S. V. (1973) The modification of abnormal beliefs. *British Journal of Medical Psychology*, **46**, 359–363.

WESSELEY, S., BUCHANAN, A., REED, A., *et al* (1993) Acting on delusions I: Prevalence. *British Journal of Psychiatry*, **163**, 69–76.

WIENGAERTNER, A. M. (1971) Self-administered aversive stimulation with hallucinating hospitalised schizophrenics. *Journal of Consulting and Clinical Psychology*, **36**, 422–429.

WINCZE, J. P., LEITENBERG, H. & AGRAS, W. S. (1972) The effects of token reinforcement and feedback on the delusional verbal behaviour of chronic paranoid schizophrenics. *Journal of Applied Behaviour Analysis*, **5**, 247–262.

WOLFF, R. (1971) The systematic application of the satisfaction procedure to delusional verbiage. *Psychological Record*, **21**, 459–463.

YOUNG, H. F., BENTALL, R. P., SLADE, P. D., *et al* (1987) The role of brief instructions and suggestibility in the elicitation of auditory and visual hallucinations in normal and psychiatric subjects. *Journal of Nervous and Mental Diseases*, **175**, 41–48.

5 Emotional disorders in primary care

L. M. MYNORS-WALLIS and D. H. GATH

The emotional disorders presenting in primary care do not fit easily into the current diagnostic categories of mental disorder. In this chapter the term emotional disorder is applied to the broad range of non-psychotic psychological conditions that are seen and treated by general practitioners (GPs). The chapter begins with a brief review of the frequency and nature of these conditions. The point is then made that GPs do not always recognise these disorders, but they can be trained to do so effectively. The chapter concludes with a review of the psychological treatments commonly used to treat emotional disorders in primary care, and reference is made to the feasibility and efficacy of such treatments.

The frequency and nature of emotional disorders in primary care

Emotional disorders are common among people consulting their GPs. Various studies have used self-report questionnaires to screen for psychiatric disorders in primary care; these studies have found prevalence rates ranging from 16% to 43% of general practice attenders (Barrett *et al*, 1988). In the third National Morbidity Survey of England and Wales (RCGP *et al*, 1987), emotional disorders were found to be the third most common cause of consultation in primary care (the first two causes being disorders of the respiratory system and of the cardiovascular system). In the UK emotional disorders certainly form a considerable part of a GP's workload. In the course of a year an average GP sees about 300 patients with emotional problems; some of these patients are seen several times a year.

It was originally thought that nearly all emotional disorders seen in primary care were transient responses to life's crises. It is now recognised that not all of these conditions have a good prognosis. In

Warwickshire, Mann and colleagues (1981) carried out a one-year follow-up of 100 people diagnosed by their GP as having an emotional disorder (89 being diagnosed as having an anxiety or depressive disorder). The outcome for these people was not uniformly good: a quarter of them recovered in the first months of the follow-up and did not relapse, about half had intermittent relapses, and a quarter had a chronic course with persisting symptoms and regular consultations. An 11-year follow-up was completed for this cohort (Lloyd *et al*, 1996) which found that about half had had a chronic course. Patients with neurotic disorder not only had a high psychiatric morbidity but also a high consultation rate for physical illness and an increased mortality from all causes. In a south London general practice, the outcome of emotional disorders over five years was determined from the practice records. It was found that a large proportion of emotional disorders ran a chronic or relapsing course. Thus, for patients given a new psychiatric diagnosis, 18% of the men and 35% of the women received a psychiatric diagnosis in each subsequent year (Cooper *et al*, 1969).

In primary care, the common symptoms of emotional disorders have been identified by Goldberg & Huxley (1980), who studied 88 people diagnosed as having a mental disorder in primary care. The most common symptoms were anxiety and worry (82 people), while despondency and sadness were also frequent (71 people). Other common symptoms were fatigue (71), sleep disturbance (50), and irritability (38). Psychological symptoms were often accompanied and masked by somatic symptoms. It is now well recognised that in primary care many people with emotional disorders present somatic rather than psychological symptoms. Thus, among 125 new attenders diagnosed as having an emotional disorder, 42% presented with somatic symptoms (Wright, 1990).

Among the people seen in primary care, considerable social impairment can be caused by emotional disorders, particularly by depressive disorders. In a British study, a consecutive series of 207 attenders with depressive disorders were identified by GPs in six Manchester practices (Johnson & Mellor, 1977). Over half of the people were unable to continue with their normal lives and had to make a major change in their lifestyle, such as discontinuing normal work. In North America, data from the Medical Outcome Study were used to compare two groups of people seen in primary and secondary care. One group consisted of attenders with depression; the other consisted of attenders with any of eight chronic medical conditions (hypertension, diabetes, advanced heart disease, angina, arthritis, back problems, lung problems and gastrointestinal disorders) (Wells *et al*, 1989). It was found that people with depression had significantly worse social functioning than did the people with chronic medical conditions.

Compared with people in six of the eight medical groups, the depressed people spent more days in bed. Patients with depressive symptoms, as distinct from depressive disorders, also had significant social impairment.

The financial cost of emotional disorders is considerable. An estimate was made of the economic cost of non-psychotic disorders seen in general practice in the UK in 1985 (Croft-Jeffreys & Wilkinson, 1989). Direct treatment costs were £372 million; taking into account lost productivity, however, the total cost was £5.6 billion.

In summary, anxiety and depressive disorders present commonly in general practice, and often run a chronic course, at considerable cost socially and economically to the individual and the country.

Recognition of emotional disorders by general practitioners

An important finding has been that emotional disorders often go undetected in primary care. Some of these disorders may become chronic if not treated. Thus, in a London survey it was found that depressive disorders lasted longer if they were not detected by the GP (Freeling *et al*, 1985). In Holland, a comparison was made between patients with recognised/unrecognised depression. Those with unrecognised depression were less likely to receive mental health interventions, and had worse outcomes in terms of psychopathology and social functioning (Ormel *et al*, 1990).

In a suburban London practice it was found that even a well motivated GP did not detect one-third of psychiatric cases (Goldberg & Blackwell, 1970). In Manchester a survey of 91 GPs showed that about 45% of attenders with mental illness (identified by high scores on the General Health Questionnaire) were missed by the GP. A second finding was that GPs varied widely in their ability to diagnose emotional disorders accurately (Marks *et al*, 1979).

Goldberg & Huxley (1992) identified two ways of determining how accurately a GP recognises emotional disorders. The first way is to measure specificity; that is, how well the GP can distinguish between cases and non-cases of emotional disorder. The second is to measure sensitivity; that is, how far the doctor over-identifies or under-identifies psychiatric illness. Several features characterise the consultation style of doctors who can best identify emotionally distressed attenders. These features are: more eye contact throughout the interview; less avoidance, with a more relaxed posture; making facilitatory noises while listening; less urgency and hurry initially; and not giving information early in the interview.

Other interviewing skills are important in increasing accurate recognition of emotional disorders. They include: clarifying the complaint, dealing with over-talkativeness and interruptions, detecting verbal and non-verbal cues, asking directive and closed 'psychiatric questions', and making supportive comments (Goldberg & Huxley, 1992). It is important to stress that these interview skills can be taught to GPs.

It has been shown that the use of video feedback can improve interview skills in both experienced GPs and GP trainees (Gask *et al*, 1987, 1988). Thus, a group of 10 experienced GPs received a training course consisting of 36 hours' tuition over 18 weeks. After this course, there was a statistically significant improvement in their use of direct psychosocial questioning, their ability to clarify comments, and their ability to detect and develop the main problem (Gask *et al*, 1987).

Psychological treatments of emotional disorders in primary care

Once an emotional disorder has been recognised by the GP, a decision has to be made about appropriate management. Medication may have a role in treatment, particularly for specific disorders such as depressive disorder and panic disorder. Many patients, however, are unwilling to take medication because of side-effects, fears about dependence and a belief that their symptoms are caused by social difficulties that will not be resolved by medication.

Simple support and advice by the GP is probably a part of the treatment of most patients with emotional disorders. It is difficult to control for such an intervention which is part of a normal consultation. Catalan *et al* (1984) showed that listening, explanation, advice and reassurance by the GP, were as effective in the treatment of recent onset anxiety disorders, as anxiolytic medication, and no more demanding of the GP's time.

Some patients, however, may benefit from a psychological intervention over and above usual GP care. There are now several studies of psychological interventions for emotional disorders in primary care and these will now be reviewed.

Counselling

Counselling involves a wide variety of interventions, and is provided by practitioners with varying professional backgrounds and skills. There are, however, basic components common to all counselling. Some of these components have been summarised as guidelines for counsellors (Murgatroyd, 1986):

(1) A person in need has come to you for help.
(2) In order to be helped they need to know that you have understood how they think and feel
(3) They also need to know that, whatever your own feelings about who or what they are or about what they have or have not done, you accept them as they are (unconditional positive regard).
(4) In the light of this knowledge about your acceptance and understanding of them they will begin to open themselves to the possibility of change and development.

Within this client-centred, accepting, listening framework, several specific skills may be used:

(1) Open questioning: exploring problems and emotions.
(2) Reflection: echoing back the last few words, or making a paraphrase of these words, to encourage the client to say more about a particular subject.
(3) Clarification: summarising what has been said, in order to check and clarify a discussion for both the counsellor and the client.

The British Association for Counselling describes counselling as the skilled and principled use of relationships to develop self-knowledge, emotional acceptance and growth, and personal resources. The overall aim is to live more fully and satisfyingly. Counselling may be concerned with addressing and resolving specific problems, making decisions, coping with crises, working through feelings or inner conflict or improving relationships with others (Rowland, 1993).

There has been a large increase in the numbers of counsellors working in primary care. A survey of over 1500 general practices in England and Wales found that 31% of practices had a practice counsellor (Sibbald *et al*, 1993). The qualifications of the counsellors were varied. Uncontrolled studies of conselling in primary care have shown that the treatment is valued by both patients and GPs (Anderson & Hasler, 1979; Waydenfeld & Waydenfeld, 1980; Martin & Mitchell, 1983; Trepka & Griffiths, 1987). A descriptive study from Dorset (Baker *et al*, 1998) showed that anxious and depressive symptoms improved more in counselled patients than in patients on a waiting list. Randomised controlled trials have evaluated counselling both for the treatment of depressive disorders alone, and for the treatment of a broader range of patients with anxious and depressive symptoms.

Three studies have evaluated the role of counselling in the treatment of depressive disorders in primary care. Corney (1987) compared social work counselling with treatment as usual for a group of 80 depressed women in general practice. The overall results showed little difference in outcome between the two groups, 60% of women in both groups being clinically improved at six months. One subgroup of women – those who had major marital problems and who were suffering from 'acute on chronic' depression – did benefit from the social work. In a trial of counselling for women with postnatal depression (68% of them meeting Research Diagnostic Criteria for major depression), eight sessions of counselling by a health visitor were found to be more beneficial than treatment as usual (Holden *et al*, 1989). Thus the counselled group had a significantly greater reduction in mean scores on depression measures, while significantly more counselled mothers recovered.

In Edinburgh, 121 people with major depression were randomly assigned to one of four treatments – social work counselling, cognitive therapy from a psychologist, amitriptyline from a psychiatrist, or treatment as usual from the GP (Scott & Freeman, 1992). After four weeks, recovery rates were significantly better after social work counselling than after treatment as usual from the GP. The results were also better after amitriptyline from a psychiatrist than after the usual treatment from the GP. After 16 weeks (end of treatment) only social work counselling was more effective than GP care. Individuals in the social work group had received 12 hours of counselling as against the 50 minutes received by the people treated by the GP.

Four randomised controlled trials from UK primary care have compared counselling with GP's treatment as usual for a broad range of emotional disorders. Ashurst (1982) in a study of 726 patients found no difference in symptom outcome, demand on GP's time, nor psychotropic drug prescription between the two groups. Boot *et al* (1994) did find a more favourable outcome in the counselling group, but methodological concerns have been raised about this study (Harvey *et al*, 1998). Friedli *et al* (1997) in a study of 136 patients found no difference in overall outcome in terms of psychological symptoms and social adjustment between patients who received up to 12 sessions of counselling and those who received GP treatment as usual. However, patients who were cases of depressive disorder on entry to the study did better in the counselled group. Harvey *et al* (1998), in a sample of 162 patients, reported no difference in clinical outcome or cost between GP usual care and up to six sessions of counselling. In an Australian study of people with psychological symptoms of at least six months duration, neither brief dynamic psychotherapy nor counselling from the GP was more effective than GP usual care (Brodaty & Andrews, 1983).

In summary, counselling has not been shown to offer clear benefit for emotional disorders in primary care. Counselling may be of value for certain depressive disorders. No study, however, has controlled for the non-specific effects of therapy, in particular therapist attention.

Cognitive–behavioural treatments

Cognitive–behavioural treatments have been successful in primary care. These treatments are structured and time-limited, and they focus on the here and now rather than the past. All aspects of therapy are made explicit to the client. The therapist and client work together in planning strategies to deal with clearly identified problems (Hawton *et al*, 1989). One of these treatments, cognitive therapy, has been reported as effective for major depression in primary care (Blackburn *et al*, 1981; Teasdale *et al*, 1984; Scott & Freeman, 1992). Cognitive therapy is time consuming and requires specialist training. It is usually given by psychologists rather than doctors. A clinical psychology service can operate successfully in primary care (Robson *et al*, 1984), but many general practices do not have the resources to provide such a service for the many attenders who might benefit.

Psychiatric nurses with specialised training in behaviour therapy can successfully treat people with phobias and obsessive–compulsive disorders in primary care (Ginsberg *et al*, 1984). Nurses with such training are not widely available.

Problem-solving treatment is a simple cognitive–behavioural treatment that has been evaluated in Oxford for use in primary care. The problem-solving approach is based on the common observation that emotional symptoms are generally induced by problems of living. The treatment encourages people to formulate ways of dealing with such problems, both psychologically and practically. People learn to use their own skills and resources to cope with both present and future problems.

A course of problem-solving treatment starts by eliciting the person's symptoms. A list is then made of all the problems that the person is facing. These problems commonly relate to personal relationships, work and money. The therapist and client identify links between these problems and the client's symptoms. The therapist stresses that, if the client's problems can be satisfactorily resolved, the symptoms will improve. The resolution of particular problems is brought about in a structured way using the following stages.

Stage 1: *Explanation of the treatment and its rationale.*
Stage 2: *Clarification and definition of problems.*
    Listing the problems in a clear and concrete form and

breaking down large problems into smaller and more manageable parts.

Stage 3: *Choice of achievable goals.*
Specific goals are set to be achieved both quickly (before the next treatment session), and more slowly (over the course of treatment).

Stage 4: *Generating solutions.*
Consider any relevant solutions to achieve the goals set (brain-storming).

Stage 5: *Choice of preferred solution.*

Stage 6: *Implementation of the preferred solution.*
Any steps required to implement the preferred solution should be listed clearly and precisely. The therapist and patient should agree homework tasks for the patient to carry out before the next session.

Stage 7: *Evaluation.*
The patient and therapist evaluate the patient's success of lack of success in the assigned homework tasks.

A more detailed description of problem-solving treatment as evaluated in primary care can be found in Gath & Mynors-Wallis (1997). Four studies have evaluated problem-solving treatment in primary care. The first study compared problem-solving treatment with usual treatment by the GP for patients with emotional disorders of poor prognosis (Catalan *et al*, 1991). Patients in this study were selected if they were still unwell, defined as a score of 12 or above on the Present State Examination (Wing *et al*, 1974) one month after their initial consultation. At both end of treatment and six month follow-up the patients treated with problem solving showed significantly greater improvement on all standardised measures. They also reported greater satisfaction with their treatment.

A second study evaluating problem-solving in primary care focused on depressive disorders (Mynors-Wallis *et al*, 1995). This study set out to determine whether problem-solving was an effective treatment for patients with major depression by comparison with amitriptyline and drug/psychological placebo. A second objective was to determine whether the treatment could be given by GPs trained in problem-solving techniques as well as by a research psychiatrist. Ninety-one people with major depression were recruited from general practice and randomly allocated to receive one of three treatments: (a) problem-solving treatment; (b) amitriptyline in a dose of 150 mg; (c) drug and psychological placebo. All treatments were delivered in six sessions over 12 weeks either by a research psychiatrist or by research GPs trained in the treatment techniques. The first session was scheduled to last 60 minutes, with subsequent sessions lasting 30 minutes.

At the end of treatment there were four important findings:

(1) Problem solving was at least as effective as amitriptyline in the treatment of major depression in primary care, on measures of depressive severity and of social outcome.

(2) Problem solving was more effective than a placebo treatment which combined the non-specific effects of both drug and psychological interventions. This indicates that there is something specific about problem solving which facilitates recovery in major depression.

(3) Problem solving was equally effective when given by research GPs trained in the techniques as when given by a research psychiatrist.

(4) Patient satisfaction with problem solving was high, as demonstrated by low drop-out rates and high satisfaction ratings on a self-report questionnaire.

No factors predicted which patients did better with medication and which with problem-solving treatment (Mynors-Wallis & Gath, 1997).

Although problem-solving treatment is a time-limited psychological treatment and in the studies described above was delivered in four to six sessions, this is still too lengthy a treatment to be given by most GPs. Problem-solving treatment could be made more widely available if non-medical members of the primary care team could be trained to use the technique effectively. A third study has been completed to answer two questions:

(a) Can community nurses be successfully trained in the techniques of problem-solving treatment?

(b) After training, how effectively can community nurses give problem-solving treatment to primary care patients with emotional disorders, in comparison with GP's usual treatment? (Mynors-Wallis *et al*, 1997).

This study showed that community nurses could be trained to deliver problem-solving treatment appropriately. Seventy patients with an emotional disorder were then randomly allocated to receive either problem-solving treatment from a trained community nurse or treatment as usual from their GP. There was no difference in the clinical outcome between the two groups at either eight or 26 weeks. However, patients who received problem-solving treatment had fewer disability days and fewer days off work.

A fourth study is being completed. Four treatments for major depression in primary care have been compared: (a) problem-solving alone given by a GP; (b) problem-solving alone given by a community nurse; (c) antidepressant medication alone given by a GP; (d) problem-solving given by a community nurse in combination with antidepressant medication given by a GP.

Other studies that are in progress evaluating the use of problem-solving treatment include group and individual problem-solving treatment for a European community sample of depressive disorders (Dowrick *et al*, 1998), and individual problem-solving for patients with dysthymia in the USA.

Interpersonal psychotherapy and interpersonal counselling

Interpersonal psychotherapy is a structured psychological treatment that focuses on interpersonal problems (Klerman *et al*, 1984). Problems are categorised as involving bereavement, role disputes, role transitions or interpersonal deficits. Schulberg *et al* (1996) in the United States compared interpersonal psychotherapy with antidepressant medication and physician's usual care in a sample of 275 patients with major depression in primary care. Patients who received interpersonal psychotherapy or medication did better than those receiving usual care throughout the eight-month follow-up. Patients receiving antidepressant medication recovered more quickly than patients receiving interpersonal psychotherapy.

Interpersonal counselling is a modification of interpersonal psychotherapy, designed for administration by nurse practitioners in primary care. Interpersonal counselling comprises a maximum of six half-hour sessions which are focused on recent changes in the person's life, including sources of stress in the family home, workplace and neighbourhood.

A clinical trial was carried out among people enrolling in a Health Maintenance Organisation in Boston, USA. The subjects were people with a score of six or above on the 30-item version of the General Health Questionnaire (Goldberg & Hillier, 1979). People receiving interpersonal counselling were compared with a group of similar people left untreated. The treated people showed a greater reduction in GHQ scores over three months than did untreated people. Interpersonal counselling proved feasible in primary care, and was easily learnt by experienced nurse practitioners in a short training programme of 8–12 hours (Klerman & Budman, 1987).

Group treatments

Group treatment, if acceptable to patients, would be a potentially cost-effective way of providing psychological treatment in primary care.

Anxiety management groups have been described in general practice (Adams & Dixey, 1988), but they are not always effective in reducing symptoms (Trepka *et al*, 1986). In primary care a comparison was made between group therapy and treatment as usual for mothers who attended frequently with pre-school children; group therapy led to a reduction in their consultation rates (Benson & Turk, 1988). The use of a group to prevent child neglect among at risk mothers has been described (Beswick & Richardson, 1992).

Group treatment remains as yet a largely unevaluated treatment option.

Conclusions

Emotional disorders are common in primary care and a significant cause of psychological and social morbidity. Many of these disorders resolve spontaneously but a significant proportion become chronic. Patients with these disorders may be helped by a time-limited psychological intervention in primary care. Interpretation of the research to date is hampered by the heterogeneous patient groups enrolled in many studies. Research that has focused on a specific psychiatric disorder, such as depressive disorder, has shown that a range of psychological interventions are effective, often as effective as antidepressant medication. However, it has proved more difficult to demonstrate that brief psychological treatments are more effective than GP's usual care for the broad range of emotional disorders presenting as distress. This may be because the interventions are ineffective. Alternatively it may be that among those patients who are benefiting from the treatment, there is a group with only minimal symptoms who get better anyway, and another group with long-standing, entrenched symptoms who are unlikely to be helped by the brief interventions described above. Future research needs to be directed at helping the GP decide which patients are most likely to be helped by the brief psychological treatments available.

References

ADAMS, A. & DIXEY, D. (1988) Running an anxiety management group. *Health Visitor*, **61**, 375–376.

ANDERSON, S. A. & HASLER, J. C. (1979) Counselling in general practice. *Journal of the Royal College of General Practitioners*, **29**, 352–356.

ASHURST, P. (1982) Counselling in general practice. In *Psychiatry and General Practice* (eds A. Clare & M. Lader), pp. 77–88. London: Academic Press.

BAKER, R., ALLEN, H., GIBSON, S., *et al* (1998) Evaluation of a primary care counselling service in Dorset. *British Journal of General Practice*, **48**, 1049–1054.

BARRETT, J. E., BARRETT, A., OXMAN, T. G., *et al* (1988) The prevalence of psychiatric disorders in a primary care practice. *Archives of General Psychiatry*, **45**, 1100–1106.

BENSON, P. & TURK, T. (1988) Group therapy in a general practice setting for frequent attenders. *Journal of the Royal College of General Practitioners*, **38**, 538–541.

BESWICK, K. & RICHARDSON, P. (1992) *Liaison in Primary Care: Early Detection of Difficulties in the Prevention of Depression and Anxiety* (eds R. Jenkins, J. Newton & R. Young). London: HMSO.

BLACKBURN, I. M., BISHOP, S., GLENN, A. I. M., *et al* (1981) The efficacy of cognitive therapy in depression. *British Journal of Psychiatry*, **139**, 181–189.

BOOT, D., GILLIES, P., FENELON, J., *et al* (1994) Evaluation of the short term impact of counselling in general practice. *Patient Education and Counselling*, **121**, 531–539.

BRODATY, J. & ANDREWS, G. (1983) Brief psychotherapy in family practice. *British Journal of Psychiatry*, **143**, 11–19.

CATALAN, J., GATH, D. H., EDMONDS, G., *et al* (1984) The effects of non-prescribing of anxiolytics in general practice. *British Journal of Psychiatry*, **144**, 593–602.

———, ———, BOND, A., *et al* (1991) Evaluation of a brief psychological treatment for emotional disorders in primary care. *Psychological Medicine*, **21**, 1013–1018.

COOPER, B., FRY, J. & KALTON, G. (1969) A longitudinal study of psychiatric morbidity in a general practice population. *British Journal of Preventative and Social Medicine*, **23**, 210–217.

CORNEY, R. H. (1987) Marital problems and treatment outcome in depressed women. A clinical trial of social work intervention. *British Journal of Psychiatry*, **151**, 652–659.

CROFT-JEFFREYS, C. & WILKINSON, G. (1989) Estimated costs of neurotic disorders in UK general practice in 1985. *Psychological Medicine*, **19**, 549–558.

DOWRICK, C., CASEY, P., DALGARD, O., *et al* (1998) Outcomes of Depression International Network (ODIN). Background, methods and field trials. *British Journal of Psychiatry*, **172**, 359–363.

FREELING, P., RAO, B. M., PAYKEL, E. S., *et al* (1985) Unrecognised depression in general practice. *British Medical Journal*, **290**, 1880–1883.

FRIEDLI, K., KING, M. B., LLOYD, M., *et al* (1997) Randomised control assessment of non-directive psychotherapy versus routine general practitioner care. *Lancet*, **350**, 1662–1665.

GASK, L., MCGRATH, G., GOLDBERG, D., *et al* (1987) Improving the psychiatric skills of established general practitioners. *Medical Education*, **21**, 362–368.

———, ———, ———, *et al* (1988) Improving the psychiatric skills of the general practice trainee: an evaluation of a group training course. *Medical Education*, **22**, 132–138.

GATH, D. H. & MYNORS-WALLIS, L. M. (1997) Problem-solving treatment in primary care. In *Science and Practice of Cognitive Behaviour Therapy* (eds D. M. Clark & C. G. Fairburn). Oxford: Oxford University Press.

GINSBERG, G., MARKS, I. & WATERS, H. (1984) Cost–benefit analysis of a controlled trial of nurse therapy for neurosis in primary care. *Psychological Medicine*, **14**, 683–690.

GOLDBERG, D. P. & BLACKWELL, B. (1970) Psychiatric illness in general practice. A detailed study using a new method of case identification. *British Medical Journal*, **261**, 439–443.

——— & HILLIER, V. F. (1979) A scaled version of the General Health Questionnaire. *Psychological Medicine*, **9**, 139–145.

——— & HUXLEY, P. (1980) *Mental Illness in the Community: The Pathway to Psychiatric Care.* London: Tavistock.

——— & ——— (1992) *Common Mental Disorders – A Bio-Social Model.* London: Tavistock/ Routledge.

HARVEY, I., NELSON, S. J., LYONS, R. A., *et al* (1998) A randomised controlled trial and economic evaluation of generic counselling in primary care. *British Journal of General Practice*, **48**, 1043–1049.

HAWTON, K., SALKOVSKIS, P., KIRK, J., *et al* (1989) *Cognitive Behaviour Therapy for Psychiatric Problems.* Oxford: Oxford University Press.

HOLDEN, J. M., SAGOVSKY, R. & COX, J. L. (1989) Counselling in a general practice setting; controlled study of health visitor intervention in the treatment of post-natal depression. *British Medical Journal*, **298**, 223–226.

JOHNSON, D. & MELLOR, M. (1977) The severity of depression in patients treated in general practice. *Journal of the Royal College of General Practitioners*, **27**, 419–422.

KLERMAN, G. L., WEISSMAN, M. M., ROUNSAVILLE, B. J., *et al* (1984) *Interpersonal Psychotherapy of Depression.* New York: Basic Books.

—— & BUDMAN, S. (1987) Efficacy of a brief psychological intervention for symptoms of stress and distress among patients in primary care. *Medical Care*, **25**, 1078–1088.

LLOYD, K. R., JENKINS, R. & MANN, A. (1996) Long term outcome of patients with neurotic illness in general practice. *British Medical Journal*, **313**, 26–28.

MAGUIRE, P., ROE, P. & GOLDBERG, D. (1978) The value of feedback in teaching interviewing skills to medical students. *Psychological Medicine*, **8**, 695–704.

MANN, A. N., JENKINS, R. & BELSEY, E. (1981) The 12 month outcome of patients with neurotic illness and general practice. *Psychological Medicine*, **11**, 535–550.

MARKS, J., GOLDBERG, D. & HILLIER, V. (1979) Determinants of the ability of general practitioners to detect psychiatric illness. *Psychological Medicine*, **9**, 337–353.

MARTIN, E. & MITCHELL, H. (1993) A counsellor in general practice: a one year survey. *Journal of the Royal College of General Practitioners*, **33**, 366–367.

MURGATROYD, S. (1986) *Counselling and Helping.* London: British Psychological Society/Methuen.

MYNORS-WALLIS, L. M., GATH, D. H., LLOYD-THOMAS, A. R., *et al* (1995) Randomised control trial comparing problem-solving treatment with amitriptyline and placebo for major depression in primary care. *British Medical Journal*, **310**, 441–445.

—— & —— (1997) Predictors of treatment outcome for major depression in primary care. *Psychological Medicine*, **27**, 731–736.

——, DAVIES, I., GRAY, A., *et al* (1997) A randomised control trial and cost analysis of problem-solving treatment for emotional disorders given by community nurses in primary care. *British Journal of Psychiatry*, **170**, 113–119.

ORMEL, J., VAN DEN BRINK, W., KOETER, M. W. J., *et al* (1990) Recognition, management and outcome of psychological disorders in primary care: a naturalistic follow-up study. *Psychological Medicine*, **20**, 909–923.

RCGP, OPCS & DHSS (1987) *Morbidity Statistics from General Practice – Third National Morbidity Survey 1981–182.* London: HMSO.

ROBSON, M. H., FRANCE, R. & BLAND, M. (1984) Clinical psychology in primary care: a controlled clinical and economic evaluation. *British Medical Journal*, **288**, 1805–1808.

ROWLAND, N. (1993) What is counselling? In *Counselling in General Practice* (eds R. Corney & R. Jenkins). London: Routledge.

SCHULBERG, H. C., BLOCK, M. R., MADONIA, M. J., *et al* (1996) Treating major depression in primary care practice. *Archives of General Psychiatry*, **53**, 913–919.

SCOTT, A. I. F. & FREEMAN, C. P. L. (1992) Edinburgh primary care depression study: treatment outcome, patient satisfaction, and cost after 16 years. *British Medical Journal*, **304**, 883–887.

SIBBALD, B., ADDINGTON-HALL, J., BRENNEMAN, D., *et al* (1993) Counsellors in English and Welsh general practices: their nature and distribution. *British Medical Journal*, **306**, 29–33.

TEASDALE, J. D., FENNELL, M. J. W., HIBBERT, G. A., *et al* (1984) Cognitive therapy for major depressive disorder in primary care. *British Journal of Psychiatry*, **144**, 400–406.

TREPKA, C., LAING, I. & SMITH, S. (1986) Group treatment of general practice anxiety problems. *Journal of Royal College of General Practitioners*, **36**, 114–117.

—— & GRIFFITHS, T. (1987) Evaluation of psychological treatments in primary care. *Journal of the Royal College of General Practitioners*, **37**, 215–217.

WAYDENFELD, D. & WAYDENFELD, S. W. (1980) Counselling in general practice. *Journal of the Royal College of General Practitioners*, **30**, 671–677.

WELLS, K. B., STEWART, A., HAYS, R. D., *et al* (1989) The functioning and well-being of depressed patients: results from the Medical Outcomes Study. *Journal of the American Medical Association*, **262**, 914–919.

WING, J. K., COOPER, J. E. & SARTORIUS, N. (1974) *The Measurement and Classification of Psychiatric Symptoms.* Cambridge: Cambridge University Press.

WRIGHT, A. (1990) A study of the presentation of somatic symptoms in general practice by patients with psychiatric disturbance. *British Journal of General Practice*, **40**, 459–463.

6 Psychological interventions in HIV infection

JOSE CATALAN

In many regions of the world, HIV infection is a major health and social problem (Mann *et al*, 1992). While the UK has so far reported rates of HIV infection which are lower than in other developed countries, the extent and implications of the epidemic of HIV infection have important consequences. For example, in the UK, about 15 000 cases of AIDS had been reported by the end of March 1998, the majority in people aged 25 to 44 years, leading to a rapidly increasing number of years of working life lost, in particular for men (Communicable Disease Report, 1998). In the USA AIDS is now one of the leading causes of death for men aged 25 to 44 (Centers for Disease Control, 1993).

As in the case of other potentially fatal disorders, HIV infection can be accompanied by significant psychiatric and social disturbance, including an increased risk of suicide (Catalan, 1990*a*; Maj, 1990; Marzuk, 1991; Catalan *et al*, 1995), made worse by the social stigmatisation of those infected and by the risk of developing HIV-related neuropsychiatric disease (Burgess & Riccio, 1992; Catalan & Thornton, 1993). Reports from New York City indicate that HIV infection is present in a small but significant proportion of psychiatric patients: Sacks *et al* (1992) found 7% of acute psychiatric in-patients to be seropositive and Empfield *et al* (1993) found a seroprevalence of 6.4% among homeless severely mentally ill, while Susser *et al* (1993) reported that 19.4% of men in a community shelter for psychiatric patients were HIV infected. The possible presence of HIV infection among psychiatric patients can lead to complex practical and ethical problems (Catalan, 1990*b*).

Psychological morbidity in HIV infection

While not all individuals with HIV infection (or those who regard themselves as being at risk of acquiring the infection) experience psychological problems, a substantial proportion suffer transient or persistent periods of psychological disturbance. A variety of factors are known to be associated with the likelihood of HIV positive people developing psychological problems. They include (a) disease-related factors: when a positive test result is notified or when symptomatic disease develops; (b) factors related to the individual: a past psychiatric history or previous difficulties coping with problems; (c) interpersonal and social factors, such as lack of perceived social supports or poor social adjustment (Catalan *et al,* 1992*a,b*). Early identification and treatment of people likely to experience HIV-related psychological difficulties is therefore an important task for those involved in the care of individuals with HIV infection.

Psychological interventions also have a place in the prevention of spread of HIV infection in relation to sexual and injecting drug use behaviours, in particular for those individuals who experience difficulties changing their behaviour in the direction of lower risk activities (Stimson, 1991; Thornton & Catalan, 1993).

Range of psychological interventions in HIV infection

Psychological interventions and techniques well known to mental health workers, such as cognitive–behavioural therapy, brief focal psychotherapy, crisis intervention or psychodynamic therapies, are all being employed to deal with the problems created by HIV infection. However, novel approaches to the delivery of psychological care have been developed in the context of the infection, to a large extent as a result of the involvement of voluntary, non-governmental organisations.

Peer group-led individual and group support (both formal and informal) for people living with HIV infection, and support for partners and relatives, in particular after bereavement, are now a standard part of the range of psychological services available in many developed countries. Voluntary organisations exist that provide support and care for gay men, injecting drug users, women, and partners of infected individuals, among others. A unique example of this non-statutory form of psychological care is provided by the case of the 'buddy', a trained and supervised volunteer who provides regular, personal emotional support and practical advice, often for long periods of time (Arno, 1986; Williams, 1988; King, 1993). Non-profit making organisations have provided much invaluable support and care which statutory bodies would not have found possible to deliver alone. This model of care developed in relation to HIV infection could well be applied to other severe disorders (McCullum *et al,* 1989).

The term counselling is much used in the context of HIV infection, but unfortunately often in a vague and all-inclusive way, which makes it difficult to understand what it actually involves. There are at least three kinds of activities covered by the term counselling: (a) counselling about the significance and consequences of testing for HIV antibodies; (b) counselling about HIV risk reduction; and (c) counselling to deal with the psychological and social consequences of HIV infection. Clearly the knowledge and skills needed for each of these forms of counselling are different, and it can not be assumed that a given 'AIDS counsellor' will be equally at home in the three modalities. Detailed discussion of theoretical and practical aspects of counselling are provided by Green & McCreaner (1989) and Bor *et al* (1992).

Psychological interventions at the time of HIV testing

Pre-test counselling about the significance of HIV testing

There is evidence that individuals who regard themselves as being at risk of HIV infection and who seek testing have higher than expected rates of lifetime psychopathology, in particular mood disorders and substance misuse problems (Perry *et al*, 1990*a*; Riccio *et al*, 1993). A substantial proportion report suicidal ideas (Perry *et al*, 1990*b*) and anecdotal reports have documented the occurrence of completed suicide following notification of a positive HIV test result (Pierce, 1987). The presence of such psychological vulnerability in people coming forward for testing highlights the need to ensure careful evaluation of the reasons for seeking testing, risk perception, and in particular assessment of how the person is likely to cope with the result of the test. The World Health Organization (WHO) (Catalan, 1993) has stressed the need for informed consent in HIV testing and has rejected mandatory testing programmes.

Counselling before HIV testing should include explanation of the significance of the test, including what it means regarding possible progression to symptomatic disease, and the possible advantages of knowing the result (i.e. access to early treatment to prevent progression or ability to make a decision about continuation of pregnancy), as well as its disadvantages (Miller & Pinching, 1989; Bor *et al*, 1991; Meadows *et al*, 1993). Establishing the likelihood of the person having HIV infection will require enquiring about behaviours associated with high risk – history of unprotected anal or vaginal intercourse with casual partners, sharing of injecting drug using equipment such as needles and syringes, blood transfusion or use of blood products, rather than membership of so-called 'risk groups', which may not only tend to stigmatise those thought to belong to such groups but, more importantly may lead to failure to identify those who are really at risk because of their behaviour (Catalan, 1990*b*). Issues concerning confidentiality, and the likely personal and social reactions to a positive result need to be explored (Perry & Markowitz, 1988). For example, there are real concerns about the implications for the person's chances of obtaining life insurance after undergoing HIV testing, even when the results are negative. Pre-test counselling is sometimes regarded as a complex and highly skilled procedure which requires a good deal of time. In practice, most individuals considering HIV testing will not need intense and lengthy counselling, although some will need more careful and detailed counselling before they make up their mind (Miller & Bor, 1992).

Post-test counselling about the implications of test result

Counselling following HIV testing may require more time than pre-test counselling, in particular when the person is found to be HIV positive. Post-test counselling will include notification of the result, some help to reduce stress, discussion of how to prevent spread of infection, consideration of the practical implications, including to whom to tell the result, and an offer of further opportunities for discussion (Perry & Markowitz, 1988).

Perry *et al* (1991) compared three different interventions to reduce distress after HIV testing in a study involving 1307 individuals. All subjects received standard pre- and post-test counselling, and after notification of the results, they were randomly allocated to one of the following: (a) six weekly individual 'stress prevention training' sessions; (b) three weekly 'interactive video programme' sessions; and (c) standard post-test counselling alone. Three months later significant reductions in levels of distress were seen in the three conditions for both HIV seropositive and seronegative subjects, although seropositive subjects who had received stress prevention training showed greater reductions in psychological distress.

Risk reduction counselling

Counselling to modify sexual and drug using behaviours in the direction of lowering the risk of acquiring or transmitting HIV infection is often provided at the time when individuals consider HIV testing, although it can be provided in other situations. Counselling will involve information about risky behaviours, assessment of the person's risk perception and obstacles to risk reduction, as well as provision of practical help in the form of condoms, needles and syringes, and access to cleaning materials and exchange of injecting equipment.

It is often wrongly assumed that risk reduction counselling is only necessary when a person is found to be HIV positive: people who are found to be seronegative, in particular after practising risky behaviours, may become overconfident as a result of a negative test and thus fail to alter their behaviour. There is disturbing empirical evidence to indicate that in the six months following HIV testing and post-test counselling, seronegative individuals increase their rates of sexually transmitted disease, while seropositives experience a reduction (Otten *et al*, 1993). One possible reason for the increase in risky sexual behaviour in those found to be seronegative may be their falsely increased sense of confidence in their ability to avoid HIV infection in spite of having taken risks. By contrast, those found to be seropositive, as a group, may be initially too distressed and shocked to engage in sexual activity of any kind, let alone unprotected sex. Risk reduction counselling can be associated with favourable changes regardless of testing, although the results vary considerably with the population counselled and the behaviours considered (Higgins *et al*, 1991; Perkins *et al*, 1993; Simpson *et al*, 1993). Encouraging results have been published about the value of counselling to prevent HIV transmission in heterosexual couples where one of the partners is infected (Padian *et al*, 1993). (See below for further discussion of risk reduction interventions.)

Abnormal beliefs in people seeking HIV testing

Among people seeking HIV testing some present with persistent concerns about being infected, often in spite of repeated negative tests. Reassurance and basic counselling provides minimal relief, the individual soon returning to a state of distress about HIV infection. Many different terms have been used to describe these individuals or the syndromes they suffer, often adding to the confusion, rather than helping to clarify the problem. A good example is provided by the unfortunate term 'the worried well', which was originally introduced before HIV testing was available to refer to a mixed group of individuals including some who had been sexual partners of people with AIDS but who had no symptoms at the time and had no way of knowing if they were likely to develop AIDS, as well as others with hypochondriacal preoccupations (Forstein, 1984; Morin *et al*, 1984). What at the time was a good attempt at dealing with a new problem, is now an unhelpful label with derogatory connotations.

Worrying beliefs about HIV infection which do not subside after a negative test result and appropriate counselling about its significance should be regarded as a symptom rather than a diagnosis: for example, they may be part of an adjustment reaction, obsessional disorder, somatisation disorder or hypochrondriasis; they may be delusional and occur in the context of an affective disorder or schizophrenic illness; or they may present in someone with a personality disorder. People with hypochondriasis have received a good deal of attention in the HIV literature (Davey & Green, 1991) compared with those with delusional or other disorders, perhaps reflecting the prevalence of syndromes. Miller *et al* (1988) in a study of 19 cases found the majority to be men, and that a primary diagnosis of depression was given to almost three-quarters. Sexual guilt, usually involving marital infidelity was common. Interestingly, as a group they had been involved in behaviours with low risk of HIV infection, partly because of their long-standing concerns. A past psychiatric history was present in more than half of the people.

Psychological interventions will clearly depend on the nature of the principal diagnosis, cognitive–behavioural approaches being the treatment of choice in hypochondriasis and obsessional or phobic disorders (Salkovskis & Warwick, 1986; Miller *et al*, 1988; Logsdail *et al*, 1991), while explanation and change in misguided attitudes may be all is needed in less complex or well established cases (Bor *et al*, 1989).

HIV testing in psychiatric settings

The association between HIV infection and psychiatric disorder means that HIV-infected individuals will present in psychiatric settings, regardless of whether their HIV status is known to them or their carers. Psychiatrists and other mental health workers will be faced with questions about when to think about the possibility of HIV-related psychiatric disorders, how to proceed when it is probable that the patient has HIV infection, and how to manage known seropositive individuals (Catalan, 1990*b*). Testing psychiatric patients for HIV infection, as in any other case, should include the need for explicit consent, and provision of pre- and post-test counselling, as outlined in official documents – see General Medical Council (1988), Royal College of Psychiatrists (Catalan *et al*, 1989) and WHO (Catalan, 1993).

Testing without the patient's explicit consent would only be justified in very rare cases, whether in psychiatric settings or in other situations. In psychiatry the question may arise when someone with a psychiatric disorder is unwilling (for example in the case of a manic patient) or unable (as in the case of someone with marked cognitive impairment) to give consent. Faced with such situations, psychiatrists should attempt to clarify to what extent the patient's immediate treatment would be influenced by knowledge of HIV status, the degree to which testing would be in the patient's interest, and whether knowing the HIV status would make any difference to the safety of staff or other patients. The answers to these questions are not always obvious, and discussion with the rest of the clinical team and with a physician with experience in the management of HIV infection will be important. If a decision to test without consent is made, careful documentation of the decision-making process and consultation with a legal advisor would be highly desirable (Catalan, 1990*b*).

Psychological interventions for HIV-infected individuals

The care of psychological problems in HIV infection should be part of the overall clinical management of the condition. Doctors and nurses involved in providing day-to-day care will be in a good position to identify and deal with common psychological and social problems in HIV-infected individuals and their relatives, and only a proportion of people will need more intensive or specialised help. It is a matter of regret that GPs, who are usually well placed to provide long-term care to people with HIV and their families, have only had a limited role in the management of people with HIV infection, although there are encouraging changes taking place (King, 1989). Social workers, health advisers and a variety of other hospital and community-based professionals form a second level of intervention, dealing with psychological and social problems requiring more time and skills. Specialised mental health workers can provide assessment and care of more severe or complex problems, as well as be available to help other professionals.

Mental health interventions for people with HIV infection will depend on the nature of the psychiatric problem and the causal factors involved. As discussed above, a variety of factors contribute to psychiatric morbidity in people with HIV infection, some related to the disease itself, some to the individual's own vulnerability, and some to the social consequences and correlates of the disease. Provision of specialised psychiatric care is not always accessible. A WHO survey of European professionals involved in the care of people with HIV infection has highlighted the inadequacies in the provision of specialist mental health interventions, in particular in emergencies, when dealing with injecting drug users (Catalan, 1993).

In common with other potentially serious and fatal conditions such as cancer, the physical consequences of the disease and its treatment will be a fundamental element in the development of problems (see chapter 8). Those involved in providing psychological care to people with HIV infection will need to become familiar with the specific medical complications and treatments of the condition as well as with the medical terminology generated by the disease. Unfortunately, standard medical textbooks are usually out of date in relation to HIV and its treatment, and those outside treatment centres may have difficulty keeping up with the literature. Lack of such knowledge will not only make it difficult to understand an individual's predicament, but it will do little to enhance the therapist's credibility in that person's eyes.

General psychological interventions

Psycho-educational interventions

Discussion of the implications of having HIV infection or explaining the nature of treatments, likely complications and their effects may be more complex than expected. While many people with HIV infection are well informed about such matters, misguided media reporting and negative social attitudes may have led some to hold inaccurate beliefs. Methods of transmission of infection to others (i.e. unprotected anal and vaginal intercourse) should be avoided, as well as the sharing of drug injecting equipment, and concerns about infection of social contacts will need to be addressed (for example sharing crockery, shaking hands, touching or kissing are all safe). Discussion of risks to unborn children and family planning advice may be necessary. Advice about keeping healthy, including diet, exercise and minimisation of the effects of substance misuse should be included. Much of the advice given by professionals and by voluntary organisations regarding lifestyle changes is generally sensible and may help the person acquire a greater sense of mastery over his or her life, but it has to be stressed that it is not clear that such changes will have a significant effect in preventing disease progression. Some individuals will have known others who have died as a result of HIV infection, and their fears will need to be noted, including concerns about developing dementia. Partners and relatives may need to be involved in the discussions (Perry, 1993).

Problem-solving interventions

HIV infection is characterised by the seemingly inevitable development of health-related problems leading to gradual or sudden changes in personal autonomy, work, social life and income, to name a few possible problems. A problem-solving approach of the type that has been shown to be effective in general practice and other settings (Green & McCreaner, 1989; Hawton & Kirk, 1989; Catalan *et al*, 1991) could help the person develop strategies to cope with a range of moving targets at different stages of disease. For example, in the early stages individuals often feel overwhelmed by multiple concerns about how long they have been infected, who was responsible for their infection, how long they are going to live, who should be told about their status, how parents will respond, what they should do with their remaining years, to list a few. The role of the therapist would be to help people identify their concerns, prioritise them in terms of urgency, and then take each one at a time to look at possible solutions. By breaking the problems down into manageable tasks, the person can gain a sense of control and mastery which will allow him or her to tackle the more difficult issues that will arise as the disease progresses.

Cognitive–behaviour therapy

There is encouraging evidence from controlled investigations for the value of relatively brief cognitive–behavioural interventions for people with HIV infection. Group cognitive–behaviour therapy and support group brief therapy for depressed individuals were found to be superior to the control condition (Kelly *et al*, 1993). Individual approaches have also been reported to be effective (see Thornton & Flynn, 1993, for review).

Brief psychotherapy

Brief focused psychotherapy is sometimes used for people with HIV infection, both in hospital-based services and, possibly more, in non-profit AIDS organisations. While there has been no research of the kind carried out in other physical disorders (Guthrie *et al*, 1993), clinical experience suggests that brief psychotherapy can be of value.

Supportive therapy and support groups

Lack of social supports is an important contributor to psychiatric morbidity, and not surprisingly, access to a confiding relationship, whether with professionals or with others with HIV infection, can be very effective in preventing psychiatric disorder (Mulleady *et al*, 1989; Viney *et al*, 1991; Kelly *et al*, 1993). Sometimes, long-term contact with a 'buddy' or with a counsellor from a voluntary organisation will be all that is required, but in the case of vulnerable individuals with limited coping resources more skilled help may be needed.

Other therapies

Interventions to deal with relationship problems (see chapter 3), psychosexual dysfunction, children and family difficulties, and with the problems associated with bereavement may be required in people with HIV and their relatives (see Green & McCreaner, 1989). Psychological interventions in palliative care are discussed elsewhere in this volume (chapter 8). A wide range of complementary therapies are available for people with HIV infection, including such techniques as aromatherapy, reflexology, and massage. While there is no doubt that they are popular and reported to be psychologically beneficial, there are no empirical data supportive of their value.

HIV-specific psychological interventions

Particular problems related to the disease or its consequences may need specific attention. Some examples are considered below.

Breaking the bad news

As with other serious conditions, particular sensitivity will be needed when discussing the implications of an AIDS diagnosis, preparing people for the possibility of future problems, or when attempting to answer a person's questions about life expectancy or further treatments (Bor *et al*, 1993).

The significance of laboratory tests indicating decline in health

Progress in our understanding of HIV infection has led to identifying predictors of progression before a clinical decline in health, and notification of such changes may have important psychological results (Miller *et al*, 1991). For some people, being told that early treatment is available may increase the sense of hope in the chances of remaining well for longer, while others may see it as a sign of impending disease, and this may lead to psychological distress.

Kaposi's sarcoma and other disfiguring conditions

Skin cancer, in particular when it affects visible parts of the body, severe scarring or weight loss can lead to dramatic loss of self-esteem, avoidance of social situations and depression. Intensive help may be needed to help people mobilise resources and face feared situations, as well as practical cosmetic advice (Bor, 1993).

HIV-associated cognitive impairment

Fear of developing dementia is common among people with HIV infection and their relatives, although the prevalence of severe cognitive impairment is far less common than was originally feared

(Catalan & Thornton, 1993). Providing accurate information about the risk of dementia will be an important part of the counselling. Clear and sensitively given counselling will be needed in those cases where cognitive impairment occurs, in particular in the early stages, when the person may be fairly aware of what is happening. Relatives and carers will need to be involved in counselling (Green & Kocsis, 1988).

Risk reduction

Many factors can contribute to changes in behaviours likely to affect the spread of HIV infection, including demographic and cultural factors, levels of knowledge about risk, social norms, and attitudes to behaviour change (Thornton & Catalan, 1993). While specifically psychological interventions may not be necessary in many instances, it is clear that understanding of the contribution of psychological factors such as attitudes to risk-taking, search for excitement, low self-esteem, low mood and search for immediate gratification (Kelly *et al*, 1991; Gold & Skinner, 1992) can provide the basis for psychological intervention in the case of individuals who experience difficulties initiating and maintaining low risk behaviours.

In the case of injecting drug users, a variety of preventive strategies have been introduced with the aim of reducing the risk of acquiring or spreading HIV infection and to minimise the harm associated with drug taking. These include outreach work; access to voluntary and confidential HIV counselling and testing; education about risk behaviours; access to supply and return of needles and syringes; education about decontamination of syringes; motivational inter-viewing; and use of methadone prescribing for prevention (see Mulleady, 1992, for detailed description of psychological interven-tions). While it is difficult to isolate the relative contribution of the various interventions, there is evidence for behaviour change among injecting drug users (Stimson, 1991), and for the value of needle and syringe exchange programmes (Heimer *et al*, 1993; Keene *et al*, 1993). Sadly, there is very little evidence about the efficacy of psychological interventions to change sexual behaviour in injecting drug users in the direction of safer sex.

Preventing the sexual spread of HIV infection has generated interesting forms of social and psychological intervention. A good example of psycho-educational programmes for school children was reported by Walter & Vaughan (1993), who evaluated a six-lesson package for 12 to 20-year-olds which included a predominant proportion of non-whites in New York City. The study involved 1316 students who were randomly allocated to experimental intervention or to no formal intervention groups. The six lessons included information about methods of transmission of HIV, consequences of the infection, how to avoid infection, including discussion of safer sex activities and safer injecting drug use practices. Three months after the intervention, significant advantage for the experimental condition was apparent for knowledge, beliefs, perceived self-efficacy and risk behaviour.

In an example of community intervention, Kelly *et al* (1992) showed the value of training key opinion leaders in the gay community to communicate risk reduction advice: the rates of risky behaviours (anal intercourse, non use of condoms) declined significantly in the cities where the experiment took place, by comparison with the control ones.

Cognitive–behavioural approaches, similar to those used in other appetitive behaviours such as obesity and smoking, have been used in a number of controlled studies. Kelly *et al* (1989) evaluated a 12-week group intervention programme for gay men which included education about risk, identification of triggers to risky behaviour, teaching of cognitive and behavioural skills to manage trigger situations, assertiveness training to negotiate sexual encounters, and problem solving related to lifestyle. The experimental condition was successful in reducing the frequency of risky behaviours and increasing condom use, and change was maintained at 16-month follow-up. A similar intervention was shown to be effective for runaway male and female adolescents (Rotherham-Borus *et al*, 1991). Interventions aimed at sexual behaviour change among injecting drug users have so far been disappointing (Stimson, 1991; Thornton & Catalan, 1993).

Conclusions

The epidemic of HIV infection has raised many challenges for the health and social services, and in particular for those working in mental health. There is good evidence for the presence of psychological difficulties in people with the infection, their partners and relatives, and a wide range of psychological interventions have been developed to provide care and enhance the person's ability to cope. Unfortunately, there has been little in the way of systematic research to tease out the most effective elements in the various treatments used, and this remains an outstanding task of mental health workers dealing with HIV infection. Another potentially fertile area for both practice and research concerns risk reduction. As has been said many times before, HIV infection is essentially a behaviourally acquired condition, and as such, it should be possible to reduce its spread by changes in behaviour. The mental health services have many of the skills necessary to improve the possibilities for effective intervention, and thus have a duty to take an active part in the struggle against the spread of HIV infection and to minimise its consequences.

References

ARNO, P. S. (1986) The non-profit sector's response to the AIDS epidemic: community-based services in San Francisco. *American Journal of Public Health*, **76**, 1325–1330.

BOR, R. (1993) Counselling patients with AIDS-associated Kaposi's sarcoma. *Counselling Psychology Quarterly*, **6**, 91–98.

——, PERRY, L., MILLER, R., *et al* (1989) Strategies for counselling the "worried well" in relation to AIDS: discussion paper. *Journal of the Royal Society of Medicine*, **82**, 218–220.

——, MILLER, R. & JOHNSON, M. (1991) A testing time for doctors: counselling patients before an HIV test. *British Medical Journal*, **303**, 905–907.

——, —— & GOLDMAN, E. (1992) *Theory and Practice of HIV Counselling*. London: Cassell.

——, ——, ——, *et al* (1993) The meaning of bad news in HIV disease: counselling about dreaded issues revisited. *Counselling Psychology Quarterly*, **6**, 69–80.

BURGESS, A. & RICCIO, M. (1992) Cognitive impairment and dementia in HIV-1 infection. *Baillière's Clinical Neurology*, **1**, 155–174.

CATALAN, J. (1990*a*) Psychiatric manifestations of HIV disease. *Baillière's Clinical Gastroenterology*, **4**, 547–562.

—— (1990*b*) HIV and AIDS-related psychiatric disorder: what can the psychiatrist do? In *Dilemmas and Difficulties in the Management of Psychiatric Patients* (eds K. Hawton & P. Cowen), pp. 205–217. Oxford: Oxford Medical Publications.

—— (1993) *HIV Infection and Mental Health Care: Implications for Services*. Copenhagen: World Health Organization Regional Office for Europe.

——, RICCIO, M. & THOMPSON, C. (1989) HIV disease and psychiatric practice. *Psychiatric Bulletin*, **13**, 316–332.

——, GATH, D., ANASTASIADES, P., *et al* (1991) Evaluation of a brief psychological treatment for emotional disorders in primary care. *Psychological Medicine*, **21**, 1013–1018.

——, KLIMES, I., BOND, A., *et al* (1992*a*) The psychosocial impact of HIV infection in men with haemophilia. *Journal of Psychosomatic Research*, **36**, 409–416.

——, ——, DAY, A., *et al* (1992*b*) The psychosocial impact of HIV infection in gay men. *British Journal of Psychiatry*, **161**, 774–778.

—— & THORNTON, S. (1993) Whatever happened to HIV-associated dementia? *International Journal of STD and AIDS*, **4**, 1–4.

——, BURGESS, A. & KLIMES, I. (1995) *Psychological Medicine of HIV Infection*. Oxford: Oxford University Press.

CENTERS FOR DISEASE CONTROL (1993) Update: mortality attributable to HIV infection/AIDS among persons aged 25–44 years, US, 1990 and 1991. *Morbidity Mortality Weekly Report*, **42**, 481–486.

COMMUNICABLE DISEASE REPORT (1998) AIDS and HIV infection in the United Kingdom. *Communicable Disease Report. CDR Review*, **8**, 155–158.

DAVEY, T. & GREEN, J. (1991) The worried well: ten years of a new face for an old problem. *AIDS Care*, **3**, 289–293.

EMPFIELD, M., COURNOS, F., MEYER, I., *et al* (1993) HIV seroprevalence among homeless patients admitted to a psychiatric inpatient unit. *American Journal of Psychiatry*, **150**, 47–52.

FORSTEIN, M. (1984) AIDS anxiety in the "worried well". In *Psychiatric Implications of AIDS* (eds S. Nichols & D. Ostrow), pp. 49–60. Washington, DC: American Psychiatric Press.

GENERAL MEDICAL COUNCIL (1988) *HIV infection and AIDS: The Ethical Considerations*. London: General Medical Council.

GOLD, R. & SKINNER, M. (1992) Situational factors and thought processes associated with unprotected intercourse in young gay men. *AIDS*, **6**, 1021–1030.

GREEN, J. & KOCSIS, A. (1988) Counselling patients with AIDS-related encephalopathy. *Journal of the Royal College of Physicians of London*, **22**, 166–168.

—— & McCREANER, A. (1989) *Counselling in HIV Infection and AIDS*. Oxford: Blackwell Scientific Publications.

GUTHRIE, E., CREED, F., DAWSON, D., *et al* (1993) A randomized controlled trial of psychotherapy in patients with refractory irritable bowel syndrome. *British Journal of Psychiatry*, **163**, 315–321.

HAWTON, K. & KIRK, J. (1989) Problem-solving. In *Cognitive Behaviour Therapy for Psychiatric Problems* (eds H. Hawton, R. Salkovskis, J. Kirk, *et al*), pp. 406–426. Oxford: Oxford Medical Publications.

HEIMER, R., KAPLAN, E. & KHOSHNOOD, K. (1993) Needle exchange decreases the prevalence of HIV-1 Proviral DNA in returned syringes in New Haven, Connecticut. *American Journal of Medicine*, **95**, 214–220.

HIGGINS, D., GALAVOTTI, C., O'REILLY, K., *et al* (1991) Evidence for the effects of HIV antibody testing and counselling on risk behaviours. *Journal of the American Medical Association*, **266**, 2419–2429.

KEENE, J., STIMSON, G., JONES, S., *et al* (1993) Evaluation of syringe-exchange for HIV prevention among injecting drug users in rural and urban areas of Wales. *Addiction*, **88**, 1063–1070.

KELLY, J., MURPHY, D., ROFFMAN, R., *et al* (1989) Behavioural intervention to reduce AIDS risk activities. *Journal of Counselling and Clinical Psychology*, **57**, 60–67.

——, ST LAWRENCE, J. & BRASFIELD, T. (1991) Predictors of vulnerability to AIDS risk behaviour relapse. *Journal of Consulting and Clinical Psychology*, **59**, 163–166.

——, —— & STEVENSON, L. (1992) Community AIDS/HIV risk reduction: the effects of endorsement by popular people in three cities. *American Journal of Public Health*, **82**, 1438–1489.

——, MURPHY, D., BAHR, G., *et al* (1993) Outcome of cognitive–behavioural and support brief therapies for depressed HIV infected persons. *American Journal of Psychiatry*, **150**, 1679–1686.

KING, E. (1993) *Safety in Numbers*. London: Cassell.

KING, M. (1989) Psychological and social problems in HIV infection: interviews with general practitioners in London. *British Medical Journal*, **299**, 713–717.

LOGSDAIL, S., LOVELL, K., WARWICK, H., *et al* (1991) Behavioural treatment of AIDS-focused illness phobia. *British Journal of Psychiatry*, **159**, 422–425.

MAJ, M. (1990) Psychiatric aspects of HIV infection and AIDS. *Psychological Medicine*, **20**, 547–563.

MANN, J., TARANTOLA, D. & NETTER, T. (1992) *A Global Report: AIDS in the World*. Cambridge, Mass: Harvard University Press.

MARZUK, P. (1991) Suicidal behaviour and HIV illnesses. *International Review of Psychiatry*, **3**, 365–371.

McCULLUM, L. W., DYKES, J., PAINTER, L., *et al* (1989) The Ankali project: a model for the use of volunteers to provide emotional support in terminal illness. *Medical Journal of Australia*, **151**, 33–38.

MEADOWS, J., CATALAN, J. & GAZZARD, B. (1993) HIV antibody testing in the antenatal clinic. *Midwifery*, **9**, 17–27.

MILLER, D., ACTON, T. & HEDGE, B. (1988) The worried well: their identification and management. *Journal of the Royal College of Physicians of London*, **22**, 158–165.

—— & PINCHING, A. (1989) HIV tests and counselling: current issues. *AIDS*, **3** (suppl. 1), S187–S193.

MILLER, R., BOR, R., SALT, H., *et al* (1991) Counselling patients with HIV infection about laboratory tests with predictive values. *AIDS Care*, **2**, 159–164.

—— & —— (1992) Pre-HIV antibody testing – too much fuss? *Genitourinary Medicine*, **68**, 9–10.

MORIN, S., CHARLES, K. & MALYON, A. (1984) The psychological impact of AIDS on gay men. *American Psychologist*, **39**, 1288–1293.

MULLEADY, G. (1992) *Counselling Drug Users about HIV and AIDS*. Oxford: Blackwell Scientific Publications.

——, RICCIO, M. & HOGARTH, S. (1989) HIV infection and drug users: setting up support groups. *Counselling Psychology Quarterly*, **2**, 53–57.

OTTEN, M. W., ZAIDI, A. A., WROTEN, J., *et al* (1993) Changes in sexually transmitted disease rates after HIV testing and post-test counselling, Miami, 1988 to 1989. *American Journal of Public Health*, **83**, 529–533.

PADIAN, N., O'BRIEN, T., CHANG, Y., *et al* (1993) Prevention of heterosexual transmission of HIV through couple counselling. *Journal of AIDS*, **6**, 1043–1048.

PERKINS, D., LESERMAN, J., MURPHY, C., *et al* (1993) Psychosocial predictors of high risk sexual behavior among HIV-negative homosexual men. *AIDS Education and Prevention*, **5**, 141–152.

PERRY, S. (1993) Psychiatric treatment of adults with HIV infection. In *Current Psychiatric Therapy* (ed. D. L. Dunner), pp. 475–482. Philadelphia: W. B. Saunders.

—— & MARKOWITZ, J. (1988) Counselling for HIV testing. *Hospital and Community Psychiatry*, **39**, 731–739.

——, JACOBSBERG, L., FISHMAN, B., *et al* (1990*a*) Psychiatric diagnosis before serological testing for HIV. *American Journal of Psychiatry*, **147**, 89–93.

——, —— & —— (1990*b*) Suicidal ideation and HIV testing. *Journal of the American Medical Association*, **263**, 679–682.

——, FISHMAN, B., JACOBSBERG, L., *et al* (1991) Effectiveness of psycho-educational intervention in reducing emotional distress after HIV antibody testing. *Archives of General Psychiatry*, **48**, 143–147.

PIERCE, C. (1987) Underscore urgency of HIV counselling: several suicides follow positive test. *Clinical Psychiatry News*, 1.

RICCIO, M., PUGH, K., JADRESIC, D., *et al* (1993) Neuropsychiatric aspects of HIV-1 infection in gay men: controlled investigation of psychiatric, neuropsychological and neurological status. *Journal of Psychosomatic Research*, **17**, 819–830.

ROTHERAM-BORUS, M., KOOPMAN, C. & HAIGNERE, C. (1991) Reducing HIV sexual risk behaviors among runaway adolescents. *Journal of the American Medical Association*, **266**, 1237–1241.

SACKS, M., DERMATIS, H., LOOSER-OTT, S., *et al* (1992) Undetected HIV infection among acutely ill psychiatric inpatients. *American Journal of Psychiatry*, **149**, 544–545.

SALKOVSKIS, P. & WARWICK, H. (1986) Morbid preoccupations, health anxiety and reassurance: a cognitive–behavioural approach to hypochondriasis. *Behaviour Research and Therapy*, **24**, 597–602.

SIMPSON, D., KNIGHT, K. & RAY, S. (1993) Psychosocial correlates of AIDS-risk drug use and sexual behaviours. *AIDS Education and Prevention*, **5**, 121–130.

STIMSON, G. (1991) Risk reduction by drug users with regard to HIV infection. *International Review of Psychiatry*, **3**, 401–415.

SUSSER, E., VALENCIA, E. & CONOVER, S. (1993) Prevalence of HIV infection among psychiatric patients in New York City men's shelter. *American Journal of Public Health*, **83**, 568–570.

THORNTON, S. & CATALAN, J. (1993) Preventing the sexual spread of HIV infection – what have we learned? *International Journal of STD and AIDS*, **4**, 311–316.

—— & FLYNN, R. (1993) Psychological management and HIV infection: Berlin 1993 summaries. *AIDS Care*, **4**, 497–500.

VINEY, L., ALLWOOD, K. & STILLSON, L. (1991) Reconstructive group therapy with HIV-affected people. *Counselling Psychology Quarterly*, **4**, 247–258.

WALTER, H. & VAUGHAN, R. (1993) AIDS risk reduction among a multiethnic sample of urban high school students. *Journal of the American Medical Association*, **270**, 725–730.

WILLIAMS, M. J. (1988) Gay men as "buddies" to persons living with AIDS and ARC. *Smith's College Studies in Social Work*, **59**, 38–52.

7 Emotional disorder in chronic illness: psychotherapeutic interventions

ELSPETH GUTHRIE

Emotional disorder is common in individuals suffering from physical illness. Among general medical in-patients, most of whom have quite severe physical illness, the prevalence of psychiatric disorder varies from 23–39% depending upon age and gender. Among general medical out-patients, the pattern is slightly different; only 15% of people with a definite physical diagnosis suffer from psychological disorder in comparison with nearly half (45%) of those people with unexplained somatic symptoms.

Chronic physical illness, such as diabetes or rheumatoid arthritis, is a long-term stressor, and between 20–25% of people suffering from these kinds of disorders, have some form of psychological disturbance. The prevalence is not very high, but the importance of emotional distress in chronic illness lies with more subtle effects resulting in greater demands on medical, social and psychiatric services.

Types of emotional disturbance

The kinds of emotional disorder associated with physical illness fall into two main groups: 'psychological reaction to physical illness' and 'somatic presentation of psychological disorder'.

Psychological reaction to physical disorder

The psychological reaction to any physical disorder is a transitional process moving from initial shock and denial to a gradual assimilation of the information and adjustment to the new disease state. Within this process, individuals react very differently. Adjustment disorders, anxiety states and

This paper was first published in the *British Journal of Psychiatry* (1996), **168**, 265–273.

depressive states are a common consequence of physical disease, and sexual dysfunction is found in nearly one-third of medical male in-patients.

Depressive disorders are sometimes difficult to detect in the medically ill as less reliance can be placed on biological symptoms. Other symptoms, such as low mood, morning depression, hopelessness, suicidal ideation and social withdrawal help discriminate the depressed medically ill from non-depressed controls. If depression is detected, it should be treated with appropriate antidepressant medication.

The type and intensity of any psychological intervention depends upon both the kind of psychological disorder and nature of the underlying physical condition.

Interventions at the early stage of illness

Any form of psychological intervention in people with a sudden onset of illness must be brief and aimed to facilitate the individual's natural adjustment to his/her new physical status. The systematic investigation of such interventions in the acute stage of illness has been remarkably limited. One area to receive attention, however, has been in people with myocardial infarction (MI).

There are now several controlled intervention studies that have employed brief, mainly behavioural, treatments in post-MI people (e.g. Oldenburg *et al*, 1985). Their findings suggest that psychological intervention during the acute phase of illness is beneficial, although the results must be viewed with caution, as these studies have various methodological flaws including small numbers, lack of random assignment, and failure to define the treatment intervention.

A more recent study by Thompson & Meddis (1990) prospectively evaluated an in-hospital programme of counselling provided to first-time MI patients by coronary care nurses. In this study, the psychological intervention was carried out by staff already working on the unit, rather than by psychologists or counsellors brought in from outside. Subjects were randomised in cohorts of 10 either to the counselling intervention, or to an 'as usual' control group. Subjects who received the counselling reported significantly lower levels of anxiety than controls, both immediately following the MI and when re-assessed six months later. They also reported less anxiety about returning to work, and their spouses, who were also evaluated, reported significantly lower levels of anxiety than the spouses of controls.

The counselling was focused on the person's reactions to and feelings towards the heart attack. Expression of both positive and negative feelings was actively encouraged. The person was helped to reflect upon any losses and explore positive coping mechanisms to deal with them. Fear and uncertainty were reduced by providing clear information about the person's illness, the staff, equipment, routines and general environment in the cardiac care unit (CCU). The person was given an optimistic, albeit realistic, outlook regarding recovery, and was involved in decision-making aspects of care.

The key point about this study is that it demonstrates that a relatively simple psychological intervention, conducted by staff already involved in the care of the patient, can have a significant long-term impact on patients' well-being.

A study of women awaiting mastectomy for breast cancer has also demonstrated the powerful effect of a simple intervention (Burton *et al*, 1991). In this study 200 women were randomly allocated to one of four groups; preoperative psychological assessment interview plus a 30 minute psychotherapeutic intervention; preoperative assessment plus a 30 minute 'chat' to control for the effects of attention; preoperative assessment only; or routine hospital care. The therapy and 'chat' were carried out by a surgeon and the psychological assessment (45 minutes) was carried out by an experienced clinical psychologist.

The preoperative assessment with or without additional 30 minute intervention from the surgeon was found to have lasting protective effects against body image distress and Hospital Anxiety and Depression Scale (HADS: Zigmond & Snaith, 1983) anxiety scores at three months and one year post-surgery. Little benefit was found in outcome for the psychotherapeutic intervention over the chat except that significantly fewer women were depressed at one year follow-up.

The striking finding from this study is the powerful, long-term, protective effect of a *simple* psychological intervention, targeted at a *specific* group of patients during the *acute* stage of an illness. It suggests, as with the study on patients with MI, that self-disclosure and exploration of emotional issues during the acute illness, are the key factors in conveying protection against later emotional distress.

There is now a substantial body of work from Maguire's team in Manchester (Maguire *et al*, 1982) that counselling by a nurse pre- and post-operatively can reduce the overall cost of mastectomy for breast cancer. Nurse counselling itself did not reduce the psychiatric morbidity in cancer patients, but resulted in a much higher detection rate and subsequent treatment. National Health Service (NHS) costs were almost wholly covered by savings made because counselled subjects who developed psychiatric problems were recognised and treated much earlier than control patients.

Interventions with chronic illness

The evidence for the efficacy of psychological treatment in chronic physical disorders is less clear. Most work has centred upon the traditional 'psychosomatic disorders', such as diabetes, peptic ulcer, asthma, ulcerative colitis, etc. Previously, psychosocial conflicts were thought to be the underlying cause of these conditions, while modern understandings emphasise pathophysiological mechanisms. Recent psychological interventions have focused upon bringing about better physiological control or alleviating coexisting emotional distress, rather than attempting cure.

Diabetes

Diabetes has received the most attention and psychodynamic, cognitive–behavioural, a variety of different group interventions, and family therapies have all been tried.

There are many case reports of psychoanalytic or psychodynamic treatment in people with diabetes resulting in more favourable control but few empirical studies. Ryle's team have used brief cognitive–analytical psychotherapy to help people understand the complex interactions between their diabetic control and underlying psychological conflicts (Ryle *et al*, 1993). The outcome of this work is currently being evaluated.

A more intensive dynamic approach with poorly controlled teenagers with diabetes has been described by Moran & Fonagy (1993). An in-patient programme of combined psychoanalytic psychotherapy and ward management was compared with admission to a medical ward with no psychoanalytic treatment or ward management programme in 22 patients.

The psychotherapy group showed evidence of better diabetic control than the comparison group at follow-up one year later. As the authors themselves point out, there are many methodological shortcomings of this study, the most obvious being the difference in the amount of professional attention that the treatment group received in comparison to controls.

A wide variety of different behavioural interventions have been described in the literature although there is a paucity of good quality outcome data. Progressive muscle relaxation and electromyographic feedback has been described as reducing serum glucose levels in two small studies, each of five diabetic patients (Lammers *et al*, 1984; Landis *et al*, 1985). Other workers have reported similar improvement with non-insulin dependent diabetics but less success with diabetic patients selected for their poor control and emotional disorders.

Cognitive therapy has been described as being effective in people with a combined problem of diabetes and an eating disorder (Peveler & Fairburn, 1989), but there is no systematic evaluation. It must be recognised, however, that a systematic evaluation in this group of people would be very difficult because of the rarity of the joint condition.

The role of group and family work in people with diabetes has never been carefully evaluated, although a number of influential case reports and studies have appeared in the literature. Supportive groups for young adults with diabetes have been described and reported to improve compliance. Minuchin's (Minuchin *et al*, 1975) pioneering work using family therapy with children whose diabetes was poorly controlled, and who required repeated hospital admissions is well documented. A proportion of children were found to attain diabetic stability very quickly after being removed from the family environment.

Other chronic disorders

Case reports of psychological interventions in patients with chronic disease other than diabetes abound in the literature but there are only sporadic accounts of controlled evaluations (Table 7.1).

The results of these studies are conflicting, with some showing quite clear evidence that psychological intervention is helpful (Sjodin, 1983) and others demonstrating that it is not (Rosser *et al*, 1983; Johnston *et al*, 1993). Psychological treatments were least effective with patients who were physically very ill and who found it difficult to concentrate or engage in treatment. Greer *et al's* (1992) study suggests psychological intervention was helpful in a subsample of patients with cancer, but not all patients. Again the most physically ill were excluded from the study or declined to participate.

In summary, there is some evidence that brief, well timed psychological interventions during the initial state of an acute illness may have a protective effect against the subsequent development of psychological disorder. The evidence that psychotherapy is helpful in more chronic conditions or those that carry a long-term threat to life is less convincing. Research in this area is difficult and challenging, as there are many confounding variables and it is often difficult to recruit patients because of their poor health.

Somatic presentation of psychological disorder

The somatic manifestation of psychological distress is extremely common. In the majority of cases the symptoms are transient but in a significant minority are persistent, associated with distress, disability and tenacious health care seeking. In severe cases patients may receive extensive investigations and treatment, with little relief of symptoms.

There is evidence that certain groups of people with symptoms of pain respond to antidepressant medication; however, this review focuses upon the efficacy of psychological treatment approaches.

TABLE 7.1
Controlled evaluations of psychotherapeutic interventions in patients with physical disease

Author; type of illness	Type of therapy	No. of patients	Length (weeks)	Follow-up (months)	Outcome
Rosser *et al* (1983) Chronic bronchitis	Dynamic *v.* support *v.* nurse *v.* control	65	8	Nil	Nurse group less breathless/ support group less psychological distress
Ewer & Stewart (1986) Asthma	Hypnosis: low *v.* high susceptibility	39	6	Nil	High susceptibility group better than low group
Van Montfrans *et al* (1990) Mild hypertension	Relaxation training *v.* controls	42	8	12	No difference between groups
Sjodin (1983) Peptic ulcer disease	Dynamic therapy plus routine treatment *v.* routine treatment	101	12	12	Therapy patients better than controls
Johnston *et al* (1993) Hypertension	Stress management *v.* controls	96	10	Nil	No difference
Greer *et al* (1992) Cancer	CBT plus routine *v.* routine alone	174	8	4	CBT patients less anxious depressed than controls

CBT, cognitive–behavioural therapy.

Individuals in the community with somatic complaints are no more psychologically disturbed than their symptom-free counterparts. Those individuals, however, who seek advice and treatment from their doctor, not only complain of more severe symptoms, but are also more psychologically distressed than those people who choose to deal with their symptoms themselves. The degree of psychological distress is independent of symptom complaints.

Different treatment interventions must be designed to treat people at different levels of the referral process. An intensive psychological intervention is inappropriate for a person with mild symptoms attending a hospital out-patient appointment for the first time. Such people are likely to improve with simple management, and a controlled evaluation of a psychological treatment in this group is unlikely to show any appreciable benefit over standard treatment.

Treatment of people with chronic functional somatic symptoms

There is an increasing body of research which suggests that psychological interventions can be extremely effective in people with functional somatic symptoms (FSS). Malone & Strube (1988) conducted a meta-analysis of non-medical treatments for chronic pain. They included 109 published studies, but only had enough information to calculate effect sizes on 48 of them. Types of pain included migraine, back pain, joint pain, and facial pain. Techniques evaluated included relaxation, stress management packages, biofeedback, hypnosis, cognitive therapy and operant behavioural interventions. They concluded that effect sizes were, generally, positive and of modest magnitude. Mood and the number of subjective symptoms consistently showed greater responses to treatment than did pain intensity, pain duration, or frequency of pain.

The main kinds of psychological treatment that have been employed over the last 15 years to treat people with chronic somatic symptoms can be grouped into six areas: cognitive–behavioural, hypnosis, dynamic psychotherapy, 'pain clinic packages', couple and family work. The main randomised controlled trials of psychological treatment in people with chronic somatic symptoms are summarised in Table 7.2. All these studies included at least 30 subjects and had a minimum treatment period of six weeks.

Cognitive–behavioural interventions

Assessment focuses on the person's symptoms and associated cognitions and behaviour. The aetiological model takes into account both psychological and physiological mechanisms. The person may be asked to keep a diary of these and then a formulation is constructed

Table 7.2

Controlled evaluations of psychotherapeutic interventions in patients with functional somatic symptoms

Authors; type of illness	Type of therapy	No. of patients	Length (weeks)	Follow-up (months)	Outcome
Svedlund (1983) IBS	Dynamic plus routine v. routine alone	101	12	12	Therapy plus routine better than routine alone
Whorwell *et al* (1984) Refractory IBS	Hypnosis v. supportive therapy	30	6	Nil	Hypnosis better than support
Harvey *et al* (1989) IBS	Individual hypnosis v. group	33	7	3	Both groups improved, no difference
Pilowsky & Barrow (1990) Chronic pain	AMI+therapy v. AMI+support v. placebo+therapy v. placebo+support	102	12	Nil	AMI reduced pain, therapy improved productivity but pain worse
Klimes *et al* (1990) Atypical chest pain	CBT v. assessment only	31	4–11	6	Therapy better than no treatment
Guthrie *et al* (1991) Refractory IBS	Dynamic therapy v. support	102	12	12	Therapy group better than support
Corney *et al* (1991) IBS	Behaviour therapy v. routine medical treatment	42	6–15	9	Both groups mild improvement, no difference
Taug *et al* (1994) Functional dyspepsia	CBT v. nil	100	10	12	Therapy better than nil

AMI, amitriptyline; IBS, irritable bowel syndrome; CBT, cognitive–behavioural therapy.

about how the person's thoughts, behaviour and physiological responses are interlinked to perpetuate his/her symptoms, distress and disability.

This approach has now been evaluated in a variety of different somatic conditions. Klimes *et al* (1990) have demonstrated its effectiveness with people with atypical chest pain referred either from general practitioners or hospital out-patient clinics. Bennett & Wilkinson (1985) found that cognitive–behavioural therapy was as effective as routine medical care in newly referred out-patients with irritable bowel syndrome (IBS), but psychological treatment was more cost-effective. This study was notable for including an economic evaluation, but the number of subjects was small.

A controlled study by Taug *et al* (1994) has shown that cognitive–behaviour therapy (CBT) is superior to 'no treatment' in people with mild to moderate symptoms (at least three months) of functional dyspepsia. The absence of a control condition, however, means that the non-specific effects of psychotherapy could not be assessed.

Corney *et al* (1991) failed to show any difference between behavioural treatment versus routine treatment in consecutive out-patients with IBS.

It is not surprising that some of the above results are conflicting as the studies employed different methodologies and recruited people with differing severity and chronicity of symptoms. Further studies with better selection criteria that identify subgroups of patients are required. In particular, there are no studies of CBT that have selected patients on the basis of chronicity of symptoms or unresponsiveness to treatment. These patients have a low placebo response rate and are the group that physicians most want help with managing.

There are currently several controlled studies employing behavioural techniques to treat people with chronic fatigue syndrome being conducted in the UK.

Hypnosis

Hypnosis has been a widely used and popular treatment for over 100 years. Its usefulness in alleviating somatic symptomatology has, however, rarely been evaluated. There have been several publications describing striking effects using hypnosis to treat IBS (Whorwell *et al*, 1984; Harvey *et al*, 1989).

When used to treat functional bowel symptoms, the kind of hypnosis employed focuses entirely on the problematic symptom, and does not involve exploration of the person's state of mind. Hypnosis has been demonstrated to relieve symptoms in people with refractory IBS, previously unresponsive to a variety of different treatments. It seems to be less effective in people who complain of severe pain, those with coexisting psychological problems, and in elderly subjects.

The impressive results achieved by using hypnosis are interesting. The work has often been carried out by physicians or non-clinically trained psychologists in medical clinics. The subjects never have to see a psychiatrist or other psychological health professional and there is no discussion about psychological matters. The hypnosis is administered almost like a drug. The trials carried out to date have included only small numbers of people, and the rates of psychiatric morbidity in the trial groups have been lower than expected. None of the studies recruited people on a consecutive basis suggesting they may have been selected on the grounds of suitability for hypnosis. Another difficulty in evaluating the findings of these studies is the absence of a detailed psychological assessment at the beginning and end of the treatment intervention.

Dynamic psychotherapy

As with the other kinds of psychological interventions there are a plethora of case reports suggesting dynamic therapy can be helpful in people with somatic symptoms, but few randomised controlled evaluations.

There have been two controlled trials of dynamic therapy in people with chronic pain. Bassett & Pilowsky (1985) compared 12 sessions of dynamic psychotherapy with six sessions of supportive therapy in 26 people attending a pain clinic. They had great difficulty recruiting people to the study, and a high drop-out rate, with only four people in the control group completing the full number of sessions. The number of patients in the study was too small to show a significant difference between the two groups.

In the second study, the same group of researchers (Pilowsky & Barrow, 1990) employed a more complex design. They compared the effects of four different interventions (antidepressant plus psychotherapy *v.* antidepressant plus support *v.* placebo plus psychotherapy *v.* placebo plus support) in 102 people with chronic pain. The results indicated that antidepressant medication was effective in both reducing pain and increasing people's activity levels. The effect of psychotherapy was more equivocal: psychotherapy appeared to improve people's productivity but increase their reports of pain.

As with the previous study, recruitment was difficult and over 400 people were approached to take part in the study but only a quarter accepted. People who attend pain clinics are by definition an extremely chronic and disabled group. Even if psychotherapy is effective and helpful in a small proportion of pain patients it cannot be recommended as a general treatment because most pain patients would refuse it. Specific treatment packages for pain patients will be discussed in the next section.

Dynamic therapy, however, has been demonstrated to be both acceptable and effective in people with refractory IBS. Two randomised controlled trials, both with over 100 subjects, have shown that brief dynamic therapy is superior to either routine medical treatment (Svedlund, 1983), or support plus routine treatment (Guthrie *et al*, 1991). In the second study, out of 113 consecutive patients only four refused to enter the trial. Recruitment of patients was made easier by the therapist's presence in the gastrointestinal clinic, and by an initial emphasis on the patient's physical as opposed to psychological problems. Patients with overt symptoms of depression or anxiety did particularly well and improvement in bowel symptomatology was mediated via an improvement in psychological status. Patients with so-called atypical gastrointestinal symptoms and more chronic symptoms were less likely to respond, and in many respects resembled patients with chronic pain. Detailed statistical analysis of the results of this study suggested that the process of improvement began with an improvement in psychological symptomatology which then led to improved bowel symptomatology. In other words, psychological change was the key therapeutic factor. Both studies included a follow-up assessment at one year which confirmed that long-term improvement was maintained.

Pain clinic packages

People with chronic and disabling symptoms usually require more intensive treatment. They commonly complain of severe pain, which can be experienced in any part of the body. The different treatment approaches have been reviewed recently by Benjamin (1989). The particular components of treatment packages vary from one centre to another but can be classified into two main groups. The first group of therapies are based on the theoretical concept of operant conditioning. This suggests that the experience of, and behaviour related to, pain can be positively reinforced by certain consequences such as increased attention and care, and avoidance of responsibility or work. Treatment involves identifying the reinforcers then changing environmental contingencies to stop reinforcing learned pain behaviours. Alternative positive behaviours are encouraged and positively rewarded.

The second group of therapies adopt a cognitive–behavioural approach. Negative and inappropriate beliefs and expectations about pain are identified and challenged. Specific cognitive skills are used to replace the negative cognitions with more appropriate ideas and coping strategies.

Pain programmes can result in significant improvements in physical and work activity and reductions in analgesic consumption and analgesic demand. There is, however, little agreement about the efficacy of such programmes in reducing pain intensity.

Most of the evaluation of intensive in-patient pain programmes has been conducted in the United States. The recent changes in the NHS, with many psychiatric services suffering reductions in beds and staffing, have meant restrictions on the kinds of treatment available for people with functional somatic symptoms. The emphasis has shifted to out-patient based programmes. Skinner *et al* (1990) have reported encouraging results from an out-patient based CBT treatment package for people with chronic pain, but further evaluation is needed.

Couple therapy

Spouses of people with chronic functional somatic symptoms often unwittingly collude with their abnormal illness behaviour or reinforce maladaptive ways of coping with illness. There have been surprisingly few studies in the mainstream literature that have evaluated the efficacy of couple intervention. Preliminary reports have suggested that spouse involvement in the form of couple therapy could improve the efficacy of treatment in people with chronic pain.

In a controlled study of an out-patient group receiving treatment for chronic pain, spouse involvement was not found to enhance the immediate outcome of the treatment (Moore & Chaney, 1985). Saarijarvi *et al* (1992) reported the outcome of a controlled evaluation of couple therapy in people with chronic back pain. Sixty-three couples entered the study and only four out of 33 defaulted from the couple therapy. The treatment was practically and structurally orientated and consisted of five monthly sessions conducted by two family therapists.

Although the immediate results of treatment were not very striking, the psychological distress in the couple group gradually decreased over time whereas it gradually increased in the control group. There was no difference between the groups, after treatment, or at follow-up five years later, in scores of marital adjustment and communication. Pain, disability and clinical scores remained unchanged during the follow-up period with no difference in outcome between the trial groups.

Although the results of this study suggest psychological distress may be reduced by a couple intervention, the overall outcome in terms of disability was disappointing. Couple therapy, however, would seem a fruitful avenue to explore in terms of the development of new treatment approaches for people with chronic functional somatic symptoms. The powerful reinforcing effects of some spouses on their partners' illness behaviour would seem more likely to be ameliorated by involvement of the spouse in treatment, rather than exclusion. Future work should be encouraged.

In summary, there is now evidence suggesting that a number of different psychological interventions are helpful for people with functional somatic symptoms. Poor compliance or unwillingness to participate in psychological treatment are the two main reasons for poor outcome, no matter what type of psychological treatment. A very long history of physical symptoms with entrenched support systems reinforcing illness behaviour suggests out-patient treatment of any kind will be unsuccessful.

People who acknowledge emotional distress in relation to their physical symptoms respond well to a brief dynamic approach. Although there is no empirical evidence as yet, it would seem reasonable to assume from clinical experience that these people would also respond favourably to a cognitive approach, provided they could be engaged in the treatment process. There are no comparative studies of cognitive versus dynamic treatment in this field, so there are little empirical data to suggest which patients respond better to which treatment.

Implications for future research

In any future trial of psychotherapy, it will be important to control for the non-specific effects of therapy (e.g. spending time with a supportive and helpful professional) by the inclusion of an active control condition. Unless this is done, improvement cannot be attributed to the specific effect of the therapy itself. Only seven out of the 14 studies reviewed in this paper actually included a control condition (Tables 7.1 and 7.2).

The recent introduction of therapy manuals has meant that therapies can now be standardised. Cognitive–behavioural treatments are easier to manualise than dynamic approaches which are less structured and use concepts such as transference which are difficult to measure. It is to be hoped that therapy manuals will be developed for dynamic therapy which will help to standardise the therapy without eliminating the essence of the whole enterprise, i.e. the individual and unique relationship formed between each therapist and client.

In any future research, the recruitment of subjects must be described in detail and the numbers of people who refuse must be recorded. The chronicity, severity, and responsiveness of their symptoms to previous interventions should be described. Only when that is done can the results of the study be generalised in a meaningful way. In this field it is probably more important to record the chronicity of people's physical symptoms than the description of specific psychiatric diagnoses.

Both self-report and independent assessments should be employed and a follow-up of at least six months should be mandatory for any condition which is chronic or relapsing. Only six studies in the current review included a follow-up assessment of this duration.

Only one study included an economic evaluation and it will be important that any future research addresses this neglected area. When conducting evaluation, the inclusion of a 'treatment as usual' group is important to compare the economic benefit of introducing a new treatment with whatever option is currently available.

Conclusion

There is limited evidence to date for the effectiveness of psychotherapy, of any school, in people with chronic physical illness. Psychological therapies may be effective for particular subgroups of people with physical illness, but empirical studies are required to confirm this. People who are severely debilitated by their illness respond poorly to psychotherapy.

People with certain kinds of chronic functional somatic symptoms appear to respond to brief psychological interventions, of either a dynamic or cognitive nature, although better quality studies are required. The current choice of treatment is more likely to be determined by its practical availability in a particular area and individual preference rather than by any discernible therapeutic difference.

People with a very long history of symptoms and marked abnormal illness behaviour are unlikely to respond to a brief out-patient intervention. More intensive treatments need to be developed and tested for this group of people, who are small in number, but utilise a great deal of resources.

References

BASSETT, D. & PILOWSKY, I. (1985) A study of brief psychotherapy for chronic pain. *Journal of Psychosomatic Research*, **29**, 259–264.

BENJAMIN, S. (1989) Psychological treatment of chronic pain: a selective review. *Journal of Psychosomatic Research*, **33**, 121–131.

BENNETT, P. & WILKINSON, S. (1985) A comparison of psychological and medical treatment of the irritable bowel syndrome. *British Journal of Clinical Psychology*, **24**, 215–216.

BURTON, M. V., PARKER, R. W. & WOLLNER, J. M. (1991) The psychotherapeutic value of a "chat": a verbal response modes study of a placebo attention control with breast cancer patients. *Psychotherapy Research*, **1**, 39–61.

CORNEY, R. H., STANTON, R., NEWE, R., *et al* (1991) Behavioural psychotherapy in the treatment of irritable bowel syndrome. *Journal of Psychosomatic Research,* **353**, 461–469.

EWER, T. C. & STEWART, D. E. (1986) Improvement in bronchial hyper-responsiveness in patients with moderate asthma after treatment with a hypnotic technique: a randomised controlled trial. *British Medical Journal,* **293**, 1129–1132.

GREER, S., MOOREY, S., BARUCH, J. D., *et al* (1992) Adjuvant psychological therapy for patients with cancer: a prospective randomised trial. *British Medical Journal,* **304**, 675–680.

GUTHRIE, E. A., CREED, F. H., DAWSON, D., *et al* (1991) A controlled trial of psychological treatment for the irritable bowel syndrome. *Gastroenterology,* **100**, 450–457.

HARVEY, R. F., HINTON, R. A., GUNARY, R. M., *et al* (1989) Individual and group hypnotherapy in treatment of refractory irritable bowel syndrome. *Lancet, i,* 424–425.

JOHNSTON, D. W., GOLD, A., KENTISH, J., *et al* (1993) Effect of stress management on blood pressure in mild primary hypertension. *British Medical Journal,* **306**, 963–966.

KLIMES, I., MAYOU, R. A., PEARCE, M. J., *et al* (1990) Psychological treatment for atypical non-cardiac chest pain: a controlled evaluation. *Psychological Medicine,* **20**, 605–611.

LAMMERS, C. A., NALIBOFF, B. D. & STRAATNEYER, A. J. (1984) The effects of progressive relaxation on stress and diabetic control. *Behaviour Research and Therapy,* **8**, 641–650.

LANDIS, B., JOVANOVIC, L., LANDIS, E., *et al* (1985) Effect of stress reduction on daily glucose range in previously stabilised insulin-dependent diabetic patients. *Diabetes Care,* **8**, 624–626.

MAGUIRE, P., PENTOL, A., ALLEN, D., *et al* (1982) Cost of counselling women who undergo mastectomy. *British Medical Journal,* **284**, 1933–1935.

MALONE, M. D., STRUSE, M. J. & SVOGIN, F. K. (1988) Meta-analysis of non-medical treatment for chronic pain. *Pain,* **34**, 231–244.

MINUCHIN, S., BAKER, L. & ROSMAN, B. (1975) A conceptual model of psychosomatic illness in children. *Archives of General Psychiatry,* **32**, 1031–1038.

MOORE, J. E. & CHANEY, E. F. (1985) Outpatient group treatment of chronic pain. Effects of spouse involvement. *Journal of Consulting Clinical Psychology,* **53**, 326–334.

MORAN, G. S. & FONAGY, P. (1995) A psychoanalytic approach to the treatment of brittle diabetes in children and adolescents. In *Psychological Treatment in Disease and Illness* (eds M. Hodes & S. Moorey), pp. 166–192. London: The Royal College of Psychiatrists and The Society for Psychosomatic Research.

OLDENBURG, B., PERKINS, R. J. & ANDREWS, G. (1985) Controlled trial of psychological intervention in myocardial infarction. *Journal of Consulting and Clinical Psychology,* **53**, 852–859.

PEVELER, R. C. & FAIRBURN, C. G. (1989) Anorexia nervosa in association with diabetes mellitus: a cognitive–behavioural approach to treatment. *Behaviour Research and Therapy,* **27**, 95–99.

PILOWSKY, I. & BARROW, C. G. (1990) A controlled study of psychotherapy and amitriptyline used individually and in combination in the treatment of chronic intractable 'psychogenic pain'. *Pain,* **40**, 3–19.

ROSSER, R., DENFORD, J., HESLOP, A., *et al* (1983) Breathlessness and psychiatric morbidity in chronic bronchitis and emphysema: a study of psychotherapeutic management. *Psychological Medicine,* **13**, 93–100.

RYLE, A., BOA, C. & FOSBURY, J. (1993) Identifying the causes of poor-management in insulin dependent diabetics: the use of cognitive-analytic therapy techniques. In *Psychological Treatment in Disease and Illness* (eds M. Hodes & S. Moorey), pp. 157–165. London: The Royal College of Psychiatrists and the Society for Psychosomatic Research.

SAARIJARVI, S., ALANEN, E., RYTOKOSKI, U., *et al* (1992) Couple therapy improved mental well-being in chronic low back pain patients. A controlled, five year follow-up study. *Journal of Psychosomatic Research,* **36**, 651–656.

SJODIN, I. (1983) Psychotherapy in peptic ulcer disease: a controlled outcome study. *Acta Psychiatrica Scandinavica,* **67** (suppl. 307).

SKINNER, J. B., ERSKINE, A., PEARCE, S., *et al* (1990) The evaluation of a cognitive behavioural programme in out-patients with chronic pain. *Journal of Psychosomatic Research,* **34**, 13–19.

SVEDLUND, J. (1983) Psychotherapy in irritable bowel syndrome. A controlled outcome study. *Acta Psychiatrica Scandinavica*, **67** (suppl. 306).

TAUG, T. T., SVEBAK, S., WILHELMSEN, I., *et al* (1994) Psychological factors and somatic symptoms in functional dyspepsia. A comparison with duodenal ulcer and healthy controls. *Journal of Psychosomatic Research*, **38**, 281–292.

THOMPSON, D. R. & MEDDIS, R. (1990) A prospective evaluation of in-hospital counselling for first time myocardial infarction in men. *Journal of Psychosomatic Research*, **34**, 237–248.

VAN MONTFRANS, G. A., KAREMAKER, J. M., WIELING, W., *et al* (1990) Relaxation therapy and continuous ambulatory blood pressure in mild hypertension: a controlled study. *British Medical Journal*, **300**, 1368–1372.

WHORWELL, P. J., PRIOR, A. & FARAGHER, E. B. (1984) Controlled trial of hypnotherapy in the treatment of severe intractable bowel syndrome. *Lancet*, *ii*, 1232–1234.

ZIGMOND, A. S. & SNAITH, R. P. (1983) The Hospital Anxiety and Depression Scale. *Acta Psychiatrica Scandinavica*, **67**, 361–370.

8 Psychotherapy of patients with cancer

PETER MAGUIRE

People with a cancer diagnosis have to overcome several psychological hurdles if they are to avoid becoming chronically distressed or suffering from an anxiety disorder or depressive illness. Despite the demands and possible complications of surgery, radiotherapy and chemotherapy they have to try to maintain a reasonable quality of life during and after treatment. An important minority of people seek to use the cancer predicament as an opportunity for positive reappraisal of their lives and personal growth. This chapter will discuss how psychological therapies may help people achieve these aims. It will also illustrate how people who are already highly distressed or have developed treatment complications (like body image problems or conditioned responses) or an affective disorder may be helped.

Whatever the aim of the intervention the first step is to establish a therapeutic alliance. People are likely to be more preoccupied with worries about treatment and survival than their psychological welfare, and difficult situations will inevitably need to be faced by their therapists. Some guidelines are provided here.

Establishing a therapeutic alliance

This can be done by demonstrating an accurate knowledge and understanding of the main hurdles that people with cancer have to face in relation to their diagnosis. The key is to ask appropriate questions as you assess the individual. Unless you ask these questions people will hide these concerns and wrongly believe that you are unaware of the problems associated with a cancer diagnosis and treatment.

It is also important to check how a person is coping with each of these hurdles because failure to deal with any one of them markedly increases the risk of the person developing a generalised anxiety disorder and/or depressive illness.

Hurdles

Uncertainty

People with cancer have to try and put thoughts about the inherent uncertainty of their prognosis to the back of their minds. This can be difficult given the reality that many people will die from their disease within a few years even when aggressive treatments are used. Worries about their mortality may be fuelled by stories they hear on television or read in a newspaper about people who have died despite 'fighting their cancer'. Similarly, every clinic visit may fuel worries that signs of recurrence may be found. Some people become plagued by this uncertainty. It dominates their lives and can lead to a generalised anxiety disorder or depressive illness.

To elicit whether or not the person is struggling with this uncertainty it is useful to ask 'How do you see your illness working out?' A question like 'What did the doctor tell you?' can be helpful but does not elicit the individual's own view of the prognosis.

Control

A major concern of people with cancer is what they can do to contribute to their own survival. This is not an easy question to answer given that there are few clear risk factors and therefore, little that people can do to lessen the chance of recurrence. However, those with cancer who adopt self-help approaches like meditation, relaxation, a more healthy lifestyle or diet will generally feel more in control and less vulnerable psychologically than those who feel there is little they can do to contribute to their survival. The latter tend to feel helpless and hopeless about their predicament and are more at risk of developing a depressive illness.

To elicit an individual's attitude to this issue of control it is helpful to ask 'Do you feel that there is anything you can do to contribute to your own survival?'

Search for meaning

Many patients react by asking why they have been singled out for misfortune, particularly if they develop cancer at an earlier than expected age. They may worry that this is because of past misdeeds and, therefore, a punishment from God or other sources. Since there is no satisfactory explanation for the development of most cancers there is a danger that people will fill this vacuum with their own theories. Common theories include notions that people brought about their cancer through having some flaw in their personality, being unable to express feelings like anger, or having some unresolved long-standing problems. Alternatively, they may blame other people for putting them under stress, for example, a partner who was unable to hold a steady job or had substance misuse problems.

People who become preoccupied by self-blame or blaming others find it much more difficult to adapt psychologically to their predicament. So, ask people if they have any theories as to why they developed the disease.

Openness

While most people with cancer feel able to talk to their partners, close relatives and friends about their diagnosis and treatment some are loath to do so. They fear that it is unacceptable and that they will be rejected by family and friends. Alternatively, they may be secretive in order to protect loved ones from the distress that talking about the disease and treatment may cause. Lack of openness is associated with poor psychological adaptation. People should, therefore, be asked 'Have you been able to talk to other people about your illness?'

Stigma

A diagnosis of cancer causes some patients to feel stigmatised. They feel unclean and contagious and worry that society wants to shun and isolate them. They tend to reduce their social activities to minimise the risk of encountering rejection. Their fears of being unclean or contagious are reinforced by current medical theories that some cancers may be caused by viruses. The stigma of cervical cancer may also be reinforced by the belief that it is caused by promiscuity.

A feeling of being stigmatised or out of control can lead to a marked lowering of self-esteem. It is helpful to ask 'Has having your illness affected in any way how you feel about yourself?'

Reaction of others

Close relatives and friends may find it hard to continue to relate at the same level to the person because they find it too distressing to talk about the reality of what is happening. It also confronts them with thoughts of their own mortality which they may find too painful. Instead of giving more support they may reduce the amount of face to face contact, especially if the illness is stormy, the prognosis uncertain and treatment unpleasant. So, ask routinely 'How much are you seeing of your close relatives and friends compared with before your illness?'

Medical support

It should be expected that people with cancer would have increased practical and emotional support from those health professionals involved in their care. However, doctors and nurses often find it hard to maintain a supportive relationship with cancer patients because they are reluctant to engage in any psychological enquiry. They fear that such enquiry will provoke strong emotions which they will not be able to contain or deal with. Moreover, it may reactivate their own doubts about the value of specific treatments for cancer and concerns about the failure of high technology medicine to combat this disease. Thus, it is important to ask 'Have you been getting as much support as you would have liked from those involved in your care?'

Concerns about treatment

Surgical treatment of cancer may lead to the loss of an important part of the body or function and cause profound body image problems. In assessing people it is important to be aware that three types of body image problem can exist separately or in combination. First, the person may be unable to tolerate feeling less than physically whole and this can make them feel vulnerable psychologically. Second, they may experience a heightened self-consciousness where they worry that other people have only to look at them to know that they have lost the relevant body part or function. Third, it may have an adverse effect on their feelings of masculinity or femininity, on their sexual relationship and functioning. For example, up to a quarter of people who lose a breast or have a colostomy have persisting body image problems unless given adequate psychological help.

Many patients have to endure chemotherapy in combination which can cause adverse side-effects, particularly nausea, vomiting and diarrhoea. Chemotherapy can also cause the development of conditioned responses where any stimulus that reminds the person of therapy causes them to experience the symptoms reflexively. Some people then develop phobic reactions to treatment and may opt out of a treatment that would have been curative.

Other people find radiotherapy difficult because it makes them feel exhausted, causes soreness of the skin and intensifies their worries that some of the cancer may have been left behind.

As with the hurdles related to diagnosis people withhold these concerns unless they are interviewed in a proactive way. Thus, in assessment it is important to ask people about the exact impact of treatment on them physically, on their daily lives, on their mood and on their relationships. Since they are often ambivalent about revealing the true impact of treatments it is important to use precision ('How exactly did chemotherapy affect you?').

Recent research has emphasised the importance of trying to elicit people's current concerns and helping them resolve them. There is a strong relationship between the number of unresolved concerns, their severity and the likelihood that the person will develop a generalised anxiety disorder or depressive illness (Parle & Maguire, 1995).

Handling difficult situations

When assessing people with cancer you may encounter certain specific difficulties. These will need to be resolved before therapy can start on a sound footing.

Handling difficult questions

In the course of assessment it is likely that the cancer patient will ask difficult questions such as 'Have they cured me?' or 'Am I dying?' While it is tempting to duck the question and suggest the person asks the treating clinician it is better to explore why the person is asking the question ('Before I try and answer your question could you tell me why you are asking me this?'). This will usually reveal that the person has good reasons. It is then helpful to ask if there are any other reasons in order to confirm that the person has a good basis for asking the question. You are then in a position to confirm that the person's concerns, for example, about having a terminal illness may be correct. You should then pause to allow the person to assimilate and react to the confirmation. Then acknowledge the distress and explore the concerns that have been provoked before trying to help the person resolve them.

Handling uncertainty

Often the therapist is faced with a situation where the treating clinician cannot say with any certainty how the patient is going to fare in the long term. There is no point in pretending that there is certainty when there is none but allowing the person to talk about feelings about the uncertainty may be helpful. It is worth asking the person if he or she would like to monitor possible markers of a recurrence (that is, indications of what signs or symptoms would herald a recurrence) and be given regular markers of progress (that is, detailed feedback about the results of any investigations), or whether he or she would prefer to forget about their illness unless (or until) some new symptoms appear. My experience is that people who want markers benefit from being given them, contrary to what the clinicians may fear, they do not become phobic about their illness and are able to postpone worry about their predicament until the marker signs or symptoms appear. However, it is important that people who ask for markers have easy and rapid access to the treating clinician so that if worrying symptoms arise they can be seen quickly and investigated appropriately.

Those who prefer to put things to the back of their mind cope better when information is not imposed upon them. However, it is important to check when they have any further needs for information at each session since this can be an evolving and dynamic situation.

Handling denial

Between 10 and 20% of people with cancer cope with their diagnosis by denying it. They are often able to cope well day to day despite this. However, a situation may arise, for example when important decisions have to be made because of the possibility of premature death. When denial becomes a problem you may need to challenge it. There are two methods that can be used with reasonable safety but it is important to remember that denial may be adopted because the person finds the reality too painful to face.

The first way to confront denial is to review the history in detail with the person and challenge the inherent inconsistencies to see if that will help the person become aware of the gravity of his or her predicament. For example, you might say 'Given you say it was a benign tumour why do you think they are giving you all this radiotherapy?'

When this fails to provoke any awareness it is worth checking to see if there is 'a window on denial'. Here, you might say 'I know you say you are convinced that there is no cancer there but is there any time during the day or even when you are asleep that it crosses your mind that things may not be so simple?' Many people who appear to be in total denial will admit that there are some moments when they do have doubts. It is then important to negotiate whether they can bear to discuss this further by saying, for example, 'A major part of you wants to deny what is happening but a little part of you is aware of what is going on. Can you bear to talk more about your illness?' If the person can it is possible to help them enlarge their awareness and begin to face their predicament and the associated concerns. However, some people will continue to deny the gravity of their illness and further confrontation will be unhelpful.

Dealing with collusion

A considerable proportion of people with cancer are the victims of collusion to withhold the diagnosis. The collusion is usually initiated by relatives who believe genuinely that their loved one cannot take the news of their cancer and cannot bear to see the person distressed. For these reasons they beseech the doctor not to tell the person the truth. However, over time relatives usually find this imposes a great emotional strain on them and also leads them to feel they are growing apart from the person at a time when they want to be more loving and also deal with any practical or emotional unfinished business.

Continued collusion increases the risk of development of affective disorders in the person with cancer and may lead to unresolved grief in relatives and subsequent psychiatric morbidity.

The first step is to ask relatives to consider what the costs of the collusion have been. They usually include the psychological strain of lying, or at least withholding the truth and the distress that may result from an increase in interpersonal distance. The next step is to ask the relatives' permission to check how much the person knows, on the understanding that you will not tell the person that they have cancer but will concentrate on checking the person's awareness.

In assessing people's awareness it is important to ask them about their perception of what is going on rather than asking what the doctor has told them. This will usually indicate that the person has realised what is wrong but is protecting the relative as much as the relative is protecting the person with cancer.

It is then important to negotiate with the couple whether they are prepared to sit down together with you as the therapist and talk through their concerns and feelings together to determine the help they now need. Some couples prefer to be left alone but most welcome help to promote open dialogue and help them handle the distress and concerns that arise inevitably.

Reducing emotional distress

Individual supportive counselling

Psychological support may be offered to people with cancer from the time of diagnosis and through the phase of active treatment. It is usually provided by specialist nurses or social workers, and involves providing information about the nature of the disease and treatments; helping the person to adapt to any complications of treatment; and offering people a chance to discuss their problems and feelings. Counselling does not reduce the psychological and psychiatric morbidity associated with cancer but controlled trials of counselling and monitoring by specialist nurses (Maguire *et al*, 1980; Wilkinson *et al*, 1988) have found that it markedly increases the identification and referral of people needing psychological and psychiatric help. Subsequent psychological and psychiatric help reduces psychological and psychiatric morbidity three to four times that found in the control groups because the specific interventions used (antidepressant medication, anxiety management training, cognitive–behavioural therapy, Masters and Johnson conjoint therapy) are all effective interventions.

Relaxation and imagery

In a study by Bridge *et al* (1988) 154 women with breast cancer were randomised to a control group, relaxation, or relaxation and imagery. Their mood was assessed on the Profile of Mood States (McNair & Lorr, 1964) and Leeds Scales for the self-assessment of Anxiety and Depression (Snaith *et al*, 1976). At six weeks their total mood score was significantly less in those given relaxation or relaxation plus guided imagery and least in those who had a combination of relaxation and guided imagery.

Group support

Providing support in a group has several potential advantages over individual counselling. Group members can serve as role models for each other. By listening to and observing one another members can learn new ways of tackling shared problems and thus increase their repertoire of coping strategies, a process important to the success of many self-help groups. Members also benefit from the experience of helping one another. Groups provide an opportunity for members to give as well as receive. Seeing themselves contribute to others' well-being enhances a sense of worth and value and reduces feelings of powerlessness and uselessness. Participation in a group with other people who face the same life-threatening conditions provides a sense of community and reduces the sense of isolation.

In their group approach Spiegel *et al* (1981) offered weekly support in an out-patient setting to women with metastatic breast cancer. Groups consisted of seven to ten members and two leaders, a psychiatrist or a social worker and a counsellor with a past history of breast cancer.

The groups were designed to be supportive. There was a high degree of cohesion, and little confrontation or here and now interpersonal exploration. The main emphasis was on the disclosure and sharing of mutual fears and concerns. There were frequent phone calls among members between meetings and visits to any members admitted to hospital. The content included discussions about death and dying, related family problems, difficulties in obtaining treatment, communication with physicians and living as richly as possible in the face of a terminal illness.

In a controlled study people were randomised to these weekly support groups for one year or a control condition. People were assessed before randomisation and at four-monthly intervals thereafter. Those attending the groups had significantly lower mood disturbance scores on the Profile of Mood States, reported fewer maladaptive coping responses like eating or drinking too much and were less phobic than the control group.

In another group intervention which consisted of a six week structured programme for people after surgery for malignant melanoma, Fawzy and colleagues (1990) used an intervention which consisted of health education, enhancement of problem solving skills, stress management and psychological support. Although experimental subjects still displayed some emotional distress, they had higher vigour scores and used more active behavioural coping strategies than the control group. At six months follow-up the intervention subjects showed significantly lower depression, fatigue, confusion and total mood scores. They were using significantly more active behavioural and active cognitive coping strategies than the control group.

Alleviating psychological morbidity

When the person with cancer fails to surmount any of the hurdles to successful adaptation already discussed, or has developed image problems or sexual difficulties it is worth considering cognitive–behavioural therapy (Tarrier & Maguire, 1984). If they are also suffering from a severe depressive illness it is important to treat this with antidepressant medication first. Otherwise, they will be unable to think positively and challenge their irrational thinking. Even those with moderately severe depression will benefit from medication since the risk of relapse of the depression is less than when cognitive therapy is used alone.

In clinical practice cognitive–behavioural therapy both helps people with cancer surmount hurdles and overcome problems and gives them confidence that they can cope with any future difficulties.

A particular method of cognitive–behavioural therapy has been developed by Moorey and colleagues (Moorey & Greer, 1980). It is intended for use across a broad spectrum of people who may be suffering from adjustment disorders, moderate or marked depression or anxiety, sexual or marital problems, or conditioned responses to chemotherapy.

In six to twelve sessions each of an hour, people are taught the cognitive model of adjustment to cancer and helped to see how their thoughts are contributing to the distress they are experiencing.

The aim is to provide people with new coping strategies. Each session begins by setting an agenda to help people deal with one or more of their concerns. Homework assignments are used to give them experience of challenging maladaptive fantasies, and developing and testing out new coping strategies. For example, a person who was avoiding intimacy with her husband because she believed he would reject her was advised to test her theories by asking her to review if there had been any actual changes in his behaviour towards her since her treatment for cancer of the cervix. This revealed that he had tried to be more considerate and loving.

People are also taught to examine evidence for their beliefs about cancer. A statement like 'I know I am no longer attractive to my husband' is tested by considering the evidence for and against this belief.

Other components of therapy are: giving people an opportunity to express feelings associated with the key concerns, relaxation, distraction, graded task assignments, visualisation and activity scheduling.

In visualisation they imagine their cancer and mobilise their bodily defences, like macrophages, to attack it. Overall, the aim is to help people find ways of coping with their disease and treatment.

Conditioned responses commonly develop in people receiving chemotherapy, particularly when drugs are used in combination. They become apparent after two to three courses when the person reports that any stimulus which reminds him of chemotherapy causes him to re-experience side-effects like nausea and vomiting. This provokes much anxiety. Progressive muscular relaxation coupled with guided imagery, where the person is encouraged by suggestions of comfort and relaxation, have been found to be effective in alleviating these responses whether or not they are combined with hypnosis (Redd & Andrykowski, 1982). Systematic desensitisation using a hierarchy of situations, beginning with the person entering the room for chemotherapy, has also been effective. The value of those behavioural methods cannot be explained by non-specific factors (Lyles *et al*, 1982).

Personal problems unrelated to cancer

Some people with cancer wish to use the experience of having a cancer as an opportunity to deal with unresolved personal issues from the past in order to make the most of the life that is left. You have to be realistic in determining what issues might be susceptible to change and avoid making a herculean bid to resolve deep-rooted problems. A woman, for example, with breast cancer who is a capable person but has had problems in asserting her needs and who now wants to become more assertive can be helped to do so within the framework of eight to ten sessions of brief psychotherapy using the therapeutic relationship as a vehicle for her to explore the fears of being assertive, test out being assertive within the sessions, and then generalising this to friends and relatives outside.

A common issue that often presents in people with cancer is the wish to deal with an unresolved bereavement. This usually responds to a mixture of forced mourning techniques and dynamic psychotherapy. Thus, a nurse who developed cervical cancer asked for help because she had felt 'dead inside' since losing her father three years ago. Her grief had been blocked because she found it too painful. She felt she had grown apart from her husband. She reluctantly agreed to look at photographs but this failed to provoke any grief. However, at the third session she became very angry because the therapist was five minutes late. She was furious because she felt abandoned by him. Exploring this elicited that she had felt full of rage at her father deserting her. This and other aspects of her grief were explored and expressed in the subsequent seven sessions. Over this time she noticed a marked lessening in the frequency and intensity of her waves of grief.

Cancer as an opportunity for personal growth

Some people report that the experience of cancer allows them to reappraise their lives in a positive way and permit personal growth so that they feel more fulfilled and effective as individuals. Yet, there has been little systematic study of psychotherapy used for this purpose. Pilot work has suggested that a combination of the methods described by Hobson in his conversational model of psychotherapy coupled with strategies used in cognitive analytic therapy may be useful in helping individuals pursue these goals (Sheard, personal communication).

Counselling for couples

There has been little research into the effect of dyadic therapy for couples when a partner has cancer. However, Christensen (1983) carried out a controlled study where 20 couples were randomly assigned to an experimental or control condition after women had had a mastectomy for breast cancer.

Treatment consisted of four sessions. The first session began with an informal discussion and then focused on the couple's relationship history, particularly how they demonstrated affection, how they approached problems, and what it was they appreciated about their partner.

Session two began with a discussion of a reading assignment on myths about the psychosexual effects of mastectomy which deals in a non-threatening way with common misconceptions that may be affecting the couple's relationships. The couple are then encouraged to identify areas of change they wish to make in the way they relate and to do so through suggestion, role play and behavioural practice.

Session three builds on the previous two relationships by exploring the impact of mastectomy on the couple's relationship in terms of self-image, reviews the previous week's assignment and determines what has happened to the relationship. The main focus of session three is the couple's exploration of how they view themselves and their spouse. An expressive technique is utilised to enrich the fullness of their self and spouse's image. First, each is asked to scan magazines and cut out pictures they feel portray themselves or aspects of themselves. These are then arranged on a poster board to form collages entitled 'How I see myself'. A second collage is constructed entitled 'How I see my partner'. The portrayals are then discussed with the emphasis being on clarifying each person's thoughts, feelings, beliefs and fantasies about themselves and their spouses.

The last session emphasises an integration of the new information the couple have gained into their relationship. The intervention condition reduced emotional discomfort in both partners, reduced depression in the women and increased sexual satisfaction of both partners. However there is no discussion of any adverse effects on the couples.

Working with those at risk

Worden & Weisman (1984) sought to screen out-patients at risk of high levels of emotional distress by using a screening instrument which they had developed in previous research.

They chose people with newly diagnosed cancer from consecutive admissions to the medical and surgical services of the Massachusetts General Hospital. Within ten days of initial diagnosis these people were screened by a social worker to identify those at risk for high levels of emotional distress during the second through to the sixth month after diagnosis. The screening interview covered 20 variables. These were church attendance, marital status, living arrangements, family members in the vicinity, socioeconomic status, total of current physical symptoms, history of alcohol problems, history of depressed mood, mental health history, history of illness, optimism/pessimism, past regrets, anatomical staging, health concerns, religious concerns, work–finance concerns, family concerns, relationship concerns, friendship concerns and self-appraisal concerns.

Those people deemed to be at high risk were assigned to one of two short-term intervention programmes.

The first intervention was based on a psychotherapeutic model which was client-centred, focused on specific problems a person was facing and the ways people could resolve such problems. The therapist's role was to facilitate the identification of problems, encourage the expression of appropriate affect and engage the person in exploring various ways of problem solving. The intervention could include behaviour reversal and role playing. The therapy emphasised four components: clarification, cooling off, confrontation and collaboration.

The second intervention was more didactic, drawing from cognitive–behavioural therapy. Each person was offered the opportunity to learn a specific, step by step approach to problem solving, then to apply the method learned to personal problems related to the illness. The intervention focused on problems people with cancer encountered in general in the course of coping. The problems were represented pictorially with one illustration showing the problem and another illustrating the same problem solved. Therapy concentrated on the intermediate steps necessary for the person to move from the problem to considering alternative solutions and then to resolution. The second intervention also included training in progressive body relaxation. Both interventions were limited to four sessions.

The control group received no intervention. All three groups were followed up and assessed by interview and questionnaire. There was a significant reduction in the level of emotional distress in the intervention groups as compared with the control groups. There was also a significant increase in the level of problem resolution in the intervention groups but no difference between the two interventions.

Psychological intervention and survival

Psychological interventions which aim to enhance effective coping and reduce distress seem to have beneficial effects on survival. Spiegel *et al* (1989) reported that their weekly group support conferred a definite survival advantage of some months in women with metastatic carcinoma. Fawzy *et al* (1983) found that control subjects had a significantly greater death rate (10/34) compared with people participating in their group intervention (3/34). This effect requires confirmation in much larger studies where stage of disease, prognostic and treatment variables are rigorously controlled for.

References

BRIDGE, L. R., BENSON, P., PIETRONI, P. C., *et al* (1988) Relaxation and imagery in the treatment of breast cancer. *British Medical Journal,* **297**, 1169–1172.

CHRISTENSEN, D. N. (1983) Postmastectomy couple counselling: An outcome study of a structured treatment protocol. *Journal of Sex and Marital Therapy,* **9**, 266–275.

FAWZY, F. J., COUSINS, N., FAWZY, N. W., *et al* (1990) A structured psychiatric intervention for cancer patients. *Archives of General Psychiatry,* **47**, 720–725.

FAWZY, I. F., FAWZY, N. W., HYUN, C. S., *et al* (1993) Malignant melanoma: Effects of an early structured psychiatric intervention, coping and affective state on recurrence and survival 6 years later. *Archives of General Psychiatry,* **50**, 681–689.

LYLES, J. N., BURISH, T. G., KROZELY, M. G., *et al* (1982) Efficacy of relaxation training and guided imagery in reducing the aversiveness of cancer chemotherapy. *Journal of Consulting and Clinical Psychology,* **50**, 509–524.

MAGUIRE, P., TAIT, A., BROOKE, M., *et al* (1980) Effect of counselling on the psychiatric morbidity associated with mastectomy. *British Medical Journal,* **281**, 1454–1456.

McNAIR, D. M. & LORR, M. (1964) An analysis of mood in neurotics. *Journal of Abnormal and Social Psychology,* **69**, 620–627.

MOOREY, S. & GREER, S. (1989) *Psychological Therapy for Patients with Cancer.* Oxford: Heinemann Medical Books.

PARLE, M. & MAGUIRE, P. (1995) Exploring relationships between coping and demands of cancer. *Journal of Psychosocial Oncology,* **13**, 27–50.

REDD, W. H. & ANDRYKOWSKI, M. A. (1982) Behavioural intervention in cancer treatment: controlling aversion reactions to chemotherapy. *Journal of Consulting and Clinical Psychology,* **50**, 1018–1029.

SNAITH, R. P., BRIDGE, G. W. K. & HAMILTON, M. (1976) The Leeds Scales for the self-assessment of anxiety and depression. *British Journal of Psychiatry,* **128**, 156–165.

SPIEGEL, D., BLOOM, J. R. & YALOM, I. (1981) Group support for patients with metastatic cancer. *Archives of General Psychiatry,* **38**, 527–533.

——, ——, KRAEMER, H. C., *et al* (1989) Effect of psychosocial treatment on survival of patients with metastatic breast cancer. *Lancet,* **2**, 888–891.

TARRIER, N. & MAGUIRE, P. (1984) Treatment of psychological distress following mastectomy. *Behaviour Research and Therapy,* **22**, 81–84.

WILKINSON, S., MAGUIRE, P. & TAIT, A. (1988) Life after breast cancer. *Nursing Times,* **84**, 34–37.

WORDEN, W. & WEISMAN, A. (1984) Preventive psychosocial intervention with newly diagnosed cancer patients. *General Hospital Psychiatry,* **6**, 243–249.

9 Psychological treatments for eating disorders

JANET TREASURE

> Therapeutic work with eating disorder patients may become a fruitful training experience in developing patience, frustration tolerance, perseverance and flexibility. And it cures you of omnipotence fantasies. . . . (Vandereycken, 1993)

Epidemiological studies have shown that there is a large range of eating disorders which lie both within and outside the current clinical diagnostic criteria. Even inside the criteria the range of clinical severity and psychosocial impairment is large. Some people present for treatment for their anorexia nervosa in wheelchairs, unable to walk because of proximal myopathy secondary to emaciation. Others are reluctant to schedule any time for treatment because their professional lives are so busy and demanding. Eating disorders occur at a time of rapid developmental change. Some people develop the illness when they are still children dependant upon their parents and with immature cognitive and physical development. Others develop their illness in maturity. Although the spectrum of illness in bulimia nervosa is somewhat narrower, there are hints that subgroups may be present. For example, patients with impulsive personality disorder/borderline disorder have a poorer prognosis and different needs in treatment than those with no comorbidity. Those who lie at the anorexic end of the weight spectrum respond to treatment differently from those who are obese. We do not know what treatment works for the younger adolescent with bulimia. It is impossible to provide the same blanket approach to treatment for all these conditions.

In an ideal world we would have a clearly defined model which was able to match clinical variables to treatment form/content and intensity. After assessing our patient we would be able to key in the relevant clinical details and obtain a rational plan of treatment. This matching of patient to treatment is at the stage of a philosophical idea rather than a practical reality at the current time. The most important aim will be to have resources for health care distributed equitably and efficiently.

The extent to which the interventions will consume resources and intrude upon a person's life will be counterbalanced by the desire to give an adequate intensity of treatment. Balancing budgets leads us to question whether a treatment that is more expensive or demanding produces a sufficiently superior outcome to warrant the additional cost or personal investment.

Apart from these practical and economic restraints there is also the drive to make clinical practice more evidence based. Eligible procedures are judged by the randomised controlled trial. However, the randomised controlled trial is limited in the information it can produce (Black, 1996) and is plagued by pitfalls in an illness such as anorexia nervosa which has such a broad range of clinical presentations. Even if efficacy of a treatment has been proven by a randomised controlled trial it may not be possible to translate this into effectiveness in clinical practice. (This is discussed for bulimia nervosa by Mitchell *et al* (1996).)

Most clinical trials are performed using people with clear-cut diagnoses, who are previously untreated and sufficiently motivated to comply with the regime. In real life people often have co-morbidity such as substance abuse which may reduce the applicability of trial results. Individual preferences may conflict with what is best treatment according to scientific evidence and it is inappropriate for the physician to insist on the one best option which may increase the person's resistance to treatment and disrupt the therapeutic alliance. For example the majority of young women are reluctant to take psychotropic medication. Many families refuse to accept family therapy or the person herself may insist 'I do not want my family involved'.

The two conditions anorexia nervosa and bulimia nervosa are at greatly different stages of maturity in terms of the level of scientific knowledge about how to treat them and how this is best adopted into health policy. Although bulimia nervosa was only identified as an illness under 20 years ago the scientific quality of knowledge about its management has far outstripped that of anorexia nervosa.

Bulimia nervosa

The setting of treatment (individual, group, family and in-patient approaches)

The first reports of a treatment for bulimia nervosa involved a group intervention (Boskind-Lodahl & White, 1978). Not only have treatments for eating disorders developed in the context of worldwide rationalisation of services but they also have been influenced by feminist ideas (Root *et al*, 1986; Johnson, 1991; Fallon *et al*, 1994). There is thus a sensitivity to hierarchical/power differentiated relationships and a preference for more collaborative approaches in which female psychological development and current roles and expectations are clearly addressed. There has also been a focus on relationships, for example involving the families of origin of adult clients and groups. Affective expression is encouraged with the use of experiential therapies (Hornyak & Baker, 1989).

Both group and individual approaches have been developed. The content of individual approaches has included psychoeducational, behavioural, cognitive and interpersonal techniques. The model of group treatment has often been a structured approach including these techniques but with the additional concept that interpersonal factors can be used to facilitate the treatment response.

Randomised controlled trials of group treatment for bulimia nervosa are shown in Table 9.1 and those for individual therapies are shown in Table 9.2. It is difficult to compare studies because the sample size and power is low. Many of the group treatment approaches have studied active treatment against waiting list whereas the individual therapies have often studied two forms of active treatment and a variety of outcome measures have been used. Geometrical and linear scales of binging and vomiting have been used. In the tables the difference in score at the beginning and end of treatment is expressed as a ratio of the original score. Problems with the expression of symptom frequency can be overcome by using abstinence as an outcome parameter, however, the duration of abstinence required varies between studies from one week to six months.

In terms of effectiveness and drop-out there appears to be very little difference between the two forms of treatment. Group treatments produce an abstinence rate ranging from 25–80% with an impressive reduction in symptoms. Furthermore, the results appear to be maintained into the follow-up period. The intensity of group treatment ranges from the minimum of 9 hours shared with six people to a maximum of 80 hours. There appears to be a relationship between treatment intensity and outcome. This was confirmed in a large study which found that treatments which have an emphasis on abstinence have high initial levels of abstinence but that the intensity of treatment is important to maintain abstinence (Crosby *et al*, 1993).

Set against the economical arguments that favour group treatment are the practical difficulties in setting up a group. It can be very difficult to organise a sufficient number of patients who can start and attend together. The study which had the greatest number of cases held all their groups in the evening and was very intensive. It therefore may be

TABLE 9.1
Controlled outcome studies of group treatment for bulimia nervosa

Date	Comparison	Number	Complete	Abstinent	B reduce	V reduce	Diagnosis	Age	Duration	1yr abs	1yr b	1yr v	Intensity	Group size	Therapist no
1983 Lacey	Eclectic	15	15 (100%)	80%	93%	94%	DSM-III	21–37	3 to 18	66%			10 of 4hr	5	2
	WL	15	15 (100%)	0	0	0								6	2
1984 Yates & Sambrailo	CBT	12	8 (66%)	25%	20%	?	DSM-III 1 week	29	8	?	?	?	6 of 1.5	6	2
	CBT instruct	12	8 (66%)	0	28%	?					?	?			
1985 Kirkley	CBT	14	13 (93%)	?	96%	90%	DSM-III 2 week	28	9	38%	?	?	16 of 1.5	7	2
et al	Non-directive	14	11 (78%)	?	63%	69%				11%	?				
1986 Wilson	CR. EVP	9	6 (67%)	?	91%	93%	DSM-III 1 week	20	?		100%	100%	16 of 1.5	?	?
et al	CR	8	6 (75%)	?	69%	69%				?		?			
1986 Lee & Rush	CBT	15	8 (53%)	28%	69%	68%	DSM-III	28		?			12 of 1.5hr	1	
	WL	15		7%	0%	0%					84%	76%			
1986 Wolchik et al	CBT	13	11 (85%)		59% plus 64%	51% plus 54%	DSM-III	23	5		60% at 10	68% at 10	7 of 1.5hr plus 2	8	2
	WL	7	7 (100%)												
1990 Telch	CBT	23	19 (83%)	79%	94%	NA	DSM-III-R non purge	42	23	50% at 10	92%		10 of 1.5	?	?
et al	WL	21		0%	22%	NA									
1991 Laessle	Nut man	27	22 (82%)	50%	71%	67%	DSM-III-R	24	7.5	50%	83%	77%	15 of 2hr	5 to 8	2
et al	Stress man	28	26 (93%)	25%	70%	67%				20%	81%	81%			
1992 Wolf	CBT	15	15 (100%)	?	44%	30%	DSM-III-R 2 week	26	7	?	68%	57%	10 of 2hr	?	2
& Crowther	BT	15	15 (100%)	?	47% plus 17%	46%				?	33%	40%			
	WL	11	11 (100%)	?		42%									
1993 Mitchell	CBT plus	34	29 (85)	?	89%	84%	DSM-III 3/week	24	6				80 hr	?	?
et al	Imipramine	54	31 (67)	?	49%	45%									
	CBP imip	52	30 (75)	?	92%	89%									
	Placebo	31	26 (84)	?	3%	12%									
1993 Wilfley	CBT	18	13	28%	47%	NA	DSM-III-R non purge	44	24		55%	16 of 1.5	9	2	?
et al	IPT	18	16	44%	70%	NA					50%				
	WL	20		0%	11%	NA									

CBT, cognitive–behavioural treatment; IPT, interpersonal therapy; WL, waiting list; Nut man, nutritional management; Stress man, stress management; B reduce, reduction in binging; V reduce, reduction in vomiting; 1 yr abs, 1 year abstinence rate; 1 yr b, 1 year reduction in binging; 1 yr v, 1 year reduction in vomiting.

TABLE 9.2
Controlled outcome studies of individual treatment for bulimia nervosa

Date	Author	Comparison	Number	Complete	Abstinence	B reduction	V reduction	Diagnosis	Age	Duration	1yr FU abs	1 yr FU b	1 yr FU v	Intensity
1986	Fairburn et al	CBT	12	11 (92%)	?	87%	92%	Russell	22	2	?	100%	100%	19
		STP	12	11 (92%)	?	80%	88%				?	100%	100%	
1988	Freeman et al	CBT	32	21 (66%)		77%	86%	DSM-III 1 week	24	6				14
		BT	30	25 (83%)		86%	92%							
		Group	30	19 (63%)		87%	93% plus 21%							
		WL	20	16 (80%)		35%								
1989	Agras et al	Self	19	16 (84%)	23&		62%	DSM-III-R	29	9	18%	?	50%	14
		Monitor	22	17 (77%)	56%		73%				59%	?	80%	
		CBT	17	16 (94%)	31%		52%				20%	?	50%	
		Resp Prev WL	19	19 (95%)	6%		0%							
1991	Wilson et al	CBT	11	8 (73%)	63%	94%	90%	DSM-III-R 1 week	20	?	62%	?	79%	19
		CBT & ERP	11	9 (82%)	54%	91%	92%				66%	?	95%	
1991 & 1993	Fairburn et al	CBT	25	21 (84%)	42%	94%	95%	DSM-III-R	24	4.4	34$	?	?	19
		IPT	25	22 (88%)	28%	89%	64%				44%	?	?	
		BT	25	19 (76%)	38%	91%	95%				20%	?	?	
1992	Jansen et al	Cue	7	6 (86%)	100%			30	9					
		Self control	7	6 (86%)										
1993	Garner et al	CBT	30	25 (83%)	30%	72%	61%	DSM-III-R 1	24	6				19
		SET	30	25 (83%)	12%	69%	69%							
1994	Treasure et al	Manual 8 CBT	55	41 (74%)	22%	66%	66%	ICD-10	26	8				0
		WL		21 (75%)	24%	75%	95%							
1996a	Treasure et al	Man & 8CBT	55	46 (84%)	30%		30%	ICD-10	26	8	40%			8
		16 CBT	55	40 (72%)	30%						41%			16
1998	Thiels et al	Man & 8CBT	31	22 (71%)	6.50%	23%	29%	DSM-III-R	28	8	35%	64%	51%	8
		16 CBT	31	27 (87%)	50%	50%	48%				58%	61%	63%	16

CBT, cognitive–behavioural treatment; IPT, interpersonal therapy; WL, waiting list; STP, short-term psychotherapy; BT, behaviour therapy; Resp Prev, response prevention; ERP, exposure response prevention; Cue, cue exposure; SET, supportive expressive therapy; Man, selfhelp manual; B reduce, reduction in binging; V reduce, reduction in vomiting; 1 yr FU, 1 year abstinence rate; 1 yr FU b, 1 year reduction in binging; 1 yr FU v, 1 year reduction in vomiting.

very difficult to replicate the results obtained from these clinical trials, conducted by committed and motivated researchers into clinical practice. In the one study which compared group and individual approaches, much lower levels of compliance were found with the group treatment (Freeman *et al*, 1988). Freeman (1991) warned that group approaches may not be practicable in most clinical settings.

Individual treatments have an abstinence rate ranging from 20–60%. Again the intensity of treatment (8–19 sessions) relates to outcome. The results of individual treatment are well maintained into follow-up.

The content of treatment

Cognitive–behavioural therapy

Cognitive–behavioural therapy (CBT) is now regarded as the gold standard against which all other treatments are judged. The cognitive model which underpins this approach is shown in Figure 9.1. In essence it is the view that the disorder persists because of a tendency to judge self-worth in terms of shape and weight and the presence of low self-esteem, perfectionism and dichotomous thinking. Descriptions of this approach have been produced (Fairburn, 1985; Garner, 1986; Hsu *et al*, 1991; Fairburn *et al*, 1993; Freeman, 1995).

The first phase of the treatment is behavioural and educational and focuses on developing a normal eating pattern and includes self-monitoring, stimulus control and developing alternative behaviours. The second stage focuses more upon cognitive restructuring (examining attitudes to self, 'all or none' and other types of dysfunctional thinking) and examining the context of the symptoms and using a problem-solving approach to resolve difficulties. The final phase is consolidating maintenance strategies.

Standard practice is 20 individual sessions. It may help to engage more severely symptomatic patients if sessions begin weekly and are then tapered into a less intense twice weekly phase.

Of all the forms of treatment that have been investigated this has been found to be among the most effective and the results have been frequently replicated. The drop-out rates have ranged from 17–34% and of those remaining in treatment the abstinence rates range from 29–63% with good maintenance (Agras, 1993).

Behavioural therapy

Behavioural therapies have been based on a variety of models. The dieting/eating habit model is based upon the concept of the symptoms

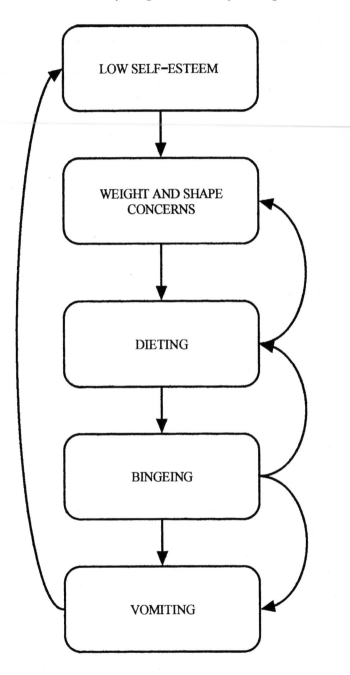

Fig. 9.1. *A cognitive–behavioural model of bulimia nervosa*

arising out of homeostatic mechanisms of appetite and weight control becoming activated by weight loss and fasting. The interpersonal stress model conceptualises that stress and 'hassles' precipitate binging which is used to regulate negative emotion. The anxiety reduction model is based on the premise that binge eating leads to anxiety which is decreased by vomiting. Self-monitoring of eating and techniques to modify eating patterns with nutritional counselling were more effective than therapy based on the stress management paradigm (Laessle *et al*, 1991). The omission of cognitive restructuring from CBT leaving a residual behavioural intervention although effective in the short term did not lead to maintained changes (Agras *et al*, 1989; Fairburn *et al*, 1991, 1995).

Exposure and response prevention, based on the anxiety reduction model, has been controversial. The technique involves exposing the client to food and eating but preventing vomiting. Although in some hands this method works well (Wilson *et al*, 1986; Leitenberg *et al*, 1988; Jansen *et al*, 1992) Agras and colleagues (1989) found that this intervention had a deleterious effect on outcome when it was added to standard CBT. Many report difficulties putting this technique into practice.

Overall behaviour therapies have drop-out rates ranging from 16–24%, abstinence rates ranging from 23–63% in the short term and 18–20% at follow-up.

Descriptions of the psychoeducational approaches that form the rationale for the dieting/eating behaviour habit model are available (Garner *et al*, 1985; Hsu *et al*, 1991).

Interpersonal therapy

Interpersonal therapy (IPT) was introduced as a contrast to cognitive–behavioural treatment as a form of treatment not based upon the cognitive/eating habits model. The rationale for using IPT for depression was transposed to bulimia, that is bulimic symptoms were maintained by interpersonal difficulties. The therapist promotes understanding and change in these relationship predicaments which are categorised into four problem areas: grief, conflicts, role transitions and interpersonal deficits. Issues about food and eating are not mentioned.

This approach was almost as effective as CBT at the end of therapy with a trend for it to become more effective over the follow-up period (Fairburn *et al*, 1991, 1995). The implication of this finding is that it is unnecessary to change dysfunctional attitudes to shape and weight in order to treat bulimia nervosa. This calls into question the validity of the cognitive–behavioural model as a necessary and sufficient explanatory paradigm for bulimia nervosa. A different form of manualised short-term psychotherapy (supportive expressive) was less effective than CBT in the short term (Garner *et al*, 1993). A large multi-centre study with IPT as one of the treatments is now in progress in the USA which will examine whether the results from Fairburn's study can be replicated.

Interpersonal therapy has been adapted for the treatment of obese binge eaters in groups (Wilfley *et al*, 1993).

A manual for IPT for depression is available (Klerman *et al*, 1984) and a chapter describing how it has been adapted for bulimia nervosa has been written by Fairburn (1993).

Other forms of therapy

Other types of individual psychotherapy have been described in uncontrolled case series: hypnosis (Vanderlinden & Vandereycken, 1990); psychoanalytical therapy (Schwartz, 1990); family therapy (Schwartz *et al*, 1985; Dodge *et al*, 1995); and the 12 step approach of Overeaters Anonymous (Malenbaum *et al*, 1988).

Minimal treatment

It became apparent to many providers of eating disorder care that although short-term psychotherapy was effective it consumed a great deal of resources in terms of trained therapist time and the amount of time invested by the client. Ideally there should be a correspondence between problem severity and the intensity of the intervention. Unfortunately we do not have the information that would allow a confident matching of treatment with need at the present time (see below).

An alternative approach to clinical algorithms of care is to have treatment arranged in a series of steps of graded intensity. A sequential model was recommended in a Royal College of Psychiatrists report with different concepts described in reviews (Garner *et al*, 1986; Tiller *et al*, 1993). A series of treatments increasing in intensity are offered. The advantages of such an approach are that it does not waste resources, in that those who respond to a minimal intervention are filtered out.

A variety of low intensity models of treatments have been developed and evaluated. A group psychoeducational intervention of five 90-minute lectures (total of 7.5 hours) with an emphasis on symptom management was developed in Canada and examined in a quasi-experimental design (Davies *et al*, 1990). This produced a 20% abstinence rate from binge eating. The minimal intervention was as effective as a more intensive treatment in the less severely affected subgroup.

An alternative approach has been to include education, cognitive–behavioural and motivational elements into a book *Getting Better Bite by Bite* (Schmidt & Treasure, 1993). This was proved to be effective in an open pilot study (Schmidt *et al*, 1993) and so it was used as the first stage in a model of sequential treatment (Stage 1: self-care manual for 8 weeks; Stage 2: up to 8 sessions individual cognitive–behavioural treatment for those who had the manual in the first stage and had failed to respond). This was compared in a randomised controlled study with 16 sessions of CBT. We found that 20% of the patients assigned to the sequential treatment were free from symptoms at the end of Stage 1 (Treasure *et al*, 1994). There were no differences in the abstinence rates (approximately 30%) between the two forms of treatment at the end of treatment and at 18-month follow-up (Treasure *et al*, 1996*a*).

A different self-care manual has also been found to be effective in an open study (Cooper *et al*, 1996). We have completed a further randomised controlled trial using a German version of *Bite by Bite* with eight sessions of CBT as a form of guided self-care in comparison with 16 sessions of CBT (Thiels *et al*, 1998). This study was undertaken in Germany where a high intensity of treatment for bulimia nervosa is the norm as either in-patient care or long-term psychotherapy. Interestingly, this model of care was not as effective in the short term at the end of treatment but the effects of both treatments were similar at the time of follow-up after six months.

The main predictors of outcome using these minimal book guided treatments were (a) severity of illness, in that those with a greater frequency of binging and vomiting fared worse, and (b) duration of illness – those who had a longer illness did better (Turnbull *et al*, 1996). Interestingly, this somewhat counterintuitive second finding had been also found in a pharmacological treatment study (Walsh *et al*, 1991). This suggests that these approaches are appropriate for the group with milder symptoms.

An important lesson from the research of Cooper *et al* (1996) is that the therapist may not require special training. The therapist they used in their study to provide 'guidance' had generic counselling skills but was not trained in the management of eating disorders nor in CBT. This suggests that a cognitive–behavioural approach combined with the use of a self-treatment book can be successful in many treatment settings. Indeed Fairburn and colleagues have piloted this in primary care (Waller *et al*, 1996).

In total three self-treatment books based on cognitive–behavioural principles are available (Fairburn, 1985; Cooper, 1993; Schmidt & Treasure, 1993).

One possible adverse effect on sequential treatment is that it can lead to the experience of failure which may lower the already fragile self-esteem and break the therapeutic alliance.

Pharmacological treatment

Pharmacological treatment for bulimia nervosa was hailed as 'New hope for binge eaters' (Pope & Hudson, 1984) but has not lived up to its earlier promise. Although antidepressants were found to be efficacious (of the 23 randomised controlled trials reported by 1995 only two failed to find a significant effect, for review see Treasure *et al*, 1996*b*). Relapse is common and maintenance therapy is either ineffective (Pyle *et al*, 1990; Walsh *et al*, 1991) or complex requiring constant changes (Pope *et al*, 1985; Mitchell *et al*, 1989). The effect size in later studies and in clinical practice was much lower than initially reported. In part this is because the recruitment process into the randomised controlled trials involved choice by both individual and doctor. A quarter to a half of eligible people failed to enter these studies. People who proved to be unreliable or placebo responders were excluded. Drop-out rates were high. Some of this was related to side-effects of the medication but this remained a problem when drugs with fewer side-effects such as fluoxetine (Fluoxetine Bulimia Nervosa Collaborative Study Group, 1992; Goldstein *et al*, 1995) were used. Of particular interest for this review is the large variability in the outcome of the placebo group in contrast to the drug effects which were constant across studies. This ranged from a deterioration of symptoms by 20% to an improvement of 50% (Walsh & Devlin, 1992). This suggests that the doctor/client interaction can have a profound effect on the outcome. What this effect could be remains speculative as the written reports give little to no detail about the baseline treatment.

It is fair to conclude that in comparison to psychotherapy the 28% abstinent rate with 8 weeks and 18% with 16 weeks produced by fluoxetine (which is the only drug so far to be licensed for the treatment of bulimia nervosa) is poor. Used conjointly drug treatment can improve the outcome of low intensity psychotherapy but a ceiling effect is observed with high intensity models (Mitchell *et al*, 1990; Walsh *et al*, 1991; Agras *et al*, 1992, reviewed by Mitchell *et al*, 1993; Abbot & Mitchell, 1993). Pharmacotherapy may increase the speed of response to treatment and help engage patients with a severe form of illness but this has not yet been evaluated.

Longer-term therapy

Although short-term treatments of up to 25 sessions are effective for approximately 50% of people with bulimia nervosa, this leaves a half of those people symptomatic. On the whole these tend to be people with personality disorders and low weight (see below). It is uncertain what should be the second line treatment for such cases. The design and execution of a study to examine this is complex. Agras and colleagues (1995) have attempted such a study with people with binge eating disorder. They found that people who had not responded to CBT did not respond when treatment was changed to IPT. Perhaps this is not surprising as IPT is not recommended for people with personality disorders. Treatments which integrate both symptom management techniques and analysis of the transference may be appropriate for this patient group. For example integrative therapies such as cognitive analytical therapy (Ryle, 1990) or schema focused therapy (Young, 1993) or Linehan's (1993) dialectical behavioural therapy may be necessary. The more severely disturbed individuals may require treatments of a duration of a year or longer. Even so the outcome is far from satisfactory (Johnson *et al*, 1987, 1990; Herzog *et al*, 1991; Tobin, 1993).

More intensive day patient and in-patient programmes have been developed. Wooley & Kearney-Cooke (1986) had an intensive programme of 35 hours of treatment each week for three weeks. The treatment involved education, body image and several individual sessions. Maddocks *et al* (1992) also report on a day hospital treatment programme which runs eight hours, five days a week with an average stay of 10 weeks. At discharge 56% were abstinent from binging and vomiting and this figure had fallen to 46% at two-year follow-up. A relapse rate of 30% was reported (Olmsted *et al*, 1994). Attempts to produce heuristic models have so far been disappointing but as the sample size is only 57 this is perhaps not surprising (Olmsted *et al*, 1996).

In Germany intensive in-patient treatments are common. These are often highly structured (Tuschen & Bent, 1995) and frequently involve cognitive–behavioural approaches (Bossert *et al*, 1989). Fichter and colleagues (1992) reported on the outcome of 250 people with bulimia nervosa admitted for in-patient care based on intensive broad spectrum behavioural therapy. The focus of this treatment was to improve interoceptive and emotional perception, expression of emotions, training of social communicative skills and nutritional management. These patients were on average aged 25 years with a duration of illness of about 8 years. The completion rate for the follow-up was impressive (98.8%). Interestingly at two-year follow-up 53% had no eating disorder i.e. were abstinent, 36% met the full criteria for bulimia nervosa and the rest had some degree of eating disturbance. Thus even high intensity in-patient care leaves 50% of people symptomatic.

Meta-analysis of treatment studies for bulimia nervosa

Laessle *et al* (1987) performed a meta-analysis of 25 outcome studies in bulimia which were reported before December 1985. Psychotherapy in general produced a mean effect size of 1.1 which was greater than the mean effect size of pharmacological therapy at 0.60. A subsequent meta-analysis of psychotherapeutic studies published before 1990 (Hartmann *et al*, 1992) found no real advantage of one setting or therapeutic approach over another. A step-wise multiple regression analysis found that 36% of the variance was explained by the number of treatment sessions in combination with 'relationship orientation'. (Relationship orientation was operationalised as the extent the symptom is connected by the therapist with relationships between the client and her self, inner objects, therapist, friend and family). They concluded that outcome was related to therapy dose, a minimum of 15 sessions was required for any clinically relevant effect and that the more severely disturbed patients require treatments of a year or longer duration.

Fettes & Peters (1992) completed a meta-analysis of 40 studies of group psychotherapy studies and found a post treatment effect size of 0.75. A meta-analysis of studies published between 1987–1993 concluded that cognitive–behavioural treatment was the most common and successful form of treatment (Whitebread & McGown, 1994). We have recently reviewed the literature addressing the cost effectiveness of interventions and how services should be planned (Treasure *et al*, 1996*b*; Treasure & Schmidt, 1998). Several more qualitative reviews have also been written (Mitchell, 1991; Garfinkel & Goldbloom, 1993; Tiller *et al*, 1993; Wilson, 1996).

Matching patients to treatment

In its next stage research into the development of treatment for bulimia nervosa will have to try to match treatment to the patient. Table 9.3 details the prognostic factors that have been evaluated in some of the treatment studies to date. None of the studies had been designed specifically to address prognostic variables and so few have the power needed to allow confidence in their findings. It is confusing to compare studies as the outcome variables used have differed. A common feature which has intuitive appeal is that the more severe the symptoms the worse the prognosis and the poorer response* to low intensity treatments.

Another intuitive finding is that low self-esteem predicts a poor outcome. A counterintuitive predictor found in both psychotherapy (Turnbull *et al*, 1996) and drug treatment (Walsh *et al*, 1991) was that a

TABLE 9.3
Controlled studies in anorexia nervosa

Date	Author	Content	No.	Complete	Good	Intermed	Poor	wt 0	wt 1 yr	Age	Duration	Adm
1987	Russell *et al*	FT	10	9 (90%)	6	3	1	68%	93%	16.6	1.2	0.9
		IT	11	4 (36%)	1	1	9	64%	80%			
		FT	10	8 (80%)	2	2	6	67%	82%	20.6	5.9	2.4
		IT	9	6 (66%)	2	2	6	65%	92%			
		FT	7	4 (57%)	0	1	6	66%	71%	27.7	3	1.8
		IT	7	7 (100%)	2	1	4	60%	80%			
		FT	9	5 (55%)	1	1	8	77%	89%	24	4	1.3
		IT	10	9 (90%)		3	7	79%	86%			
1989	Channon *et al*	CBT	8	8 (100%)	?			14.8		22	5.1	50%
		BT	8	7 (87%)	?			16.1		24	31	12%
		Cont	8	6 (75%)	?			14.9		26	7.7	37%
1991	Crisp *et al*	Inpat	30	18 (60%)				72%	82%	23	3.4	
		OP	20	18 (90%)				73%	90%	21	2.7	
		GP	20	17 (85%)				74%	93%	20	2.2	
		Control	20					75%	79%	22	2.2	
1992	Le Grange *et al*	FT	8					76%	89%	15	1.1	
		PC	8					80%	100%			
1995	Treasure *et al*	CAT	14	10 (71%)	6	5	3	15.6	18.5	25	5.3	21%
		EBT	16	10 (62%)	5	3	8	15	17.4	25	4.1	37%

FT, family therapy; IT, individual therapy; CBT, cognitive–behavioural therapy; BT, behavioural therapy; Cont, control treatment; Inpat, in-patient treatment; OP, out-patient treatment; GP, group treatment; PC, parental counselling; CAT, cognitive–analytical therapy; EBT, educational behavioural therapy; Good, Intermed (intermediate) Poor, Morgan & Russell scales; wt 0, weight on admission; wt 1 year, weight at one year; Adm, number of previous admission or percentage with prior admissions.

long duration of illness was associated with a good outcome. A consistent finding from pharmacological treatment studies and psychotherapy studies is that people who have a lower body mass index are less likely to respond to treatments (Agras *et al*, 1987; Pope & Hudson, 1987; Davis *et al*, 1992; FBNCSG, 1992; Fichter *et al*,1992; Fahy *et al*, 1993). An additional consistent factor is that comorbid personality disorders are a negative prognostic factor (Fichter *et al*, 1992; Rossiter *et al*, 1993; Fahy *et al*, 1993; Wonderlich *et al*, 1994). In particular the group with so-called multi-impulsive bulimia (three or more of six impulsive behaviours: (a) suicide attempts; (b) episodes of self-harm; (c) one or more episodes of stealing; (d) severe abuse of alcohol; (e) promiscuity (five or more sexual partners in two years or 10 since puberty); (f) drug abuse) have a poorer prognosis even with high intensity in-patient treatment (Fichter *et al*, 1994). This group use more medical resources and yet also drop out of treatment.

Anorexia nervosa

Anorexia nervosa is much more heterogeneous than bulimia nervosa which means that the strategies for management are more varied and planning care is more complex.

The setting of treatment: in-patient, out-patient

The main variables which contribute to the decision about which setting is appropriate are the age of onset and the severity of the illness.

Developmental age

If the illness begins in childhood and is of a short duration then chronological and developmental age are in synchrony and the level of physical and cognitive emotional immaturity is overt. The parents will need to show the degree of authority and care that is developmentally appropriate. It is therefore obvious that the family will be actively engaged in treatment.

However, the situation becomes more complex when the illness began in childhood with an ominous course which leaves physical and cognitive emotional development many years behind chronological age. In this case it is probable that the family will need to be involved but what level of parenting behaviour is appropriate needs to be more carefully judged. There will be a clash between the expectations and assumptions made because of the chronological age and the confusion, difficulty with abstract reasoning and judgement which are present because of the cognitive immaturity. There are no easy rules and guidelines but it is important that the clinician and the family are sensitive to the issues.

If the illness develops during maturity then the family can be involved but with much less parenting responsibility than in the cases above.

Severity of the illness

The severity of anorexia nervosa can be tracked on several different dimensions, physical and social. A simple rule of thumb is that it is sensible to match the intensity of the intervention with the severity of the illness. Severe weight loss requires urgent intense attention because the risk of death is high. In addition the course of the illness contributes to the dimension of severity so an individual with an illness which has required in-patient treatment for many years because of unremitting weight loss will need high intensity treatment.

The broad range of developmental age and severity of illness mean that treatment has to be diverse. This makes it difficult to compare treatments using randomised controlled trials hence the number of such studies is small (see Table 9.4). The study of Russell and colleagues (1987) tried to overcome some of these difficulties by dividing the subjects into four different groups based upon developmental age and severity. These were (a) subjects with age of onset less than 18 and duration of less than 3 years; (b) onset less than 18, duration greater than 3 years; (c) onset after age 19 years; (d) bulimia nervosa. Other studies have investigated those who have better prognostic features in that they are young with a short duration (Crisp *et al*, 1991; Le Grange *et al*, 1992) or with less severe weight loss. One of the problems with all these studies is that the numbers are small which has meant that the power to detect differences between the treatments has been very low. Compliance with treatment has also been variable ranging from 36–100% (median 80%). Also, it is very difficult from the reports to establish the intensity of treatment given. In some of the studies from the Maudsley Hospital the duration of therapy (over a year) rather than the number of sessions was described. This makes it difficult to estimate cost effectiveness and plan services.

In-patient treatment

'Moral' management in which nurses and doctors used their authority to ensure that the patients ate was advocated by physicians at the turn of the century. Later operant conditioning programmes were developed in which in-patients were deprived of material and/or social reinforcers. The reinforcers were reintroduced contingent upon weight gain (Eckert *et al*, 1979). Unfortunately some of these programmes were taken to the extreme with patients nursed in seclusion deprived of everything but a mattress. In specialist units there has been a swing against such approaches as more lenient approaches are as effective and more humane (Vandereycken & Pieters, 1978; Touyz *et al*, 1984). The prevailing view at present is that in-patient treatment for anorexia nervosa is successful in the short term and it remains the standard treatment defined in the American Psychiatric Association Guidelines (APA, 1993). Nevertheless the relapse rates are high (McKenzie & Joyce, 1990). Also many patients are reluctant to accept in-patient treatment.

Crisp and colleagues (1991) attempted to compare the effectiveness of in-patient care with out-patient treatment (see Table 9.4). The interpretation of the study is difficult as 60% of those allocated to in-patient treatment refused this approach despite being offered no other form of treatment. Nevertheless the outcome of all subjects and of those who complied with treatment was no better in those allocated to in-patient treatment than for those given out-patient treatment. These results need to be tempered by the fact that those allocated to in-patient treatment were older and with a longer duration of illness and a lower mean weight, all factors known to be associated with a poor prognosis. The intensity and cost of the various interventions used in this study differ widely as the extra cost of an in-patient stay of several months would be between £16 000–£24 000. An important conclusion from these results is that people with good prognostic features can be managed with out-patient treatment. Matching of the person's need with the intensity of treatment will be an important part of cost-effective management of anorexia nervosa.

In the short term in-patient treatment leads to full recovery of weight but in the majority of cases these changes are not maintained. Several studies have addressed the issue of therapy to prevent relapse after in-patient treatment. In adolescents, family therapy prevented relapse after in-patient care, whereas individual therapy was more effective in older people (Russell *et al*, 1987). There was a trend for these immediate benefits to persist over five years of follow-up (Eisler *et al*, 1997). A further study which compares focal dynamic therapy with supportive therapy and family therapy in the older group is in progress (Dare & Eisler, 1995). The preliminary results from this study suggest that a family therapy approach can be effective in the older group with an early onset of illness. Other approaches to the problem of relapse in cases with poor prognosis include aftercare in a specialist hostel.

Managed care has led to a decrease in the length of hospital stay in the USA, however it has been argued that this may increase the overall burden of illness (Baran *et al*, 1995). In the UK, private insurers are

TABLE 9.4
Studies looking at predictors of outcome

Study	Treatment	Outcome variable(s)[1]	Statistical analysis			Pre-treatment predictors of poor outcome
			N	Statistical tests	No. of predictors[2]	
Blouin *et al* (1994)	Group CBT	% decrease: (a) binging, (b) vomiting, (c) EDI cognition subscales	69	18 multiple regressions + path analysis	29	Highly controlled or discordant family environment
Collings & King (1994)	Double-blind trial of the anti-depressant mianserin	Fully recovered or not according to DSM-III-R criteria	37	About 20 chi-squares followed by a logistic regression	5	↓ social class negative family history of alcoholism
Fairburn *et al* (1993)	Individual CBT, behavioural or interpersonal therapy	a) symptom severity b) severity within normal range c) abstinence from all symptoms	50	3 stepwise multiple regressions	10	↓ self esteem ↑ disturbed attitude
Baell & Wertheim (1992)	Group CBT	Binge frequency post-treatment	21	Correlations + discriminant function analysis	4	↓ self esteem ↑ EDI ineffectiveness ↑ binging frequency
Davis *et al* (1992)	Group psycho-education	Frequency of binging, vomiting and laxative abuse	41	Correlations + stepwise discriminant function	40	↑ psychotic depression ↑ vomiting frequency ↑ maturity fears ↑ passive–aggressive
Keller *et al* (1991)	Various (naturalistic study)	Recovery from BN (no or minimal symptoms)	30	Cox regression	not stated	↑ EDI global score ↓ social support
Garner *et al* (1993)	Individual CBT or psycho-dynamic	Binge frequency (good or bad)	50	MANOVAs	39	↑ binging frequency ↑ EDI ineffectiveness
Fairburn *et al* (1987)	Individual CBT or short-term focal therapy	a) global symptoms score b) PSE symptom score c) EAT symptom score d) depressive symptoms	24	8 correlations + 4 stepwise multiple regressions	12	↓ selfesteem

1. EDI, Eating Disorders Inventory (Garner *et al*, 1983); PSE, Present State Examination (Wing *et al*, 1974); EAT, Eating Attitudes Test (Garner & Garfinkel, 1979).
2. The total number of predictor variables entered into the analyses.

limiting the amount of money paid for treatment for anorexia nervosa. For example, if there has been a failure to gain weight during in-patient treatment, then financial support is withdrawn.

This drive to decrease the intensity of treatment for anorexia nervosa is not supported by any research evidence. We are awaiting the results from a naturalistic outcome study of the treatment of anorexia nervosa in Germany which involved 51 institutions and 1500 people. The preliminary data suggest that there is a relationship between treatment length, treatment amount and outcome (Kordy & The German Collaborative Study Group on Eating Disorders, 1996).

Family therapy

There are two classic texts which influenced the development of family therapy for anorexia nervosa. The first was that of Salvador Minuchin who developed a model of the 'psychosomatic family' of which anorexia nervosa was the paradigm (Minuchin *et al*, 1978). The model has three factors:

> First the child is physiologically vulnerable. . . . Second, the child's family has four transactional characteristics: enmeshment, overprotectiveness, rigidity and a lack of conflict resolution. Third, the sick child plays an important role in the families' pattern of conflict resolution: and this role is an important source of reinforcement for his symptoms. (Minuchin *et al*, 1975, p. 1033)

Selvini-Palazzoli (1974) emphasised the function that anorexia nervosa served within the family, as if there was a need for a perfect child, with the anorexia nervosa serving the function of coping with the difficulties caused by generational or cultural conflict. Further models of family therapy have been developed and discussed (Dare & Eisler, 1995; Eisler, 1995*a,b*).

The advantage of having clearly defined models is that they are useful for teaching and so have been the source of much current clinical practice. Also they can be empirically tested. It is here where some of the models fall. For example there is no evidence that these transactional patterns are specific for anorexia nervosa and some features may be an adaptive response to having a sick child. Eisler (1995*b*) has concluded "Family studies in eating disorders have been hampered by the attempts to find the elusive 'anorexogenic family'. Such a quest is probably fruitless and is probably best abandoned". Dare & Eisler (1995) have developed a form of working with the family which has evolved from and been enriched by their research findings. In their model for young adolescents the family is seen not as a cause of the illness but an important resource to prevent the illness becoming chronic. The family who often are hopeless and helpless when they first bring their daughter to the clinic are motivated to work with the therapist, firstly by raising their anxiety about the dangers of the illness and then by suggesting that they have a choice of helping the child themselves or admitting the child to an in-patient unit. The therapist weights the choice by suggesting that in-patient treatment is only successful in the short term and may lead to chronicity.

Two styles of family intervention have been examined: family counselling (in which the parents and anorexic child were seen separately) and classical family therapy (Le Grange *et al*, 1992; Dare & Eisler, 1995). The families themselves preferred the family counselling approach. Also, family counselling was more successful at reducing the number of critical comments in families who were high in expressed emotion. The structural approach derived from Minuchin's model often involved encouraging the families to resolve their conflicts within the session. This often led to open confrontation, deadlock and distress. Family counselling offers the opportunity to train the parents in ways of managing problems more effectively.

The form of family therapy used for young adolescents was ineffective in the older group (Russell *et al*, 1987). However, an approach which did not expect the parents to control the symptoms was more effective (reported in Dare & Eisler (1995) in the latter group). In our practice on an adult in-patient unit we encourage the parents to develop the skills of motivational interviewing which fosters negotiation rather than confrontation (Treasure, 1997).

Individual out-patient therapy

Three small studies complement the findings of Crisp and colleagues reported above in that they have shown that out-patient treatment alone can be effective in adult anorexia nervosa (Hall & Crisp, 1987; Channon *et al*, 1989; Treasure *et al*, 1995). A variety of models of treatment were used: nutritional counselling, dynamic psychotherapy, CBT, behavioural therapy and cognitive analytical therapy.

We are in the process of collecting the follow-up data from a study of out-patient treatment of anorexia nervosa in which three forms of specialised treatment, family therapy, cognitive analytical therapy and focal dynamic treatment, were compared against supportive therapy. All specialised treatments were equally effective whereas little weight gain was attained in the group given supportive therapy. A greater number of the latter required in-patient treatment. Interestingly, although the outcomes are similar there were differences in the amount of therapy given with cognitive analytical therapy (20+5 sessions) and focal dynamic weekly therapy for a year (approx. 40 sessions).

Practice guidelines

The American Psychiatric Association (1993) produced practice guidelines for the management of eating disorders using a review of the literature up to 1990. A summary statement was:

> Anorexia nervosa is a medically, psychopathologically and interpersonally complex, serious and often chronic condition that requires ongoing commitment and attention to multiple, interdigitating diagnosis and to a comprehensive plan that involves medical management, individual psychotherapy and family therapy. At the present time the best initial results appear linked to weight restoration accompanied by individual and family psychotherapies when the patient is medically ready to participate.

They also discussed setting:

> Although some underweight patients who are less than 20% below average weight for height may be successfully treated outside of the hospital, such treatment usually requires a highly motivated patient, cooperative family and brief duration of symptoms. Such patients may be treated in out-patient programmes with close monitoring for several weeks to assess their response. Most severely underweight patients and those with physiological instability require in-patient medical management and comprehensive treatment for support of weight gain.

These statements need to be questioned in the light of the recent research findings. For example the need for full weight restoration to be the primary goal before other issues can be worked upon does not appear to be supported by the research evidence in that the one year outcome after in-patient treatment is not improved for cases of intermediate severity (Crisp *et al*, 1991). Also, out-patient care can be successfully used for people with intermediate prognostic features, that is a body mass index below 15 kg/m² and a duration of over 3 years.

The high mortality and morbidity rate of severe untreated anorexia nervosa makes in-patient treatment the most usual treatment setting but it remains uncertain what intensity of treatment is required after discharge. In our practice we find that a specialist hostel can help in the maintenance phase post discharge.

Conclusions

The complexities of conducting randomised controlled trials for anorexia nervosa means that it is unlikely that evidence-based practices will emerge from this methodology (Treasure & Kordy,

1998). Large scale naturalistic outcome studies may provide the answers that we need and it is pleasing that there is a large multinational European study in progress (Treasure, 1995). Similarly for bulimia nervosa, in order to make further progress we need to move from efficacy studies with their tightly defined and restricted case mix to studies that reflect clinical practice. Interventions that will allow for flexibility and patient treatment matching will need to be developed. We need to move away from the fixed intensity model, whether it be three months of in-patient treatment for anorexia nervosa or 20 sessions of cognitive–behavioural treatment for bulimia nervosa, to a service which offers a range of services from those which facilitate self-help to those which offer long-term rehabilitation.

References

ABBOT, D. W. & MITCHELL, J. E. (1993) Antidepressants vs. psychotherapy in the treatment of bulimia nervosa. *Psychopharmacology Bulletin*, **29**, 115–19.

AGRAS, W. S. (1993) Short term psychological treatments for binge eating. In *Binge Eating: Nature Assessment and Treatment* (eds C. G. Fairburn & G. T. Wilson), pp. 122, 270–286. New York: Guilford Press.

——, DORIAN, B., KIRKLEY, B. G., et al (1987) Imipramine in the treatment of bulimia: a double-blind controlled study. *International Journal of Eating Disorders*, **6**, 29–38.

——, SCHNEIDER, J. A., ARNOW, B., et al (1989) Cognitive behavioural therapy with and without exposure plus response prevention in the treatment of bulimia nervosa. *Journal of Consulting and Clinical Psychology*, **57**, 215–221.

——, ROSSITER, E. M., ARNOW, B., et al (1992) Pharmacological and cognitive–behavioral treatment for bulimia nervosa: A controlled comparison. *American Journal of Psychiatry*, **149**, 82–87.

——, TELCH, C. F., ARNOW, B., et al (1995) Does interpersonal therapy help patients with binge eating disorders who fail to respond to cognitive–behavioural therapy. *Journal of Consulting and Clinical Psychology*, **63**, 356–360.

AMERICAN PSYCHIATRIC ASSOCIATION (1993) Guidelines. *American Journal of Psychiatry*, **150**, 208–228.

BAELL, W. K. & WERTHEIM, E. H. (1992) Predictors of outcome in the treatment of bulimia nervosa. *British Journal of Clinical Psychology*, **31**, 330–332.

BARAN, S. A., WELTZIN, T. E. & KAYE, W. H. (1995) Low discharge weight and outcome in anorexia nervosa. *American Journal of Psychiatry*, **152**, 1072–1077.

BLACK, N. (1996) Why we need observational studies to evaluate the effectiveness of health care. *British Medical Journal*, **312**, 1215–1218.

BLOUIN, J. H. CARTER, J., BLOUIN, A. G., et al (1994) Prognostic indicators in bulimia nervosa treated with cognitive behavioural group therapy. *International Journal of Eating Disorders*, **15**, 113–123.

BOSKIND-LODAHL, M. & WHITE, W. C. (1978) The definition and treatment of bulimarexia in college women. A pilot study. *Journal of American College Health*, **27**, 84–97.

BOSSERT, S., SCHNABEL, E. & KRIEG, J. C. (1989) Effects and limitation of cognitive behavioural therapy in bulimia inpatients. *Psychotherapy and Psychosomatics*, **51**, 77–82.

CHANNON, S., DE SILVA, P., HEMSLEY, D., et al (1989) A controlled trial of cognitive behavioural and behavioural treatment of anorexia nervosa. *Behaviour Research and Therapy*, **27**, 529–535.

COLLINGS, S. & KING, M. (1994) Ten-year follow-up of 50 patients with bulimia nervosa. *British Journal of Psychiatry*, **164**, 80–87.

COOPER, P. (1993) *Bulimia Nervosa.* London: Robinson.

COOPER, P. J., COKER, S. & FLEMING, C. (1996) An evaluation of the efficacy of supervised cognitive behavioral self-help for bulimia nervosa. *Journal of Psychosomatic Research*, **40**, 281–287.

CRISP, A. H., NORTON, K., GOWERS, S., *et al* (1991) A controlled study of the effect of therapies aimed at adolescent and family psychopathology in anorexia nervosa. *British Journal of Psychiatry*, **159**, 325–333.

CROSBY, R. D., MITCHELL, J. E., RAYMOND, N., *et al* (1993) Survival analysis of response to group psychotherapy in bulimia nervosa. *International Journal of Eating Disorders*, **13**, 359–368.

DARE, C. & EISLER, I. (1995) Family therapy. In *Handbook of Eating Disorders. Theory, Treatment and Research* (eds C. Dare, G. Szmukler & J. Treasure), pp. 333–349. Chichester: Wiley.

DAVIS, R., OLMSTED, M. P. & ROCKERT, W. (1990) Brief group psychoeducation for bulimia nervosa: assessing the clinical significance of change. *Journal of Consulting and Clinical Psychology*, **58**, 882–885.

———, ——— & ——— (1992) Brief group psychoeducation for bulimia nervosa: II prediction of clinical outcome. *International Journal of Eating Disorders*, **11**, 205–211.

DODGE, E., HODES, M., EISLER, I., *et al* (1995) Family therapy for bulimia nervosa in adolescents: an exploratory study. *Journal of Family Therapy*, **17**, 59–77.

ECKERT, E. D., GOLDBERG, S. C., HALMI, K. A., *et al* (1979) Behaviour therapy in anorexia nervosa. *British Journal of Psychiatry*, **134**, 55–59.

EISLER, I. (1995*a*) Combining individual and family therapy in adolescent anorexia nervosa: a family systems approach. In *Treating Eating Disorders* (ed. J. Werne). San Francisco, CA: Jossey-Bass.

——— (1995*b*) Family models of eating disorders. In *Handbook of Treatment of Eating Disorders: Theory, Treatment and Research* (eds G. Szmukler, C. Dare & J. L. Treasure), pp. 155–176. Chichester: Wiley.

———, DARE, C., RUSSELL, G. F. M., *et al* (1997) A five year follow-up of a controlled trial of family therapy in severe eating disorder. *Archives of General Psychiatry*, **54**, 1025–1030.

FAHY, T. A., EISLER, I. & RUSSELL, G. F. M. (1993) Personality disorder and treatment response in bulimia nervosa. *British Journal of Psychiatry*, **162**, 765–770.

FAIRBURN, C. G. (1985) Cognitive behavioural treatment for bulimia nervosa. In *Handbook of Psychotherapy for Anorexia Nervosa and Bulimia* (eds D. M. Garner & P. E. Garfinkel), pp. 160–192. New York: Guilford Press.

——— (1993) Interpersonal psychotherapy for bulimia nervosa. In *New Applications of Interpersonal Psychotherapy* (eds G. L. Klerman & M. M. Weissman), pp. 353–378. Washington, DC: American Psychiatric Press.

———, KIRK, J., O'CONNOR, M., *et al* (1986) A comparison of two psychological treatments for bulimia nervosa. *Behaviour Research and Therapy*, **24**, 629–643.

———, ———, ———, *et al* (1987) Prognostic factors in bulimia nervosa. *British Journal of Clinical Psychology*, **26**, 223–224.

———, JONES, R., PEVELER, R. C., *et al* (1991) Three psychological treatments for bulimia nervosa: a comparative trial. *Archives of General Psychiatry*, **48**, 463–469.

———, MARCUS, M. D. & WILSON, G. T. (1993) Cognitive behaviour therapy for binge eating and bulimia nervosa: A comprehensive treatment manual. In *Binge Eating: Nature Assessment and Treatment* (eds C. G. Fairburn & G. T. Wilson), pp. 361–404. New York: Guilford Press.

———, NORMAN, P. A., WELCH, S. L., *et al* (1995) A prospective study of outcome in bulimia nervosa and the long term effects of three psychological treatments. *Archives of General Psychiatry*, **52**, 304–312.

FALLON, P., KATZMAN, M. A. & WOOLEY, S. C. (eds) (1994) *Feminist Perspectives on Eating Disorders.* New York: Guilford Press.

FETTES, P. A. & PETERS, J. M. (1992) A meta analysis of group treatments for bulimia nervosa. *International Journal of Eating Disorders* **11**, 97–110.

FICHTER, M. M., QUADFLEIG, N. & RIEF, W. (1992) The German Longitudinal Bulimia Nervosa Study I. In *The Course of Eating Disorders* (ed W. Herzog), pp. 133–149. Heidelberg: Springer.

——, —— & —— (1994) Course of multi-impulsive bulimia. *Psychological Medicine*, **24**, 591–604.

FREEMAN, C. P. (1991) A practical guide to the treatment of bulimia nervosa. *Journal of Psychosomatic Research*, **35**, 41–49.

—— (1995) Cognitive therapy. In *Handbook of Eating Disorders* (eds C. Dare, G. Szmukler & J. Treasure), pp. 309–332. Chichester: Wiley.

FREEMAN, C. P. L., BARRY, F., DUNKELD-TURNBULL, J., *et al* (1988) Controlled trial of psychotherapy for bulimia nervosa. *British Medical Journal*, **296**, 521–525.

FLUOXETINE BULIMIA NERVOSA COLLABORATIVE STUDY GROUP (FBNCSG) (1992) Fluoxetine in the treatment of bulimia nervosa. A multicentre, placebo-controlled, double-blind trial. *Archives of General Psychiatry*, **49**, 139–147.

GARNER, D. M. (1986) Cognitive therapy for bulimia nervosa. *Annals of the American Society for Adolescent Psychiatry*, **13**, 358–390.

——, ROCKERT, W., OLMSTED, M. P., *et al* (1985) Psychoeducational principles in the treatment of bulimia and anorexia nervosa. In *Handbook of Psychotherapy for Anorexia Nervosa and Bulimia* (eds D. M. Garner & P. E. Garfinkel), pp. 513–572.

——, GARFINKEL, P. E. & IRVINE, M. J. (1986) Integration and sequencing of treatment approaches for eating disorders. *Psychotherapy and Psychosomatics*, **46**, 67–75.

——, ROCKERT, W., DAVIS, R., *et al* (1993) A comparison of cognitive–behavioural and supportive–expressive therapy for bulimia nervosa. *American Journal of Psychiatry*, **150**, 37–46.

GARFINKEL, P. E. & GOLDBLOOM, D. S. (1993) Bulimia nervosa. A review of therapy and research. *Journal of Psychotherapy Practice and Research*, **2**, 38–50.

GOLDNER, E. M. & BILSKER, D. (1995) Evidence based psychiatry. *Canadian Journal of Psychiatry*, **40**, 97–101.

GOLDSTEIN, D. J., WILSON, M. G., THOMPSON, V. L., *et al* (1995) Long term fluoxetine treatment of bulimia nervosa. *British Journal of Psychiatry*, **166**, 660–666.

HALL, A. & CRISP, A. H. (1987) Brief psychotherapy in the treatment of anorexia nervosa: outcome at one year. *British Journal of Psychiatry*, **151**, 185–191.

HARTMANN, A., HERZOG, T. & DRINKMANN, A. (1992) Psychotherapy of bulimia nervosa: What is effective? A meta-analysis. *Journal of Psychosomatic Research*, **36**, 159–167.

HERZOG, T., HARTMANN, A., SANDHOLZ, A., *et al* (1991) Prognostic factors in outpatient psychotherapy of bulimia. *Psychotherapy and Psychosomatics*, **54**, 48–55.

HORNYAK, L. M. & BAKER, E. K. (1989) *Experimental Therapies for Eating Disorders*. New York: Guilford Press.

HSU, L. K. G., SANTHOUSE, R. & CHESLER, B. E. (1991) Individual cognitive behavioural therapy for bulimia nervosa: The description of a programme. *International Journal of Eating Disorders*, **10**, 273–283.

JANSEN, A., BROEKMATE, J. & HEYMANS, M. (1992) Cue exposure vs self control in the treatment of binge eating: A pilot study. *Behavior Research and Therapy*, **30**, 235–241.

JOHNSON, C. (1991) *Psychodynamic Treatment of Anorexia Nervosa and Bulimia Nervosa*. New York: Guilford Press.

——, CONNORS, M. E. & TOBIN, D. L. (1987) Symptom management of bulimia. *Journal of Consulting and Clinical Psychology*, **55**, 668–676.

——, TOBIN, D. L., DENNIS, A. (1990) Differences in treatment outcome between borderline and non-borderline bulimics at one year follow-up. *International Journal of Eating Disorders*, **9**, 617–627.

KELLER, M. B., HERZOG, D. P., LAVORI, P. W., *et al* (1991) The naturalistic history of bulimia nervosa: Extraordinary high rates of chronicity relapse recurrence and psychosocial morbidity. *International Journal of Eating Disorders*, **12**, 1–9.

KIRKLEY, B. G., SCHMEIDER, J. A., AGRAS, W. S., *et al* (1985) Comparison of two group treatments for bulimia. *Journal of Consulting and Clinical Psychology*, **53**, 43–48.

KLERMAN, G. L., WEISSMAN, M. M., ROUNSVILLE, B. J., et al (1984) *Interpersonal Psychotherapy of Depression.* New York: Basic Books.

KORDY, H. AND THE GERMAN COLLABORATIVE STUDY GROUP ON EATING DISORDERS (1996) Towards psychotherapy for eating disorders of high quality and affordable costs. *European Psychiatry,* **11** (Suppl. 4), 221s.

LACEY, L. H. (1983) Self-damaging and addictive behaviour in bulimia nervosa. A catchment area study. *British Journal of Psychiatry,* **163,** 190–194.

LAESSLE, P. J., BEUMONT, P. J. V., BUTOW, P., et al (1991) A comparison of nutritional management with stress management in the treatment of bulimia nervosa. *British Journal of Psychiatry,* **159,** 250–261.

LAESSLE, R. G., ZOETTLE, C. & PIRKE, K. M. (1987) Meta analysis of treatment studies for bulimia. *International Journal of Eating Disorders* **6,** 647–653.

LEE, N. F. & RUSH, A. J. (1986) Cognitive–behavioral group therapy for bulimia. *International Journal of Eating Disorders,* **5,** 599–615.

LE GRANGE, D., EISLER, I., DARE, C., et al (1992) Evaluation of family treatments in adolescent anorexia nervosa: a pilot study. *International Journal of Eating Disorders,* **12,** 347–357.

LEITENBERG, H., ROSEN, J. C. & GROSS, J. (1988) Exposure plus response prevention treatment of bulimia nervosa. *Journal of Consulting and Clinical Psychology,* **56,** 535–541.

LINEHAN, M. M. (1993) *Cognitive Behavioural Treatment of Borderline Personality Disorder.* New York: Guilford Press.

MADDOCKS, S. E., KAPLAN, A. S. & WOODSIDE, D. B. (1992) Two year follow-up of bulimia nervosa: the importance of abstinence as the criteria of outcome. *International Journal of Eating Disorders,* **12,** 133–141.

MALENBAUM, R., HERZOG, D., EISENTHAL, S., et al (1988) Overeaters anonymous. *International Journal of Eating Disorders,* **7,** 632–637.

MCKENZIE, J. M. & JOYCE, P. R. (1990) Hospitalisation for anorexia nervosa. *International Journal of Eating Disorders,* **11,** 235–241.

MINUCHIN, S., BAKER, L., ROSMAN, B. L., et al (1975) A conceptual model of psychosomatic illness in children. *Archives of General Psychiatry,* **32,** 1031–1038.

——, ROSMAN, B. L., LIEBMAN, R., et al (1978) *Psychosomatic Families: Anorexia Nervosa in Context.* Harvard, MA: University Press.

MITCHELL, J. E. (1991) A review of the controlled trials of psychotherapy for bulimia nervosa. *Journal of Psychosomatic Research,* **35,** 23–31.

——, CHRISTIANSON, G., JENNINGS, J., et al (1989) A placebo controlled, double blind crossover study of naltrexone hydrochloride in outpatients with normal weight bulimia. *Journal of Clinical Psychopharmacology,* **83,** 94–97.

——, PYLE, R. L., ECKERT, E. D., et al (1990) A comparison study of antidepressants and structured intensive group psychotherapy in the treatment of bulimia nervosa. *Archives of General Psychiatry,* **47,** 149–157.

——, ——, POMEROY, C., et al (1993) Cognitive behavioural group psychotherapy of bulimia nervosa: Importance of logistical variables. *International Journal of Eating Disorders,* **3,** 277–287.

——, HOBERMAN, H. N., PETERSON, C. B., et al (1996) Research on the psychotherapy of bulimia nervosa: Half empty or half full. *International Journal of Eating Disorders,* **20,** 219–230.

OLMSTED, M. P., KAPLAN, A. S. & ROCKERT, W. (1994) Rate and prediction of relapse in bulimia nervosa. *American Journal of Psychiatry,* **151,** 738–743.

——, ——, ——, et al (1996) Rapid responders to intensive treatment of bulimia nervosa. *International Journal of Eating Disorders,* **19,** 279–285.

POPE, H. G. & HUDSON, J. I. (1984) *New Hope for Binge Eaters: Advances in Understanding and Treatment of Bulimia.* New York: Harper Row.

——, ——, JONAS, J. M., et al (1985) Antidepressant treatment of bulimia: a two-year follow-up study. *Journal of Clinical Psychopharmacology,* **5,** 320–327.

—— & —— (1987) Antidepressant medication in the treatment of bulimia nervosa. *Psychopathology,* **20** (suppl. 1), 123–129.

PYLE, R. L., MITCHELL, J. E., ECKHERT, E. D., *et al* (1990) Maintenance treatment and 6-month outcome for bulimia patients who respond to initial treatment. *American Journal of Psychiatry*, **147**, 871–875.

ROOT, M. P. P., FALLON, P. & FREIDRICH, W. N. (1986) *Bulimia: A Systems Approach to Treatment.* New York: WW Norton.

ROSSITER, E. M., AGRAS, W. S., TELCH, C. F., *et al* (1993) Cluster B personality disorder characteristics predict outcome in the treatment of bulimia nervosa. *International Journal of Eating Disorders*, **13**, 349–358.

RUSSELL, G. F., SZMUKLER, G. I., DARE, C., *et al* (1987) An evaluation of family therapy in anorexia nervosa and bulimia nervosa. *Archives of General Psychiatry*, **44**, 1047–1056.

RYLE, A. (1990) *Cognitive Analytic Therapy: Active Participation in Change.* Chichester: Wiley.

—— (1995) *Cognitive Analytic Therapy: Developments in Theory and Practice.* Chichester: Wiley.

SCHMIDT, U., TILLER, J. & TREASURE, J. L. (1993) Self treatment of bulimia nervosa: a pilot study. *International Journal of Eating Disorders*, **13**, 273–277.

—— & TREASURE, J. L. (1993) *Getting Better Bite by Bite.* Hove: Lawrence Erlbaum.

—— & —— (1996) *A Clinicians Guide to Getting Better Bite by Bite.* Hove: Lawrence Erlbaum.

SCHWARTZ, H. J. (1990) *Psychoanalytical Treatment and Theory, 2nd edn.* Madison, CT: International University Press.

SCHWARTZ, R. C., BARRETT, M. J. & SABA, G. (1985) Family therapy for bulimia. In *Handbook of Psychotherapy for Anorexia Nervosa and Bulimia* (eds D. M. Garner & P. E. Garfinkel), pp. 280–310. New York: Guilford Press.

SELVINI-PALAZZOLI, M. (1974) *Self-starvation: From the Intrapsychic to the Transpersonal Approach.* London: Chaucer.

TELCH, C. F., AGRAS, W. S., ROSSITER, E. M., *et al* (1990) Group cognitive–behavioral treatment for the nonpurging bulimic: An initial evaluation. *Journal of Consulting and Clinical Psychology*, **58**, 629–635.

THIELS, C., SCHMIDT, U., TREASURE, J., *et al* (1998) Guided self-change for bulimia nervosa incorporating a self-treatment manual. *American Journal of Psychiatry*, **155**, 947–953.

TILLER, J., SCHMIDT, U. & TREASURE, J. (1993) Treatment of bulimia nervosa. *International Review of Psychiatry*, **5**, 75–86.

TOBIN, D. L. (1993) Psychodynamic treatment and binge eating. In *Binge Eating: Nature Assessment and Treatment* (eds C. G. Fairburn & G. T. Wilson), pp. 97–122. New York: Guilford Press.

TOUYZ, S. W., BEAUMONT, P. J. V., GLAUN, D., *et al* (1984) A comparison of lenient and strict operant conditioning programmes in refeeding patients with anorexia nervosa. *British Journal of Psychiatry*, **144**, 520–527.

TREASURE, J. (1995) European co-operation in the fields of scientific and technical research. COST B6 Psychotherapeutic Treatment of Eating Disorders. *European Eating Disorders Review*, **3**, 119–120.

—— (1997) *Escaping from Anorexia Nervosa: A Self Treatment Book for Sufferers and Carers.* Hove: Lawrence Erlbaum.

——, SCHMIDT, U., TROOP, N., *et al* (1994) First step in managing bulimia nervosa: controlled trial of a therapeutic manual. *British Medical Journal*, **308**, 686–689.

——, TODD, G., BROLLY, *et al* (1995) A pilot study of a randomised trial of cognitive analytical therapy vs educational behavioural therapy for adult anorexia nervosa. *Behaviour Research and Therapy*, **33**, 363–367.

——, SCHMIDT, U., TROOP, N., *et al* (1996a) Sequential treatment for bulimia nervosa incorporating a self care manual. *British Journal of Psychiatry*, **168**, 94–98.

——, TROOP, N. A. & WARD, A. (1996b) An approach to planning services for bulimia nervosa. *British Journal of Psychiatry*, **169**, 551–554.

—— & KORDY, H. (1998) Modelling care for eating disorders across Europe. *European Eating Disorders Review* (submitted).

————— & SCHMIDT, U. (1998) Beyond effectiveness and efficacy lies quality in services for eating disorders. *European Eating Disorders Review* (in press).

TURNBULL, S., WARD, A., TREASURE, J. L., *et al* (1996) The demand for eating disorder care: An epidemiological study using the General Practice Research Database. *British Journal of Psychiatry,* **169**, 705–712.

TUSCHEN, B. & BENT, H. (1995) Intensive brief inpatient treatment of bulimia nervosa. In *Comprehensive Textbook of Eating Disorders and Obesity* (eds K. D. Brownell & C. G. Fairburn). New York: Guilford Press.

VANDEREYCKEN, W. (1993) Naughty girls and angry doctors. *International Review of Psychiatry,* **5**, 13–18.

————— & PIETERS, G. (1978) Short term weight restoration in anorexia nervosa through operant conditioning. *Scandinavian Journal of Behavioural Therapy,* **7**, 221–236.

VANDERLINDEN, J. & VANDEREYCKEN, W. (1990) The use of hypnosis in the treatment of bulimia nervosa. *International Journal of Clinical and Experimental Hypnosis,* **XXXVIII**, 101–111.

WALLER, D., FAIRBURN, C. G., MCPHERSON, A., *et al* (1996) Treating bulimia nervosa in primary care – a pilot study. *International Journal of Eating Disorders,* **19**, 99–103.

WALSH, B. T., HADIGAN, C. M. & DEVLIN, M. J. (1991) Long term outcome of antidepressant treatment for bulimia nervosa. *American Journal of Psychiatry,* **148**, 1206–1212.

————— & DEVLIN, M. J. (1992) The pharmacological treatment of eating disorders. *Psychiatric Clinics of North America,* **15**, 149–160.

WHITBREAD, J. & MCGOWN, A. (1994) The treatment of bulimia nervosa: What is effective. A meta analysis. *Indian Journal of Clinical Psychology,* **21**, 32–44.

WILFLEY, D. E., AGRAS, W. S., TELCH, C. F., *et al* (1993) Group cognitive–behavioral therapy and group interpersonal psychotherapy for the nonpurging bulimic individual: a controlled comparison. *Journal of Consulting and Clinical Psychology,* **61**, 296–305.

WILSON, D. G. T. (1996) Treatment of bulimia nervosa: When CBT fails. *Behavior Research and Therapy,* **34**, 197–212.

WILSON, ROSSITER, E., KLEINFIELS, E. I., *et al* (1986) Cognitive behavioral treatment of bulimia nervosa: a controlled evaluation. *Behavior Research and Therapy,* **24**, 277–288.

—————, ELDREDGE, K. L., SMITH, D., *et al* (1991) Cognitive behavioral treatment with and without response prevention for bulimia. *Behavior Research and Therapy,* **29**, 579–583.

WING, J. K., COOPER, J. E. & SARTORIUS, N. (1974) *Measurement and Classification of Psychiatric Symptoms: an Instruction Manual for PSE and Catego Program.* London: Cambridge University Press.

WOLCHIK, S. A., WEISS, L. & KATZMAN, M. A. (1986) An empirically validated short term psychoeducational group treatment programme for bulimia. *International Journal of Eating Disorders,* **5**, 21–31.

WOLF, E. M. & CROWTHER, J. H. (1992) An evaluation of behavioural and cognitive behavioural group interventions for the treatment of bulimia nervosa in women. *International Journal of Eating Disorders,* **11**, 3–15.

WONDERLICH, S. A., FULLERTON, D., SWIFT, W. J., *et al* (1994) Five year outcome from eating disorders: relevance of personality disorders. *International Journal of Eating Disorders,* **15**, 233–243.

WOOLEY, S. C. & KEARNEY-COOKE, A. (1986) Intensive treatment of bulimia and body image disturbance. In *Handbook of Eating Disorders* (eds K. D. Brownell & J. P. Foreyt), pp. 476–502. New York: Basic Books.

YATES, A. J. & SAMBRAILO, L. (1984) Bulimia nervosa: A descriptive and therapeutic study. *Behavior Research and Therapy,* **22**, 503–517.

YOUNG, J. E. (1993) *Cognitive Therapy for Personality Disorders: A Schema Focused Approach.* Sarasota FL: Professional Resource Exchange.

10 Victims and perpetrators of child sexual abuse

M. R. HILTON and G. C. MEZEY

Victims of sexual abuse

Prevalence

The lack of uniformity between researchers in the definition of sexual abuse has led to wide discrepancies in stated prevalence. Baker & Duncan (1985), interviewing a sample of over 2000 men and women, found that 12% of women and 8% of men reported being sexually abused before the age of 16 years, mostly by a family member. Russell (1984) surveyed a community sample of over 900 women and found that 28% had been sexually abused before the age of 13 years and 38% before the age of 17 years; only 2% of the incest cases and 6% of the extra-familial cases of abuse were ever reported. The most common form of sexual abuse is father–daughter incest, although there is increasing recognition of the abuse of boys and of sexual abuse by women.

Identification

Given the high rate of childhood sexual abuse reported in clinical populations, clinicians need to be aware of symptoms and behaviour that may signal sexual abuse (Briere, 1988), such as a sudden change in social and/or academic functioning or the emergence of truancy, delinquency and other conduct disorders. The presence of repetitive sexual play and sexual precociousness, including sexual abuse of other children, is a more direct indicator, but such evidence may not always

---

This paper was first published in the *British Journal of Psychiatry* (1996), **169**, 408–415.

be present. An important part of skilled intervention is therefore being sensitive to signs of child sexual abuse and creating a therapeutic environment that is sufficiently safe for memories to be revealed, while avoiding the creation of false memories (British Psychological Society, 1995).

The effects of sexual abuse

The experience of sexual abuse during childhood is associated with disturbing subsequent problems in some victim's lives. However, it should also be noted that generally about one-third of survivors consistently report no long-term negative effects (Kendall-Tackett *et al*, 1993). Certain features appear to predict a more severe outcome: abuse by a father or step-father, as opposed to a stranger or sibling (Finkelhor, 1979); the use of violence during abuse (Russell, 1986); penetrative sexual acts (Bagley & Ramsay, 1986); and bizarre abuse using pseudo-religious rituals or particularly repugnant acts (Briere, 1988). The circumstances of disclosure, reactions to this by significant others, and the amount of support available to the child as well as their attributional style and temperament are additional factors which affect the likelihood of developing long-term pathology (Carson *et al*, 1989; Wolfe *et al*, 1989).

A wide range of symptoms have been reported by adult survivors of sexual abuse, who show higher rates of depression, guilt, feelings of inferiority, impaired feelings of inter-relatedness and lower self-esteem than the general population (Briere, 1989; Mullen *et al*, 1993). They frequently manifest anxiety and chronic tension, sexual problems and a tendency towards re-victimisation (Runtz & Briere, 1986; Briere, 1989; Finkelhor *et al*, 1989).

High prevalence rates of sexual abuse have also been found in 'disordered' or clinical populations presenting with alcoholism, sexual dysfunction, anorexia, self-cutting and suicidal attempts (Briere, 1984; Oppenheimer *et al*, 1985; Bryer *et al*, 1987; Palmer *et al*, 1993). Sexual abuse may give rise to post-traumatic stress disorder (Lindberg & Distad, 1985) and dissociative states, including multiple personality disorder (Jehu, 1988; Wolfe *et al*, 1989).

Male survivors of abuse describe similar long-term problems following abuse to those of female survivors. There is some evidence that male survivors are more likely to react by projecting their anger outwards, whereas women are more likely to internalise feelings of anger and express these in self-destructive behaviour, self-hatred, low self-esteem and suicidal thoughts or attempts (Carmen *et al*, 1984). Specific problems of male survivors include confusion and anxiety over sexual identity, inappropriate attempts to assert masculinity and repetition of the victimisation experience, either as victims or perpetrators (Watkins & Bentovim, 1992). Although there is a growing awareness of the problem, male victims remain disadvantaged in terms of the lack of resources available to help them (Mezey & King, 1992).

Intervening in child sexual abuse

The extent to which the child or adult is further damaged by disclosure will be affected by whether they are believed and how well they are supported. Various enquiries have highlighted the necessity of providing a supportive network of agencies working together, and have criticised overzealous interventions leading to more traumatisation (Butler-Sloss, 1988). Children frequently feel that they have caused the problem and wish that they had never spoken out. The police, social services and child health services have been encouraged to draw up joint plans and procedures so that each agency is clear about its roles and responsibilities.

Helping the child victim

The investigation of allegations should proceed with as little disruption to the child as possible. However, in cases where the perpetrator and his/her partner are unwilling to be separated, the child may need to be removed from the home in order to ensure his/her safety. Disclosure of abuse can be extremely frightening for the victim. Fears about being disbelieved, or being accused of having been sexually provocative or encouraging the abuse, all deter disclosure. The need to obtain reliable evidence in order to bring the perpetrator to court provides a situation which, if not sensitively handled, can further traumatise the victim. There is often considerable pressure to achieve disclosure in the shortest possible time, particularly if sessions are video-taped and attended by the police and social worker. However, such considerations should never take precedence over the need to give the victim time to feel comfortable and to develop trust in the people assessing him/her. Certain techniques have been objected to by the courts who are concerned that children's evidence can easily be distorted and rendered invalid. In response to such concerns, a range of interviewing techniques with child victims of abuse is proposed (Vizard *et al*, 1987).

In recent years, greater awareness of the impact of court proceedings on the child have led to changes in the legal process, allowing children's evidence to be given in court via a video link, although in practice this is rarely used.

Therapy with children

Therapy with abused children needs to be tailored to their developmental level. Play materials are useful with children under 10 years of age, or with less articulate older children. Other methods include getting them to play-act, write letters, speak into a cassette recorder, make up stories, or discuss other people's stories. With adolescents, group psycho-drama can be extremely helpful in enabling them to explore different identities and to enact different aspects of their stories and their family life. Assertiveness and communication skills may also be helpful. The aims of treatment are to enable the child to cope emotionally with the experience and repercussions of the abuse and to identify and correct damaging and self-punitive cognitive distortions.

Family therapy

Family systems theorists have frequently noted the blurring of boundaries and role reversal that occur in abusing families, the collusive role of the non-offending partner and secondary gain for the family through the scapegoating of the identified victim. This means that a treatment approach should generally involve family members (Giaretto, 1981).

Good prognostic factors in family work are indicated by maternal support of the child, lack of scapegoating, willingness to cooperate, availability of appropriate treatment resources and a potential for multi-agency collaboration. Family therapy is unlikely to be successful if the abuser's paedophiliac tendencies are very entrenched, if there is clear rejection of the child and if members of the family are uncooperative and undermining the treatment. The Great Ormond Street Treatment Project defined approximately 25% of their 120 abusive families as falling within the latter group, indicating a 'hopeless' prognosis (Bentovim, 1991).

Group and individual therapy with adolescents and adults

There are several texts which offer useful suggestions for providing effective assessment and treatment for survivors of child sexual abuse and which discuss a wide range of issues including the sex of the therapist and legal considerations (Hall & Lloyd, 1989; Sanderson, 1990).

Therapeutic groups have been used with survivors of all ages, but may be particularly helpful with adolescents and adults as a means of reducing their sense of isolation and of being different and unacceptable to others. The knowledge that others have suffered similar experiences may facilitate a sense of trust and building of self-esteem. This may be much more difficult to achieve if clients perceive the therapist as someone who is likely to denigrate and humiliate them, or deny their reality and whose experiences are totally different from their own. For many survivors, group treatment may be too threatening initially and the extent of their own needs may preclude the possibility of empathising with or coping with hearing about the experiences of others.

There is often a need to help the patients to reframe their feelings and behaviour during the abuse in order to understand that the strategies they employed enabled them to survive and cope with what was happening. Education, using books and videos, can facilitate a greater knowledge of child sexual abuse and its effects, reducing the sense of isolation, building trust and empowering the individual to achieve greater control in his/her life. Various methods have been suggested for facilitating disclosure and recall and to assist emotional processing of the abuse. Specific skills training may also be needed, for instance training in assertiveness or anger management, as may treatment for depression, eating disorders, sexual functioning and self-destructive behaviour.

Ethical issues in working with survivors of sexual abuse

Therapists who work with survivors of sexual abuse, particularly children, are often faced with complex ethical decisions: whether they should encourage disclosure if the victim is not amenable and whether they should recommend legal proceedings, often many years after the alleged abuse occurred. Once a disclosure has been made by a child, legal sanctions are automatically initiated, often in the form of child-care proceedings which may be experienced by the child as abusive. Recent legislation has put the child's interests and wishes firmly on the agenda but cannot fully protect the abused child who becomes embroiled in legal proceedings. The current ethic argues that the perpetrator of child sexual abuse needs to be subject to legal restraint, if not prosecution, even if this runs counter to the expressed wishes of the victim.

Many clinicians experience a tension between their role as clinician and evidence gatherer. In cases where abuse has been disclosed, it could be argued that the therapist has a duty to pass on this information regardless of the wishes of the client, where failure to do so could be putting another child at risk. Therapists may be concerned that such action would represent a breach of confidentiality, to the possible detriment of the therapeutic process, and may be perceived as a further abuse of trust. Instead of receiving help, the victim may unwittingly begin a chain of events which results in ostracism by his/her family and friends. It is crucial that all carers address this issue realistically with awareness of both the needs of the survivor and of the children considered to be at risk, so that an ethical response can be agreed.

Perpetrators of sexual abuse

Offender characteristics

Child sex abusers are usually men. Although generally not mentally ill, many have a disorder of personality, which may interfere with their capacity to form intimate relationships with partners of the appropriate age. They are often regarded as inadequate, passive and dependent; their contact with children represents an attempt to reassure themselves of a potency, power and control that they are unable to attain in any other sphere of their lives.

There is increasing recognition that incest offenders may abuse children outside as well as inside the home. In a community sample of over 500 self-admitted male sexual offenders, Abel and colleagues (1987) found that 23.3% of men had offended against both family and non-family members; 12% had offended exclusively against family members. Most abusers targeted either male or female victims and remained fairly fixed in their sexual preference; 20% were bisexual, suggesting a greater degree of sexual pathology.

Child sex abuse is multifactorial. Finkelhor (1984) proposed four preconditions for sexual abuse to occur; emotional congruence, sexual arousal, and the removal or undermining of both perpetrator and victim resistance. Most abusers experience sexual and emotional gratification, a release of tension and a sense of excitement associated with the act. Sexual contact with children can become a compulsive activity; the perpetrator arranges his life around children, and creates opportunities to abuse them.

Children's friendliness and wish for physical comfort, along with their natural inquisitiveness and curiosity, may be misinterpreted as a desire for sexual contact. One reason for such misunderstanding may relate to male sex role socialisation, which leads to men in our culture being socialised in adolescence to respond to emotionally intimate relationships as potentially sexual ones (Finkelhor, 1986).

The strategies used by abusers to gain access to children include 'targeting' (seeking out and selection of vulnerable children, who lack protective adult carers) and 'grooming' (gradually increasing intimacy with selected children to gain their trust through bribery, persuasion and encouragement, thus reducing their resistance to subsequent sexual contact). Typically one sees an escalation of behaviour, or 'try-outs', over a period of time, each subsequent contact involving a greater degree of intimacy, until the sexual offence occurs. The child's secrecy is assured through appealing to his/her sense of loyalty (if the perpetrator is a caretaker or family member), through intimidation by threats, actual physical violence and/or emotional manipulation, e.g. 'if they send me to prison I'll probably kill myself', or 'if you tell your mother she'll be really upset'. The sexual activity, often referred to as a game or harmless fun, becomes known as the child's 'secret'.

Victim to victimiser cycle

A significant number of child sex abusers report a history of sexual victimisation. Histories of abuse are particularly common in paedophiles whose preferred targets are boys (Knopp, 1984). There is some evidence that the more 'deviant' the population, the higher the rates of past reported victimisation. Histories of past victimisation also appear to be higher among adolescent perpetrators (Davis & Leitenberg, 1987; Johnstone, 1988). The choice of victim and his/her physical characteristics, including age of the chosen victim, often replicate the offender's own experience of abuse.

The association between early abuse and later offending behaviour is complex, and includes identification with the aggressor, a conditioning of sexual responsiveness to forced or coercive sex, and a defence against feelings of vulnerability engendered through the experience of victimisation (Mezey *et al*, 1991). Early traumatic sexual experiences may facilitate emotional congruence towards children, one of the four preconditions necessary for sexual abuse to take place (Finkelhor, 1984). Histories of early physical or sexual abuse are particularly common in adults with a diagnosis of borderline personality disorder which may represent a final common pathway for future impulsive and aggressive offending behaviour (Ogata *et al*, 1990; Shearer *et al*, 1990). A compulsion to repeat early trauma may be a manifestation of the re-experiencing phenomena of post-traumatic stress disorder (Deblinger *et al*, 1989).

The victim to victimiser cycle does not account for the protective factors that inhibit the development or expression of subsequent abusive behaviour nor does it explain why most sex abusers are men while the majority of victims are female.

Assessment

Victims' statements, police reports, information on previous convictions and reports from other agencies such as social services and the probation service are important sources of information. Victims' statements are particularly crucial, enabling the abuser to be confronted with discrepancies between his account and that of his victim, in order to explore the child's perceptions and reactions and to encourage greater openness. Prior to interviewing the abuser, the issue of confidentiality and the circumstances in which information will be shared with others must be discussed, as well as reasons for carrying out the assessment, who has commissioned the report and who the report will be made available to.

The tendency of sex offenders to deny various aspects of their behaviour, either because of shame or guilt, or in the hope of manipulating the therapist, can make assessment and treatment extremely difficult. Experienced clinicians can frame questions in such a way as to encourage disclosure and break down denial. With non-incest child abusers, for instance, it could be stated "from research and my own experience I know that by the time someone is arrested for abusing children they have usually offended with a large number of different children. Tell me about other children you have touched sexually". Questions exploring and challenging the offender's belief systems can be helpful, e.g. "You say you knew that what you were doing was wrong; so how did you give yourself permission to carry on?" Hypothetical situations can be presented in order to encourage openness, e.g. "I wonder if, when she asked to sit on your lap, you may have felt that she was wanting to be tickled and touched by you?" It can be useful to refer to information from victims' statements in order to explore faulty cognitions. For instance, "you said that you believed that she was enjoying the abuse, yet in her statement she said that she lay very still because she was terrified. Why do you think she said that?" Such questioning needs to be sensitive to the risk of eliciting false or misleading accounts from vulnerable or suggestible individuals.

Perkins (1991) emphasises the importance of being persuasive rather than bullying, of establishing common goals, using open, closed and evaluating questioning, and avoiding challenging too early in the therapeutic contact. When confrontation is used, it is important to try to convey that its purpose is to enable individuals to gain greater awareness and insight rather than to humiliate and catch them out.

The failure to communicate with other agencies and to share information is often justified on the basis of the confidentiality of the doctor–patient relationship. Child sex abusers are skilled at exploiting this situation, and therapists may easily get drawn into a collusive and conspiratorial relationship with the abuser. Mechanisms for counteracting this tendency include paired work with individual abusers, preferably using a male *and* female therapist, or group work, where fellow abusers may be expected to challenge each other's deceptions, rationalisations and denials. Sharing information on risk assessment with colleagues, with other agencies and with professionals who have an interest in ensuring child protection is a crucial component of sex offender treatment.

Assessment should involve detailed and thorough investigation of the individual's pattern of offending behaviour as well as the origins of offending, both historical and current. Attitudes and beliefs concerning offending and its effects on the victim are important to identify, as are situational triggers and disinhibiting factors such as substance abuse. In addition, it is important to identify factors that are likely to impede or encourage change, including the person's motivation.

Interviews can usefully be supplemented by psychometric assessment, including pencil and paper tests of attitudes, mood and personality. In addition, penile plethysmography, which measures arousal to various stimuli by examining changes in penile tumescence, has been found to be useful in eliciting disclosure as well as monitoring the success of treatment and pointing to potential risk factors (Launay, 1994).

Treatment approaches

A thorough and comprehensive assessment should enable treatment targets to be identified for the individual client. A prerequisite is that the person recognises that there is a problem, and has some motivation to explore this.

Where applicable, it may be useful to encourage clients to recount their own experiences of abuse in order to begin to challenge unhelpful and distorted cognitions about the child enjoying, needing or initiating sexual activity and about the benign nature of such contact. With some clients, where there is an abnormally high libido or compulsion to offend, it may be helpful to consider the use of anti-libidinal medication to provide some measure of control (Bradford, 1990). If such medication is contraindicated or not acceptable to the client, an aversive behavioural procedure such as masturbatory satiation

(Marshall, 1979) or covert sensitisation (Cautela, 1967) should be considered. Similarly, where motivation is good and masturbatory fantasy is believed to be an important factor in offending, orgasmic reconditioning (Marquis, 1970) can be implemented.

Once adequate motivation and self-control have been promoted and reinforced, there is a range of techniques that can be used to increase self-awareness, reduce denial, challenge cognitive distortions and increase empathy for victims. Good accounts can be found in Salter (1988) and Marshall & Barbaree (1990). Relapse prevention techniques also appear effective in work with sex offenders (Laws, 1989; Pithers, 1990).

Although some aspects of treatment, such as orgasmic reconditioning, are best done individually, the group treatment of sex offenders has many advantages. In particular, group work enables individuals to be challenged by their peers on their views and attitudes relating to child sexual offending and its origins. The offenders' denial, distorted cognitions and attitudes can often be confronted more effectively by peers than by professionals. Groups can also promote peer support as well as reducing the offender's isolation and fear of rejection. Most group treatments offer a cognitive–behavioural approach but are fundamentally eclectic and flexible, often drawing on a knowledge of group dynamics to understand and contain the evolving relationships between participants and therapists.

Treatment evaluation

There are clearly many problems in evaluating treatment, including differences in outcome measures used, length of follow-up, presence of a control group and offender characteristics. Despite these difficulties, there are some recent studies which provide some evidence that treatment can effect change. Pithers (1990) reported on a 5-year follow-up of 160 sex offenders, 147 of whom were child molesters. A recidivism rate of only 4% was found following relapse prevention treatment incorporating external monitoring by others. A recent report commissioned by the Home Office examined the efficacy of group treatment programmes for sex offenders based on seven separate programmes run mainly by probation services (Beckett *et al*, 1994). Good outcome was associated with high levels of group cohesiveness, high levels of task orientation, clear structure of the group, explicit roles for the men and offering the men respect and encouragement as individuals. They found that with more serious and deviant offenders, treatment needs to be long-term. A residential programme offering an average of 462 hours of therapy was particularly successful.

Abel and colleagues (1988) have proposed five factors which predict failure of treatment of child sex abusers: molestation of girls and boys; failure to accept increased communication with adults as a treatment goal; contact and non-contact offences; divorced status; and the involvement of familial and non-familial victims.

More treatment evaluation studies are needed, in particular to address the question of the extent to which treatment affects recidivism rates, what other markers can be used as evidence of treatment efficacy, what treatment model works best, what factors predict response to treatment and whether any apparent short-term benefits continue to be apparent in the long term.

Therapist qualifications

Working with sex abusers is liable to evoke strong emotions which may include fear, dread or disgust. It can be difficult to maintain a stance of therapeutic neutrality, let alone empathy and respect, which may result in a punitive, rather than a therapeutic, approach. Therapists may emotionally and intellectually distance themselves from their work, avoid thinking about the material presented during sessions, collude in denial, blame the victim or become excessively punitive within sessions, perhaps motivated by a wish to make the abuser experience what the victims may have felt. Many therapists feel de-skilled, overwhelmed by the material that they are forced to listen to. They may feel helpless, as if the patient is in control, a dynamic that replicates the original abuse. Therapists need to be aware of these factors and the potential for the therapist 'acting out', through the process of training and supervision (Roundy & Horton, 1990).

Therapists must be able to critically examine their own beliefs and attitudes in this area. A stance of therapeutic neutrality is not appropriate if clients are denying or minimising their behaviour and its effects, but to balance confrontation with support is a skilled task. Therapists must be secure in their own sexuality and comfortable in talking openly about all aspects of sexuality, and must be skilled in a range of intervention techniques.

References

ABEL, G. G., BECKER, J. V., MITTLEMAN, M. S., *et al* (1987) Self-reported sex crimes of non-incarcerated paraphiliacs. *Journal of Interpersonal Violence*, **2**, 3–25.
——, MITTLEMAN, M. S. & BECKER, J. V. (1988) Predicting child molesters' response to treatment. *Annals of the New York Academy of Science*, **528**, 223–234.
BAGLEY, C. & RAMSAY, R. (1986) Sexual abuse in childhood: psychological outcomes and implications for social worker practices. *Journal of Social Work and Human Sexuality*, **4**, 33–47.

BAKER, A. W. & DUNCAN, S. P. (1985) Child sexual abuse: a study of prevalence in Great Britain. *Child Abuse and Neglect*, **9**, 457–467.

BECKETT, R., BEECH, A., FISHER, D., *et al* (1994) *Community-Based Treatment for Sex Offenders: An Evaluation of Seven Treatment Programmes*. London: HMSO.

BENTOVIM, A. (1991) Clinical work with families in which sexual abuse occurred. In *Clinical Approaches to Sex Offenders and their Victims* (eds C. R. Hollin & K. Howells), pp. 179–208. Chichester: Wiley.

BRADFORD, J. M. W. (1990) The anti-androgen and hormonal treatment of sex offenders. In *Handbook of Sexual Assault. Theories and Treatment of the Offender* (eds W. L. Marshall, D. R. Laws & H. E. Barbaree), pp. 297–310. New York: Plenum Press.

BRIERE, J. (1988) The long-term clinical correlates of childhood sexual victimisation. In *Human Sexual Aggression: Current Perspectives* (ed. R. Prentky), pp. 327–334. New York: Annals of the New York Academy of Sciences.

—— (1989) *Therapy for Adults Molested as Children: Beyond Survival*. New York: Springer.

BRITISH PSYCHOLOGICAL SOCIETY (1995) *Recovered Memories*. Leicester: British Psychological Society.

BRYER, J. B., NELSON, B. A., MILLER, J. B., *et al* (1987) Childhood sexual and physical abuse as factors in adult psychiatric illness. *American Journal of Psychiatry*, **144**, 1426–1430.

BUTLER-SLOSS, E. (1988) *Report of the Enquiry into Child Abuse in Cleveland (1987)*. London: HMSO.

CARMEN, E. H., RIEKER, P. P. & MILLS, T (1984) Victims of violence and psychiatric illness. *American Journal of Psychiatry*, **141**, 378–383.

CARSON, D. K., COUNCIL, J. R. & VOLT, M. A. (1989) Temperament as a predictor of psychological adjustment in female adult incest victims. *Journal of Clinical Psychology*, **45**, 330–335.

CAUTELA, J. (1967) Covert sensitization. *Psychological Reports*, **20**, 459–468.

DAVIS, G. E. & LEITENBERG, H. (1987) Adolescent sex offenders. *Psychological Bulletin*, **101**, 417–427.

DEBLINGER, E, McLEEN, S. V., ATKINS, M. S., *et al* (1989) Post-traumatic stress in sexually abused, physically abused and non-abused children. *Child Abuse and Neglect*, **13**, 403–408.

FINKELHOR, D. (1979) *Sexually Victimised Children*. New York: Free Press.

—— (ed.) (1984) *Child Sexual Abuse: New Theory and Research*. New York: Free Press.

—— (1986) *A Source Book on Child Sexual Abuse*. Pp. 129. London: Sage.

——, HOTALING, G. T., LEWIS, I. A., *et al* (1989) Sexual abuse and its relationship to later sexual satisfaction, marital status, religion and attitudes. *Journal of Interpersonal Violence*, **4**, 379–399.

GIARETTO, H. (1981) A comprehensive child sexual abuse treatment programme. In *Sexually Abused Children and their Families* (eds P. B. Mrazek & C. H. Kemp), pp. 179–198. Oxford: Pergamon Press.

HALL, L. & LLOYD, F. (1989) *Surviving Child Sexual Abuse*. London: Falmer Press.

JEHU D. (1988) *Beyond Sexual Abuse: Therapy with Women who were Childhood Victims*. Chichester: Wiley.

JOHNSTONE, T. C. (1988) Child perpetrators: children who molest other children: preliminary findings. *Child Abuse and Neglect*, **12**, 219–229.

KENDALL-TACKETT, K. A., MEYER-WILLIAMS, L. & FINKELHOR, D. (1993) Impact of sexual abuse of children: a review and synthesis of recent empirical findings. *Psychological Bulletin*, **113**, 164–180.

KNOPP, S. H. (1984) *Retraining Adult Sex Offenders: Methods and Muddles*. Syracuse, New York: Safer Society Press.

LAUNAY, G. (1994) The phallometric assessment of sex offenders: some professional and research issues. *Criminal Behaviour and Mental Health*, **4**, 48–70.

LAWS, D. M. (1989) *Relapse Prevention with Sex Offenders*. London: Guilford Press.

LINDBERG, F. H. & DISTAD, L. J. (1985) Post-traumatic stress disorders in women who have experienced childhood incest. *Child Abuse and Neglect,* **9**, 329–334.

MARQUIS, J. N. (1970) Orgasmic reconditioning: changing sexual object choice, through controlling masturbation fantasies. *Journal of Behaviour Therapy and Experimental Psychiatry,* **1**, 263–271.

MARSHALL, W. L. (1979) Satiation therapy: a procedure for reducing deviant sexual arousal. *Journal of Applied Behaviour Analysis,* **12**, 10–22.

―――― & BARBAREE, H. E. (1990) Outcome of comprehensive cognitive–behavioural treatment programs. In *Handbook of Sexual Assault. Issues, Theories and Treatment of the Offender* (eds W. L. Marshall, D. R. Laws & H. E. Barbaree), pp. 363–385. New York: Plenum Press.

MEZEY, G. C., VIZARD, E., HAWKES, C., *et al* (1991) A community treatment programme for convicted child sex offenders: a preliminary report. *Journal of Forensic Psychiatry,* **2**, 12–25.

―――― & KING, M. B. (1992) *Male Victims of Assault.* Oxford: Oxford University Press.

MULLEN, P. E., MARTIN, J. C., ANDERSON, S. E., *et al* (1993) Childhood sexual abuse and mental health in adult life. *British Journal of Psychiatry,* **163**, 721–732.

OGATA, S. N., SILK, K. R., GOODRICH, S., *et al* (1990) Childhood sexual and physical abuse in adult patients with borderline personality disorder. *American Journal of Psychiatry,* **147**, 1008–1013.

OPPENHEIMER, R., HOWELLS, K. J., PALMER, R. L., *et al* (1985) Adverse sexual experiences in childhood and clinical eating disorder: a preliminary description. *Journal of Psychiatric Research,* **19**, 357–361.

PALMER, R. L., COLEMAN, L., CHALONER, D., *et al* (1993) Childhood sexual experiences with adults. A comparison of reports by women psychiatric patients and general practice attenders. *British Journal of Psychiatry,* **163**, 499–504.

PERKINS, D. (1991) Clinical work with sex offenders in secure settings. In *Clinical Approaches to Sex Offenders and their Victims* (eds C. R. Hollin & K. J. Howells), pp. 151–178. Chichester: Wiley.

PITHERS, W. D. (1990) Relapse prevention with sexual aggressors: a method for maintaining therapeutic gain and enhancing external supervision. In *Handbook of Sexual Assault. Issues, Theories and Treatment of the Offender* (eds W. L. Marshall, D. R. Laws & H. E. Barbaree). New York: Plenum Press.

ROUNDY, L. M. & HORTON, A. L. (1990) Professional and treatment issues for clinicians who intervene with incest perpetrators. In *The Incest Perpetrators: A Family Member No One Wants to Treat* (eds A. L. Horton, B. L. Johnson, L. M. Roundy, *et al*), pp. 164–189. London: Sage.

RUNTZ, M. & BRIERE, J. (1986) Adolescent 'acting out' and childhood history of sexual abuse. *Journal of Interpersonal Violence,* **1**, 326–334.

RUSSELL, D. E. H. (1984) *Sexual Exploitation.* Beverly Hills, California: Sage.

―――― (1986) *The Secret Trauma: Incest in the Lives of Girls and Women.* New York: Basic Books.

SALTER, A. C. (1988) *Treating Child Sex Offenders and Victims.* London: Sage.

SANDERSON, C. (1990) *Counselling Adult Survivors of Child Sexual Abuse.* London: Jessica Kingsley.

SHEARER, S. L., PETERS, C. P., QUAYTMAN, M. S., *et al* (1990) Frequency and correlates of childhood sexual and physical abuse histories in adult female borderline inpatients. *American Journal of Psychiatry,* **147**, 214–216.

VIZARD, E., BENTOVIM, A. & TRANTER, M. (1987) Interviewing sexually abused children. *Adoption and Fostering,* **11**, 21–25.

WATKINS, B. & BENTOVIM, A. (1992) Male children and adolescents as victims: a review of current knowledge. In *Male Victims of Sexual Assault* (eds G. C. Mezey & M. D. King), pp. 27–66. Oxford: Oxford University Press.

WOLFE, V. V., GENTILE, C. & WOLFE, D. A. (1989) The impact of sexual abuse on children: a P.T.S.D. formulation. *Behaviour Therapy,* **20**, 215–228.

11 The offender

CHRISTOPHER CORDESS

To be recognised as offending against the law requires that the illegal behaviour be brought to the attention of the criminal justice system: this may happen by confession or as a result of detection. The matter may rest there and, for example, a caution may be given, or if the evidence is strong and the offence serious, charges may be brought. Prosecution may result in conviction or in acquittal. There is a large rate of attrition along this path and only a minority of potentially criminal activities end in a conviction. Self-report studies, especially among sexual offenders, for example, make this all too clear (Abel *et al*, 1987). The 'iceberg of crime' is, indeed, very much larger than its visible part. Also, crime varies across jurisdictions and with time, as some behaviour is decriminalised and others criminalised. For example, homosexual acts in private between consenting males of any age were an offence in the UK up until their decriminalisation for those of 21 years and over in the Sexual Offences Act (1967); this was reduced to 18 years in the Criminal Justice and Public Order Act (1994).

In this chapter I address the clinical and psychotherapeutic aspects of the offender and of offending behaviour, and the issue of selection for the range of psychotherapeutic treatments. It should be emphasised, however, that the psychotherapy of the offender is but one part of a range of other necessary provision which may include general education (frequently at the level of basic reading, writing and numeracy skills), specialist education (e.g. sexual information), and sociotherapy including social skills and occupational training. In the relatively few cases of offenders who suffer from mental illness and the psychoses (as opposed to the personality disorders) psychiatric treatment will be indicated in conjunction with the psychotherapies.

Psychiatric and forensic psychotherapy practice has concentrated on violent and sexual offenders, partly because psychological and psychiatric disorders are more prevalent in this subgroup; also, offences against the person leave a toll of victimisation and are more shocking than 'property offences', and psychological explanations for them are consequently more frequently sought. This chapter will take violence as a paradigm: sexual offending is covered in chapter 10, and will only be referred to here in regard to its aggressive and frequently violent components.

Contemporary sentencing policy is based upon the conflicting philosophies of punishment, retribution and utilitarian deterrence, mixed in varying proportions, with considerations of rehabilitation and – in some cases – clinical management and treatment. Psychotherapy is but one part of the 'rehabilitative ideal', which itself has been much attacked in recent decades. It is therefore unsurprising that when psychotherapy is offered within the criminal justice system it is invariably complicated by conflicting demands upon the offender, as well as frequently by his or her own ambivalence or poor motivation. For example, for many offenders – and most particularly for adolescents – it is very important to cling defensively to a 'macho' or 'bad' image rather than have offensive and antisocial behaviour re-interpreted as symptomatic – and a sign of social failure and psychological vulnerability, with the consequent need for help. Only a minority of offenders – at least, initially – ask for social, psychological and emotional assistance. However, in practice an individual's motivation frequently changes and those who have been emphatically resistant may later come to welcome offers of psychotherapeutic help.

Timing of interventions aimed at engaging an individual offender in any form of therapeutic alliance can be crucial, as it is, in different ways, in the psychotherapies of non-offender patients. People tend to ask for help when they recognise they are in trouble and offenders may experience crises, or the criminal justice system may precipitate them, at many points along the way. The context and the setting need careful consideration, for example, whether the individual is in prison or in the community, or whether a particular treatment is best offered as an in-patient or as an out-patient. The skills of therapists, their level of training and the standard of supervision and support are especially important with an offender, who may create anxiety and be extremely disturbing to even the most experienced therapist. Team work of some form is essential, and no therapist should try to 'go it alone'. The case for the recognition of different levels of psychotherapy training and competence is well made by Pedder (1993). The qualities that make for excellence in psychotherapy supervision have been empirically researched by Shanfield *et al* (1993).

In many cases the offender will suffer significant levels of symptomatology and of distress. In others, distress may be absent or minimised by the offender, and the difficult therapeutic task is to try to overcome the self-idealisation and lack of concern for others which sanctions the frequently repeated antisocial behaviour. Modern dynamic psychotherapy attempts to bring the offender to accept responsibility and to achieve a state of concern for his victims and for himself. This requires the offender to relinquish the feeling of superiority and triumph which his offending behaviour is frequently aimed, however, briefly, to award him. To take a simple example, the sexual exhibitionist feels enormously powerful at the point of his act of 'exposure'. Characteristically, however, he feels very low self-esteem at other times, and, in particular, directly after an episode of exposing, when shame – and sometimes guilt – take over. His victim will frequently feel humiliated and attacked. Psychotherapy will aim to give the man a greater sense of his own worth, and an affective as well as a cognitive understanding of how he is experienced by his victim: it will also show him how he undermines his own sense of esteem, and will attempt to break the cycle of the need to re-offend.

Ethical considerations are central. Although any treatment of the offender must give primacy to the offender's interests, those of potential future victims have to be fully considered.

Many offenders are victims of their own antisocial behaviour, as well as frequently victims of others' earlier exploitation. The overlap, therefore, of offending behaviour and victimisation is great, and forensic psychotherapy seeks to address both. As Gunn & Taylor (1993) remark, 'Most patients who come to forensic psychiatrists are victims of one sort or another . . . (they) have often suffered multiple victimisation in the sense that they have suffered earlier psychological trauma, usually in childhood. (Their) deleterious experiences include poverty, social deprivation, inconsistent discipline, violence or sexual abuse, or as adolescents or adults inadequate or harsh treatment for primary problems (such as schizophrenia and behaviour disorders)'.

Huesmann *et al* (1984) found that aggression was perpetuated in families across three generations, and Mullen (1990), Mullen *et al* (1993), and Herman *et al* (1989) among many others, have recently provided empirical evidence of some of the long-term sequelae of abuse in childhood. They include personality disorder, anxiety, depression and eating disorders, as well as patterns of abusive behaviour perpetrated against others. Shetzky (1990) has provided a comprehensive review of the long-term effects of child sexual abuse.

It should be emphasised that the fact that violent and sexual offenders have frequently been victims of similar behaviour themselves does not reduce their responsibility for their actions (Cordess, 1993). Clinically, however, it is clearly of great significance in the individual case.

There is a conceptual dissonance, and there are frequently many practical difficulties, when the law and psychological ways of thinking meet. For strong pragmatic reasons the psychological model most used in British courts has been the psychiatric–phenomenological one, relying on such dichotomies as 'mental illness–personality disorder', 'psychotic–neurotic illness' and 'endogenous–exogenous aetiology'. There is a certain psycho-legal value in such dichotomies since the courts and the Mental Health Act necessarily require them, but forcing such categorical distinctions becomes clinically artificial. An alternative model – the dimensional one – avoids 'forcing dimensional reality into categorical fiction' (Eastman, 1992). The dimensional approach is far more appealing to the majority of clinicians and psychotherapists who are involved in work with the offender, who, like psychiatric services generally, 'mostly see patients whose dissatisfactions, distress and social censure results from recurrent misbehaviour or failed relationships, and not from recognisable illness' (Tantam, 1988).

The setting

The ethical and moral dilemmas of treatment for offenders hardly arise where the treatment is voluntary and the individual is well motivated. In these conditions the usual prerequisites for psychotherapy or, indeed, for any therapeutic or medical treatment, obtain, namely that the person suffers and seeks help. Such voluntary treatment may be as an out-patient or residentially based such as within a therapeutic community, for example, the Henderson Hospital in London.

More commonly, in practice, offenders are subject to some degree of external expectation, and to varying pressures, and sometimes to frank coercion in starting and then in the continuation of their treatment. This may be as an out-patient, for example on a probation order with a condition of treatment; or it may be within an institution, for example a regional secure unit, a maximum security special hospital or a prison. Most worryingly, in modern Britain, it may be conducted within private profit-making organisations. For adolescents, placement in residential care, in youth treatment centres, or in young offender institutions provides increasingly severe sanction with elements of coercive or compulsory treatment. Compared with, for example, voluntarily contracted psychotherapy, where the maximum degree of personal freedom and privacy is regarded as essential and is fundamentally preserved, there are a number of inevitable complications. These may be summarised as:

(1) coercion
(2) loss of total confidentiality within the extended system
(3) conflicts of loyalty
(4) dangers of 'pseudo-change', e.g. mere compliance

(5) the effects which are wrought on the transference, counter-transference relationship i.e. upon the therapist–client interactions.

For these reasons it is essential to clarify an ethical standpoint as the first stop in the provision of psychotherapy for offenders. Harding (personal communication) emphasises that a clearly conceptualised value system be made explicit for all treatment, research or evaluation of offenders. He warns against therapeutic regimes which (a) involve 'rewards' and 'punishments' superimposed upon a system (such as a prison) which is based anyway on principles of retribution and 'just desserts', or (b) involve the development of treatment models specific to closed institutions. For example, there have been disturbing instances of malpractice in homes for delinquent adolescents in Britain, where there has been a failure to apply even minimally recognised standards of supervision and training.

Psychotherapy for the offender must be considered within the overall context of health care for those involved in the criminal justice process. The Department of Health & Home Office Report (1992), the *Reed Report*, states that the standard of care for the offender should be of a similar standard to that for any other person. Therapists must therefore maintain their independence, according to criteria which correspond to health-based values. The difficulty of holding to this task, and at the same time achieving some impact, for example, within a prison, is given by Hinshelwood (1993) specifically from a psychodynamic perspective.

The importance of the multidisciplinary and team approach to clinical and psychotherapeutic work with offenders cannot be over-emphasised. Glover (1960), for example, spoke of the benefits of the 'distributed transference', when working with frequently difficult, demanding and sometimes very provocative people. On the other hand, such team work offers ample opportunity for the 'splitting' of staff – particularly, but not by any means exclusively, in residential settings – as the acting out of 'part object' relationships (Gabbard, 1989). At its worst this can result in confusion, demoralisation and consequent withdrawal by staff working within these institutions – in short, 'burn-out': for this reason, among others, our maximum secure hospitals had gained, until the real changes of recent years, a reputation for therapeutic bankruptcy. One authority has written, albeit of the American system, that 'quasi-criminal institutions (i.e. those for offender patients) have been a terrible failure: not only in the sense that they often failed to offer meaningful treatment, but also because they typically created an environment worse than prisons or mental institutions' (Stone, 1975). It is our task to be fully aware of these dangers and to combat and overcome them. It is for this reason that 'institutional' shared experiences, for example, the therapeutic community therapy, and in its diluted form 'milieu' therapy, and group therapy approaches have an especially important part to play.

Cox (1983) makes the case for the presence of the psychotherapist as a constituent member of the eclectic, multidisciplinary team, basing his model on work in a Special hospital, to which however it is not confined. He describes the mutual contributions which the forensic psychiatrist and the dynamic psychotherapist can offer one another.

Aims

For Gunn & Taylor (1993) a major task for the psychiatrist and psychologist is to gain understanding of different types of crime in order to assist in policies directed at reducing the conditions for it, as much as devising therapeutic strategies for individual offenders.

Much psychotherapeutic work with offenders involves the provision of psychological 'support', although how that is done is the source of much debate: evaluation of this is even more difficult than the evaluation of 'change'. Psychodynamically the work of Winnicott (1965) and the 'holding' environment, and Bion (1984) and the 'container and contained', are central concepts. The concepts of 'projective identification', well described in a demystified way by Jureidini (1990), and of splitting are also crucial. Etchegoyen (1992) remarks that (psychological) 'support is the most common instrument of psychotherapy, the one most available to the general practitioner (or simply to anyone who has to do with interpersonal relations)'.

For the psychoanalytic psychotherapist the (deceptively simple) aim of every moment of every session is to put clients in touch with as much of their true feelings as they can bear: put another way, the aim of psychodynamic therapy is to achieve affective (and thereby cognitive) recognition of 'facts'. However, although psychoanalytic theory, with its concept of 'acting out', can account for how phantasy (unconscious) and fantasy (conscious) moves from impulse to action, it often does not have an adequate, or pragmatically useful account of why a particular behaviour is sometimes enacted – and why sometimes it is not – in any given case. In offender populations, in which severe narcissistic, schizoid, borderline and antisocial personalities are common, the achievement of insight may remain only partial and so striving for this goal may be less important than the provision of emotional and psychological support. By being provided with a therapeutic relationship which is safe, understanding and accepting, without in any way being collusive, the individual offender may feel less need to 'act out' his antisocial impulses and may achieve some adaptation to his surroundings, and regulation of his behaviour. Although psychoanalytic psychotherapists primarily focus on the affective and emotional life of the patient, by the use and interpretation of transference and countertransference interactions, they necessarily also thereby aim to change cognitions.

Cognitive therapists emphasise such aspects as perception, appraisal, assumption and attribution in their theory of thinking. These different cognitive events are the mental building blocks of our different behaviours, and 'cognitive restructuring' can change antisocial behaviour. Whereas anxiety and depression have been the affects predominantly addressed in mainstream psychiatry and psychology, the negative emotions have been relatively neglected, except by psychodynamic psychotherapists. Cognitive therapists have begun to focus more recently on anger, and its management, with offenders, in a productive way (see below). Pfafflin (1992), an experienced forensic psychotherapist, has expressed the provocative view that with some offenders (it does not) 'matter much whether one works along behavioural or psychoanalytic lines or a combination of both . . . as long as one accepts that (some offending behaviour) is a coping mechanism which once served a vital purpose and has since developed into a non-specific way of reacting to stress. . . '. He emphasises the necessity of listening to the patients' predicaments and history in all their complexity in order to gain an understanding and assessment of the deprivation and traumata which they have suffered earlier in their lives.

We need to be clear about the primary and secondary aims of psychotherapy: in a given case, is it the removal of the symptom (the offending behaviour), or the relief of an underlying condition (for example depression), or is it a more holistic, existential goal – responding to the subject's experience in order to improve the individual's general sense of well-being, and thereby his adaptation to the environment (i.e. his social relationships and social functioning)? Aims are multiple and vary according to circumstances, but we cannot and should not aim only to reduce the rate or gravity of re-offending, even though that is a hoped for consequence. Robertson (1989), for example, specifically argues against the use of re-offending rates in the evaluation of any treatment of the offender, and states that the criteria used to judge therapeutic effectiveness for offenders should not differ from those used in all other forms of care.

Holmes (1992) quotes Parsons (1951), to the effect that the role of general psychotherapy within society is "to help those whose socialisation has gone awry: the central issue appears to be that of belonging and the key question is not so much 'who am I?' but, 'where do I fit in?'". Indeed, forensic psychotherapy could be described as primarily involved in the vicissitudes of failed interpersonal attachment.

These include: lack of trust and fear of (further) traumatisation, fear of dependency, excessive fear of (further) loss and separation; the pathologies of love (e.g. morbid jealousy); and the many and various defensive manoeuvres against the experience of (further) shame, humiliation and guilt – both conscious and unconscious. Forensic psychotherapy may then be seen to function towards one end of the spectrum of 'those whose socialisation has gone awry', and specifically with those whose failure has been to act on and against society and to have caused serious offence. Violence as a manifestation of experiences of traumatising, skewed or failed early and later attachment – as 'attachment gone wrong' – and, as a defence against vulnerability and further psychic pain and traumatisation, has been well described by de Zulueta (1993).

One worrying aspect is that by the very act of offending, attention is gained where previously the environment, for example family, and later the health and welfare systems, had been experienced as dismissive. It is not uncommon for patients to tell you that they had to offend in order to be noticed and taken seriously: for a larger number this motive is less consciously known. Winnicott (1965) remarked that 'the easiest way to get help is provocatively and through violence'. There is, therefore, a strong argument for the provision of better general and preventative therapeutic services.

The peak age of offending is within the middle years of adolescence and this is when preventative efforts should be focused. In point of fact child and adolescent psychiatric services in Britain are being cut, and delinquents are not well catered for therapeutically. Overall, some 5% of the mental health budget nationally (in Britain) is spent on child mental health, although children under 16 years make up approximately 20% of the population. Instead more punitive policies are at present being introduced. Rose (1993) writes "Hitherto control efforts have been focused almost exclusively on the deviant minorities (. . . those with behavioural disorders, the criminally aggressive, and so on). This alienation of the extremists is attractive to public and politicians, since it affirms the normality and innocence of the majority; but as a basis for prevention it has been a failure". Estimates of some form of recidivism by youngsters after release from young offender institutions are in the range of 80% across the board.

Assessment

Neither the seriousness of offending, nor the gravity of some forms of psychiatric illness, for example, chronic psychoses or depression, nor indeed evidence of low intellectual performance (Sinason, 1992), should preclude assessment and consideration for some form of psychotherapeutic help, alongside the involvement of other professionals providing a range of different treatments. The question is: what sort of psychotherapy and when? Cox & Theilgaard (1987) have written of the importance of the therapist's attentiveness and accurate empathy, to be attendant upon the moments when an offender patient may be receptive to offers of 'talking' therapy and support, or to the prospect of change which psychological treatments can offer: moments like these may be brought about for example, by acute feelings of depression, of appropriate shame or of guilt. Such attentiveness should be the aim of all staff who are in contact with offender patients. Within a National Health Service (NHS) forensic psychiatry secure unit, where the patients are typically psychotic and have behaved violently, frequently including killing, it is the nurses and occupational therapists who provide the continuing day-to-day, and night, patient contact – the so-called 'other 23 hours' (Stanton & Schwarz, 1954). They provide the therapeutic front line and are likely to be the first recipients of a patient's intimate feelings. They require supervision by the psychotherapist, as well as the support of all other staff: a good working relationship between staff members within such settings is the basis upon which any more specialised family, group or individual psychotherapy relies. Interventions may then include dynamic, cognitive or behaviourally based treatments. Later, after discharge into independent living, a range of these psychotherapeutic interventions are likely to be necessary at different times.

The relationship between the offending behaviour and psychological state is invariably complex. Part of the specifically forensic psychotherapeutic task consists of the elucidation of this relationship by understanding the individual and the context in which the offending occurs. Common to most clinical analyses of offending behaviour is an analysis of:

(1) the offender himself – his behaviour, cognitions and personal psychodynamics, and the relation of these to personal and family history and present circumstances
(2) the criminal act
(3) the situation and environmental conditions in which it occurs.

For example, in a given act of violence, the assessor will want to know what the perpetrator feels he did it for: was it self-protective (reactive) or was it in the pursuit of gratification (i.e. sadistic)? He will want to know the minute details of the antecedents to the act, the act itself and what happened afterwards; also, is this a recurrent behaviour and are there specific, repeated characteristics, for example of the type of victim(s) or of the circumstances. Following Walker (1991) he will wish to consider whether the offender is only 'conditionally dangerous' (i.e. if he finds himself in a particular relationship or set of circumstances), or whether he seeks out opportunities to offend, or worse, actually contrives to create opportunity. A rule of thumb categorisation might be into:

(1) Mood or anxiety disorders, e.g. a depressive illness, with consequent 'acting out'.
(2) Social and psychological stress leading to unbearable anxiety and 'acting out', as in (1) above: frequently the offence will be partly understandable as an expression of this intrapsychic anxiety (Tuovinen, 1973), although other factors and variables will be needed for a full explanation of why the crime was actually enacted rather than being merely thought about.
(3) Psychotic illness, including episodic, reactive psychotic states in the context of a severe personality disorder.
(4) Personality disorder of narcissistic, borderline or antisocial type, or character pathology with, for example, deviations of sexual behaviour.
(5) 'Career' criminality, i.e. criminality which is 'ego-syntonic', and which in its established form would usually be considered inappropriate for attempts at psychotherapeutic intervention.

The psychotherapist has a part to play in the assessment and treatment of all these groups, except the last, in a number of varying roles.

A complicating factor in the assessment of those who commit violence is that of partial or total amnesia for the act and surrounding events. In cases of homicide this may occur in over half the cases: the phenomenon is quite distinct from straight lying. Taylor & Kopelman (1984) invoke 'a variety of mechanisms to account for (this) amnesia, including repression, dissociation and alcoholic blackouts'. The assessor and therapist will need to respect the psychological need for this failure by the person to be able to recall certain horrific events (e.g. the killing of a spouse or a child), while offering the person the opportunity to fill-in or reconstruct events. The literature on the subject is reviewed from a research perspective by Schacter (1986).

Management and treatment

The first step is necessarily one of management and of containment within the least restrictive environment which provides safety for the patient as well as for society: this may be achieved emotionally within a 'holding' relationship or may require physical containment e.g. admission to a locked ward. Although community and out-patient ('ambulant') treatment of the offender is the aim – where it is practicable – it is frequently the case that treatment will begin as an in-patient, or in residential care, as part of a plan of working towards later care for the particular individual in the community. In Winnicott's phrase 'there is first a need for environmental care and then for psychotherapy' (Winnicott, 1956). Only when these preconditions are satisfied, can assessment and therapeutic work begin. Winnicott adds that therapists need to be realistic about what can be achieved because of the amount of 'secondary' gain that accrues to offending behaviour.

The fact that many offenders are contained for long periods of time within intensively staffed settings provides, at least, the external conditions for their engagement in an extended treatment alliance. By contrast some of the apparently more motivated offenders who present to out-patient settings often break off treatment peremptorily for what they think are compelling reasons. While, rarely, this may be a reasonable reaction to external demands, sabotage of offers of help by leaving therapy is a common hazard in the psychotherapeutic treatment of the offender, since he or she frequently deals with emotions and psychological stress by action rather than words.

People with psychoses being treated with medication present different challenges to those of the borderline and antisocial, personality disordered, person. In these cases psychotherapy will be but one among several therapeutic ingredients, including the use of physical treatments. Too frequently the use of medication has been seen as in opposition to psychodynamic psychotherapy rather than complementary: in severely ill populations there is a need to study the benefits of the combined effects of pharmacotherapy and psychotherapy (Karasu, 1982).

Kraemer (1988), writing of the impossibility in his view of combining statutory responsibility and psychotherapeutic potency and efficacy (specifically, in this case, when working with abusive families), makes a powerful general case for a division of labour – between administrative and psychotherapeutic functions – when working with any offender. The psychotherapist, he says, needs to feel free to 'take leaps in the dark if real discoveries are to be made'. Further, 'therapists have the privilege of inactivity when in doubt, yet action is just what is required when a child is in danger'. Issues of management necessarily impinge on forensic psychotherapy, since they are central to the subject of the offender. An extreme but instructive example of where 'management' went 'wrong' is the case of Tarasoff (Stone, 1984; Menninger, 1990), in which a therapist in California was found legally negligent of not warning a third party that he was in potential danger from the patient; homicide ensued. The case went to several appeal courts: the final ruling was that therapists have a duty to protect potential victims. Although Britain has not adopted this law (but at least eight states in the USA have), we may be moving towards such practice whether legislated or not. Appelbaum *et al* (1989) provide a stimulating discussion of the implications of such legal rulings and of different approaches in the USA to the limitation of therapists' liability and responsibility for their clients' violent acts.

Violence and the anti-social personality

A central challenge for the clinician working with the offender is to address those people labelled as 'Personality Disorder'. Frequently, such people suffer also from neurotic symptoms and sometimes psychotic episodes; addictive problems, conflicts of identity and gender identity are not uncommon. The severely personality disordered patient taxes the training and skills of the clinician, and may expose him, particularly in the present political climate in Britain, to unreasonable or ill-informed censure if re-offending occurs (Coid & Cordess, 1992).

Rutter (1987) has proposed the abandonment of trait-defined categorisations and suggests, instead, the lumping together of the personality disorders as mainly defined by a pervasive difficulty in establishing and maintaining adequate and rewarding social relationships. This view has been given support from a psychotherapy point of view by Higgitt & Fonagy (1992). From a specifically forensic standpoint Blackburn (1989) states that 'personality disorders are not diseases and their treatment is more analogous to remedial education than to medical treatment'. Personal change rather than 'cure' is therefore the appropriate goal.

Dolan & Coid (1993) have comprehensively reviewed the treatment and research issues of psychopathic, antisocial personality disorders. Their conclusions are cautiously optimistic. They counter the rather nihilistic mood of the last two decades that 'nothing works' with psychopathic antisocial personality disordered offenders, which was itself based upon insufficient evidence from criminological studies of treatment programmes in American correctional institutions. They argue particularly for standardised assessments, incorporating the three overlapping elements of personality disorder, clinical syndromes and behaviour as the basis for the appraisal of different treatment interventions.

A brief overview of different typological descriptions and treatment methods follows, but they should be regarded as provisional and are necessarily partial.

Psychodynamic

Yarvis (1972) distinguished between three "distinctly different psychological constellations of a cohort of character-disordered offenders": Group I, the neurotic-character group, were characterised by a relative achievement of interpersonal and work stability but with "impulses (which were) previously under control exploding into an isolated criminal outburst". They could all distinguish between reality and fantasy and in none was there evidence of 'psychotic ego functioning', although they suffered a range of neurotic symptomatology; Group II, the narcissistic-character Group, for whom antisocial conduct was 'ego-syntonic', in contrast to those in Group I 'lacked evidence of psychic pain or of current psychiatric symptomatology'. Put another way, they showed little or no internalised conflict but rather expressed their conflicts exclusively in "combative interactions with their environment". 'Treatment' among these patients was valued only for its "heuristic potentials – (for example) special privileges during incarceration, an opportunity to impress a parole board to earn early release, and the like, (and) real treatment motivation was rare"; Group III patients, the ego-disturbance Group, showed a mixture of incapacitating psychiatric distress and social turmoil, with considerable psychic symptoms and gross evidence of social deviance of a violent and sexual type. Their psychopathology was noticeable from an early age and half had been in some contact with psychiatric services in childhood. Yarvis comments that "if Group I represents penology's walking wounded, Group III patients represent its major casualties . . . they are its perennial recidivists . . . (who) constitute the criminal justice system's worst headache".

Gallwey has described a broad categorisation of the psychopathology of 'borderline personality' (an ever-widening label, described by him as 'atypical such and such') from a practical psychotherapeutic point of view (Gallwey, 1985). He describes two main types whose common denominator is that they present with "dual personalities in which a 'false self' or pseudo-normal ego is in dynamic balance with a more pathologically disordered area of the self". Type A are false self individuals who are ego deficient, with impoverished social and work relationships and whose antisocial conduct may be either the consequence of their traumatised, deprived core selves or of the often fragile defensive organisation of the false self. Type B, by contrast, present as apparently healthier, with a stronger ego structure often resulting in relative worldly success, but who have separated off an encapsulation of psychotic, disturbed functioning. Typically these are the cases who, quite out of the blue, commit serious, bizarre, and violent, sometimes quasi-sexual offences much to the surprise of others and also themselves. After the event they and those who know them typically use such phrases as 'I was beside myself', 'It wasn't the man I know', 'He wasn't himself' in an attempt to explain the apparently inexplicable. Gallwey (1992) has also provided a descriptive overview of 'psychopathic' offenders and some of the implications for their psychodynamic treatment.

Kernberg (1992) describes the range of intensity of the therapist's countertransference according to the 'regression' (or, alternatively, psychologically primitive state) of the severely personality disordered person. Symington (1980), in similar vein, has described the countertransference evoked by a person with a psychopathic (antisocial personality) disorder as stages of initial 'collusion', later 'disbelief' (at the attack on the therapist) and finally 'condemnation' with the consequent danger of rejection. The therapist needs to be fully aware that the transference object relations of the psychotic (borderline) personality are frequently precipitate, labile, but frequently tenacious and that such people may become intensely dependent. Psychotic and erotic transference needs to be addressed early and clearly, by acknowledging the person's fantasy but underlining the reality of the professional relationship.

Cognitive–behavioural

In those offenders in whom the violent and antisocial behaviour is less pervasive and where problem areas and symptoms can be well defined – and in whom there are personality strengths as well as global weaknesses – cognitive–behavioural approaches have become popular. The cognitive model and its therapeutic strategies adopt a problem-oriented approach focusing on an individual's emotions, cognitions and behaviour. They have been successfully applied to the treatment of depression (Beck *et al*, 1985) and anxiety (Chambless & Gillis, 1993), and many clinicians have attempted to employ these concepts to the treatment of offenders. Most comprehensive is Novaco's model of aggression (Novaco, 1975, 1977) based on Meichenbaum's 'stress inoculation training' (Meichenbaum, 1986). In a review paper, Novaco & Welsh (1989), using an information processing approach, postulate that anger and aggression can be viewed in terms of five information-processing biases:

(1) Attentional cueing whereby the arousal of anger may result in attention being directed to aggressive cues.
(2) Perceptual matching describes a readiness to perceive aggressiveness cues following prior exposure to aggressive stimuli. Indirect support for this is given by those using a post-traumatic stress disorder (PTSD) framework to analyse the traumatising effects of violence. Collins & Bailey (1990) for example found that when demographic and other factors such as problem drinking were controlled, there was a relationship between PTSD and its symptoms, and serious expressive violence. Furthermore, Burton *et al* (1994) found a significant relationship between exposure to violence and post-traumatic stress symptoms (including hypervigilance) in male juvenile offenders.
(3) Attribution error describes a tendency for aggressive individuals to routinely attribute the behaviour of others to dispositional characteristics as opposed to situational causes.
(4) False consensus refers to a bias in the way that an aggressive individual may perceive events to have undue relevance for himself (i.e. deficiencies in perspective-taking).
(5) Anchoring effects result in a resistance to changing one's initial judgement even when subsequent information dictates that revision.

They maintain that these processes have largely been ignored in previous work but that they are highly relevant to the assessment and treatment of anger. As regards assessment, the information-processing approach casts doubt on the reliance of consciously accessible thoughts (and, therefore, the use of self-report inventories) and requires that other methods be considered, such as role-play and videotape reconstruction, to facilitate the assessment of cognitive determinants of anger. Identification of particular cognitive biases would then determine which interventions are applied and may include contingent reinforcement, activity scheduling, relaxation, modelling, problem-solving, self-instructional training, thought-monitoring, challenging negative thoughts, reality testing, and re-attribution of beliefs (Mark *et al*, 1989).

From a practical assessment and treatment point of view the cognitive–behavioural approach may be described in three stages:

(1) Cognitive preparation. Here, the emphasis is primarily educational: diaries are used to identify the antecedents of anger and its interaction with behaviour is explored.

(2) Skill acquisition. In this phase, angry appraisals are challenged and modified; calming 'self-statements' are encouraged. In addition, a variety of behavioural strategies are taught.
(3) Application. Here, a hierarchy of progressively complex real-life anger situations are identified and skills are practised using both imaginal and role-play methods.

Novaco (1976) in a study of anger compared the effect of cognitive, relaxation and combined treatment, with a non-treatment control group. The results suggest that cognitive therapy produced greater changes than the relaxation method, and a number of other outcome studies have indicated a reduction in anger following the use of such cognitive methods (Schlicter & Horan, 1981; Nomellini & Katz, 1983; Hazaleus & Deffenbacher, 1986). Linehan (1993) has used a similar approach in her treatment of patients with borderline personality disorder.

Other approaches

Ryle (1991) attempts a synthesis of these different modes by combining a variety of theoretical sources in what he titles cognitive–analytic therapy. This has not been used specifically with offender patients to date.

To summarise, the different functions of the psychotherapies in relation to the offender patient include:

(1) The provision of a 'holding' environment, whether including residential placement or not, which is reliable, regular and non-moralistic, where a confiding relationship can grow and in which the offender patient feels that he is listened to and taken seriously, and in which psychotic and/or bizarre phenomena may be able to be made meaningful for both the patient and the staff.
(2) Contributing to the multidisciplinary team by providing psychodynamic and other psychological understanding in order to help in the organisation of the treatment plan.
(3) Offering selected patients group, family or individual psychotherapy or one of the art therapies. This may be of a psychodynamic or, if considered more appropriate, a cognitive–behavioural type. Only rarely, with selected offenders, in the right setting (where the risks of acting out can be minimised), can classical psychoanalytic principles be followed without adaptation. This was recognised early by such pioneers as Edward Glover, one of the founding fathers of the Portman Clinic. Family therapy in a regional secure

unit which was effectively the treatment of offenders and their family victims has been described by Cordess (1992). Bentovim (1992) describes his extensive out-patient experience of families traumatised by offending behaviour. Group therapy with offenders is described by several authors including Welldon (1994).

(4) Finally, independently of direct patient contact, the psychotherapist may function as consultant to in-patient units, by supporting and developing the work of the staff and the ward culture; this may or may not include the more delineated role of supervisor of different types of psychotherapy (Cox, 1983).

Research and audit

Maxwell (1984) listed a number of criteria by which a psychotherapy service may be judged. These were:

(1) relevance or appropriateness
(2) equity (for example, the relative failure to provide psychotherapy services to members of ethnic minorities)
(3) accessibility
(4) acceptability
(5) effectiveness
(6) efficiency.

The questions asked of psychotherapy services are often muddled or over-simplified but are increasingly based upon questions of cost-effectiveness. Parry (1992) has emphasised the need in this regard to make distinction between "service evaluation, operational research, professional audit, service audit, quality assurance and total quality management".

The evaluation of psychotherapeutic interventions with offender patients provides even greater methodological and practical difficulties than the challenges of psychotherapy research generally. One problem is the inadequacy of currently used outcome measures: there is, as previously stated, general agreement that re-offending rates lack validity as well as clinical appropriateness. The point has been well made that no-one would think if evaluating the efficacy of neuroleptic medication in offenders merely by recidivism rates rather than overall clinical and mental state, and the same goes for psychotherapeutic interventions.

Another difficulty is the length of time for follow-up: recidivism increases in virtually all studies which use long-term follow-up. The massive number of variables that come into play over time, both personal and situational, within an offender's life, make the focus on one variable alone – the psychotherapeutic intervention – nonsensical. Long-term follow-up and a range of social and other interventions are the ideal, and can be pursued, for example, in those cases where a long-term restriction order (Section 41) of the Mental Health Act 1983 is in place. Drop-out rates of voluntary patients for follow-up are high.

Third, there is the difficulty of instituting cost-effective analyses. This is an important area for emphasis in future forensic research, since, for example, in-patient forensic services are extremely costly – whether merely custodial or those attempting treatment. Where such studies have been attempted (Menzies *et al*, 1993; in their case researching a therapeutic community (the Henderson Hospital)) clinical and cost effectiveness has been well demonstrated. A central question arises: what long-term psychotherapeutic intervention, if effective, could possibly cost as much in economic, not to mention human, terms as the frequently failed years of short-term placements in, for example, care, foster parenting, residential care, assessment centre and then penal detention, of the recidivist delinquent?

Finally there are the methodological problems connected with distinguishing statistical from clinical significance. A number of authors consider that the controlled trial is not an appropriate methodology for researching medium or long term NHS-based psychodynamic psychotherapy in general (Higgitt & Fonagy, 1992). The same, only perhaps more so, goes for people who are offenders. These authors favour large scale, service-based, observational or individualised and naturalistic studies, as in the work with offenders of Dolan *et al* (1992). Such studies give sufficient acknowledgement of the multidimensional, deeper and long-lasting nature of the change aimed at by psychotherapy and sociotherapy.

Peay & Shapland (1992) state that "the historical lessons in clinical criminology of the attempts to evaluate treatment have shown that proper individual therapy is ethically almost always impossible to combine with rigorous evaluation where all is held constant but the treatment". However, there have been some evaluations of outcome of groups of offenders treated in different types of therapeutic community.

For example, McCord (1983) reported a significant reduction in recidivism among young delinquents treated within a therapeutic community, and Copas & Whiteley (1976), in a follow-up study of 194 men and women admitted to the Henderson Hospital, showed that 41% had been neither convicted nor admitted to hospital after three years. This 'success' rate increased to 71% for those who stayed more than nine months: there was no control group, but the recidivism rates compare favourably with general rates. One explanation, common to other studies, is that those who stayed the course were more highly motivated and that the more highly motivated do better in any psychological treatment. Copas *et al* (1984) conclude that there is evidence of success for this form of therapeutic community treatment for those suffering from personality disorder, and particularly for the subgroup of better motivated, emotionally expressive individuals. They emphasise its cost effectiveness for this damaged, disturbed and damaging group.

Robertson & Gunn (1987) in their study of Grendon Underwood, a therapeutic prison within the British prison system, found no absolute quantitative affect on recidivism, but an improvement in mental state and attitude while offenders were detained: after release the severity of re-offending was found to be reduced at 10-year follow-up. Further, Cullen (1992) has produced preliminary data from Grendon Underwood to show both clinical improvement and reduced recidivism in prisoners who had remained in therapy for 18 months or more, compared with other groups. Genders & Player (1993) in their study of Grendon conclude that 'Grendon can be of substantial benefit to some individual prisoners'.

The Netherlands provides the best examples of a range of sociotherapeutic and psychotherapeutic institutions for offender patients, although systems of continuing follow-up and support have proved problematic. In the Mesdagklinik, a clinic for seriously violent offenders, an eclectic programme offers the range of social, educational and occupational therapies, and intensive dynamic psychotherapy for three or more sessions per week for more than half of those detained. The re-offending rate is better than for unmatched but similar offenders in ordinary prisons, but still is probably higher than would be considered acceptable within the British system, which detains many more people for longer durations.

In general there is a body of evidence, some of it empirical, some anecdotal, that offenders who become engaged in treatment of whatever type tend to re-offend less while that treatment continues; re-offending may recur when treatment stops, when staff move on, or during temporary breaks in treatment, as in the necessary holiday breaks of psychoanalytic or other forms of psychotherapy.

The provision of long-term supportive therapy attempts to address these findings, as does the cognitive–behavioural 'relapse prevention' model which aims to increase self-control by enhancing self-knowledge of risk situations, and by the development of corresponding strategies to either avoid or to cope with those situations (Pithers, 1990).

Strupp (1986) makes the important point that when research is undertaken in the clinical setting it combats dogmatic and authoritarian practices and encourages an attitude of tentativeness and respect for evidence.

Finally, two points need to be emphasised. First, the necessity for adequate training of non-specialists in dealing with people who are offenders. The general services are frequently, after all, the first port of call. Second, the need for professional and financial resources to be allocated to prevention and to comprehensive community care, including psychotherapies, for medium and long-term follow-up and support. It is here that the treatment of the offender finally belongs.

Acknowledgement

I would like to thank Joanna Brook for help with the cognitive and behavioural aspects of this chapter.

References

ABEL, G., BECKER, J., MITTLEMAN, M., *et al* (1987) Self-reported sex crimes of non-incarcerated paraphiliacs. *Journal of Interpersonal Violence*, **2**, 3–25.

APPELBAUM, P., ZONANA, H., BONNIE, R., *et al* (1989) Statutory approaches to limiting psychiatrists liability for their patients' violent acts. *American Journal of Psychiatry*, **146**, 821–828.

BECK, A., HOLLON, S., YOUNG, J., *et al* (1985) Treatment of depression with cognitive therapy and amitriptyline. *Archives of General Psychiatry*, **42**, 143–148.

BENTOVIM, A. (1992) *Trauma Organised Systems: Physical and Sexual Abuse in Families*. London: Karnac Books.

BION, W. (1984) Container and contained. In *Attention and Interpretation*, pp. 72–82. London: Maresfield Reprints.

BLACKBURN, R. (1989) Psychopathy and personality disorder in relation to violence. In *Clinical Approaches to Violence* (eds K. Howells & C. Hollin), pp. 61–87. Chichester: Wiley.

BURTON, D., FOY, D., BWANAUSIC, C., *et al* (1994) The relationship between traumatic exposure, family dysfunction, and post-traumatic stress symptoms in male juvenile offenders. *Journal of Traumatic Stress*, **7**, 83–93.

CAPLAN, H. (1984) Annals of Law. The Insanity Defense. *The New Yorker*. 2 July, pp. 46–78.

CHAMBLESS, D. L. & GILLIS, M. M. (1993) Cognitive therapy of anxiety disorders. *Journal of Consulting and Clinical Psychology*, **62**, 248–260.

COID, J. & CORDESS, C. (1992) Compulsory admission of dangerous psychopaths. Psychiatrists are damned if they do and damned if they don't. Editorial. *British Medical Journal*, **304**, 1581–1582.

COLLINS, J. J. & BAILEY, S. L. (1990) Traumatic stress disorder and violent behaviour. *Journal of Traumatic Stress*, **3**, 203–220.

COPAS, J. B. & WHITELEY, J. S. (1976) Predicting success in the treatment of psychopaths. *British Journal of Psychiatry*, **129**, 388–392.

——, O'BRIEN, M., ROBERTS, J., *et al* (1984) Treatment outcome in personality disorder. The effects of social, psychological and behavioural measures. *Personality and Individual Differences*, **5**, 565–573.

CORDESS, C. (1992) Family therapy with psychotic offenders and family victims in a forensic psychiatry secure unit. *Proceedings of the 17th International Congress of the International Academy of Law and Mental Health*, pp. 366–380. Leuven, Belgium.

—— (1992) Pioneers in forensic psychiatry. Edward Glover (1888–1972): psycho-analysis and crime – a fragile legacy. *Journal of Forensic Psychiatry*, **3**, 509–530.

—— (1993) Understanding: exoneration and condemnation. *Journal of Forensic Psychiatry*, **4**, 423–426.

COX, M. (1983) The contribution of dynamic psychotherapy to forensic psychiatry and vice versa. *International Journal of Law and Psychiatry*, **6**, 89–99.

—— & THEILGAARD, A. (1987) *Mutative Metaphors in Psychotherapy. The Aeolian Mode.* London: Tavistock.

CULLEN, E. (1992) The Grendon Reconviction Study, Part I. *Prison Service Journal*, **90**, 35–37.

DEPARTMENT OF HEALTH (1989) Medical Audit. Working Paper 6 of *Working for Patients*. London: HMSO.

DEPARTMENT OF HEALTH, HOME OFFICE (1992) *Review of Health and Social Services for Mentally Disordered Offenders and Others Requiring Similar Services.* (Reed Report.) Cmnd 2088. London: HMSO.

DOLAN, B., EVANS, C. & WILSON, J. (1992) Therapeutic community treatment for personality disordered adults: changes in neurotic symptomatology on follow-up. *International Journal of Social Psychiatry*, **38**, 243–250.

—— & COID, J. (1993) *Psychopathic and Antisocial Personality Disorders: Treatment and Research Issues.* London: Gaskell.

EASTMAN, N. (1992) Psychiatric, psychological and legal models of man. *International Journal of Law and Psychiatry*, **15**, 157–169.

ETCHEGOYEN, R. H. (1992) *The Fundamentals of Psychoanalytic Technique.* London: Karnac Books.

FOUCAULT, M. (1975) *Discipline and PUNISH. The Birth of the Prison.* Peregrine, Penguin Books.

FREUD, S. (1914) *Remembering, Repeating and Working-Through.* Vol. 12. *The Standard Edition.* London: The Hogarth Press and the Institute of Psychoanalysis.

GABBARD, G. O. (1989) Splitting in hospital treatment. *American Journal of Psychiatry*, **146**, 444–451.

GALLWEY, P. (1985) The psychodynamics of borderline personality. In *Aggression and Dangerousness* (eds D. P. Farrington & J. Gunn), pp. 127–152. London: Wiley.

—— (1992) The psychotherapy of psychopathic disorder. *Criminal Behaviour and Mental Health*, **2**, 159–168.

GENDERS, E. & PLAYER, E. (1993) Rehabilitation in prisons: a study of Grendon Underwood. In *Current Legal Problems*. Vol. 46 (eds M. Freeman, B. Hepple & R. Halson). Oxford: Oxford University Press.

GLOVER, E. (1960) *The Roots of Crime. Selected Papers on Psychoanalysis. Volume II.* New York: International Universities Press.

GUNN, J. & TAYLOR, P. (1993) *Forensic Psychiatry. Clinical, Legal and Ethical Issues.* London: Butterworth Heinemann.

HAZALEUS, S. L. & DEFFENBACHER, J. L. (1986) Relaxation and cognitive treatments of anger. *Journal of Consulting and Clinical Psychology*, **54**, 222–226.

HERMAN, J., PERRY, J. & VAN DER KOLK, B. (1989) Childhood trauma in borderline personality disorder. *American Journal of Psychiatry*, **146**, 490–495.

HIGGITT, A. & FONAGY, P. (1992) Psychotherapy in borderline and narcissistic personality disorder. *British Journal of Psychiatry*, **161**, 23–43.

HINSHELWOOD, R. (1993) Locked in role: a psychotherapist within the social defence system of a prison. *Journal of Forensic Psychiatry*, **4**, 427–440.

HOLMES, J. (1992) *Textbook of Psychotherapy in Psychiatric Practice.* London: Routledge.

—— (1993) Attachment theory: A biological basis for psychotherapy? *British Journal of Psychiatry*, **163**, 430–438.

HOME OFFICE (1993) *Criminal Statistics. England and Wales 1991.* London: HMSO.

HUESMANN, L., ERON, L., LEKKOWITZ, M., *et al* (1984) Stability of aggression over time and generations. *Developmental Psychology*, **20**, 1120–1134.

JUREIDINI, J. (1990) Projective identification in general psychiatry. *British Journal of Psychiatry*, **157**, 656–660.

KARASU, T. B. (1982) Psychotherapy and pharmacotherapy: Toward an integrative model. *American Journal of Psychiatry*, **139**, 1102–1111.

KERNBERG, O. (1992) *Aggression in Personality Disorders and Perversions.* New Haven: Yale University Press.

KRAEMER, S. (1988) Splitting and stupidity in child sex abuse. *Psychoanalytic Psychotherapy*, **3**, 247–257.

LINEHAN, M. M. (1993) *Cognitive-Behavioural Treatment of Borderline Personality Disorder*. New York: Guilford Press.

MARK, J., WILLIAMS, G. & MOOREY, S. (1989) The wider application of cognitive therapy: the end of the beginning. In *Cognitive Therapy in Clinical Practice* (eds J. Scott, J. M. G. Williams & A. T. Beck), pp. 227–250. London: Routledge.

McCORD, W. M. (1983) *The Psychopath and Milieu Therapy*. New York: Academic Press.

MAXWELL, R. J. (1984) Quality assessment in health. *British Medical Journal*, **288**, 1470–1472.

MEICHENBAUM, D. (1986) Self-instructional methods. In *Helping People Change: A Textbook of Methods* (eds F. Kanfer & A. Goldstein), pp. 357–392. New York: Pergamon Press.

MENNINGER, K. (1990) Law. *Current Opinion in Psychiatry*, **3**, 762–765.

MENZIES, D., DOLAN, B. & NORTON, K. (1993) Are short term savings worth long term costs? Funding treatment for personality disorders. *Psychiatric Bulletin*, **17**, 517–519.

MULLEN, P. E. (1990) The long term influence of sex assault on the mental health of victims. *Journal of Forensic Psychiatry*, **1**, 13–34.

——, MARTIN, J., ANDERSON, J., *et al* (1993) Childhood sexual abuse and mental health in adult life. *British Journal of Psychiatry*, **163**, 721–732.

NOMELLINI, S. & KATZ, R. C. (1983) Effects of anger control training on abusive patients. *Cognitive Research and Therapy*, **7**, 57.

NOVACO, R. W. (1975) *Anger Control*. Lexington, MA: D. C. Heath.

—— (1976) Treatment of chronic anger through cognitive and relaxation controls. *Journal of Consulting and Clinical Psychology*, **44**, 681.

—— (1977) A stress innoculation approach to anger management in the training of law enforcement officers. *Journal of Community Psychology*, **5**, 327–346.

—— & WELSH, W. N. (1989) Anger disturbances: Cognitive mediation and clinical prescriptions. In *Clinical Approaches to Violence* (eds K. Howells & C. R. Hollin), pp. 39–60. Chichester: Wiley.

PARRY, G. (1992) Improving psychotherapy services: Applications of research, audit and evaluation. *British Journal of Clinical Psychotherapy*, **31**, 3–19.

PARSONS, T. (1951) *The Social System*. New York: Free Press.

PEAY, J. & SHAPLAND, J. (1992) Introduction: Special Issue: Clinical Criminology. *International Journal of Law and Psychiatry*, **15**, 125–128.

PEDDER, J. (1993) Entrance requirements for psychotherapy training: Rationale and objectives. *British Journal of Psychotherapy*, **9**, 310–316.

PFÄFFLIN, F. (1992) What is a symptom? A conservative approach in the therapy of sex offenders. *Journal of Offender Rehabilitation*, **18**, 5–17.

PITHERS, W. D. (1990) Relapse prevention with sexual aggressors. In *Handbook of Sexual Assault. Illness, Theories and Treatment of the Offender* (eds W. C. Marshall, D. R. Laws & H. E. Barakee), pp. 343–361. New York: Plenum Press.

POWER, M. & BREWIN, C. (1991) From Freud to cognitive science: A contemporary account of the unconscious. *British Journal of Clinical Psychology*, **30**, 289–310.

ROBERTSON, G. (1989) Treatment for offender patients: how should success be measured? *Medicine, Science and the Law*, **29**, 303–307.

—— & GUNN, J. (1987) A ten-year follow-up of men discharged from Grendon Prison. *British Journal of Psychiatry*, **151**, 674–678.

ROSE, G. (1993) Mental disorder and the strategies of prevention. *Psychological Medicine*, **23**, 553–555.

RUTTER, M. (1987) Temperament, personality and personality disorder. *British Journal of Psychiatry*, **150**, 443–458.

RYLE, A. (1991) *Cognitive-Analytic Therapy: Active Participation in Change. A new integration in brief psychotherapy*. Chichester: Wiley.

SCHACTER, D. (1986) Amnesia and crime. *American Psychologist*, **3**, 286–295.

SCHETSKY, D. H. (1990) A review of the literature on the long term effects of childhood sexual abuse. In *Incest Related Syndromes of Adult Psychopathology* (ed. R. P. Khift), pp. 35–54. Washington, DC: American Psychiatric Press.

SCHLICTER, K. J. & HORAN, J. J. (1981) Effects of stress innoculation on the anger and aggression management skills of institutionalised juvenile delinquents. *Cognitive Therapy and Research*, **5**, 359–365.

SHANFIELD, S., MATTHEWS, K. & HETHERLY, V. (1993) What do excellent psychotherapy supervisors do? *American Journal of Psychiatry*, **150**, 1081–1084.

SINASON, V. (1992) *Mental Handicap and the Human Condition. New Approaches from the Tavistock.* London: Free Association Books.

STANTON, A. & SCHWARZ, M. S. (1954) *The Mental Hospital.* London: Tavistock.

STONE, A. (1975) *Mental Health and Law: A System in Transition.* Washington, DC: NIMH.

—— (1984) *Law, Psychiatry and Morality.* Washington, DC: American Psychiatric Press.

STRÜPP, H. H. (1986) Psychotherapy. Research, practice and public policy (how to avoid dead ends). *American Psychologist*, **41**, 120–130.

SYMINGTON, N. (1980) The response aroused by the psychopath. *International Review of Psychoanalysis*, **7**, 291–298.

TANTAM, D. (1988) Personality Disorders. In *Recent Advances in Clinical Psychiatry* No. 6 (ed. K. Granville-Grossman), pp. 111–133. Edinburgh: Churchill Livingstone.

TAYLOR, P. & KOPELMAN, M. (1984) Amnesia for criminal offences. *Psychological Medicine*, **14**, 581–588.

TUOVINEN, M. (1973) Crime as an attempt at intrapsychic adaptation. Oulu, Finland: University of Oulu.

WALKER, N. (1991) Dangerous mistakes. *British Journal of Psychiatry*, **158**, 752–757.

WELLDON, E. V. (1994) Forensic psychotherapy. In *The Handbook of Psychotherapy* (eds P. Clarkson & M. Pokorny). London: Routledge.

WINNICOTT, D. (1956) The antisocial tendency. In *Deprivation and Delinquency* (1984) (eds C. Winnicott, R. Shepherd & M. Davis), pp. 120–135. London: Tavistock.

—— (1965) The theory of the parent-infant relationship. In *The Maturational Process and the Facilitating Environment*, pp. 37–55. London: The Hogarth Press.

—— (1970) Residential care as therapy. In *Deprivation and Delinquency* (1984) (eds C. Winnicott, R. Shepherd & M. Davis), pp. 220–228. London: Tavistock.

YARVIS, R. (1972) A classification of criminal offenders through use of current psychoanalytic concepts. *Psychoanalytic Review*, **59**, 549–563.

DE ZULUETA, F. (1993) *The Traumatic Roots of Destructiveness. From Pain to Violence.* London: Whurr Publishers.

12 Learning disability and developmental disorders

SHEILA HOLLINS and VALERIE SINASON

In this chapter we explore the relevance of particular disabling conditions on the presentation and treatment of psychiatric disorder and emotional upset. We try to illuminate some of the diagnostic and assessment challenges which may face the psychotherapist, and which arise because of the co-existence of a condition causing developmental learning disability (formerly called mental handicap) with psychiatric disorder. We present a series of case studies each followed by a discussion of the diagnosis and of appropriate treatment.

Research and clinical experience with individual, group, couple and family therapy (Symington, 1981; Szymanski & Kiernan, 1983; Sinason, 1986, 1992; Thomson, 1986; Hollins & Evered, 1990) reveals that this client group can make use of a similar range of treatments as other groups. Psychoanalytic psychotherapy requires an emotional ability and a wish to make sense of experiences (Sinason, 1992) rather than cognitive intelligence. Consequently the level of cognitive handicap does not preclude psychoanalytic psychotherapy.

Creative therapies including music therapy (Heal, 1989; Eisler, 1990) and art therapy (Buckley, 1989) may be excellent ways of engaging people with learning disabilities emotionally. The use of milieu therapy or of technology such as a voice synthesiser may create major transformations.

Behavioural and cognitive approaches are successfully used in anger management (Bates, 1992), treatment of phobias, or of sexual offending (Murphy & Clare, 1991).

Assessment

We consider the therapist's assessment of his or her own ability to tolerate the patient the most crucial aspect of the assessment. Those with emotional disturbance combined with severe or profound learning disability often communicate their feelings and thoughts in concrete physical ways. Spitting, dribbling, smearing, biting, head-banging, rocking, vomiting and wetting are disturbed primitive infantile modes of communication. They stir up powerful responses and people vary in their abilities to deal with such issues. One therapist will cope well with self-mutilation but will find it impossible to deal with urinating or vice-versa.

In assessing such clients the constraints of personality of the therapist may be more relevant than those of the client. Where the therapist is the main resource she needs to honestly evaluate her own tolerance of the patient's behaviour.

The assessment also needs to try and differentiate between the organic disability and the secondary handicap (Sinason, 1992). Sometimes the reality of the organic deficit is ignored and the client is expected to manage what is mentally impossible. At other times everything is attributed to the organic problem and the possibility of emotional improvement is ignored.

Case history 1

Paul Adams, aged 32, has cerebral palsy and a mild learning disability since birth. With support, he successfully lives in a community home. During the last holidays he answered the door when he was alone in his house. He recognised the man at the front door although he did not know his name and let him in. He was sadistically abused by the man and lay hurt for a couple of hours until other people returned home. Within that same week his epilepsy, which had previously been under control, deteriorated rapidly and he was admitted to a general medical ward for stabilisation.

The epilepsy did not respond to treatment and medical staff suspected pseudo-epilepsy. Paul's speech and language were difficult to understand, but he had told the nursing staff that he kept hearing a man's voice. The consultant decided that he must be hallucinating and prescribed neuroleptic medication.

This brief vignette is an extremely familiar one and there are other men like Paul Adams who present and are treated in a similar way. They had a real organic basis to their learning disability – in this case cerebral palsy with epilepsy (as the most common additional medical complication) – and there is an extra vulnerability to sexual abuse (Brown & Craft, 1989; Brown & Turk, 1992; Sobsey, 1994).

However, professionally, there is a more disturbing way in which we find this to be a familiar scenario. Where an individual has a learning disability with a real organic basis there is often great diagnostic difficulty and a resistance to understanding the emotional aspects of the individual's experience.

Diagnosis: Post-traumatic stress disorder (PTSD).

In fact, the voice that Paul Adams was hearing was not hallucinatory. A therapeutic exploration revealed that the voice in his head was the voice of his abuser playing over and over again without relief. Such flashbacks are an intrinsic part of PTSD of which sexual abuse is an all too common precipitant for people with developmental/learning disabilities. PTSD has been estimated to occur in 1% of the general population (Helzer *et al*, 1987). Estimates of the prevalence in people who have experienced a traumatic event varies between 3.5% and 23.6% (Helzer *et al*, 1987; Breslau *et al*, 1991). DSM–III–R diagnostic criteria include the presence of a traumatic event, persistent re-experiencing of the event, persistent avoidance of stimuli associated with the traumatic event, persistent symptoms of hyperarousal and duration of at least one month. Ryan (1994) found that 16.5% of 310 consecutive people with learning disability who had all suffered significant abuse or trauma met DSM–III–R criteria for PTSD.

Treatment

Ryan (1994) recommends a six-point treatment protocol for PTSD. This is not described fully here but two of the points will be explored. She recommends brief focal psychotherapy to work through the trauma and grief issues and to find ways to feel safe, using whatever communication style the patient feels most comfortable with. Secondly, she recommends habilitative changes to control dissociative triggers. Sometimes triggers related to extended periods of abuse are a real challenge to identify, and almost impossible to eliminate. Ryan describes a woman who had been repeatedly scalded from a kettle as a child, and who became distressed as an adult every time she heard running water or a boiling kettle.

Case history 2

Pauline Atkins (not her real name) was blind and severely learning disabled. She was referred at 21 by her parents following a psychotic breakdown. They had been deeply concerned to find her several stone underweight on their return from a 3-month visit abroad visiting her ill maternal grandmother. On taking her back home she spoke of being sexually abused by one of the workers. The police were unwilling to take action because of her handicap, a common experience for people with a learning disability who are abused (Buchanan & Wilkins, 1991), and she was referred for therapy.

Differential diagnosis: PTSD, affective psychosis.

Affective psychosis is thought by some writers to be underdiagnosed in this client group (Sovner & Hurley, 1983; McLaughlin & Bhate, 1987). Fraser & Nolan (1994) describe the full range of affective disorders in people with learning disabilities with depressed mood being the commonest of the psychiatric symptoms which present. Associated delusions tend to be naive in their form.

Treatment

During therapy it became apparent that her florid psychotic episode occurred when she tried to tell her social worker about the abuse and was not believed. Our experience (Sinason, 1993) mirrors that of Varley (1984) who found learning disabled patients were more vulnerable to a psychotic breakdown when their case was not taken up.

After one year in therapy we could understand her hallucinations in a different way as well as appreciate the changes in them. This is illustrated in the following extract from a treatment session:

Pauline: He's here. In the room.
Therapist: Who's here?
Pauline: That man. Mr X (the alleged abuser)
Therapist: So Mr X is here?
Pauline: (laughing) Yes
Therapist: Are you pleased he's here?
Pauline: Yes. Because he keeps me company now. He used to hurt me but now he says sorry.
Therapist: He used to hurt you but now he says sorry.
Pauline: I don't want him to go because he keeps me company now. I don't want him to go to prison.
Therapist: Are you worried that if Mr X goes to prison the Mr X in your head will also go away?
Pauline: Yes. I like his voice.

We were able to understand that Pauline had transformed a traumatic memory into an eroticised one that cushioned her from her original sense of hurt and betrayal. By enjoying Mr X in her head she was showing her own agency. After this had been worked through he slowly disappeared from her thinking.

Case history 3

A young couple in their thirties had been supported by their parents in the early years of their marriage. The man had psychosexual problems, and despite specialist counselling and medical investigations the marriage was never fully consummated. He had several psychiatric admissions for treatment of depression, and his wife began to enjoy these regular respites from her husband's jealous and sometimes aggressive behaviour. Eventually the marriage broke down and the husband returned home to live with his widowed mother. His wife had a prolonged episode of tearfulness with feelings of regret and guilt about her marriage and several times tried to persuade her husband to return. Later she was placed in supported employment where she met a married man who befriended her.

He began to visit her at home at 2 or 3 a.m. to have sex with her, and she willingly left the door unlocked for him. Her mood was inappropriate and she saw no need to use contraceptives.

Diagnosis: bipolar affective disorder.

In the UK we have yet to see many people with learning disabilities being sentenced for being drunk and disorderly. This is because people with a learning disability have not had much access to alcohol. Most of the ways that 'normal' people harm themselves such as by smoking, drinking and being promiscuous are just as damaging and self-abusive as head-banging or biting. However, because enough of the ordinary population commit such acts the disturbance in them is often minimised. As normalisation leads to 'normal abuses' it took a while for professionals to realise that the wife's promiscuity was not a matter of healthy liberation. Therefore normalisation can lead to 'normal abuses' which would be recognised as emotional disturbance more easily. However, as Fraser & Nolan (1994) point out the infectious gaiety typically associated with mania is less commonly seen in people with learning disabilities.

Treatment

An individual counselling approach is recommended in similar situations where long-term support is needed. The woman in this case scenario was also offered group therapy, but was unable to make a commitment to attend regularly. Psychotropic medication may be a useful adjunct to psychotherapeutic approaches.

Case history 4

Melanie Curtis was admitted to a hostel following the death of her mother. She was a middle-aged woman with severe learning disability of unknown aetiology. Like many handicapped people she suffered a double loss with the loss of a parent coinciding with the loss of a home (Kloeppel & Hollins, 1989; Hollins & Sireling, 1991; Oswin, 1991). The hostel had low morale and a speedy turnover of semi-trained staff. A year after her mother's death a psychiatrist was asked to make an emergency call on a bank holiday. Melanie had not slept the previous night and was reported to have been aggressive to a staff member and to have destroyed property in her room. The GP had been called twice but the sedatives prescribed had had no effect. It was in fact inappropriate to give neuroleptics to someone simply to sedate them without having made a formal diagnosis. However, the GP did not know what else to do. When the psychiatrist arrived she found Melanie in her room sitting on a bed full of broken glass from a picture.

Diagnosis: Grief.

This identikit is a familiar one. Faced with a person with a disability in a disturbed state it is all too frequent for the doctor to treat the behaviour or see it as part of the disability, rather than to understand the subtle mixture of the organic and the emotional.

A therapeutic exploration revealed that Melanie's key worker had worked his last night before emigrating to Canada. A party was held for him the previous night while he was on duty, the residents having been informed of his imminent departure earlier the same day. It was also close to the first anniversary of Melanie's mother's death.

Many schools for ordinary children in the UK still avoid telling classes their teacher is going until the last day 'in case they get upset'. Within the field of learning disability the concept that separation and loss need time to work through is even more difficult to find room for. No wonder Melanie was so mad with grief after such multiple bereavement within the context of gross insensitivity.

Treatment

Bereavement counselling for people with learning disabilities was pioneered at St George's and is now more widely available. Bereavement counsellors use the same skills with people with learning disabilities as they do with other bereaved people but need to understand the multiple losses that this client group have to cope with (Sinason, 1986; Hollins & Grimer, 1988) such as their dependency on others and loss of control over their own future lives including where they actually live. Oswin (1991) found that people with learning disabilities bereaved of their last surviving carer may be moved five or more times in the year following the bereavement. Marris (1993), studying factors which were predictive of poor outcome in bereaved adults in the general population, found lack of control over one's own life to be one of five distinguishing factors.

Case history 5

Darren James was a gentle, talkative and outgoing 19-year-old with Down's syndrome who had done well in a special school, and made particular progress in independent living skills. His parents were encouraged to send him to a residential college with the longer term aim of him leaving home. After 4 months his distressed parents removed their mute, behaviourally disturbed and uncooperative son from the college believing that something abusive must have happened. The college staff were unable to give any insight into the changes in his behaviour and personality. The learning disability psychiatrist initially prescribed a major tranquilliser but over the next two years also added a tricyclic antidepressant for a few weeks and provided in-patient 'respite' care in a locked ward. His parents described the damage he caused to objects and furniture at home, his continuing reluctance to speak with any words spoken seeming inappropriate and his refusal to attend any educational or social activities outside the home. There was no improvement in his condition.

Diagnosis: Unrecognised grief and depression.

A therapeutic exploration revealed that his maternal aunt had died 3 weeks after he started college – just 2 days before his first weekend at home. The funeral took place 2 days after his return to college. His family reported that until that weekend their telephone contact with Darren had been very satisfactory with Darren sharing lots of information about his life at college. They said they had not allowed his aunt's death to spoil the weekend and had given him a good time. She had been like a grandmother to the family and had been Darren's primary carer for the first year of his life because his mother had had severe postnatal depression, probably connected to her difficulty in accepting a child with Down's syndrome. In an ongoing study by Hollins & Esterhuyzen (1997) 70% of carers did not recognise symptoms of bereavement. Darren's parents could not make the link between his aunt's death and his later anger and despair.

Unfortunately, in this case, Darren's GP, psychiatrist and social worker all failed to make the link as well. In our experience this is typical of the attack on links which must be understood by mental health professionals working with people with learning disabilities.

Treatment

Individual bereavement counselling, and antidepressant medication are all indicated. An active guided mourning approach to bereavement counselling is likely to be most successful (Sireling *et al*, 1988; Hollins & Sireling, 1994*a,b*, 1991) with the use of as many visual cues as possible to ensure Darren's understanding of the finality of his aunt's death. A memorial service involving Darren and his extended family would provide another opportunity for him to share in his family's grief, and is not inappropriate even 2 years after the death. Family sessions may be needed to allow the family to explore their inability to acknowledge Darren's emotional capacity, and to work together to plan a memorial service (Thomson, 1986). Such work helps families to prepare for later significant losses which are inevitable, and thus has a preventative element to it.

Case history 6

Ellen Logan, aged 28, became severely depressed following a violent incident in her group home. Her parents had a poor relationship with each other and towards her and there was a lot of physical violence towards her when she stayed with them at weekends. After a trusted key worker left for maternity leave Ellen became verbally perseverative. This would show itself in the way she repeated the ordinary courtesies of life ad infinitum. 'I would walk in my centre and I would say "Good morning, Mary Brown" and Mary Brown, she would say to me "Good morning, Ellen Logan. How are you?" And I would say "I am very well thank you Mary Brown and how are you?" And she would say to me, Mary Brown would, she would say to me "Thank you for asking, thank you for asking Ellen Logan"'.

Diagnosis: Depression.

This carried on in an anaesthetising way so that any initial live interest anyone felt in Ellen would disappear. However, in one group session Ellen was able to show where that symptom had come from. 'My dad last night he threw plates at my mum he did and all the food went on the floor it did. And the plates broke into pieces they did and all the pieces of food went onto the carpet. And my dad shouted at my mum he did and I went and cried in my room I did. And then I came back and said 'Would you please Dad like a cup of tea please" and he answered me "Well, thank you Ellen, I would indeed like a cup of tea please, thank you very much"'.

Treatment

Ellen's coping strategies were rather fragile, and incidents which reminded her of earlier conflicts often precipitated a breakdown in her emotional adjustment. Depressive symptomatology may be responsive to antidepressant medication although idiosyncratic responses may occur (Menolascino, 1989; Dosen, 1990). An adequate trial of more than one type of antidepressant is necessary before considering alternative medication, and effective treatment should be reviewed regularly. Issues of consent must be remembered particularly with respect to any side-effects. Pharmacological treatment of depression should never be given in isolation. Unresponsiveness to treatment for major depression may be due to an associated but unrecognised medical condition such as hypothyroidism (Krah, 1988), and a full medical evaluation should be done. An holistic treatment approach should be used including social and environmental measures, and counselling or psychotherapy. In Ellen's case group therapy was effective in helping her to work through some of the distress and disappointments in her earlier family relationships. She was enabled to ·explore her feelings of being responsible for causing family arguments – a common feeling for people with learning disabilities who are aware of being a disappointment to their parents (Vanier, 1984).

Case history 7

George Daley's family requested family therapy to help them develop some consistent parental strategies to manage his difficult behaviour. He was 13 with a diagnosis of fragile X. His behaviour was characterised by restless, fidgety, impulsive and overactive features. He was aggressive and rude, constantly interrupting his parents when they talked to each other or to his sister. When he was particularly frustrated or excited, he would bite his hand. His 8-year-old sister was doing well academically and was a model of good behaviour.

Diagnosis: Fragile X and pervasive developmental disorder within a dysfunctional family system.

The behaviours exhibited by George are characteristic of children with fragile X particularly when the degree of learning disability is severe (Einfeld *et al*, 1991). Poor concentration and attentional skills tend to improve with age (Turk *et al*, 1994). Impairments of social functioning and communication are similar to those found in autism, with a significant minority of individuals with fragile X also having the diagnosis of autism (Bregman *et al*, 1988; Reiss & Freund, 1990). Cohen *et al* (1989) suggest that the commonly described aversion to eye contact is a consequence of the increased relational difficulties and associated general sensory defensiveness of people with this condition. This case highlights the importance of an understanding of the behavioural phenotype for a particular disorder causing developmental learning disability of which fragile X is one example. Other well described behavioural phenotypes include Noonan's syndrome, Lesch–Nyhan syndrome, tuberous sclerosis and Rett's syndrome.

Treatment

Pharmacological interventions have included the use of psychostimulants such as methylphenidate with research showing considerable improvement in attentional deficits in up to two-thirds of children (Hagerman *et al*, 1988). Folic acid is also reported to improve disturbed behaviour (Turk *et al*, 1994). In this case study, family therapy was an effective additional treatment which focused on the relational aspects of a system which had become disordered because of the exceptional stresses imposed by the characteristic behavioural phenotype of fragile X. It was also important to explore the meaning of the diagnosis of fragile X to the different family members. For example, George's mother blamed herself for his disability because she was the carrier for the condition. His sister had had the genetic transmission of fragile X explained to her when she was 6. She was found not to be a carrier. At the age of 8 her understanding was that she was not like her Mum (i.e. an unaffected carrier) and so she must be like her brother, and she thought she would gradually become like him.

Conclusion

Children and adults with learning disability can make use of the same range of therapies available to the rest of the population. However, although creative, cognitive and psychodynamic therapies have all proven to be efficacious there is still a shortage of such resources. Even in areas where there are resources people with a learning disability are still sometimes not referred under the misapprehension that cognitive ability is needed to make use of such treatment. Alternatively, the handicap itself is blamed for the emotional disturbances that coexist in the client and this rules out the thought of referral for psychological treatment.

Where someone needs help in coping with a life event or a mental illness a multidisciplinary assessment is essential. There needs to be psychiatric screening for depression or other states which may require chemical treatment as well as psychological assessment. Where mental illness or severe disturbance co-exists with a learning disability a treatment package might include a range of therapies.

This chapter has addressed some of the issues to be faced in work with people with learning disabilities and their families or carers. The counselling and psychotherapy needs of people with learning disabilities are in many respects similar to those of other adults, and in some ways different.

Indications for counselling generally concern the need for help in adjusting to change or accepting the self. For people with learning disabilities the four 'secrets' of disability and dependency, of sexuality and of mortality are the commonest themes in psychotherapy. Treatment may be brief focal psychotherapy, e.g. to help someone through a difficult bereavement, transition or trauma; or it may be longer term with a more developmental perspective.

Carers may try to protect people with learning disabilities from knowledge or experience in any of these areas although such conspiracies of silence may compound feelings of low self-esteem and lack of control in their own lives. Counselling may empower people with learning disabilities. A major emphasis must be placed on the communication difficulties often experienced in working with this group, and non-verbal ways of communicating with people for whom spoken language is difficult must be developed.

Psychotherapy and counselling by their nature benefit greatly from supervision but many professionals working with people with learning disabilities may be relatively untrained and without adequate supervision. Investment in training and supervision is especially advisable for this client group whose needs are more rather than less complex. Those in the wider circle of the person in therapy will also need considerable support to avoid them undermining the therapeutic relationship.

References

BATES, R. (1992) Psychotherapy with people with learning difficulties. In *Psychotherapy and Mental Handicap* (eds A. Waitman & S. Conboy-Hill). London: Sage.

BREGMAN, J. D., LECKMAN, J. F. & ORT, S. I. (1988) Fragile X syndrome: genetic predisposition to psychotherapy. *Journal of Autism and Developmental Disorder*, **18**, 343–354.

BRESLAU, N., DAVIS, G. C., ANDRESKI, P., *et al* (1991) Traumatic events and post-traumatic stress disorder in an urban population of young adults. *Archives of General Psychiatry*, **48**, 216–222.

BROWN, H. & CRAFT, A. (1989) *Thinking the Unthinkable: Papers on Sexual abuse and People with Learning Disabilities.* London: FPA Education Unit.

—— & TURK, V. (1992) Defining sexual abuse as it affects adults with learning disability. *Mental Handicap*, **20**, 44–55.

BUCHANAN, A. & WILKINS, R. (1991) Sexual abuse of the mentally handicapped. *Psychiatric Bulletin*, **15**, 601–605.

BUCKLEY, A. (1989) In *Unconscious Imagery: How Art Increases Understanding in Mutual Respect* (ed. D. Brandon). Good Impressions Publishing.

COHEN, I. L., VIETZE, P. M., SUDHALTER, V., *et al* (1989) Parent–child dyadic gaze patterns in Fragile X males and in non-Fragile X males with autistic disorders. *Journal of Child Psychology and Psychiatry*, **30**, 845–856.

CROSSLEY, R. (1994) *Facilitated Communication Training.* London: Teachers College Press, Eurospan.

DONNELLAN, A., SABIN, L. & MAJURE, L. (1992) Facilitated communication. Beyond the quandary to the questions. *Topics in Language Disorders*, **12**, 1.

DOSEN, A. (1990) *Treatment of Mental Illness and Behavioural Disorder in the Mentally Retarded* (eds A. Dosen, A. Van Gennep & G. J. Zwanniken). Leiden: Logon Publications.

EINFELD, S., HALL, W. & LEVY, F. (1991) Hyperactivity and the Fragile X syndrome. *Journal of Abnormal Child Psychology*, **19**, 253–262.

EISLER, J. (1990) Creative music therapy for the mentally handicapped or emotionally disturbed child. In *Creative Arts and Mental Disability* (eds S. Stanley & A. B. Segal). Academic Publishers.

FRASER, W. & NOLAN, M. (1994) Psychiatric disorder in mental retardation. In *Mental Health in Mental Retardation* (ed. N. Bouras), pp. 79–92. Cambridge: Cambridge University Press.

HAGERMAN, R. I., MURPHY, M. A. & WITTENBERGER, M. D. (1988) A controlled trial of stimulant medication in children with the Fragile X syndrome. *American Journal of Medical Genetics*, **30**, 377–392.

HEAL, M. (1989) In *In Tune with the Mind in Mutual Respect* (ed. D. Brandon). Good Impressions Publishing.

HELZER, J. E., ROBINS, L. N. & MCEVOY, L. (1987) Post-traumatic stress disorder in the general population. *New England Journal of Medicine*, **317**, 1630–1634.

HOLLINS, S. & EVERED, C. (1990) Group process and content: The challenge of mental handicap. *Group Analysis*, **23**, 55–67.

—— & ESTERHAUSEN, A. (1997) Bereavement and grief in people with learning disabilities. *British Journal of Psychiatry*, **170**, 497–501.

—— & GRIMER, M. (1988) *Going Somewhere: Pastoral Care for People with Learning Disabilities.* London: SPCK.

—— & SIRELING, L. (1994a) *When Mum Died.* 2nd edn. Books Beyond Words. London: Gaskell.

—— & —— (1994b) *When Dad Died.* 2nd edn. Books Beyond Words. London: Gaskell.

KLOEPPEL, D. A. & HOLLINS, S. (1989) Double handicap: Mental retardation and death in the family. *Death Studies*, **13**, 31–38.

KRAHN, D. D. (1988) Affective disorder associated with subclinical hypothyroidism. *Psychosomatics*, **28**, 440–441.

MARRIS, P. (1993) *Loss and Change.* London: Routledge.

MCLAUGHLIN, I. & BHATE, M. S. (1987) A case of affective psychosis following bereavement in a mentally handicapped woman. *British Journal of Psychiatry*, **151**, 552–554.

MENOLASCINO, F. J. (1989) Model services for treatment/management of the mentally retarded – mentally ill. *Clinical Care Update*, **25**, 145–155.

MURPHY, G. & CLARE, I. (1991) M.I.E.T.S (2) Psychological assessment and treatment, outcome for clients and service effectiveness. *Mental Handicap Research*, **4**, 180–206.

OSWIN, M. (1991) *Am I Allowed to Cry. A Study of Bereavement Amongst People who have Learning Difficulties.* London: Human Horizons.

REISS, A. L. & FREUND, L. (1990) Fragile X syndrome DSM–III–R and autism. *Journal of the American Academy of Child and Adolescent Psychiatry*, **29**, 885–891.

RYAN, R. (1994) Post-traumatic stress disorder in persons with developmental disabilities. *Community Mental Health Journal*, **30**, 45–54.

SINASON, V. (1986) Secondary mental handicap and its relationship to trauma. *Psychoanalytical Psychology*, **2**, 131–154.

––––– (1992) *Mental Handicap and the Human Condition: New Approaches from the Tavistock.* London: Free Association Books.

––––– (1993) The special vulnerability of the handicapped child and adult: with special reference to mental handicap. In *Clinical Paediatrics, International Practice and Research, Child Abuse* (eds C. J. Hobbs & J. M. Wynne). London: Baillière Tindall.

SIRELING, L., COHEN, D. & MARKS, I. (1988) Guided Mourning for Morbid Grief: A controlled replication. *Behaviour Therapy*, **19**, 121–132.

SOBSEY, D. (1994) *Violence and Abuse in the Lives of People with Disabilities: The End of Silent Acceptance?* London: Jessica Kingsley Publications.

SOVNER, R. & HURLEY, A. (1983) Do mentally retarded suffer from affective illness? *Archives of General Psychiatry*, **40**, 61–67.

SYMINGTON, N. (1981) The psychotherapy of a subnormal patient. *British Journal of Medical Psychology*, **54**, 187–199.

SZYMANSKI, L. S. & KIERNAN, W. E. (1983) Multiple family group therapy with developmentally disabled adolescents and young adults. *International Journal of Group Psychotherapy*, **33**, 521–534.

THOMSON, S. (1986) *Families and Mental Handicap.* London: Institute of Family Therapy.

TURK, J., HAGERMAN, R., BARNICOAT, A., *et al* (1994) The Fragile X Syndrome. In *Mental Health in Mental Retardation* (ed. N. Bouras), pp. 135–153. Cambridge: Cambridge University Press.

VANIER, J. (1984) *Man and Woman he Made them.* London: Darton, Longman and Todd.

VARLEY, C. K. (1984) Schizophreniform psychoses in mentally retarded adolescent girls following sexual assault. *American Journal of Psychiatry*, **141**, 593–595.

13 Sexual dysfunctions

KEITH HAWTON

The conceptualisation and treatment of sexual dysfunctions have undergone remarkable changes in the past four decades. At one time sexual dysfunctions were thought to arise almost entirely from childhood experiences, especially abnormalities in sexual development, often because of disturbed relationships with parents. Individual psychoanalytically orientated therapy was then regarded as the treatment of choice. This focused on providing patients with insight into unconscious conflicts. A major change occurred in the late 1950s and early 1960s, largely with the advent of behaviour therapy. Learning theory explanations of sexual problems were that they could be acquired at any stage of life. Treatments using some of the original methods of behaviour therapy, such as systematic desensitisation, were then introduced.

The situation underwent a notable change in 1970 when Masters and Johnson's book *Human Sexual Inadequacy* was published. This described a novel treatment approach for couples with sexual dysfunction, together with very impressive outcome data, and heralded the advent of sex therapy. This approach is based on the notions that sexual dysfunction can occur because of a wide range of factors (e.g. poor education about sexuality, early traumatic experiences, unrealistic expectations or performance concerns, impaired communication between partners) and that these can be tackled effectively with a treatment programme which combines education, homework assignments and counselling. Sex therapy was greeted with great enthusiasm on both sides of the Atlantic. Both clinical application and research investigations of the approach proliferated, although in retrospect it is clear that clinical enthusiasm for the approach far outstripped research. The demand for help for sexual dysfunctions grew rapidly during the 1970s. This was probably partly as a result of changing attitudes to sexuality and partly because of the availability of what appeared to be a

A short version of this chapter was first published in the *British Journal of Psychiatry* (1995), **167**, 307–314.

relatively effective form of treatment. In this country, sex therapy began to be offered in psychiatry and psychology departments and also in family planning clinics. Subsequently Marriage Guidance (now Relate) gradually developed a major training programme in sex therapy and is now probably the main source of help for people with sexual dysfunctions, although developments in physical treatments, especially for erectile dysfunction, have drawn urologists into this field. Now there seems to be somewhat less interest in sex therapy within psychiatry. This may be partly because of increasing focus on physical methods of treatment in general and also because it is extremely difficult to obtain funding for research in this area, although there are more challenges than ever. Clinicians have commented that over the years they have seen an increasing proportion of patients with complicated problems for which sex therapy alone may be insufficient.

This chapter includes a brief description of the nature of sexual dysfunctions and their assessment which is then followed by an overview of the nature and results of sex therapy for couples, including the effects of modifying the original Masters and Johnson approach and factors associated with outcome. Subsequently the treatment of individuals without partners, group treatment, methods of augmenting sex therapy, bibliotherapy and new applications of sex therapy are reviewed, together with a summary of research findings concerning each approach.

The nature of sexual dysfunctions and their assessments

A reasonable, although not entirely satisfactory, definition of sexual dysfunction is 'the persistent impairment of the normal patterns of sexual interest or response'. Sexual dysfunctions are distinguished from sexual variations ('deviations'), which are sexual behaviours which are regarded as qualitatively (or sometimes quantitatively) abnormal and which may be harmful to other people.

It is now customary to clarify sexual dysfunction into four categories according to the aspect of sexual function which is involved: disorders of sexual desire, of arousal, difficulties concerning orgasm and other problems which cannot be included in the first three categories. The ICD–10 disorders are shown according to these categories in Table 13.1.

Referrals to sexual dysfunction clinics

The problems of erectile dysfunction and female low sexual desire predominate among referrals to sexual dysfunction clinics. Thus in a series of 200 consecutive couples referred to a sexual dysfunction clinic

TABLE 13.1
Sexual dysfunctions according to ICD–10

Aspect of sexuality affected	Males	Females
Sexual desire/interest	Lack or loss of sexual desire	
Sexual arousal	(Failure of genital response)	
	Erectile disorder	Sexual arousal disorder
Orgasm	Premature ejaculation	Orgasmic dysfunction
	Inhibited orgasm	
Other	Sexual aversion and lack of sexual enjoyment	
		Vaginismus
		Dyspareunia

Modified from ICD–10 (WHO, 1992).

in Oxford, of the 95 in which the male partners appeared to have the main problem erectile dysfunction was identified in 63%, premature ejaculations in 16%, low sexual desire in 8% and retarded ejaculation in 6%. In the 105 couples in which the female partners seemed to have the main problem, 61% had low sexual desire, 14% vaginismus, 11% dyspareunia and 9% orgasmic dysfunction (Catalan *et al*, 1990). In this study female arousal disorder was not recorded as a separate entity. In recent years many clinicians have reported an increase in the frequency which they are referred men with low sexual desire and a marked decrease in the frequency of presentation of female orgasmic dysfunction.

Assessment of couples presenting with sexual dysfunction

In assessing couples with sexual dysfunctions it is most important to spend a substantial amount of time interviewing the partners separately. This allows them to be more forthright, thus increasing the opportunity for relevant information to be obtained, and provides each with an equal opportunity to air their views on the problem. The assessment must address a range of factors (see Hawton (1985) for details), including the nature and development of the sexual problem(s), desired changes (i.e. goals), family background and early childhood (including family attitudes to sexuality), sexual development and experiences (including traumatic experiences), previous relationships and problems, sexual information, the nature of the relationship with the partner (both general and sexual), psychiatric and medical factors (including a physical examination and investigations when indicated), use of alcohol and drugs, and other factors where relevant (e.g. education, occupation, interests, social network and religious beliefs).

TABLE 13.2
Factors relevant to determining whether or not sex therapy is indicated

---

1 The sexual problem has persisted for at least a few months.
2 The problem is likely to be caused or maintained by psychological factors (even though physical factors may be relevant).
3 The problem is not secondary to general relationship difficulties.
4 The couple's general relationship is reasonably harmonious (sufficient for the couple to have a reasonable chance of working collaboratively on homework assignments and other aspects of treatment).
5 There is no current active major psychiatric disorder, nor serious alcohol or drug abuse.
6 The female partner is not pregnant.
7 The couple show reasonable motivation for treatment.

By no means all couples (or individuals) with sexual dysfunctions require or are appropriate for intensive sex therapy. Brief counselling is often what is required. This includes education and advice, possibly combined with the use of written material. Factors relevant to whether or not sex therapy is appropriate are listed in Table 13.2.

Sex therapy

In the 'standard' sex therapy practised these days, once a couple have been assessed and found suitable for this approach, treatment usually includes presentation of a formulation of potential aetiological and maintaining factors, a graded programme of homework assignments (including sensate focus exercises and other specific procedures), therapeutic work using cognitive and other strategies, and educational measures (recommended reading and discussion of sexual anatomy and sexual response).

Homework assignments

The homework assignments are usually largely based on the original Masters and Johnson programme. Thus they include: non-genital sensate focus, which is primarily intended to help a couple establish physical intimacy in a comfortable relaxed fashion, and to encourage communication about feelings (including anxieties) and wishes; genital sensate focus, which aims to facilitate sexually arousing caressing without undue anxiety; and vaginal containment, which is an intermediate state before full sexual intercourse begins. In addition there are various other behavioural assignments that may be used depending on the specific nature of the sexual problem. For example, a woman with vaginismus is usually encouraged to go through an individual programme of examining her genitals, both externally and internally, and practising pelvic floor muscle exercises. Couples in which the male partner has premature ejaculation may be taught the squeeze or stop–start techniques.

Psychological aspects of treatment

Success with the homework assignments usually requires specific psychological help, especially when the couple or individual encounter difficulties at particular stages. Cognitive approaches can be used very effectively in this context (see Hawton (1989) and Spence (1991) for details). This is the aspect of treatment which requires most experience and is often crucial to success.

Educational aspects of treatment

Education is also often important. Many sexual difficulties are the result of lack of information, misinformation or unreasonable expectations. While education can occur throughout treatment, it is usually especially helpful to devote a larger part of one treatment session to discussing (with visual material) sexual anatomy and response in either sex, and other aspects of sexuality particularly relevant to the specific couple (e.g. the effects of ageing). Couples are also usually recommended to read one or more of the useful books about male and female sexuality (Zilbergeld, 1980; Kitzinger, 1985).

General relationship difficulties

General relationship problems often need to be addressed in the context of sex therapy. Sometimes during therapy with a couple it becomes obvious that difficulties in their general relationship are more important than was originally apparent. It may then be necessary to stop sex therapy and change to general marital therapy.

Practical aspects of treatment

Treatment is usually conducted by one therapist (see below), treatment sessions involve both partners and mostly occur weekly (see below), at least during the early phases of therapy. The programme lasts on average between 8 and 20 sessions over a period of 3–9 months. While modifications and developments of this approach have been introduced, the core treatment strategies are usually maintained.

Several detailed practical accounts of sex therapy are available (Hawton, 1985; Gillan, 1987; Bancroft, 1989; Spence, 1991).

Case examples of the use of sex therapy

A case of vaginismus

Susan, a 23-year-old secretary, presented with her husband David, to whom she had been married for three years. She and her husband had never been able to have sexual intercourse because of her vaginismus. Despite this problem they were both able to enjoy foreplay. In the past whenever they had tried to have sexual intercourse, Susan had become very tense and attempts at vaginal penetration were very painful. In the past 18 months they had abandoned trying to have intercourse. The couple's general relationship was good except that Susan feared that David might leave her because of the sexual problem.

Susan came from a family where sex had never been discussed. At the age of 12, her 19-year-old brother had twice tried to have sex with her, which had frightened her a great deal. She had never been able to use tampons and a vaginal examination by her GP confirmed the diagnosis of vaginismus, in that she became very tense and had obvious spasm of her vaginal muscles.

During the assessment it became clear that both Susan and David were not very well informed about sexuality and that Susan was particularly ignorant of her own sexual anatomy. The therapist therefore introduced the educational component of the treatment early on. It was agreed that therapy would initially focus on helping Susan become more comfortable with her sexual anatomy, through examining herself with a mirror and later with her fingers. She was also taught to gain more control over her vaginal muscles by learning to contract and relax them.

Susan had considerable difficulties initially in examining herself. Therefore, her thoughts and fears concerning the homework assignments were explored by having her imagine she were attempting the task and then carefully finding out what feelings this evoked and subsequently what thoughts caused the negative feelings. It emerged that the main fear was of experiencing unbearable pain. Susan was then helped to see how she had total control over the situation and that were discomfort to occur, she could prevent it becoming more than this. Gradually she was able to carry out the homework assignments and came to accept that her genitals were of normal size – she had previously believed that her vagina was far too small to accommodate her husband's penis.

The sensate focus exercises were introduced and both partners found this relatively easy, until genital sensate focus began. At this point, Susan again experienced apprehension. Exploration of the reasons for this revealed that she was concerned that David might not be able to stick to the agreed limits. His repeated reassurance allowed her to relax more.

Subsequently, the couple were instructed to try vaginal containment, using the female superior position. However, Susan became very distressed at this point and it was only after she had revealed to her husband her brother's attempts at having sex with her that she felt able to progress with the programme. After some initial difficulties the couple were able to enjoy vaginal containment and a couple of weeks later were able to have full sexual intercourse.

Erectile dysfunction

Peter, a 43-year-old shop owner, presented with his wife, Pamela, because of his repeatedly losing his erection just before sexual intercourse. The problem had developed 18 months previously, after he had failed to get an erection when he tried to have sex following a party at which he had drunk a good deal. He had never been very confident about his sexual performance, having experienced premature ejaculation in previous relationships and during the early part of his relationship with Pamela. The episode of acute erectile dysfunction caused him great concern and subsequent episodes of sexual activity were accompanied by intense performance anxiety. Peter felt ashamed of the problem and found it difficult to discuss this with Pamela. She herself had no sexual difficulties, but was concerned that Peter no longer found her attractive.

Physical examination was normal and there were no factors in the history to indicate an organic cause for the problem. The initial phase of therapy concentrated on helping Peter and Pamela to discuss their sexual relationship more openly. Peter was very reassured to find that Pamela did not think him less of a man because of his problem and that she was keen to help him overcome it. Peter was provided with a simple explanation of how alcohol problems inhibit sexual response and how an episode of failure can establish further fear of failure, particularly in someone who is not fully confident about their sexuality.

The couple began sensate focus, but Peter found it very difficult to relax and enjoy Pamela's caressing. On further exploration, it emerged that he found himself feeling detached from what was going on. His thoughts at the time proved to be about whether or not he would be able to obtain and sustain an erection. He was helped to focus his mind on sensations and to allow his body to respond, rather than constantly assessing his degree of arousal. When he was able to obtain an erection, he was encouraged to let this fade away from time to time, by he and Pamela ceasing their caressing. Further caressing usually resulted in his regaining his erection, which helped improve his confidence in his erectile capacity.

As would be expected, vaginal containment proved to be an important stage in treatment. Initially, Peter did experience a couple of episodes of erectile failure, but Pamela was able to stimulate him to regain his erection and this further enhanced his confidence. Eventually, they were able to establish their sexual relationship. The therapist then spent a session exploring with them how they would deal with any further difficulties. They agreed that should the problem recur they would make sure that they discussed the difficulties and, if necessary, reinstate an abbreviated sex therapy programme.

Short-term outcome with sex therapy

Uncontrolled clinical outcome data

The remarkable initial enthusiasm for sex therapy was due not just to its novelty but also to the outstanding therapeutic results Masters and Johnson reported on the basis of treating a series of more than 500 couples and individuals without partners. Their overall initial 'failure rate' was 18.9% and in a five-year follow-up of 313 couples (all post-treatment 'non-failures') they identified an overall relapse rate of 5.1%.

However, outcome statistics reported subsequently from routine clinical practice (Duddle, 1975; Bancroft & Coles, 1976; Hawton & Catalan, 1986), which revealed overall improvement in about two-thirds of cases, and from controlled treatment studies (see review by Wright *et al*, 1977) have been more modest than those of Masters and Johnson. Factors which have been proposed to explain this discrepancy include the dubious method used by Masters and Johnson to report outcome (i.e. in terms of failures rather than successes), the uncertain nature of their outcome criteria (Zilbergeld & Evans, 1980), and possible biases in patient selection.

There are marked differences in the response of individual sexual dysfunctions to sex therapy (Bancroft & Coles, 1976; Hawton & Catalan, 1986). An excellent response is obtained in nearly every case of vaginismus (Hawton & Catalan, 1990) and a good outcome in a substantial majority of cases of erectile dysfunction of psychogenic origin (Hawton *et al*, 1992). Variable initial outcome results have been reported for lack of sexual desire (Schover & LoPiccolo, 1982, compared with Hawton & Catalan, 1986; Warner *et al*, 1987). The outcome is very often poor when the male partner has this problem. Masters and Johnson (1970) claimed excellent outcome for the treatment of premature ejaculation whereas other works have reported more modest results (Bancroft & Coles, 1976; Hawton & Catalan, 1986).

Results of comparative and controlled studies

Since most, if not all, practitioners obtain more modest results with sex therapy than those initially reported by Masters & Johnson (1970) it is important to examine the results of controlled treatment studies to determine the true effectiveness of this approach. Surprisingly few controlled outcome studies of sex therapy have included either waiting list or placebo control groups. However, one study in which changes in the sexual and general adjustment of couples who received treatment for a variety of sexual dysfunctions were compared with those of couples who were placed on a one or two-month waiting list did demonstrate a clear beneficial impact of treatment (Heiman & LoPiccolo, 1983).

Unfortunately most comparative studies of sex therapy have had serious drawbacks (Warner & Bancroft, 1986). For example, most studies have included couples with different types of sexual dysfunction, without matching for type of dysfunction across treatment groups, treatment groups have usually not been matched for other important prognostic factors, some studies have used poor outcome criteria and nearly all lack long-term outcome data.

The most sophisticated studies have been conducted in the UK by Mathews *et al* (1976) and Dow (1983), both of which compared sex therapy with treatment by self-help instructions and very limited therapist contact. The study by Mathews and colleagues also included a third treatment condition, namely systematic desensitisation plus counselling. Both studies were subject to the design faults noted above. However, their results indicated more favourable outcome for couples who received sex therapy (although the differences in outcome between the groups were modest) and, if anything, the design faults would have resulted in an underestimation of true treatment differences.

The results of modifying the original treatment approach

Several studies have evaluated modifications of the original Masters and Johnson approach. This included daily treatment sessions with both partners and treatment by co-therapists (one of each gender).

Frequency of treatment sessions

The results of two comparative studies have favoured a less frequent than daily schedule. In the first study, twice-weekly treatment sessions resulted in better immediate outcome than daily treatment (Clement & Schmidt, 1983) and in the second, weekly treatment sessions were more effective than daily sessions (Heiman & LoPiccolo, 1983). With regard to less intensive treatment, little difference in outcome was found in one study between weekly and monthly treatment sessions for couples in which the woman had 'sexual unresponsiveness' (Carney *et al*, 1978), whereas in another study women with a similar problem appeared to benefit more from weekly than monthly treatment sessions (although the male partners in this study were happier with monthly sessions) (Mathews *et al*, 1983). Overall, there appears to be reasonable evidence in support of the now customary weekly treatment schedule (at least during the initial stages of therapy).

Single versus co-therapists

In one study, sex therapy appeared to be slightly (although non-significantly) more effective when conducted by co-therapists (Mathews *et al*, 1976). All other investigations which have addressed this question, however, have not found any difference in outcome between treatment provided by co-therapists and that provided by single therapists (Crowe *et al*, 1981; Clement & Schmidt, 1983; Mathews *et al*, 1983; LoPiccolo *et al*, 1985). While inclusion of insufficient numbers of couples in such investigations could explain this finding, the absence of difference between the effects of co-therapy and single therapy in several studies increases confidence in it. Also, the men in one study reported more ease of 'sexual expression' when treatment was provided by only one therapist (Mathews *et al*, 1983). Thus in terms of both efficacy and economy of treatment there appears to be no support for the use of co-therapists (although two therapists are useful for training purposes).

Gender of the therapist

A question often asked is whether there is an interactive effect in terms of treatment outcome between the gender of the therapist and that of the presenting partner. Two studies which have examined this question have found no evidence to suggest that the gender of the therapist makes any difference to outcome (Crowe *et al*, 1981; LoPiccolo *et al*, 1985). However, most clinicians believe that there are exceptions where, because of the nature of the sexual problem, one partner would benefit from being treated by a therapist of the same sex (Arentewicz & Schmidt, 1983).

Factors associated with outcome of sex therapy

Information has accumulated in recent years concerning prognostic factors associated with the results of sex therapy for couples. This information is important not only in the selection of couples for treatment but also in the design of treatment studies, where it is desirable to match treatment groups for important prognostic variables (Warner & Bancroft, 1986).

Factors associated with entry to treatment

Even after careful assessment, some couples who are offered treatment will not engage in the treatment programme. Of 200 consecutive couples seen in a sexual dysfunction clinic in Oxford, 55% were thought suitable for and offered sex therapy. However, almost 30% of

TABLE 13.3
Prognostic factors in sex therapy

The quality of the couple's general relationship.
The motivation of the partners (especially of the male partner).
Psychiatric disorder in either partner (some studies).
Physical attraction between the partners.
Early compliance with the treatment programme (homework assignments).

these never actually entered treatment and of those that did 46% failed to complete treatment. Completion of treatment was associated with higher initial ratings of motivation for treatment and quality of the general relationship and lower initial self-ratings of anxiety by the presenting partner (Catalan *et al*, 1990).

General prognostic factors in sex therapy

Factors associated with the outcome of sex therapy in series of couples with a variety of sexual dysfunctions have been reported by several authors (Lansky & Davenport, 1975; Mathews *et al*, 1976; O'Connor, 1976; Whitehead & Matthews, 1977; Hawton & Catalan, 1986). The factors are summarised in Table 13.3. A consistent finding is the importance of the quality of couples' general relationships for outcome. In a large series of couples Hawton & Catalan (1986) found that it was specifically the female partners' pre-treatment assessments of the relationship which were significantly associated with outcome. It appeared that female partners were more accurate in their assessments, which is obviously relevant to the assessment of couples before therapy. A further interesting sex difference found by these authors was that the male partners' apparent motivation for entering treatment was highly associated with outcome whereas that of the female partners was not. This finding, which is also relevant to assessment, could be interpreted in terms of either the model of sexuality embodied in sex therapy or the process of therapy itself being more acceptable to women than to men, so that the male partner's motivation is a major determinant of whether a couple are able to engage in and benefit from the therapy programme. Psychiatric disorder in either partner has been linked to poorer outcome in some studies (O'Connor, 1976) but not all (Hawton & Catalan, 1986).

Prognostic factors in specific disorders

Specific factors are likely to be relevant to the outcome of treatment of individual sexual dysfunctions.

Female dysfunctions

The outcome of female desire disorders seems to be associated particularly with factors concerning a couple's general relationship, interpersonal communication and attraction, sexual ease and confidence, and the male partner's motivation (Whitehead & Mathews, 1986; Hawton *et al*, 1991). No specific prognostic factors were found in a treatment study of women with vaginismus, probably because the overall results of treatment were so good (Hawton & Catalan, 1990).

Male dysfunctions

Less attention has been paid to the factors associated with the outcome of sex therapy for .couples in which the male partner has sexual dysfunction. Lower socio-economic status is related to non-compliance with treatment in couples who enter sex therapy because of the male partners' erectile dysfunction (Basoğlu *et al*, 1986; Hawton *et al*, 1992). Perhaps a modified approach or alternatives to sex therapy (e.g. physical treatments) should be considered for some couples of lower socio-economic status. Hawton *et al* (1992) also found that the outcome of couples treated for erectile dysfunction was associated with the female partners' pre-treatment sexual interest and enjoyment. These findings and those of couples with female sexual dysfunction emphasise the need for therapy to focus on the non-dysfunctional (or at least non-presenting) partner as well as the dysfunctional partner.

Long-term outcome following sex therapy

As noted earlier, Masters & Johnson (1970) reported outcome data five years after therapy for their couples who had a good immediate response to treatment. It is surprising that relatively little further work has been conducted regarding long-term outcome, although methodological difficulties that are associated with long-term follow-up studies in general (Hawton, 1993) may be one reason. These include low response rates, biased samples resulting from subjects with poor outcome being more liable to refuse to be followed up, and, in some studies, use of retrospective measures to evaluate post-treatment outcome and of postal questionnaires rather than interviews to assess long-term outcome.

Remarkably consistent findings emerged, however, from two relatively thorough (although uncontrolled) follow-up studies, a postal study in America by De Amicis and colleagues (1985) three years after treatment and an interview study in the UK by Hawton and colleagues (1986) of couples one to six years (mean of three years) following treatment. These indicated that the satisfactory short-term results of sex therapy for erectile dysfunction were reasonably well sustained in the longer term whereas those for premature ejaculation less often persisted. Men with low sexual desire had a very poor long-term prognosis.

The long-term results of treatment of female low sexual desire were often disappointing, whereas those for vaginismus were excellent. Increased satisfaction with the sexual relationship at follow-up was reported by couples in both the American and UK studies and in the UK study in particular there was evidence that the improved marital adjustment associated with sex therapy initially was largely sustained at follow-up. When relapses had occurred in this study, couples reported that communication between the partners about the problem, practising the techniques learned during sex therapy and an accepting attitude were helpful ways to deal with the difficulties.

Treatment of individuals without partners

Many individuals seek help for sexual dysfunction without partners, either because they do not have one or because the partner does not wish to attend (Catalan *et al*, 1991). Sex therapy approaches for individuals have gradually been developed (see Hawton, 1985, pp. 216–223 and Cole & Gregoire, 1993) and some have been evaluated. These include self-exploration and masturbation training for women with orgasmic dysfunction (LoPiccolo & Lobitz, 1972) and masturbation training, education and exploration of attitudes for men with retarded ejaculation or erectile dysfunction (Zilbergeld, 1975; Cole & Gregoire, 1993). Masturbation training can also be used in men with premature ejaculation (Zeiss, 1978) and self-exploration and examination of attitudes in women with vaginismus (Hawton, 1985, pp. 220–221).

Clearly it is difficult to assess how effective these approaches are because their success must primarily be determined in terms of sexual behaviour with a partner. However, a relevant study was conducted by Whitehead *et al* (1987) who investigated the treatment of couples who presented because of 'lack of sexual enjoyment or response in the female partner'. Half the couples were offered conjoint sex therapy and half individual treatment of the female partner, which included self-exploration and stimulation homework assignments and encouraging the woman to share the knowledge she gained from these with her partner. Considerable improvements occurred with both treatments and there was little difference between them regarding outcome of the sexual difficulties, although improvements regarding the partners' anxiety in sexual situations were greater with the conjoint treatment.

The conjoint approach seems to be the treatment of choice for couples with this problem but treatment of the female partner alone may be a reasonable alternative if both partners cannot attend. Evaluation of individual treatment of other sexual dysfunctions is still awaited.

Treatment in groups

Group treatment was popular in the 1970s and early 1980s, but now is rarely mentioned in the literature.

Women

The initial use of a group approach was with women with orgasmic dysfunction ('pre-orgasmic women'), utilising the masturbation training programme of LoPiccolo & Lobitz (1972) plus the benefits of group interaction and support. Such treatment appears to have had very satisfactory short-term outcome in terms of orgasmic experience (Barbach, 1974). The longer-term outcome in terms of generalisation of the gains from treatment to relationships with partners have varied between studies (Wallace & Barbach, 1974; Leiblum & Ersner-Hershfield, 1977). These groups appear to have been most successful for women under 35 years of age (Schneidman & McGuire, 1976). However, as noted earlier, in recent years there has been a very marked reduction in the numbers of women now seeking help because of orgasmic dysfunction so that there is now little or no need for such groups.

Men

Group treatments for men with erectile or ejaculation difficulties were also developed during the 1970s (Zilbergeld, 1975) and in an uncontrolled study Lobitz & Baker (1979) reported reasonable gains from this treatment. In a study in which social skills training and homework assignments concerning social interaction were incorporated into the group treatment of men with secondary erectile dysfunction, Reynolds *et al* (1981) found that the erectile function of these men improved more than that of similar men in a waiting-list control group. Recently, a study of group treatment of men with a variety of sexual dysfunctions has shown that therapeutic work focused on interpersonal functioning enhances treatment directed specifically at the sexual dysfunction (Stravynski *et al*, 1997).

Couples

Group treatment has been used quite extensively in the past to treat couples presenting with either the same sexual dysfunction or with mixed dysfunctions. Group treatment of couples in which both partners had sexual dysfunction was found to be as effective as individual couple treatment, although there was a suggestion of more rapid early progress of the couples treated in the group format (Golden *et al*, 1978). Similar outcomes were reported for group and individual couple treatment of couples in which the female partners had the main sexual problems (Duddle & Ingram, 1980). A relatively recent report of an uncontrolled study of group treatment of couples in which the women had secondary orgasmic dysfunction suggested that gains in orgasmic frequency were maintained 2–6 years after treatment, although measures of 'sexual harmony' and coital frequency had returned to near their baseline levels (Milan *et al*, 1988). This study also highlighted the importance of characteristics, sexual and otherwise, of the male partners for outcome. While all these studies had design faults, it can tentatively be concluded that group treatment of couples may be as effective as individual couple treatment. Unsurprisingly, however, the acceptability of group treatment for couples is far lower than for individual couple treatment (Duddle & Ingram, 1980). Issues of confidentiality, the dangers of attraction between partners of different couples and the difficulty therapists are likely to have in allowing for the different rates of progress by couples, must all further limit the applicability of group treatment of couples. Thus, although group therapy for couples with sexual dysfunctions might save valuable therapists' time (Kaplan *et al*, 1974), and even this is questionable (Duddle & Ingram, 1980), it now seems to have little or no use, perhaps in part reflecting changes in contemporary sexual attitudes.

Bibliotherapy

There has long been interest in the extent to which couples or individuals could be helped by means of instruction manuals (an approach termed 'bibliotherapy'), or other similar means (e.g. videotaped instructions). If reasonably effective, clearly this approach might have considerable benefits in terms of saving therapists' time. There have been several well-controlled studies of bibliotherapy. The overall conclusion seems to be that it can be effective in some couples (Matthews *et al*, 1976), but probably only in couples without major general relationship difficulties (Dow, 1983). However, limited contact with the therapist, either by telephone or face to face, appears to be necessary for success in either couple or individual treatment (Lowe &

Mikulas, 1975; Zeiss, 1978; Trudel & Proulx, 1987; Trudel & Laurin, 1988). This, of course, raises questions about the efficacy of self-help manuals for sexual problems in people who do not actually seek professional help and who therefore do not have support and guidance while following a programme. It may be that they are effective in people with minor difficulties.

Sex therapy combined with marital therapy

The importance of general relationship difficulties in relation to the outcome of sex therapy has already been noted. Therefore, a combined treatment approach might be more effective than either alone. In a study of couples with mixed sexual dysfunctions who received sex therapy and marital therapy separately (in a group format) in a cross-over design, sex therapy appeared to help both sexual and marital adjustment whereas marital therapy only helped marital adjustment (Hartman & Daly, 1983). However, those couples with poorer general marital adjustment at the outset failed to show the differential response to treatment in favour of sex therapy over marital therapy.

Subsequently, Zimmer (1987) studied the effect of providing marital therapy prior to sex therapy in seriously distressed couples (two-thirds having considered separation) in which the women had secondary sexual dysfunctions (i.e. they had previously not had problems). An impressive effect of the combined marital and sex therapy was found when compared with sex therapy preceded by placebo treatment. In contrast to Hartman & Daly's (1983) finding, during the course of marital therapy considerable benefits were found in the couples' sexual adjustment, whereas sex therapy alone appeared to have less impact on general relationships. The difference between the findings of the two studies is presumably explained by differences in the degree of general relationship disharmony in the couples in the two studies, Zimmer having specifically studied very distressed couples. The results of the second study support the growing trend for offering marital therapy before sex therapy for those couples presenting with sexual dysfunction but whose general relationships are disturbed.

Other applications of sex therapy and further treatments for sexual dysfunction

Sexual problems in victims of sexual abuse

Women who have suffered childhood and later sexual abuse often develop problems concerning sexual desire and arousal and may experience phobic or aversive reactions to sexual behaviour (Jehu, 1989). A fairly comprehensive treatment programme is usually required for such women. Jehu (1988) has described one such programme which is based on cognitive–behavioural principles and which includes sex therapy for the women and their partners along with treatment for mood and interpersonal problems. As one might expect, individual or group therapy of the women alone often seem to be necessary before conjoint sex therapy can be introduced (Douglas *et al*, 1989).

Sexual disorders associated with physical illness

Sexual dysfunctions are very common in people with physical illnesses (Schover & Jensen, 1988). While sex therapy, with its focus on communication and gradual rebuilding of a sexual relationship, is an attractive approach to such problems it is surprising how little attention has been paid to its use in this context. Nevertheless, clinical experience indicates that the use of such therapeutic strategies can be helpful for problems precipitated or maintained by physical illness (Schover & Jensen, 1988).

Sexual problems in alcohol abusers

Alcohol abuse often causes sexual problems in both sexes, but especially men, in whom erectile dysfunction, low sexual desire and ejaculatory problems are common and, as Farhner (1987) found, frequently persist even after effective treatment for alcohol abuse. Farhner evaluated treatment of such men in groups where they received education, role play in relation to social behaviour, and homework assignments, including masturbation training. At the end of treatment the men showed considerable improvements in sexual knowledge and attitudes, self-reported 'sociosexual behaviour' and sexual dysfunction compared with a control group. Perhaps such treatment should be a regular part of the overall treatment of severe alcohol abuse.

Use of hormones

Hormonal treatments of sexual problems have received a great deal of attention. While there is convincing evidence of the benefits of testosterone therapy for men with erectile dysfunction due to proven hypogonadism this does not seem to be helpful in men with psychogenic erectile problems (Davidson & Rosen, 1992). However, O'Carroll & Bancroft (1984) found that some men with low sexual drive but no evidence of hormonal abnormality were helped to some degree if they took a testosterone preparation. At one time there was a great deal of interest in the use of testosterone in the treatment of women with low sexual desire (Carney *et al*, 1978; Matthews *et al*, 1983; Dow & Gallagher, 1989). The upshot of these studies is that testosterone is ineffective, unless used in doses likely to cause unacceptable androgenisation. However, in post-menopausal women with low sexual drive, especially those who have undergone a surgical menopause (oophorectomy), testosterone does seem to have beneficial effects (Sherwin *et al*, 1985).

Physical treatments for erectile dysfunction

Recent years have seen a considerable expansion in physical methods of treatment for erectile dysfunction. Most important among these are intracavernosal injections of vasoactive drugs, vacuum devices and oral agents. The intracavernosal injections are usually of prostaglandin, although other drugs may be used (Gregoire, 1992). They are mostly indicated in organic erectile dysfunction but are being used more and more to treat psychogenic cases, partly because of the ever increasing demand for treatment of this problem and partly because urologists have increasingly taken on the treatment of men with erectile difficulties. Vacuum devices help produce erections by the creation of a vacuum in a plastic cylinder surrounding the penis by using a pump, following which the device can be removed, a constriction ring then maintaining the erection (Gregoire, 1993). While again this was developed for the treatment of organic erectile dysfunction, it is also being used for the treatment of psychogenic problems (Althof & Turner, 1992). Recently a remarkable breakthrough in the treatment of erectile dysfunction has occurred with the introduction of sildenafil (Goldstein *et al*, 1998). This drug, which is taken orally, facilitates erection through inhibition of an enzyme acting cyclic GMP, an important rate limiting enzyme in the nitric oxide cycle within the corpus cavernosum of the penis which mediates vasodilatation. Sildenafil and similar future compounds are likely to revolutionise the treatment of both organic and psychogenic erectile dysfunction (Rosen, 1998).

A very important aspect of treatment of erectile dysfunction with any of the physical agents is that failure to address the psychological needs of the patient, and especially of the partner (Speckens *et al*, 1995) is likely to result in poor outcome.

Conclusions

The treatment of sexual dysfunctions has undergone some remarkable changes in the past two and a half decades, with the introduction of sex therapy in the 1970s and of new physical treatments for erectile difficulties in the 1980s and 1990s being the most notable. Sex therapy has become an established treatment approach but changes in the types of problems being seen and particularly in their complexity has meant that it is often insufficient on its own and needs to be combined with other approaches (Zimmer, 1987; and see Leiblum & Rosen, 1988). There is still room for further research evaluations of this type of treatment, particularly to identify people for whom it is most helpful and to assess its value in specific conditions such as sexual disorders related to physical illness. The recently introduced treatments for erectile dysfunction, especially sildenafil, intracavernosal injections of vasoactive drugs and vacuum devices, have undoubtedly broadened and improved the treatment of men with erectile dysfunction. There is, however, a considerable need for further investigation of the psychological aspects of such treatments, especially the extent to which attention to psychological and interpersonal factors may improve the outcome.

One further important aspect of the treatment of sexual dysfunction is the extent of opportunity, or lack of it, that psychiatrists in training have for developing skills in this area, with regard to both assessment and treatment of sexual difficulties. The skills can be taught effectively (Hawton, 1980) and can be useful with regard to treatment of other problems. However, regrettably very few psychiatric trainees appear to have opportunities for such training. This is an important deficiency in current training programmes which ought to be addressed.

References

ALTHOF, S. E. & TURNER, L. A. (1992) Self-injection therapy and external vacuum devices in the treatment of erectile dysfunction: methods and outcome. In *Erectile Disorders: Assessment and Treatment* (eds R. Rosen & S. Leiblum), pp. 283–309. New York: Guilford Press.

ARENTEWICZ, G. & SCHMIDT, G. (eds) (1983) *The Treatment of Sexual Disorders.* New York: Basic Books.

BANCROFT, J. (1989) *Human Sexuality and its Problems.* 2nd edn. Edinburgh: Churchill Livingstone.

——— & COLES, L. (1976) Three years' experience in a sexual problems clinic. *British Medical Journal,* i, 1575–1577.

BARBACH, L. G. (1974) Group treatment of pre-orgasmic women. *Journal of Sex and Marital Therapy,* 1, 139–145.

BASOĞLU, M., YETKIN, N., SERCAN, M., *et al* (1986) Patterns of attrition for psychological and pharmacological treatment of male sexual dysfunction: implications for sex therapy research and cross-cultural perspectives. *Sexual and Marital Therapy,* 1, 179–189.

CARNEY, A., BANCROFT, J. & MATHEWS, A. (1978) Combination of hormonal and psychological treatment for female sexual unresponsiveness: a comparative study. *British Journal of Psychiatry*, **132**, 339–346.

CATALAN, J., HAWTON, K. & DAY, A. (1990) Couples referred to a sexual dysfunction clinic: psychological and physical morbidity. *British Journal of Psychiatry*, **156**, 61–67.

———, ——— & ——— (1991) Individuals presenting without partners at a sexual dysfunction clinic: psychological and physical morbidity and treatment offered. *Sexual and Marital Therapy*, **6**, 15–23.

CLEMENT, U. & SCHMIDT, G. (1983) The outcome of couple therapy for sexual dysfunctions using three different formats. *Journal of Sex and Marital Therapy*, **9**, 67–78.

COLE, M. & GREGOIRE, A. (1993) The impotent man without a partner. In *Impotence: An Integrated Approach to Clinical Practice* (eds A. Gregoire & J. P. Pryor), pp. 215–227. Edinburgh: Churchill Livingstone.

CROWE, M. J., GILLAN, P. & GOLOMBOK, S. (1981) Form and content in the conjoint treatment of sexual dysfunction: a controlled study. *Behaviour Research and Therapy*, **19**, 47–54.

DAVIDSON, J. M. & ROSEN, R. C. (1992) Hormonal determinants of erectile dysfunction. In *Erectile Disorders: Assessment and Treatment* (eds R. Rosen & S. R. Leiblum), pp. 72–95. New York: Guilford.

DE AMICIS, L. A., GOLDBERG, D. C., LOPICCOLO, J., *et al* (1985) Clinical follow-up of couples treated for sexual dysfunction. *Archives of Sexual Behavior*, **14**, 467–489.

DOUGLAS, A. R., MATSON, I. C. & HUNTER, S. (1989) Sex therapy for women incestuously abused as children. *Sexual and Marital Therapy*, **4**, 143–159.

DOW, M. G. T. (1983) A controlled comparative evaluation of conjoint counselling and self-help behavioural treatment for sexual dysfunction. Unpublished Ph.D. Thesis, University of Glasgow.

——— & GALLAGHER, J. (1989) A controlled study of combined hormonal and psychological treatment for sexual unresponsiveness in women. *British Journal of Clinical Psychology*, **28**, 201–212.

DUDDLE, C. M. (1975) The treatment of marital psycho-sexual problems. *British Journal of Psychiatry*, **127**, 169–170.

——— & INGRAM, A. (1980) Treating sexual dysfunction in couples groups. In *Medical Sexology* (eds R. Forleo & W. Pasini), pp. 598–605. North Holland: Elsevier.

FAHRNER, E. M. (1987) Sexual dysfunction in male alcohol addicts: prevalence and treatment. *Archives of Sexual Behavior*, **3**, 247–257.

GILLAN, P. (1987) *Sex Therapy Manual*. Oxford: Blackwell Scientific.

GOLDEN, J. S., PRICE, S., HEINRICH, A. G., *et al* (1978) Group vs. couple treatment of sexual dysfunctions. *Archives of Sexual Behavior*, **7**, 593–602.

GOLDSTEIN, I., LUE, T. F., PADMA-NATHAN, H., *et al* (1998) Oral sildenafil in the treatment of erectile dysfunction. *New England Journal of Medicine*, **338**, 1397–1404.

GREGOIRE, A. (1992) New treatments for erectile impotence. *British Journal of Psychiatry*, **160**, 315–326.

——— (1993) External vacuum devices for the treatment of impotence. In *Impotence: an Integrated Approach to Clinical Practice* (eds A. Gregoire & J. P. Pryor), pp. 185–190. Edinburgh: Churchill Livingstone.

HARTMAN, L. M. & DALY, E. M. (1983) Relationship factors in the treatment of sexual dysfunction. *Behaviour Research and Therapy*, **21**, 153–160.

HAWTON, K. (1980) Training in the management of psychosexual problems. *Medical Education*, **14**, 214–218.

——— (1985) *Sex Therapy: A Practical Guide*. Oxford: Oxford University Press.

——— (1987) Sexual problems. In *Oxford Textbook of Medicine* (eds J. Ledingham, D. Weatherall & D. Warrell), pp. 25.40–25.43. Oxford: Oxford University Press.

——— (1989) Sexual dysfunctions. In *Cognitive Behaviour Therapy for Psychiatric Problems* (eds K. Hawton, P. Salkovskis, J. Kirk, *et al*), pp. 370–405. Oxford: Oxford University Press.

—— (1993) Long-term follow-up studies of psychological treatments. In *Research Methods in Psychiatry: A Beginner's Guide* (eds C. Freeman & P. Tyrer), pp. 233–246. London: Gaskell.

—— & CATALAN, J. (1986) Prognostic factors in sex therapy. *Behaviour Research and Therapy*, **24**, 377–385.

—— & —— (1990) Sex therapy for vaginismus: characteristics of couples and treatment outcome. *Sexual and Marital Therapy*, **5**, 39–48.

——, ——, MARTIN, P., *et al* (1986) Long-term outcome of sex therapy. *Behaviour Research and Therapy*, **24**, 665–675.

——, —— & FAGG, J. (1991) Low sexual desire: sex therapy results and prognostic factors. *Behaviour Research and Therapy*, **29**, 217–224.

——, —— & —— (1992) Sex therapy for erectile dysfunction: characteristics of couples, treatment outcome, and prognostic factors. *Archives of Sexual Behavior*, **21**, 161–175.

HEIMAN, J. R. & LOPICCOLO, J. (1983) Clinical outcome of sex therapy. *Archives of General Psychiatry*, **40**, 443–449.

JEHU, D. (1988) *Beyond Sexual Abuse: Therapy with Women who were Childhood Victims*. Chichester: Wiley.

—— (1989) Sexual dysfunctions among women clients who were sexually abused in childhood. *Behavioural Psychotherapy*, **17**, 53–70.

KAPLAN, H. S., KOHL, R. N., POMEROY, W. B., *et al* (1974) Group treatment of premature ejaculation. *Archives of Sexual Behavior*, **3**, 443–452.

KITZINGER, S. (1985) *Woman's Experience of Sex*. London: Penguin.

LANSKY, M. R. & DAVENPORT, A. E. (1975) Difficulties in brief conjoint treatment of sexual dysfunction. *American Journal of Psychiatry*, **132**, 177–179.

LEIBLUM, S. R. & ERSNER-HERSHFIELD, R. (1977) Sexual enhancement groups for dysfunctional women: an evaluation. *Journal of Sex and Marital Therapy*, **3**, 139–152.

—— & ROSEN, R. C. (1988) *Sexual Desire Disorders*. New York: Guilford Press.

LOBITZ, W. C. & BAKER, E. L. (1979) Group treatment of single males with erectile dysfunction. *Archives of Sexual Behavior*, **8**, 127–138.

LOPICCOLO, J. & LOBITZ, W. C. (1972) The role of masturbation in the treatment of orgasmic dysfunction. *Archives of Sexual Behavior*, **2**, 163–171.

——, HEIMAN, J. R., HOGAN, D. R., *et al* (1985) Effectiveness of single therapists versus cotherapy teams in sex therapy. *Journal of Consulting and Clinical Psychology*, **53**, 287–294.

LOWE, J. C. & MIKULAS, W. L. (1975) Use of written material in learning self-control of premature ejaculation. *Psychological Reports*, **37**, 295–298.

MASTERS, W. H. & JOHNSON, V. E. (1970) *Human Sexual Inadequacy*. Boston: Little, Brown.

MATHEWS, A., BANCROFT, J., WHITEHEAD, A., *et al* (1976) The behavioural treatment of sexual inadequacy: a comparative study. *Behaviour Research and Therapy*, **14**, 427–436.

——, WHITEHEAD, A. & KELLETT, J. (1983) Psychological and hormonal factors in the treatment of female sexual dysfunction. *Psychological Medicine*, **13**, 83–92.

MILAN, R. J. Jr, KILMANN, P. R. & BOLAND, J. P. (1988) Treatment outcome of secondary orgasmic dysfunction: a two- to six-year follow-up. *Archives of Sexual Behavior*, **17**, 463–480.

O'CARROLL, R. & BANCROFT, J. (1984) Testosterone therapy for low sexual interest and erectile dysfunction in men: a controlled study. *British Journal of Psychiatry*, **145**, 146–151.

O'CONNOR, J. F. (1976) Sexual problems, therapy, and prognostic factors. In *Clinical Management of Sexual Disorders* (ed. J. K. Meyer), pp. 74–98. Baltimore: Williams and Wilkins.

REYNOLDS, B. S., COHEN, B. D., SCHOCHET, B. V., *et al* (1981) Dating skills training in the group treatment of erectile dysfunction for men without partners. *Journal of Sex and Marital Therapy*, **7**, 184–194.

ROSEN, R. C. (1998) Sildenafil: medical advance or media event? *Lancet*, **351**, 1599–1600.

SCHNEIDMAN, B. & McGUIRE, L. (1976) Group therapy for non-orgasmic women: two age levels. *Archives of Sexual Behavior*, **3**, 239–247.

SCHOVER, L. R. & LOPICCOLO, J. (1982) Treatment effectiveness for dysfunctions of sexual desire. *Journal of Sex and Marital Therapy*, **8**, 179–197.

—— & JENSEN, S. B. (1988) *Sexuality and Chronic Illness: A Comprehensive Approach.* New York: Guilford Press.

SHERWIN, B. B., GELFAND, M. M. & BRENDER, W. (1985) Androgen enhances sexual motivation in females: a prospective, crossover study of sex steroid administration in the surgical menopause. *Psychosomatic Medicine,* **47**, 339–351.

SPECKENS, A. E. M., HENGEVELD, M. W., LYCKLAM À NIJEHOLT, G. A. B., *et al* (1995) Differences between partners of men with non-organic erectile dysfunction and partners of men with organic erectile dysfunction. *Archives of Sexual Behavior,* **24**, 157–172.

SPENCE, S. H. (1991) *Psychosexual Therapy: A Cognitive–Behavioural Approach.* London: Chapman and Hall.

STRAVYNSKI, A., GAUDETTE, G., LESAGE, A., *et al* (1997) The treatment of sexually dysfunctional men without partners: a controlled study of three behavioural group treatments. *British Journal of Psychiatry,* **170**, 338–344.

STUART, F. M., HAMMOND, D. C. & PETT, M. A. (1987) Inhibited sexual desire in women. *Archives of Sexual Behavior,* **16**, 91–106.

TRUDEL, G. & PROULX, S. (1987) Treatment of premature ejaculation by bibliotherapy: an experimental study. *Sexual and Marital Therapy,* **2**, 163–167.

—— & LAURIN, F. (1988) The effects of bibliotherapy on orgasmic dysfunction and couple interactions: an experimental study. *Sexual and Marital Therapy,* **3**, 223–228.

WALLACE, D. M. & BARBACH, L. G. (1986) Sex therapy outcome research: a reappraisal of methodology. 2. Methodological considerations – the importance of prognostic variability. *Psychological Medicine,* **16**, 855–863.

——, —— & MEMBERS OF THE EDINBURGH HUMAN SEXUALITY GROUP (1987) A regional clinical service for sexual problems: a three-year survey. *Sexual and Marital Therapy,* **2**, 115–126.

WARNER, P. & BANCROFT, J. (1986) Sex therapy outcome research: a reappraisal of methodology. 2. Methodological considerations – the importance of prognostic variability. *Psychological Medicine,* **16**, 855–863.

WHITEHEAD, A. & MATHEWS, A. (1977) Attitude change during behavioural treatment of sexual inadequacy. *British Journal of Social and Clinical Psychology,* **16**, 275–281.

—— & —— (1986) Factors related to successful outcome in the treatment of sexually unresponsive women. *Psychological Medicine,* **16**, 373–378.

——, —— & RAMAGE, M. (1987) The treatment of sexually unresponsive women: a comparative evaluation. *Behaviour Research and Therapy,* **25**, 195–205.

WORLD HEALTH ORGANIZATION (1992) *The Tenth Revision of the International Classification of Mental and Behavioural Disorders: Clinical Descriptions and Diagnostic Guidelines* (ICD–10). Geneva: WHO.

WRIGHT, J., PERREAULT, R. & MATHIEU, M. (1977) The treatment of sexual dysfunction. *Archives of General Psychiatry,* **34**, 881–890.

ZEISS, R. A. (1978) Self-directed treatment for premature ejaculation. *Journal of Consulting and Clinical Psychology,* **46**, 1234–1241.

ZILBERGELD, B. (1975) Group treatment of sexual dysfunction in men without partners. *Journal of Sex and Marital Therapy,* **1**, 204–214.

—— (1980) *Men and Sex.* London: Fontana.

—— & EVANS, M. (1980) The inadequacy of Masters and Johnson. *Psychology Today,* August, 29–43.

ZIMMER, D. (1987) Does marital therapy enhance the effectiveness of treatment for sexual dysfunction? *Journal of Sex and Marital Therapy,* **13**, 193–209.

14 Stress and trauma

STUART TURNER

Traumatic events in the world today are both common and increasingly widely recognised as causes of distress. In the USA, the Vietnam war experience led directly to the increased recognition of traumatic stress reactions, followed in 1980 by the inclusion of post-traumatic stress disorder (PTSD) in DSM–III (American Psychiatric Association, 1980). Similarly, in the UK, the major disasters affecting, for example, the Bradford City Football Stadium (Eaton, 1985), the Herald of Free Enterprise Ferry (Johnston, 1993), the King's Cross Station (Turner *et al*, 1993) and the Piper Alpha Oil Rig (Alexander, 1993) have all inspired media interest and service developments for survivors. This has also stimulated further the work with other victim groups including those who have experienced child physical or sexual abuse, assault, rape, political violence including torture, or who have witnessed any of these (Wilson & Raphael, 1993). It is no coincidence, therefore, that there should be new international societies or journals specialising in this field of work.

Of course, traumatic events as causes of psychological reactions have long been recognised. In his diaries in 1667, five months after the fire of London, Pepys records some of the intrusive reactions which disturbed his own sleep.

> it is strange to think how to this very day I cannot sleep at night without great terrors of fire; and this very night could not sleep till almost two in the morning through thoughts of fire. (Latham & Matthews, 1970–1983)

Trimble (1981) traces the history of soldier's heart and railway spine – both examples of traumatic stress reactions. The disorder was reported in the American Civil War and, under another misleading name 'shell shock', was an important element of the tragedy of the First World War. Horowitz (1976) has commented that the phrase 'everyone has his breaking point' comes from early combat experience. Following the Second World War, the 'concentration-camp syndrome' (Eitinger, 1980) was a further manifestation and the largely neglected histories of

Far East prisoners of war (FEPOWs) provide yet more evidence of this psychological reaction to overwhelming physical and psychological abuse.

The main investigations of prevalence have largely derived from work in the USA. In one large-scale project based on detailed face-to-face interviews, the National Vietnam Veterans Readjustment Study (Schlenger *et al*, 1992), over 15% of men and over 8% of women who had served in Vietnam were identified as suffering from PTSD 15 or more years after their military service. The high prevalence and the persistence of symptoms were both dramatically illustrated. The authors estimate that about 480 000 Vietnam veterans have PTSD. This report also underlined the important role of exposure to combat and other types of war zone stress in determining current status. In comparisons with veterans of the same era who did not serve in Vietnam (prevalence 2.5% and 1.1%) and a civilian Vietnam-era group (prevalence 1.2% and 0.3%), the effect of Vietnam combat exposure is apparent. However, even the smaller percentages in non-combat groups indicate large numbers of people on a national scale and, perhaps of more importance, these numbers are demonstrably subject to increase at times of conflict or increased rates of violence.

Traumatic stress reactions

Although a range of potential conditions are possible following traumatic events – varying from simple 'working through' to permanent personality change, two appear to be highly specific reactions to trauma.

PTSD is a syndrome characterised by six elements (DSM–IV; American Psychiatric Association, 1994). First, there is an experience of a major trauma (e.g. serious injury, threat of death) associated with a response of intense fear, helplessness or horror. This is a compromise position adopted in the latest set of criteria and incorporates both objective and subjective elements into the criterion for trauma intensity. Second, there is persistent reexperiencing in the form of thoughts, nightmares (often associated with marked sleep disturbance), or dissociative flashbacks in which the victim feels as if he or she is vividly reliving the traumatic experience. Third, there is persistent avoidance of external reminders or suppression of responses to internal prompts ('emotional numbing'). Fourth, there is increased arousal and hypervigilance. Fifth, the condition is chronic, lasting at least a month. Finally, the disturbance causes clinically significant distress or impairment.

In ICD–10, PTSD is described in similar terms, but in addition, another syndrome is included reflecting the enduring personality change sometimes seen after catastrophic experiences. This reaction is demonstrated in a number of ways, for example, a hostile or mistrustful attitude towards the world, social withdrawal, feelings of emptiness or hopelessness, chronic feelings of being on edge or estrangement. However in this chapter the emphasis will be on PTSD.

Both PTSD and enduring personality change after catastrophic experience are examples of narrow psychological constructs. Following one form of complex trauma (torture), Turner & Gorst-Unsworth (1993) have proposed a complex series of events including not only PTSD but also depressive reactions, somatoform disorders and alterations of fundamental attitudes and beliefs. However, even this list is incomplete and problems with dissociation (especially in the acute phase reaction), eating disorders, other emotional and conduct disorders, borderline and multiple personality, substance misuse, phobias and general anxiety disorders have all been described in association with PTSD following a wide range of traumatic events (Wilson & Raphael, 1993).

Trauma typology

Traumatic events can have a range of effects over wide time frames and varying degrees of pervasiveness. Usually, but not always, these are negative sequelae and may be associated with long-term disability. The paradigm for a simple trauma is a single event affecting an adult of previously good personal adjustment and development. Elsewhere in this book, sexual abuse in childhood is described and here it is obvious that not only is the trauma especially intrusive and often recurrent, it also stands to affect personal development with a greater emphasis, for example, on dissociative elements when compared with the reaction seen in adult survivors. Torture is another example of a complex trauma in which the context (e.g. threat or violence to family and friends) as well as the event itself has to be considered. In planning therapeutic interventions, it is obviously important first to assess the nature of the reaction.

There has also been a debate concerning the relative importance of personality and trauma exposure in determining the subsequent psychological reaction. On the one hand, McFarlane (1989) has reported that high neuroticism is associated more closely with PTSD than exposure in the Australian Ash Wednesday Bush Fires; on the other, Shore *et al* (1986) have demonstrated following the Mount St Helens volcano eruption, a clear dose–response relationship. Common sense suggests that the traumatic event is of primary importance

Diagnosis (continuous)

(without a trauma, there cannot be a traumatic stress reaction), but personal predisposition is one of the factors (Rachman, 1980) which determines the likelihood of any individual reacting following a mild to moderate impact trauma. Following a very severe trauma, anyone is at risk of developing problems (Davidson & Foa, 1993). This applies both to short-term and long-term traumatic stress reactions.

The apparent reluctance to acknowledge the primary role of the (psychological) traumatic event may be attributable to a combination of reluctance to accept a psychological aetiology (Trimble, 1981) and an over-reliance on the central role of early development, within the psychoanalytic literature, in the production of psychopathological reactions (Brett, 1993). Following the Second World War, many people were not compensated for psychological damage, partly because of the (incorrect) assumption that neurotic symptoms inevitably reflected a primary intrinsic weakness in the victim rather than a genuine response of a normal person to overwhelming trauma (Eitinger, 1980).

Finally, there are questions concerning the universality of the trauma reaction. It is impossible to be dogmatic in the absence of complete investigation, but it seems probable that stereotyped responses such as PTSD are more likely to develop to similar degrees following comparable traumatic events in widely different cultures than somatisation or attitude change which, following trauma, are more likely to be strongly culturally determined. This may reflect differences in the nature of the reaction with PTSD resulting from an overwhelmed common psychological process (described in the next section) and the other two examples arising from more culturally determined secondary adaptive or coping strategies.

why PTSD universal

Psychology of PTSD

One way of understanding the basis of PTSD is to examine a postulated normal psychological mechanism. It is suggested that each of us carries an internal (cognitive) representation of the external world, on which we base predictions about future events. One example of this is the ability to plan ahead and rehearse (in our minds) several options before making a final decision, an important human attribute. Sometimes, the set of predictions may not be realised. When this happens, the internal representation of the outside world is demonstrated to be incorrect and has to be changed. This process, whereby the internal representation (of the world or of self within the world) is amended, is called cognitive processing. For more extreme changes, this process may have to take place in stages. Following a bereavement, for example, it may take many months for the survivor to adapt to a world in which he or she is alone.

All the familiar places must be experienced afresh, no longer including the dead person.

There is typically an emotional component to this process of change – not always a negative emotion. Successes require processing as much as losses but, in the former, the emotional context is likely to be pleasure or happiness. Traumatic stressors are events which act upon people to produce intense pressure or tension; they are usually associated with the negative emotions of fear and sadness. In normal circumstances, the emotional reaction gradually declines and each subsequent recall of this feeling is rather less intense until eventually as a new equilibrium is reached, so the emotional reaction fades completely.

Faced with events which are perceived to be more traumatic, this adaptive mechanism may be overwhelmed. The initial emotional reaction may be so intense that the only viable reaction is to attempt to prevent or avoid these painful feelings. This may be achieved by avoiding places or objects that remind the person about the trauma, or through suppression of emotions in general – emotional numbing. These defensive reactions will rarely be completely successful, so the survivor of this sort of major catastrophe is left with painful intrusive recollections which alternate with defensive avoidance. This cyclical reaction of intrusion and avoidance is the central element of PTSD. It is possible that as the emotions are suppressed, because they are too extreme, they are not held in awareness and do not decline. The condition becomes chronic and may be frankly disabling. In addition, there may be significant and permanent challenges to personal meaning and value systems.

Rachman (1980), in his seminal paper, has described the situations which stand to affect the concept he styles as 'emotional processing'. For example, he suggests that sudden, intense, dangerous, uncontrollable, unpredictable, irregular, traumatic stimuli are likely to cause more difficulties in emotional processing. Other factors which may be important include personal state (e.g. fatigue, sleeplessness, illness), activity (e.g. concurrent stressors, heat, noise) and personality (neuroticism, introversion, inner-oriented). So PTSD may be construed as a failure to complete the task of 'emotional processing'. Rachman also outlines the range of situations likely to be beneficial to a person in this condition; chiefly these involve a need for space and time to approach the distressing memories.

Therapy

Any therapeutic intervention has to be appropriate to the condition(s) being treated and must therefore follow a sufficiently detailed assessment. A range of approaches have been adopted although very few have been subjected to outcome evaluation (Solomon *et al*, 1992). In their comprehensive review of PTSD treatments, of 255 articles identified, only 11 met the criterion of being randomised clinical trials which included a systematic assessment of PTSD. Most accounts were simple case histories, likely to be a very unreliable source, especially in this emotive area, on which to base strategies for development of treatment programmes. Even where systematic evaluation has taken place, variations in traumatic complexity may mean that results should not be over-generalised and that some methodologies work more satisfactorily with some groups of survivors, or within some cultures, than others.

Psychological approaches

Many different forms of psychotherapy have been applied to PTSD. There are some important theoretical differences but in practice many similarities in content. Direct therapeutic exposure (DTE) appears to be one important (possibly essential) component of a psychological therapy for PTSD in adults (Keane *et al*, 1992) and children (Saigh, 1992). This can include all variants of *in vivo* and imaginal exposure. Based on a conditioning paradigm, the triggers for intrusive or arousal phenomena can be treated as any other triggers for an anxiety response. Both systematic desensitisation and flooding, for example, have been used as treatments for PTSD.

All six controlled studies identified by Solomon *et al* (1992) indicate benefit from DTE (Peniston, 1986; Keane *et al*, 1989; Cooper & Clum, 1989; Brom *et al*, 1989; Boudewyns & Hyer, 1990; Foa *et al*, 1991). Indeed, in one form or another the 'trauma story' has been seen as a central element of therapy in most approaches. Since the exposure technique employed would often consist of vivid re-telling of the trauma story, if DTE is effective, then it is likely also to be a non-specific factor producing benefit in other therapeutic approaches with different theoretical bases.

Vaughan & Tarrier (1992) illustrate this approach in image habituation training. In this, the patient generates a verbal description of the traumatic event and records this on audiotape. After an initial training session with the therapist, homework sessions of self-directed exposure are employed in which the patient attempts to visualise the traumatic event in response to listening to the audiotape. In their uncontrolled study, significant reductions in anxiety between and within homework sessions were obtained, suggesting that habituation both occurred and was responsible for improvement.

Both Solomon *et al* (1992) and Keane *et al* (1992) point to differential effects of DTE on symptoms of PTSD. Flooding, and possibly other variants of exposure, appear to be most effective in intrusion and arousal symptoms and have less effect on avoidance phenomena. Pitman *et al* (1991) also point out that flooding may produce severe complications, including exacerbation of depression, relapse of alcohol misuse and precipitation of panic disorder. In addition, more complex trauma reactions, for example including shame, guilt and sadness, may not extinguish in the same way as anxiety and adjunctive or additional methods may also be required.

It is possible that behavioural techniques (DTE) may prove to be most effective in combination with a cognitive therapy (Thompson *et al*, 1995). This may be particularly relevant with more complex trauma reactions. Stress inoculation training (SIT) is a combination of several techniques – muscle relaxation, thought-stopping, breathing control, communication skills and guided self-dialogue (Solomon *et al*, 1992). The cognitive restructuring includes modification of current thinking and underlying cognitive assumptions as well as rehearsal of coping skills and discussion of stress reactions. Foa *et al* (1991) found SIT to be the most effective short-term therapy for PTSD, although DTE was superior at later follow-up (3.5 months). Cognitive processing therapy, based on an information processing theory of PTSD, has also been found to be effective in comparison with a waiting list control group (Resick & Schnicke, 1992).

In a controlled study of psychodynamic therapy, Brom *et al* (1989) found that this was associated with significant symptom reduction compared with the control group. In this study, which also investigated hypnotherapy and desensitisation, the dynamic psychotherapy differed from the other two approaches in achieving more reduction in avoidance symptoms. However in general, this approach has been inadequately evaluated for definitive conclusions to be drawn. Hypnotherapy has attracted media attention recently with interest in the possibilities of inducing false memories and the legal consequences for client, alleged perpetrator and therapist; although it has also been suggested that it is a more effective means of abreaction than drugs (Putnam, 1992).

It is likely that those complex and childhood (developmental) traumas which have more pervasive consequences require a different approach from simple adult traumas. There does seem to be scope for more developed and evaluated cognitive or insight-oriented approaches, with relatively less reliance on DTE, in these circumstances (although DTE is still likely to be an important component).

In working with survivors of torture, for example, a technique called 'Testimony' has been used and adapted widely (Cienfuegos & Monelli,

1983; Jensen & Agger, 1988). This typically starts with one or two preliminary sessions, then continues with a detailed reconstruction of the events during torture. A tape recorder may be used to record the detailed history, the typed transcript providing the starting point for the subsequent session. A long document (possibly over 100 pages) is produced and worked through for accuracy. This appears to have two key beneficial effects. In the first, there is detailed exposure to memories and triggers related to the torture experience. The DTE criterion is met. In the second, there is inevitably a process of perceptual change, with the survivor coming to regard the events and his/her role within them in a different light. The therapist actively encourages a reframing of the trauma, especially working on issues such as apparent choice and subsequent guilt reactions. This cognitive element is likely to be at least as important as DTE in overall symptom reduction.

Other therapeutic measures have been tried, including the usual range of group, individual and family therapies. A specific technique, eye movement desensitisation (Shapiro, 1995), has attracted a great deal of interest. This is a curious technique, derived originally from personal experience, which in its original form involved having the person recall a traumatic experience, with thoughts of being out of control and aware of the physical sensations of anxiety, while visually tracking the therapist's index finger, which was moved rhythmically back and forth across the line of vision from left to right 30–35 cm from the person's face, at a rate of two back and forth movements per second. The back and forth movements were repeated in sets of 12–14. This procedure has been demonstrated in controlled trials to be effective (summarised in Shapiro, 1995 and Turner *et al*, 1996). This is a rapidly developing area with new evidence emerging all the time (e.g. Scheck *et al*, 1998). The most substantial question, however, is not to do with effectiveness in general but concerns the reason for effectiveness. This is a method which includes many elements shown to be important in other therapeutic modalities, especially cognitive–behaviour therapy. It now no longer seems that eye movements are an essential part of the process and other modifications have been introduced. Could it be that this is simply a good, manualised approach with commendable rigour in training (Hyer & Brandsma, 1997)? Further basic scientific investigation is required: in the meantime this is a useful approach.

Biological approaches

There are several excellent reviews of the biological aspects of PTSD which underline the importance of understanding trauma not just as a psychological but as a psychobiological event with a number of potentially long-term neurophysiological effects (see Davidson, 1992; Solomon *et al*, 1992). As a consequence, it is hardly surprising that psychopharmacological approaches should have been considered or that these should have some evidence of effectiveness.

Davidson (1992) identifies six goals of pharmacotherapy in chronic PTSD:

(1) reduction of phasic intrusive symptoms
(2) improvement of avoidance symptoms
(3) reduction of tonic hyperarousal
(4) relief of depression, anhedonia
(5) improvement of impulse regulation
(6) control of acute dissociative and psychotic features.

Some agents would be expected to be more effective in some of these areas than others.

Tricyclic antidepressants have been shown to be effective in PTSD (Frank *et al*, 1988; Davidson *et al*, 1990, 1993). One of the few negative studies (Reist *et al*, 1989) was of short duration (4 weeks) and found improvement restricted to depressive symptoms. Davidson *et al* (1990) also found early recovery in depression scores; this raises the possibility that recovery is primarily due to improvement in comorbid depression. However, Davidson *et al* (1993) found that a good response of PTSD to amitriptyline was correlated with lower baseline levels of depression, neuroticism, anxiety, impaired concentration, somatic symptoms, guilt and PTSD symptoms. Davidson (1992) concludes that tricyclic antidepressants have modest but clinically meaningful effects on PTSD and are well-tolerated. It seems that a longer trial of treatment is required (8 weeks) to exclude a beneficial effect. A curious feature from these studies is the almost total lack of response to placebo in chronic PTSD (Davidson, 1992; Solomon *et al*, 1992).

More recently, there has been interest in the newer selective serotonin reuptake inhibitor antidepressant drugs. Nagy *et al* (1993) found improvements in all elements of PTSD in an open prospective 10-week trial of fluoxetine, with 19 of 27 patients with combat-related PTSD completing more than three weeks. De-Boer *et al* (1992) found modest improvements over a 12-week open trial of fluvoxamine, but this was a group with very long-term trauma reactions (Dutch Second World War resistance veterans). In another open trial, McDougle *et al* (1991) also reported benefit in 13 of 20 combat veterans from fluoxetine.

Monoamine oxidase inhibitors (MAOIs) have also been investigated with mixed results (Frank *et al*, 1988; Shestatsky *et al*, 1988). In the positive study, phenelzine appeared somewhat more effective than imipramine (Frank *et al*, 1988). Again it is possible that the shorter duration (4 weeks) of the other, negative, study may have explained the lack of treatment effect. The side-effects and dietary restrictions of MAOI drugs usually limit their attractiveness to people with PTSD, although there is a hope that newer drugs may be less troublesome and more effective.

Other drugs investigated have included alprazolam (effective in reducing general anxiety symptoms but not PTSD; Braun *et al*, 1990), and there have been reports of effects from carbamazepine, beta-blockers, clonidine, other benzodiazepines, lithium carbonate and neuroleptics. The available evidence suggests that these are not generally useful drugs, limited either by risk of dependence, risk of misuse, side-effects or lack of evidence of efficacy.

In their review, Solomon *et al* (1992) point out that those studies which used standardised measures of PTSD showed greater recovery. There is at least a theoretical possibility that the measures of PTSD might themselves have been therapeutic and this is the impression from at least one more recent study (unpublished data). Both Solomon *et al* (1992) and Davidson (1992) point to the need to assess over a longer rather than a shorter period as some of the studies had been restricted to 4 weeks (Reist *et al*, 1989); similarly the effects of subsequent withdrawal are worthy of further investigation.

Prevention — still controversial

Perhaps one of the most exciting opportunities in this area is in preventative work. There is a long history of using drugs in the acute setting either for abreaction or sedation (Davidson, 1992). SIT has also been used as a preventative manoeuvre together with social support (Keane *et al*, 1992).

However, most interest centres on a range of early psychological interventions, targeted especially at emergency services personnel (Mitchell & Dyregrov, 1993). This is a controversial area in which early clinical claims have not been supported by systematic research. At this stage, no firm guidance can be offered. It is likely that acknowledgement of trauma, effective support for practical difficulties, accessible information and early access to treatment for the minority with severe problems will prove to be helpful. The status of psychological debriefing is less clear-cut.

Organisational issues

Based on this opportunity to provide early interventions as well as effective treatments for established PTSD, a service is required which can also operate at these different levels. A first-line response, possibly including routine debriefing and short-term support or psychological treatment should be widely available. This could be delivered by mental health and social work liaison services working into accident & emergency areas, burns and trauma units, GP surgeries, emergency services, social services, etc. However, this has to be supplemented by a specialist level response for those with established and chronic PTSD; and this is likely to be developed in accessible and more specialised mental health units, experienced in work within a combined psychological and pharmacological treatment.

Conclusion

Traumatic stress reactions are important to consider in relation to psychotherapy for a number of reasons. Perhaps the most important is that they illustrate conclusively that otherwise normal people, subjected to an overwhelming trauma in adult life, can develop psychological symptoms sufficient to cause significant morbidity. Not all psychological difficulties reflect an underlying personal vulnerability; indeed there is a persisting controversy about the relative role of serious traumas in childhood (which may hold increasing importance) in the production of later adult symptoms.

In the light of this, specific approaches to treatment are required which concentrate on the present trauma and only investigate earlier development in so far as it appears relevant in the individual context. These approaches need to include sufficient direct therapeutic exposure for anxiety responses to habituate and must also facilitate the development of understanding and coping responses. It is likely that a combination of DTE and cognitive approaches will prove to be the most effective psychological intervention although the relative importance of these factors may vary according to the degree of complexity of the traumatic stress reaction. In the more complex conditions (e.g. following childhood or complex adult trauma such as torture) additional work on personality development or on a range of other attitude and emotional effects is likely to be required.

Preventative strategies are available although these require further evaluation before conclusive statements can be made about outcome.

Effective treatment strategies include psychotropic medication and psychological interventions. Some will prefer one approach or the other and it is helpful to have options available. Interestingly, one large prospective investigation revealed that patients with PTSD and/or substance misuse were specifically and significantly more likely to miss appointments with mental health clinic psychiatrists than other groups of psychiatric patients (Sparr *et al*, 1993). Compliance and user involvement in planning treatment are important issues to address – especially where some approaches favour exposure to anxiety-provoking stimuli (DTE) and others (psychopharmacological) tend to reduce short-term anxiety without DTE. Treatment is probably delivered most effectively in specialised centres and, in a rapidly developing area of practice, it is likely that here new developments can most easily be incorporated into treatment plans. Nonetheless, it is important that this field attracts a higher priority in all psychological therapy training than has hitherto been the case.

References

ALEXANDER, D. (1993) The Piper Alpha Oil Rig Disaster. In *International Handbook of Traumatic Stress Syndromes* (eds J. P. Wilson & B. Raphael), pp. 461–470. New York: Plenum Press.

AMERICAN PSYCHIATRIC ASSOCIATION (1980) *Diagnostic and Statistical Manual of Mental Disorders* (3rd edn) (DSM–III). Washington, DC: APA.

—— (1994) *Diagnostic and Statistical Manual of Mental Disorders* (4th edn) (DSM–IV). Washington, DC: APA.

BOUDEWYNS, P. A. & HYER, L. (1990) Physiological response to combat veterans and preliminary treatment outcome in Vietnam veteran PTSD patients treated with direct therapeutic exposure. *Behaviour Therapy*, **21**, 63–87.

BRAUN, P., GREENBERG, D., DASBERG, H., *et al* (1990) Core symptoms of posttraumatic stress disorder unimproved by alprazolam treatment. *Journal of Clinical Psychiatry*, **51**, 236–238.

BRETT, E. (1993) Psychoanalytic contributions to a theory of traumatic stress. In *International Handbook of Traumatic Stress Syndromes* (eds J. P. Wilson & B. Raphael), pp. 61–68. New York: Plenum Press.

BROM, D., KLEBER, R. J. & DEFARES, P. B. (1989) Brief psychotherapy for posttraumatic stress disorders. *Journal of Consulting and Clinical Psychology*, **57**, 607–612.

CIENFUEGOS, A. J. & MONELLI, C. (1983) The testimony of political repression as a therapeutic instrument. *American Journal of Orthopsychiatry*, **53**, 43–51.

COOPER, N. A. & CLUM, G. A. (1989) Imaginal flooding as a supplementary treatment for PTSD in combat veterans: a controlled study. *Behaviour Therapy*, **20**, 381–391.

DAVIDSON, J. (1992) Drug therapy of post-traumatic stress disorder. *British Journal of Psychiatry*, **160**, 309–314.

——, KUDLER, H., SMITH, R., *et al* (1990) Treatment of posttraumatic stress disorder with amitriptyline and placebo. *Archives of General Psychiatry*, **47**, 259–266.

——, ——, SAUNDERS, W. B., *et al* (1993) Predicting response to amitriptyline in posttraumatic stress disorder. *American Journal of Psychiatry*, **150**, 1024–1029.

DE-BOER, M., OP-DEN-VELDE, W., FALGER, P. J., *et al* (1992) Fluvoxamine treatment for chronic PTSD: a pilot study. *Psychotherapy and Psychosomatics*, **57**, 158–163.

EATON, L. (1985) Bringing balm to Bradford. *Social Work Today*, **24**, 15–17.

EITINGER, L. (1980) Jewish concentration camp survivors in the post-war world. *Danish Medical Bulletin*, **27**, 232–235.

FOA, E. B., ROTHBAUM, B. O., RIGGS, D. S., *et al* (1991) Treatment of posttraumatic stress disorder in rape victims: a comparison between cognitive–behavioural procedures and counselling. *Journal of Consulting and Clinical Psychology*, **59**, 715–723.

FRANK, J. B., KOSTEN, T. R., GILLER, E. L., *et al* (1988) A randomized clinical trial of phenelzine and imipramine for post traumatic stress disorder. *American Journal of Psychiatry*, **145**, 1289–1291.

HOROWITZ, M. J. (1976) *Stress Response Syndromes*. New York: Jason Aronson.

HYER, L. & BRANDSMA, J. M. (1997) EMDR minus eye movements equals good psychotherapy. *Journal of Traumatic Stress*, **10**, 515–522.

JENSEN, S. B. & AGGER, J. (1988) The testimony method: the use of testimony as a psychotherapeutic tool in the treatment of traumatized refugees in Denmark. *Refugee Participation Network*, **3**, 14–18.

JOHNSTON, S. J. (1993) Traumatic stress reactions in the crew of the Herald of Free Enterprise. In *International Handbook of Traumatic Stress Syndromes* (eds J. P. Wilson & B. Raphael), pp. 479–485. New York: Plenum Press.

KEANE, T. M., FAIRBANK, J. A., CADDELL, J. M., *et al* (1989) Implosive (flooding) therapy reduces symptoms of PTSD in Vietnam combat veterans. *Behaviour Therapy*, **20**, 245–260.

———, WEATHERS, F. W. & KALOUPEK, D. G. (1992) Psychological assessment of post-traumatic stress disorder. *PTSD Research Quarterly*, **3**, 1–7.

LATHAM, R. & MATTHEWS, W. (1970–1983) *The Diary of Samuel Pepys* (11 volumes). London: Bell & Hyman. Quoted in Daly, R. J. (1983) Samuel Pepys and post-traumatic stress disorder. *British Journal of Psychiatry*, **143**, 64–68.

McDOUGLE, C. J., SOUTHWICK, S. M. & CHARNEY, D. S. (1991) An open trial of fluoxetine in the treatment of posttraumatic stress disorder. *Journal of Clinical Psychopharmacology*, **11**, 325–327.

McFARLANE, A. C. (1989) The treatment of post-traumatic stress disorder. *British Journal of Medical Psychology*, **62**, 81–90.

MITCHELL, J. T. & DYREGROV, A. (1993) Traumatic stress in disaster workers and emergency personnel; Prevention and intervention. In *International Handbook of Traumatic Stress Syndromes* (eds J. P. Wilson & B. Raphael), pp. 905–914. New York: Plenum Press.

NAGY, L. M., MORGAN, C. A., SOUTHWICK, S. M., *et al* (1993) Open prospective trial of fluoxetine for posttraumatic stress disorder. *Journal of Clinical Psychopharmacology*, **13**, 107–113.

PENISTON, E. G. (1986) EMG biofeedback-assisted desensitization treatment for Vietnam combat veterans post-traumatic stress disorder. *Clinical Biofeedback and Health*, **9**, 35–41.

PITMAN, R. K., ALTMAN, B., GREENWALD, E., *et al* (1991) Psychiatric complications during flooding therapy for posttraumatic stress disorder. *Journal of Clinical Psychiatry*, **552**, 17–20.

PUTNAM, R. W. (1992) Using hypnosis for therapeutic abreactions. *Psychiatric Medicine*, **10**, 51–65.

RACHMAN, S. (1980) Emotional processing. *Behaviour Research and Therapy*, **18**, 51–60.

REIST, C., KAUFFMANN, C. D., HAIER, R. J., *et al* (1989) A controlled trial of desipramine in 18 men with posttraumatic stress disorder. *American Journal of Psychiatry*, **146**, 513–516.

RESICK, P. A. & SCHNICKE, M. K. (1992) Cognitive processing therapy for sexual assault victims. *Journal of Consulting and Clinical Psychology*, **60**, 748–756.

SAIGH, P. A. (1992) The behavioural treatment of child and adolescent posttraumatic stress disorder. *Advances in Behaviour Research and Therapy*, **14**, 247–275.

SCHECK, M. M., SCHAEFFER, J. A. & GILLETTE, C. (1998) Brief psychological intervention with traumatized young women: the efficacy of eye movement desensitisation and reprocessing. *Journal of Traumatic Stress*, **11**, 25–44.

SCHLENGER, W. E., KULKA, R. A., FAIRBANK, J. A., *et al* (1992) The prevalence of post-traumatic stress disorder in the Vietnam generation: a multimethod multisource assessment of psychiatric disorder. *Journal of Traumatic Stress*, **5**, 333–363.

SHAPIRO, F. (1989) Eye movement desensitisation: a new treatment for post-traumatic stress disorder. *Journal of Behaviour Therapy and Experimental Psychiatry*, **20**, 211–217.

——— (1995) *Eye movement desensitization and reprocessing*. New York: Guilford Press.

SHESTATSKY, M., GREENBERG, D. & LERER, B. A. (1988) A controlled trial of phenelzine in posttraumatic stress disorder. *Psychiatry Research*, **24**, 149–155.

SHORE, J. H., TATUM, B. L. & VOLLMER, W. M. (1986) Psychiatric reactions to disaster: The Mount St Helens experience. *American Journal of Psychiatry*, **143**, 590–595.

SOLOMON, S. D., GERRITY, E. T. & MUFF, A. M. (1992) Efficacy of treatments for post traumatic stress disorder: an empirical review. *Journal of the American Medical Association*, **268**, 633–638.

SPARR, L. F., MOFFITT, M. C. & WARD, M. F. (1993) Missed psychiatric appointments: who returns and who stays away. *American Journal of Psychiatry*, **150**, 801–805.

THOMPSON, J., CHARLTON, P. F. C., CAREY, R., *et al* (1995) An open trial of exposure therapy based on de-conditioning for post traumatic stress disorder. *British Journal of Clinical Psychology*, **34**, 407–416.

TRIMBLE, M. R. (1981) *Post-traumatic Neurosis: from Railway Spine to the Whiplash.* Chichester: Wiley.

TURNER, S. W. & GORST-UNSWORTH, C. (1993) Psychological sequelae of torture. In *International Handbook of Traumatic Stress Syndromes* (eds J. P. Wilson & B. Raphael), pp. 703–713. New York: Plenum Press.

——, THOMPSON, J. & ROSSER, R. M. (1993) The Kings Cross fire; early psychological reactions and implications for organizing a "phase-two" response. In *International Handbook of Traumatic Stress Syndromes* (eds J. P. Wilson & B. Raphael), pp. 451–459. New York: Plenum Press.

——, MCFARLANE, A. C. & VAN DER KOLK, B. A. (1996) The therapeutic environment and new explorations in the treatment of post-traumatic stress disorder. In *Traumatic Stress* (eds B. A. Van der Kolk, A. C. McFarlane & L. Weisaeth). New York: Guilford Press.

VAUGHAN, K. & TARRIER, N. (1992) The use of image habituation training with post-traumatic stress disorders. *British Journal of Psychiatry*, **161**, 658–664.

WILSON, J. P. & RAPHAEL, B. (1993) *International Handbook of Traumatic Stress Syndromes.* New York: Plenum Press.

WORLD HEALTH ORGANIZATION (1992) *The Tenth Revision of the International Classification of Mental and Behavioural Disorders: Clinical Descriptions and Diagnostic Guidelines* (ICD–10). Geneva: WHO.

15 Psychiatric emergencies

TOM BURNS

Psychotherapists rightly emphasise the need to construct a stable and predictable environment in which to explore and resolve long-standing problems with their clients. Similarly mental health services increasingly emphasise the value of continuity of care and a move away from what is often referred to as 'episode-based' care to a 'needs-based' or 'disability-based' care for their more severely ill clients. Most people, however, come into contact with both psychiatric and psychotherapeutic services initially at a time of personal crisis. Those who are referred on to psychotherapists from mental health services are usually through the worst of their crisis but are vulnerable to such breakdowns under stress.

'Nervous breakdowns' occur as a result of the interaction of life stresses with a particular individual's constitution or vulnerability. Psychiatrists traditionally emphasise genetic or constitutional vulnerability in severe disorders, though even here there is compelling evidence that early interpersonal experiences can contribute (Brown & Harris, 1978). There is also abundant confirmation of the role of interpersonal stresses in individual psychotic breakdowns (Leff & Vaughn, 1981).

This 'rediscovery' of the importance of patients' life experiences and situations after a couple of decades of increasingly biological approaches in psychiatry has paralleled better methods of describing them (e.g. the Camberwell Family Interview, Vaughn & Leff, 1976; the Bedford College life event schedule, Brown, 1974). Similarly there has been an increase in the range of robust and targeted psychotherapies to help individuals with significant mental health problems. The caricature of psychotherapy previously held by some psychiatrists (that it was only suitable or available for individuals with above average emotional stability, personal success and an address in north London) is now dated. The present day psychotherapist can expect to work with clients who overlap extensively with those seen in psychiatric clinics. Some may be concurrently attending out-patients.

Psychotherapy involves periods of considerable stress (for example, when defences are challenged or resistance is overcome) which carry some risk of breakdown. Psychiatric emergencies must, therefore, be accepted as an inevitable, though hopefully infrequent, aspect of the job not as a remote, frightening possibility. This chapter outlines how the psychotherapist can prepare for such emergencies and how he or she can deal with them.

Making sensible provision

Sensible provision for psychiatric emergencies involves arranging back-up in advance for an emergency and ensuring a sufficient level of suspicion to spot a developing crisis before it becomes a full-blown emergency.

Back-up arrangements

The psychotherapist must be crystal clear about who they can call upon for psychiatric aid in crises. This must have been mutually agreed either with one psychiatrist for all of their patients or, more likely, with the referring psychiatrist or GP for each patient. There will usually be an explicit agreement between psychiatrist and psychotherapist about how emergency help or assessment can be obtained.

Within National Health Service settings this agreement of the psychiatrist is of crucial importance even if the referral comes from another member of the multidisciplinary team. Present health service reforms generate all sorts of unforeseen complications. These can usually be overcome with the cooperation of senior clinicians but can cause serious problems if they are approached through routine channels.

Vignette

A self-employed artist had suffered two brief, florid paranoid psychotic breakdowns each requiring hospitalisation. The breakdowns were clearly related to major neurotic conflicts centring on his difficulty in separating from his intense, somewhat masochistic, relationship with his father. Psychotic symptoms resolved within days of admission and treatment with trifluoperazine but it was clear that there were severe ongoing difficulties. Individual, dynamic psychotherapy was arranged and he began to make good progress. As a measure of this he bought a flat several miles across London away from his parents and moved in. The psychotherapist considered the move a healthy development but one which was stretching his patient to the limit. In the event the patient, now living well outside the hospital's area, did suffer another brief but dangerous psychotic relapse. The risk had been anticipated and agreement to admit the patient given for this essential transition phase. Had this arrangement not been clarified before the breakdown the referral to the, now distant, hospital would have been refused by the duty admitting doctor. In the event the hospital and psychotherapist were able to cooperate as an efficient container of the patient's anxiety.

Monitoring

Some psychotherapists arrange for the psychiatrist to see the patient on a regular, infrequent basis. An advantage is that this confirms the back-up arrangements: the patient is 'on the books' and there is usually no problem about accessing the emergency provisions. There are, however, significant drawbacks to this approach. It readily lends itself to splitting and may generate an unrealistic estimate of what the psychiatrist can do. These risks are less if there is an identified psychiatric input (e.g. prescribing antidepressants or monitoring lithium therapy).

It is self-deluding for both patient and psychotherapist to imagine that infrequent out-patient appointments will spot deterioration early. It can also undermine acknowledgement of psychotherapy as the treatment and not just part of it, and create excessive dependence on the psychiatrist, which prevents proper termination of therapy. Handled clumsily, such monitoring can make the psychotherapist feel 'spied upon' and not trusted, or the psychiatrist feel undervalued. A better option is to discharge the patient to the care of their GP, with a clear undertaking in writing to both psychotherapist and GP for immediate access and assessment on the same conditions as a continuing out-patient.

Irrespective of the back-up arrangements, psychotherapists need to be able to come out of role occasionally and view their patients as if without the benefit of their detailed knowledge. For psychotherapists with a background in a mental health profession this means reverting briefly. Most lay therapists obtain some experience of the realities of mental illness in an acute adult service. All therapists should be able to distinguish (for example) between being able to work through a depressive episode and being completely stuck in a depressive illness, or between preoccupation with a primitive fantasy in therapy, and developing delusions.

One needs to look actively for such differences at intervals. Few find that it interferes with their work in any substantial way. Usually all that is needed is a willingness to think briefly along different lines – to shift the focus actively from the deep to the superficial. The patient who is not progressing may be exhibiting slow, inefficient thinking because of depression rather than resisting a challenging interpretation. Dynamic therapists can face a special problem here because of the highly charged vocabulary they traditionally use. Those used to talking in terms of 'murderous impulses' or 'primitive rage' need occasionally to remind themselves how these terms are used in everyday speech if they are to be alert to possible suicidal risk and so forth. Allowing yourself to notice if your patient is beginning to show signs of self-neglect or behave oddly may need an energetic wrenching away of the focus.

Vignette

> The author had been conducting an out-patient therapy group with the same members for just over 18 months and had been presenting it routinely for supervision. One evening a young man in the group turned to one of the young women and said that he was very worried about how thin she had become. With a sickening awakening the conductor realised how pale and emaciated she was. She had clearly been wasting away before his eyes without his noticing (despite two years' experience in an eating disorder unit!). A few minutes direct questioning confirmed that she had developed severe anorexia nervosa. She had lost over 12 kg in the preceding eight months and her periods had ceased over six months previously. She required urgent in-patient treatment. The group appeared to weather this brief, dramatic shift of emphasis without significant change in its culture.

Dealing with common emergencies

The four most likely emergencies that the therapist will confront are acute suicidal risk, aggression, intoxication and an acute psychotic breakdown. The first three may signal the development of a mental illness but may equally be reactions to stresses in the therapist–patient relationship. How they are dealt with will vary according to such circumstances.

Suicide risk and threat

Thoughts about suicide are common. When patients share their suicidal thoughts the therapist must make a judgement about how serious the risk is. A detailed exploration of the patient's thoughts and plans is the basis of this risk assessment. The therapist need not be inhibited from a thorough assessment as there is no evidence that talking about suicide increases the risk and there is simply no truth in the view that those who talk about suicide will not do it. Of those who attempt to take their lives, 36% have consulted their GP within the preceding week, 63% within the preceding month (Hawton & Catalan, 1987).

Suicide risk increases from patients who have thought about suicide to those who have begun to plan it. A therapist must be prepared to ask whether his patient has considered which method they might use. One who has thought about fitting a pipe to the exhaust of his car but is troubled about the impact on his family finding him is at much greater risk than one who keeps wishing he didn't wake up. The more detailed and practical the planning, the greater the risk involved.

One step up from planning suicide is having made an attempt but failed. It is a serious mistake to assume that there is any clear distinction between those who attempt suicide and those who do kill themselves. The risk of dying from suicide within a year of deliberate self-harm is 1% (100 times the normal risk; Hawton & Fagg, 1988).

When exploring a patient's suicidal thoughts it is necessary to find out what makes them want to end their life and also what is holding them back. Beck *et al* (1985) have demonstrated that hopelessness about the future is the dominating issue for most who attempt to take their own lives. Anger and frustration are particularly important with men. Concern for the feelings of family, religious scruples, fear of pain or of botching the attempt are common reasons for restraint. Examination of these issues can reveal the extent of the patient's determination and can also indicate possible strategies for strengthening their resistance and providing support.

There are well recognised risk factors for suicide. It is more common in men than women, increases with age and social isolation. It is more common after a severe loss (such as a bereavement) and in the presence of alcohol abuse or chronic painful or debilitating physical disorders (e.g. arthritis). Knowing these factors is more likely to raise the therapist's vigilance and prompt a suicide assessment rather than tip the final balance.

Having decided that the patient's suicidal preoccupations reflect real intentions rather than a means of influencing the therapeutic relationship, what is to be done? The two pressing needs are to assess the degree of risk and to exclude major mental illness (see below). If the patient has a serious disorder then the necessary treatment for that disorder must be urgently sought.

A detailed risk assessment for suicide can, in itself, bring considerable relief to the patient. It involves a detailed examination of stresses and problems, plus a cataloguing of strengths and supports. What can be achieved just now? Who can he lean upon for support? Who needs him? Drawing up a detailed problem list (financial, marital, professional, etc.) rather than focusing entirely on the immediate experience of hopelessness or self-criticism can sometimes identify small, simple steps which, once taken, restore perspective and sense of control.

Encourage the person to share their feelings with family and close friends and ensure that they mobilise what support network is available. Such a practical approach to suicidal impulses and sharing it with close friends and family also help to reduce the sense of isolation and guilt they induce. Insisting that the person stays with somebody they (and you) can trust – establishing a 'safety net' until the threat recedes – is a minimal requirement if you are seriously concerned. Your own concerns can be used to justify this:

'I think you need someone close at hand while you're feeling so desperate. It's the sort of support that people are happy to offer and I don't think that I would feel safe unless I knew there was someone there for you.'

Even if the risk is manageable with these precautions it may still be necessary to modify the therapy temporarily, being more containing and supportive. Disturbing and challenging exploration should be postponed until the person is less vulnerable. Both the therapist and the client may feel reassured with an opinion from the GP or psychiatrist.

What if there is a serious risk and the person will not comply with advice? Can confidentiality be broken? What transpires between both doctors and psychotherapists and their patients is normally confidential and cannot be disclosed to a third party without the patient's consent. This can be overruled by a court, and most doctors consider that it should be overridden if there is serious risk to the patient or to others. If there is a serious suicide risk most mental health professionals would override a patient's veto on disclosure. Psychotherapists need to address these ethical issues in their training and not wait until they are faced with a crisis.

Fears that the therapeutic alliance will be irrevocably damaged are groundless if the person is seriously suicidal. Profoundly depressed people are usually grateful when they are recovered and can resume their therapy. Even when the risk is not so great, people can usually understand (and indeed appreciate) their therapist's concern. Good GPs are often the best opinion as they have a clear and socially sanctioned responsibility for the person's welfare. Where there is an element of blackmail in the threat, however, breaking the embargo may subsequently be used as an excuse to break off therapy or to harangue the therapist. It must be questionable, however, how fruitful any relationship (therapeutic or otherwise) can be when it is constrained by such threats. Similar considerations hold when a client informs his therapist that he has just taken a serious overdose before attending the session and insists that nothing must be done.

Major mental illness

Psychotherapy requires individuals to acknowledge chaotic, often irrational thoughts and feelings. There is, however, an important distinction between these reported feelings (their 'as if' quality) and the certainty and overwhelming conviction which accompany psychotic disorders. The person who reports 'It's as if one part of me wanted to dissolve' is describing a very different experience to one who, at the start of a schizophrenic breakdown, states 'My face is melting'. Often the words and concepts used to describe the start of major mental illnesses are similar to the vivid language of neurotic fantasies. What differs is their quality, the sense of total identification with the experience.

There is no convincing evidence that psychotherapy alone is sufficient treatment for an individual experiencing a psychotic breakdown. In most psychoses and severe depressions the ability to reflect on the inner world and work on it has been exceeded. Intervention is needed. The situation can be very disturbing and frightening for the therapist – especially if they figure prominently in the person's delusions (they may be viewed variously as persecutory, all powerful or the source of all goodness). People can be probed about their delusions to determine if they have any capacity to test reality.

'You say that your body is rotting. Do you mean that you're becoming older and frailer, or do you experience bits as actually dead? In that case, how do you know it's rotting – can you smell it or does it feel different?'

People need direct reassurance that they are not unworthy or being persecuted. A reduction in the demands of the psychotherapy may restore equilibrium. Regular supportive contact should be provided if there seems no immediate risk. If there isn't demonstrable improvement within a week or so then psychiatric intervention is probably necessary and should be arranged. The risk is to be reassured by small changes from week to week, while ignoring a general trend. The therapist must pull back from his intricate knowledge of the person's inner world and concentrate on the overall picture. Paranoid states can develop in vulnerable individuals in therapy. When they do they often involve the therapist:

'Now I really understand what you've been getting at all this time. You've been feeding all this information about me to them.'

Paranoid delusions commonly betray themselves by obscure questions or allusions from the client that leave the therapist feeling perplexed or uneasy:

'You, obviously, won't be surprised to know that I've been suspended at work.'
'Why shouldn't I be surprised to hear that?'
'Don't think I don't know you've been in contact with them.'

Developing hypomanic states can catch any therapist out. Often the client appears to demonstrate a gratifying improvement that they may attribute to the therapy:

'At last I've begun to see what you've meant. I can't understand why I put off having therapy for so long. Now it's clicked I can disentangle what is going on.'

Hypomanic people are notoriously difficult to persuade into treatment as they may insist that they have never felt better. The ethical dilemma may seem even greater for the therapist than with the depressed or suicidal person. The immediate risks to the person are not to his life but the loss of his reputation, damage to relationships, gross errors of financial and sexual judgement, etc. which may have enduring consequences.

Vignette

A woman in her late forties had been medically retired several years earlier because of chronic agoraphobia and depression. After a spell in a day hospital she engaged in out-patient psychotherapy which focused on her early sexual abuse and the consequent damaged self-esteem which underlay her agoraphobia and depression. During therapy she formed an overly positive transference. In supervision it was decided not to interpret this immediately as it appeared to be enabling her to expand her very restricted life. This appeared to be paying off, although several months into her treatment she began to bring the therapist extravagant gifts which he refused. Subsequently her GP was contacted by neighbours who described a pattern of escalating disinhibition with aggression towards her husband, spending unwisely and lack of sleep. Within her sessions she kept her developing hypomania channelled into the positive transference. This additional information forced a shift in focus and an acknowledgement of the severity of the developments.

Depressive disorders usually develop very slowly with little sense of discontinuity. Their detection relies upon therapist vigilance. The person's ability to progress in therapeutic work may seize up, a sense of sadness and gloom becoming overlaid or replaced by slowness of thought or a 'tunnel vision' quality that makes everything seem circular. A monotonous voice and facial expression, weight loss and self-neglect may have crept imperceptibly into the person's demeanour.

Recognition is crucial, and once the suspicion has been aroused, direct questions about sleep, weight loss, suicidal thoughts, diminished concentration and a fixed unshiftable mood can rapidly confirm the judgement.

Psychotherapy (indeed any relationship) can be experienced as an intolerable burden by depressed people who may feel unworthy of the attention they are receiving or find thinking demoralisingly difficult. It is necessary to either interrupt therapy or shift to a more supportive and directive approach. Depressed people do not usually resist further assessment or treatment unless they are profoundly deluded. Antidepressant medication is no contraindication to psychotherapy. Studies indicate that for some depressed people antidepressants and psychotherapy together are often better than either alone (Elkin *et al*, 1989). Some caution needs to be exercised with people recovering from a very retarded depression as the suicide risk rises at the start of recovery.

Intoxication

A client may arrive at the session intoxicated by alcohol or drugs. The intoxication may be consequent on stresses aroused by the previous session and people may play on the therapist's sense of guilt and imply that it is precisely now they need help. A firm statement is required that the distress is understood but that psychotherapy cannot be conducted when the person is intoxicated and that he should come back for the next session. Not only can no useful work be done but intoxicated individuals can be aggressive. Psychiatrists soon learn that they are more likely to be assaulted by an intoxicated than a psychotic individual. If a session has unwittingly been started with an intoxicated individual then as well as trying to send them away attention should be paid to the advice about handling aggression in the following section.

Aggression

People can become aroused, hostile or threatening for a variety of reasons. Occasionally this can lead to violence. Therapists must minimise the risk of violence both for their own and for the person's protection. Volatile or unknown people should not be assessed in isolated settings. They should be booked in when there are others around to help if there are concerns. If worried about a specific person, mention should be made of it to a colleague who works nearby so that if they hear anything untoward they should pop their head round the door to check. If such arrangements are unacceptable or impractical then seriously disturbed individuals should not be accepted. Arrange the consulting room in a safe manner. This means placing furniture so that both therapist and client can easily reach the door without having to pass through the other's personal space. The therapist must be prepared to act decisively if the client's mood is getting out of hand:

'This seems to be more than either of us can handle just now. I think we should stop and come back to it when we've had time to think more.'

What can be done if the person does become aggressive? The first and only objective now is to avoid violence. Anger and fear, like all states of high arousal, tend to settle if not further inflamed. The task is to keep things neutral till the rage subsides and, if possible, to calm the situation. There are a number of techniques to use and behaviours to be aware of.

Attention

Acknowledge the existence of the problem. Demonstrate by active listening a genuine concern for what the patient is experiencing. Saying 'We'll deal with this next time' will not work. Reassurance and support are needed – a 'blank screen' approach or interpretations are not wise.

Fogging

This is the technique of defusing a direct verbal attack and is much used by politicians. It involves indicating that one has heard the criticism whilst trying to avoid engaging in the argument:
'You're too middle class to understand!'
'I may or may not be middle class but let's work on this together.'

Depersonalise the issue

This can help deflect hostility:
'You're too stuck up and orthodox to carry on our session over an hour!'
'It's a contractual rule of the institution not to exceed an hour.'
    Similarly, personalising himself can make the therapist seem less hateful or threatening:
'I have gone through some of this too when I was a bit younger.'

Delayed compliance

Ask for some work towards a future resolution of the problems:

'Can we see if this can be sorted out by the next time we meet? What needs to be done over the next couple of days to reduce this pressure on you?'

Mood matching

It can be tempting to remain very calm in frightening situations but this can be infuriating for an aroused client. The therapist may need to raise his voice both to be heard and also to indicate that he is taking seriously what is going on. The aim is to raise the voice to a level just below that of the patient and by gradually reducing the level to bring his down with it. This reduces the risk that the client may interpret the disparity in how the two are behaving as evidence of a gulf in understanding.

Mirroring

This is the physical equivalent of mood matching. The therapist stands up rather than leave the patient to tower over him, and moves with him across the room if need be. Personal instinct has to be followed in this and obviously the client should not be overcrowded.

Squaring and eye contact

One must avoid 'squaring up' to the client. Maintaining a small angle between the two means both can easily look away without it appearing shifty. Similarly, avoid crowding the patient – leave him his personal 'buffer zone'. While hard to describe, this is easy to feel and most of us do it automatically. Unbroken eye contact is very threatening in most cultures. It is much more reassuring to make and break eye contact regularly. Looking away briefly before a sentence often feels comfortable.

When interviewing hostile, potentially aggressive clients I tend to sit next to them, not opposite. This allows me to turn towards and away with ease enabling regular but not too intensive eye contact. I attempt to address their grievances but move back and forth to other matters to diffuse the tension. Totally ignoring the conflict never works. I introduce the crucial issues from my point of view repeatedly, briefly and often using different phrases each time to avoid appearing to 'nag'. Brief physical contact (a touch on the arm to emphasise a point but not an arm round the shoulder to comfort as this is likely to be misinterpreted) can be very effective but should only be attempted if it feels absolutely right. I make a point of not insisting that I'm right and also giving up quickly in a nondescript way if it's not working.

Acknowledgement

If one is frightened in a hostile situation one should admit it:

'You're frightening me so I can't help you. We'll have to stop for now.'

Inciting fear may be the purpose of the hostility and hiding it may provoke aggression. If really frightened one should leave. If the client grabs hold of one then demands for them to let go should be repeated.

'Let go of my arm – you're hurting me. Let go of my arm.'

This is much more effective than 'stop it' as there may be so much going on in the patient's mind that they may hardly have noticed that they have hold of you. Shouting 'stop it' in a loud voice is an effective call for help if repeated. It is generally accepted by most mental health professionals that if they hear raised voices in a room (and certainly if they hear someone call out 'stop it') they should go in. Psychotherapists should ensure that they and their colleagues understand such conventions. The practice is to knock on the door, go straight in and say 'Is everything all right? I thought I heard a call'.

After the crisis

After a psychiatric emergency, whether a severe breakdown or the threat of violence, a therapist is likely to feel very shaken. We may blame ourselves for precipitating it and most of us have quite unrealistic expectations about our abilities to control such situations. We feel doubly a failure. It is essential to acknowledge how badly we feel. At the very least the therapist should get someone to drive him home and ensure that someone is dealing with the client. Therapists who live alone and have been threatened should get a friend or relative to come and stay for a few days. One should be aware of the characteristics of post-traumatic stress disorder (DSM–III–R; American Psychiatric Association, 1987) and expect to experience some of the features of disturbed sleep, intrusive thoughts, emotional lability and general exhaustion for some days.

Most psychotherapists will wish to discuss such an incident with colleagues and supervisor. The debriefing needs to cover both a practical audit of what happened to identify how future risks can be minimised and also a working through of the inevitable emotional turmoil. The need for simple understanding and sympathy after such an upsetting experience is paramount. Such events do not necessarily imply a mistake. They are part and parcel of the job and a risk we all take. It is vitally important for colleagues not to blame the victim.

Psychiatric emergencies are a distressing but inevitable aspect of good psychotherapeutic practice. We should obviously do what we can to minimise them but their occurrence is a healthy sign that psychotherapists are concerning themselves with those people who most need them.

References

AMERICAN PSYCHIATRIC ASSOCIATION (1987) *Diagnostic and Statistical Manual of Mental Disorders* (3rd edn, revised) (DSM–III–R). Washington, DC: APA.

BECK, A. T., STEER, R. A., KOVACS, M., *et al* (1985) Hopelessness and eventual suicide: a 10 year prospective study of patients hospitalised with suicidal ideation. *American Journal of Psychiatry*, **145**, 559–563.

BROWN, G. W. (1974) Meaning, measurement and stress of life-events. In *Stressful Life-Events: Their Nature and Effects* (eds B. S. Dohrenwend & B. P. Dohrenwend). New York: Wiley.

—— & HARRIS, T. (1978) *Social Origins of Depression: a Study of Psychiatric Disorders in Women.* London: Tavistock.

ELKIN, I., SHEA, S., COLLINS, J., *et al* (1989) National Institute of Mental Health Treatment of Depression Collaborative Research Programme: General effectiveness of treatments. *Archives of General Psychiatry*, **33**, 766–771.

HAWTON, K. & CATALAN, J. (1987) *Attempted Suicide. A Practical Guide to its Nature and Management.* Second edition. Oxford: Oxford Medical Publications.

—— & FAGG, J. (1988) Suicide, and other causes of death, following attempted suicide. *British Journal of Psychiatry*, **152**, 359–366.

LEFF, J. P. & VAUGHN, C. (1981) The role of maintenance therapy and relatives' expressed emotion in relapse of schizophrenia: A two year follow-up. *British Journal of Psychiatry*, **139**, 102–104.

VAUGHN, C. & LEFF, J. P. (1976) The measurement of expressed emotion in the families of psychiatric patients. *British Journal of Social and Clinical Psychology*, **15**, 157–165.

16 Psychotherapy, culture and ethnicity

DINESH BHUGRA and DIGBY TANTAM

Psychotherapy is often assumed to be a particularly Western form of therapy. This may be because, for many people in the West, health professionals and lay persons alike, psychotherapy means the psychoanalytic approach. This reflects the enormous influence of psychoanalysis in developed countries in this century. In other parts of the world, psychoanalysis has made little headway, and the dominant explanations of mental disorder and their cure have continued to be, as they were in the West in previous centuries, witchcraft and spirit possession. In these cultures, 'mind healing' has involved much more than 'talking treatment'. Frank's often quoted enumeration of the non-specific factors which are common to all psychotherapies applies both to psychoanalysis and to these other approaches, and is less ethnocentric than many other definitions of psychotherapy. For the purposes of this chapter, we shall therefore define psychotherapy as a procedure to counter demoralisation which makes use of: an emotionally charged confiding relationship with a helpful person; a healing setting; a rationale, conceptual scheme, or myth; a ritual (Frank, 1993).

Frank's definition itself, in his reference to myth and ritual, reflects the impact of medical anthropology on Western practitioners' understanding of the range of cultural provisions for psychotherapy (Littlewood *et al*, 1992). Anthropologists are to society as psychotherapists are to people: both groups study subjects who attract the attitudes associated with being alien. Indeed the term alien has been applied to people with mental illnesses and is currently still applied to immigrants to the United States of America. Principal causes of alienation include class, culture, language, nationality, ethnicity, and the substantial interaction between these factors which will often be present together. In this chapter, we single out two of these causes – culture and ethnicity – for particular consideration.

Culture and psychotherapy

Havenaar (1990) concludes that "Psychotherapy . . . appears by and large to be healing by culture" and that "Training programs in psychotherapy should therefore pay more attention to the role of culture". The importance of culture is also emphasised in the titles of books on counselling people from ethnic minorities: for example, *Intercultural Therapy* (Kareem & Littlewood, 1992), *Counselling across Cultures* (Pedersen *et al*, 1981), or *Counseling the Culturally Different* (Sue & Sue, 1990). Differences in culture are one of the most salient features of the differences between different ethnic groups, and have led some psychotherapists to conclude that Western psychotherapies cannot be transferred to other cultures (Boulard, 1981).

Although there are unique – *emic* – elements which only occur in one culture, cultures also include elements which are functional adaptations to circumstances which are found throughout the world and which therefore reappear in other cultures whenever these social circumstances obtain. These *etic* cultural elements may be related to biology or to universal social institutions like the family and roles such as 'healer'. Immersion in another culture often results in two, apparently contradictory, discoveries: that what one has assumed is universal (etic) is actually only local (emic), and what one assumed to be very special and specific to one's own culture (emic) is actually world-wide (etic). Psychotherapists are similar to anthropologists in that their work often leads to the same insights at a personal level. In group psychotherapy, it is very common for people to discover that what they have always believed to be an unchangeable universal truth – for example, the children of divorced parents always end up having problems in their own marriages – turns out to be a belief that obtained in their own families, which may not be held by others. But, in the same groups, people also discover that what had always seemed to be horribly, or excitingly, unique about themselves – a sexual deviation, for example – turns out to be a characteristic of at least one, and sometimes many more, of the other group members: a universal of human behaviour, in fact.

Psychoanalysis has been criticised because it assumes that what is true of people having problems is also true of people who are not. Psychiatrists may be criticised for the reverse: that they too often assume that people who consult them have a disorder and so what is troubling them is of a separate order to what troubles 'normal' people. There is no right answer about what is universal, and what is particular. It is more a question of how one is going to use the distinction. An analogous problem occurs when considering psychotherapy in different cultures. Is there a transcultural psychotherapy, built on etic elements, that is universal?

Or does one need a different psychotherapeutic approach for each culture, the cross-cultural approach? If the latter is true, psychoanalytic psychotherapy, cognitive–behavioural therapy, and the other methods that are widely used in the developed world are only relevant to the dominant culture in the developed world. If the former is true, then there is value in applying these methods in other cultural settings, and also applying healing methods that are traditional to other cultures, to Western culture.

Referring to Western culture, or to Western methods of psychotherapy, emphasises the importance of cultural difference, but is an over-simplification. People no longer have to go abroad to find other cultures; cultures are being swirled together by international marketing, through migration, through satellite television and now, through the world-wide web. Coca-Cola signs are omnipresent in Zambia, most UK pubs have a karaoke evening, people in Pakistan watched coverage of the Gulf war put out by CNN, and so on. Traditional Muslim healers, using methods very little different from those used by their colleagues in east Africa or the Gulf, practise in Bradford and Ealing. Traditional Chinese medicine, Ayurvedic medicine, spirit healing, and divination are all practised close to most high streets in many European and North American cities. Practitioners of established, Western psychotherapies have, as yet, taken little cognisance of this phenomenon but it has stimulated some consideration of what other cultures have to offer Western psychotherapy, either for the study of cultural universals in psychotherapy (Pentony, 1981; Calvert *et al*, 1988; Gerber, 1994) or through direct borrowings of psychotherapeutic technique, most famously the network therapy approach of Speck & Attneave (1973) which was based on Navajo tribal rituals. Other writers have stressed the potential contribution of Eastern philosophical and psychological approaches to Western psychotherapy (Kang, 1990; Atwood & Maltin, 1991) and this topic merits its own review.

Ethnic barriers to effective psychotherapy

Cultural differences are not the only barrier to effective psychotherapy. Physical differences which are biologically insignificant but socially salient may also demarcate ethnic groups whose access to psychotherapy would be barred by the organisation of the psychotherapy service or by the characteristics of the practitioners. Particular barriers include racism and an ill-defined group of factors often subsumed under the heading of ethnic mismatch.

Racism

It is not possible to practise psychotherapy without espousing values such as non-discrimination and respect for difference. Few psychotherapists can therefore contemplate with equanimity the possibility that they, or their services, are racist in that they discriminate against people from ethnic groups, particularly those whose skin colour is different from their own. An important element of racism is the desire to hold on to power over others. Although ethnic minorities may form a ruling elite, this is unusual. More often than not, being in an ethnic minority also means being in a lower class, having less income, being more exposed to crime, and living in a worse neighbourhood than the majority.

Overt racism implies the open use of power over others; covert racism implies its secret or disguised use. Covert racism may operate in any situation, but is of particular concern where people are in a position to exercise power over others: for example, in appointment interviews, in selecting candidates for psychotherapy training, or in selecting people for treatment. The participants in these situations may be unaware of their racial bias which may operate on some characteristic linked to ethnicity rather than ethnicity itself. Monitoring of the appointments in the National Health Service (NHS) has become standard, and ethnic information is also obtained about attenders at NHS clinics although rarely used for auditing psychotherapeutic assessment or treatment. Private training institutions and clinics should also implement monitoring if they wish to avoid racism.

Monitoring is not a complete answer to racism because it does not address what might be called passive racism, the failure to recognise and take account of the inaccessibility of psychotherapists and their services to people from ethnic minorities. Inaccessibility may arise through lack of knowledge, through lack of time or money, or because of a bias against psychotherapy in referrers who may share the sentiments expressed by Carothers (1953) that Africans (or Asians, or other members of ethnic minorities) express distress in religious or physical terms and are therefore unable to make use of talking treatment. This belief, however benevolently it is held, is itself racist if it is based on a stereotype rather than an assessment of the particular person concerned. There are cultural differences in the likelihood that distress will be somatised, or in the acceptability of a fault-based, psychological explanation rather than, for example, a supernatural one. It may seem obvious to state that these different views are, however, to be found in every culture in some degree, and that it should not be assumed that a particular person will, or will not, hold them.

A service may also be inaccessible because it seems too distant, too unsympathetic, or too alien. Lago & Thompson (1996) describe a fictional counselling organisation 'We listen and we care' and subject it to a detailed analysis of how it perpetuates its predominantly white middle-class client base. Clinics or services wishing to address passive racism might wish to use Lago and Thompson's method for a similar analysis of their own organisation.

Ethnic mismatch

Effective psychotherapy requires that there should be enough of a common language or culture for the communication of opinion and feeling. Traditional healers do not hesitate to use translators but the importance of understanding the nuances of words for Western psychotherapies has led many practitioners to assume that useful psychotherapy requires that therapist and client are both fluent in the language chosen for the therapy. However, one study found that Spanish-speaking clients who used an interpreter to speak to their therapist said that they received more help and were understood better than bilingual Mexican–Americans who used English to speak to their therapists (Kline *et al*, 1980).

Sharing a common language falls short of sharing a common culture. It has sometimes been assumed that cultural differences are so pervasive that effective psychotherapy requires that the therapist not only shares a language, but is of the same ethnic group as the patient. Outcome studies suggest that this may result in greater uptake of services and less drop-out, but this effect tends to be more marked in less assimilated minority groups e.g. Asian–Americans in the US and is confounded by language differences (Sue *et al*, 1994). Sue *et al's* review also suggests that ethnicity functions like attractiveness, one of the factors which social psychologists recognise as influencing the development of acquaintanceship but not the evolution of acquaintances into friends. It acts as a barrier to getting acquainted but, once acquainted, is much less of a barrier to a closer relationship developing between therapist and patient.

The evidence suggests that the link between ethnic matching and the outcome of those patients who are retained in treatment is much weaker, and may vary depending on other factors which co-vary with ethnicity such as identification with a minority culture language, values, socio-economic status, and attractiveness. Ethnic matching of therapist and client may also be more important for people who are unfamiliar with the majority ethnic group which may happen in recent immigrants or in members of culturally isolated minorities.

Ethnic matching is not always a viable option, particularly in countries like the UK where the number of therapists is limited. The research evidence suggests that an alternative solution is to increase the familiarity with which members of ethnic minorities view psychotherapists and their services. Specific services or clinics might be achieved by involving influential members of local minority groups in boards of management or other positions of influence. There may also be a case for revising one of the golden rules of individual psychotherapy, and including third parties in the treatment (Roder & Hersfeld, 1995) who can act as cultural 'bridges' (Heilman & Witztum, 1994) between therapist and patient.

Considering culture in psychotherapy

Sue *et al* (1994) cite studies showing an impact of culture on presumed aetiology, symptom expression, assessment and treatment of psychological disorder. All of these affect psychotherapy and its practice. However, the cultural and historical heterogeneity of ethnic minority groups cannot be over-emphasised. It is often disturbing for a British expatriate to be lumped in with other foreign nationals – say, Russians, Danes, Italians, and Germans – as a European and to be attributed with 'European' attitudes and values. Europe has been substantially more homogeneous in its history and its religion than many other parts of the world, and generalisations about Asians or Africans are likely to be even more approximate than generalisations about Europeans.

Psychotherapists working in communities containing ethnic minorities – and that probably means anyone working in the USA or the UK – may need to have some acquaintance with the culture of each, and have some particular knowledge of what categories that culture assigns to the causes and treatment of psychological disorder. A possible structure for doing so is given by Ivey *et al* (1993). They suggest that counsellors list the 'messages' that they have received about the following: life expectations, family relations, gender rules, marriage, and language. They give the messages that an American counselling student with an Irish and an English background had received. They are strikingly different. The Irish–American messages about language include the following 'words are poetry, an expression of emotion. They have beauty but no reality and may always be traded for better ones . . . '. The 'British'-American messages are that 'Language is law . . . Words are specific and binding' (Ivey *et al*, 1993). These messages clearly have very different implications for the practice of psychotherapy or counselling.

Cultural factors in symptom expression

Particular psychological symptoms or clusters of symptoms can be associated with many cultures. In the developed world, self-poisoning, eating disorders, and borderline personality disorder are egregious examples. Earlier descriptions of these phenomena as culture-bound syndromes tended to make them curiosities and hindered an understanding of their relationship to particular personal and cultural concerns. The cannibalism of windigo, the frenzied aggression of amok, semen loss syndrome (dhat), neurasthenia and all the others can be found in psychiatric practice in the developed world, too, although they may be 'read' differently, as a component of personality disorder or a manifestation of a mood disorder.

For a psychiatrist who has grown up in the UK in a culture of physical fitness where one's shape is both one's destiny and a personal product, the motives of a person with anorexia nervosa may not be culturally dystonic. A psychiatrist who has grown up in a culture where to be thin is the general condition, and to be fat is a measure of success, may find it harder to empathise but may have less difficulty in relating to the person with neurasthenia whose exhaustion is merely an exaggeration of a condition that is endemic among people who still labour physically for their living.

The problem of culturally coded disorders is not that they are new illnesses, for which new treatments need to be developed, but expressions of common disorders in the language of a particular culture which psychotherapists need to be able to understand if they are to be able to make a therapeutic relationship. Failure of understanding may result in the failure of treatment or even, sometimes, the wrong treatment. The overdiagnosis of schizophrenia in Anglo-Caribbeans may be less of a problem since the work of Littlewood & Lipsedge (1988), but a lack of imagination on the part of clinicians unwilling to put themselves into a different culture and another person's shoes may still prevent effective treatment. Schreiber (1995) describes a patient, one of the countless Ethiopians made by the Communist government to leave their homes and to trek to new and unknown territories, whose multiple losses preceded a disorder which was first diagnosed as asthma and then psychosis, but which responded to traditional purification methods and supportive psychotherapy.

Devereux (1980) proposes that what he terms ethnic disorders have a cultural patterning which is related to impoverishment, dedifferentiation and disindividualisation. The clinician or therapist who understands the culture can predict the pattern, and therefore understand the client's distress in a cultural framework and plan appropriate interventions.

Cultural factors in presumed aetiology

Varma (1985) considers that there are differences in Indian and Western aetiologies in relation to biological needs, social interrelationships, cognitive styles and value systems. Varma cites cosmic, existential and spiritual values. Many other authors in the cross-cultural field have described the emphasis on 'spirituality' and transcendent beliefs in the explanations given to psychological disorder in many developing world cultures, and their absence from the aetiologies of the West. Psychoanalysis is a part exception, since it places considerable emphasis on values like self-control, autonomy and independence but even these remain, from the perspective of other cultures, solipsistic (Neki, 1976).

The Baganda of Lake Victoria believe that there are two forms of healing: strong and weak. Strong, or Western methods, are good for some illnesses and weak, or traditional methods, for others (Orley, 1970). It is possible for rational people to combine etic and emic explanations of disease. The doctor might take the view that sufficient psychological disturbance will lead to neurochemical changes and characteristic physiological consequences which can be detected in psychologically disordered people throughout the world, irrespective of language or culture. He or she may further take the view that loss or threat to identity or survival are universal stressors that can lead to psychological disorder. The doctor may feel no inconsistency in also thinking that the nature of the loss, or the way in which identity is vulnerable, and the personal and social measures which are taken to offset the loss or guard against the vulnerability, will be culturally encoded. The acceptability of combining physical treatment with a search for the meaning of the problem follows on from the rationality of believing that depression and anxiety are both physical disorders and indications of an existential or spiritual malaise. The traditional healer in Zanzibar who combines a plant extract with a prayer is therefore being as rational as the GP who prescribes Prozac as well as referring the patient to a counsellor.

The usual explanation for psychological disorder in Zanzibar is spirit possession. In an interview study of Zanzibari traditional healers Tantam (1993) found that most healers attributed the onset of spirit possession to travelling to Pemba (the neighbouring island), meeting a white man, or resting under a large tree. Similar symptoms in Stoke-on-Trent may also be attributed to an unfamiliar and threatening experience such as going overseas, but a UK resident may go on to say that their symptoms are due to 'shock' or being 'out of sorts'. There is a commonality about the triggering stimuli for anxiety, but no commonality about the means by which the trigger produces the symptoms.

A transcultural aetiological system has therefore to include etic, universal elements and to allow for, and respect, emic variants of expression. It is a kind of story in which the narrative has to achieve some correspondence with what others have observed and recorded, but can also include the significance of the event for the story-teller or the audience. The Zanzibari story about the baobab tree is that spirits hang around such trees, and that someone thoughtless enough to rest under one is very likely to be preyed on by a spirit looking for a home. The cognitive–behavioural story might be that a very large tree in a lonely place is an unconditioned fear stimulus, and that an anxiety-prone person, experiencing some physical symptoms of fear, may then attend to them and draw catastrophic conclusions from them. The psychodynamic story might be that a person confronted by a towering tree may feel like a child again in the presence of a parent and if that parent was punitive or rejecting, this regressive experience may trigger the same anxiety in the adult as being in the actual presence of the parent may have done in the child. Each of these stories contains the etic elements of a concept of personal vulnerability, a category of non-physical danger, a concept of disease, and a plausible account linking all three. The nature of the account contains emic elements which make particular sense in a particular culture: a spiritual account in a strongly Muslim culture, an individual account in a culture which stresses autonomy and self-control, and a developmental account in a culture which emphasises the importance of the nuclear family in shaping personality.

The validity of these accounts is not how close to the truth they are, but how true they are to the patient's own culture and personal outlook.

Cultural factors in assessment

Developed world psychotherapeutic approaches typically assume considerable self-disclosure on the part of the client, and relative anonymity on the part of the therapist. This may run counter to cultural prohibitions against self-disclosure to strangers. The psychological-mindedness and autonomy that are often considered to be indications for psychotherapy in Westernised clients (Coltart, 1987) may also be unacceptable in a culture where religious and group values are dominant, such as that in parts of India (Hoch, 1990). History-taking may itself be suspect. In some areas of Nigeria, the belief prevails that the most powerful healers know what the person's problem is before the person says anything. Taking a history is, according to this view, a symptom of therapeutic weakness.

Assessing people for psychotherapy in the developed world will usually involve technical, and culturally specific elements, such as checking for symptoms of depression or establishing psychological-mindedness, but it will also involve having the person tell their story. It is difficult to think of a culture which does not include a tradition of story-telling. Although the interpretation of why one event follows another may differ considerably from culture to culture, etic elements are strongly represented in the form of the narrative and there is a homology between these formal elements of the narrative and the human relations which are their reference (Gardner, 1972). This is true of Western culture as it is of others. Storr (1986) writes: "When we tell or read our children folk or fairy tales we set before them . . . the human ability to make patterns, to structure events which might, separately, seem to have no significance or relevance, into a connected whole . . . this is a healing gift. We are reconstructing life . . . we may deliberately set ourselves to make sense out of confusion and misery by distancing ourselves enough to give our experience shape and form".

Having people tell their story allows free play to cultural or social presumptions about causation but establishes which recent experiences the person chooses to make salient, what were their antecedents, and what have been their consequences (Hyden, 1995). Lederer (1959) illustrates this through a 16th-century case report where maintaining factors were given a religious explanation in accord with the values and beliefs prevalent at the time.

Culture and psychological treatment

Psychotherapy outcome studies consistently show that the similarities between therapies account for much more outcome variance than their differences (Stiles *et al*, 1986). There have been few comparative studies of non-Western and Western psychotherapies. In a study in Puerto Rico, Koss (1987) examined expectancy of improvement and perceived improvement in the users of community mental health centre psychotherapy and attenders at a spiritist *centro* and found that psychotherapy patients and spiritist attenders were no different in their ratings of the change from expected to perceived outcome, but the expectancies of those attending the spiritist *centro* were higher. One possible explanation is that different factors affect the engagement with treatment, and its effect. Neki *et al* (1985), in their review of the applicability of Western psychotherapies, refer to this when they write:

"After all, the therapist must attract and keep the patient before he can expect anything from him".

Elsewhere Tantam (1995) has suggested that successful psychotherapy or psychotherapy assessment requires that the 'flavour' of the treatment is palatable to the client before the 'food' value of the treatment can be absorbed. 'Flavour' has been studied both in psychotherapists and their clients. Royce & Muehlke (1991) found that psychotherapists espousing rational therapies tended to make external attributions, and exploratory therapists to make internal attributions. Davies & Drummond (1990) and Calvert *et al* (1988) found that outcome was improved when clients who externalised were treated by psychotherapists who used an external focus or when patients who internalised were treated by therapists who used an internal focus. In the terms that we have used earlier in this chapter, external *vs* internal is an emic element of the therapy, and we suggest that this is generally true: that emic elements are the flavouring of the therapy which has its greatest impact on compliance, while the 'food' elements of the treatment are those invariant elements which relate to psycho- or sociobiology. Noon & Lewis (1992) come to a similar conclusion, having compared Japanese and 'Euro/American' psychotherapies. Each approach has, according to them, comparable goals which are evidence of "universal values in the definition of the fully functioning self", but the means which Japanese people find acceptable to reach those goals differ from those of Americans because of different cultural assumptions about individualism and relationship.

Western medicine is one cultural product that has a widely acceptable flavour. Psychological treatments whose emic elements are drawn from the culture of Western medicine are therefore likely to have good cross-cultural acceptance. One such is family intervention in schizophrenia, based on a mental illness model (Zhang *et al*, 1994). Interpretative psychotherapies are, on the other hand, rich in emic elements and their flavour may be unpalatable for non-Westernised individuals. If these emic elements are essential to the approach, then this would prohibit any cross-cultural validity. However, one model of interpretative psychotherapy, the narrative model, enables etic elements to be identified even in this apparently culture-bound approach. Howard (1991) summarises some of these elements by picking out, in a literature review, authors who "see the development of identity as an issue of life-story construction; psychopathology as instances of life stories gone awry; and psychotherapy as exercises in story repair". Kirmayer (1993) proposes that the transcultural basis of psychotherapy is symbolic healing, and that this has to deal with a culturally-determined myth or story about the self and the reality of 'bodily-given experience' (etic element). Personal functioning is determined by the degree to which the myth about the self and bodily-given experience are in register, and this is determined by the metaphors – imaginative constructions or enactments – which are the emic elements which link the two. Effective psychotherapy provides new metaphors which provide a better fit with psychobiological reality, other metaphors that the client may use, and the values and beliefs of the client's culture.

There is some published evidence for the usefulness of a form of narrative therapy cross-culturally. This is 'giving testimony' which has been used in assisting torture victims to overcome the psychological sequelae of their experiences in Bosnia (Weine & Laub, 1996), in Chile, and in Cambodia (Morris *et al*, 1993).

Implications for practice

All effective psychotherapy or traditional healing must be based on the right kind of relationship between therapist and client. Values which are normally associated with this relationship in the West may not apply in other cultures, or when working with people from other cultures. Traditional healers do not, according to observations by one of us, necessarily spend time listening to clients' accounts of their symptoms (Tantam, 1993). However, they do appear to be accepting of clients and their concerns, and this may be a universal (etic) characteristic of a healing relationship. Traditional healers also occupy positions of considerable respect in their community, and this may also be a universal requirement for effective psychotherapy. Finally empathy is often cited as an important characteristic of healers in all cultures.

Healing settings differ considerably in their location, and in their physical paraphernalia. It is clear that one of the barriers to the uptake of Western psychotherapy services is the unfamiliarity of the setting to many potential users. This type of barrier is one example of 'institutional racism'. Familiarity can be increased by involvement of members of the local ethnic minorities in the service, by opportunities to visit the service informally, and by 'ethnic matching' of therapy and other staff.

Therapeutic rituals give a particular flavour to healing practices which may make them unpalatable to people of other cultures. It is good practice to recognise the limits of competence, and so to know when the rituals of Westernised psychotherapy are too foreign to the experience of potential clients. In these cases collaboration with other traditional healers may be a better option. However, what may be true of some people from a particular ethnic group may not be true of all people from that group or of people from other ethnic minorities.

Widening the cultural applicability of a particular therapeutic method should be considered as a possible response to the needs of people from cultures which did not originate the method. Possible methods of doing this involve the use of people from the culture as a 'bridge'.

According to one school of thought, Westernised psychotherapy involves myth as strongly as do other cultures' healing methods. Myths function as exemplary stories and help guide psychological treatment which is, according to this view, a process of story telling and re-telling. Practitioners who hold this view are in a strong position to be able to incorporate mythic elements from other cultures into the study that they make with the client, and may therefore be able to develop a psychotherapy which is culturally syntonic for that person while retaining the discipline of a narrative structure which is true to their own theory of psychotherapy.

Cultures are not homogeneous. To some extent, each person has their own culture. Learning about the impact of culture on psychotherapy by working with people from different ethnic groups may sensitise the therapist to issues which are relevant even to working with people from their own ethnic group.

Generalisations about cross-cultural psychotherapy very often involve stereotyping. One of the commoner generalisations, and stereotypes, is that people from ethnic groups other than white European are not psychologically-minded and cannot therefore benefit from Western 'verbally-based' psychotherapy. This assumption is not consistent with research findings (Sue *et al*, 1994) and may perpetuate racist practices.

There is considerable potential for innovations in practice and for research into cultural universals in psychotherapy in the study of the healing practices of many of the ethnic groups who are in the minority in Europe, Australasia, and North America. Cross-cultural work has been described as a fourth force (after psychodynamic, cognitive–behavioural, and existential approaches) in counselling (Ivey *et al*, 1993). It is time for more psychotherapists to recognise its significance.

Ethnic differences do have an independent effect on psychotherapy, but may be less important than culture. Progressive acculturation occurs in the second and third generation of immigrants into a culture, and with it the need for a specific psychotherapeutic approach to people from that ethnic minority diminishes (Sanchez & Mohl, 1992).

Acknowledgement

We are grateful to Emmy van Deurzen for her helpful reading of this chapter.

References

ATWOOD, J. D. & MALTIN, L. (1991) Putting Eastern philosophies into Western psychotherapies. *American Journal of Psychotherapy*, **45**, 368–382.

BOULARD, C. (1981) Non verbal approach in transcultural psychiatry (author's transl). *Medecine Tropicale*, **41**, 279–281.

CALVERT, S., BEUTLER, L. & CRAGO, M. (1988) Psychotherapy outcome as a function of therapist–patient matching on selected variables. *Journal of Social and Clinical Psychology*, **6**, 104–117.

CAROTHERS, J. (1953) *The African Mind in Health and Disease – a Study in Ethnopsychiatry*. Geneva: World Health Organization.

COLTART, N. (1987) Diagnosis and assessment for suitability for psychoanalytical psychotherapy. *British Journal of Psychotherapy*, **4**, 127–134.

DAVIES, L. & DRUMMOND, M. (1990) The economic burden of schizophrenia. *Psychological Bulletin*, **14**, 522–525.

DEVEREUX, G. (1980) Normal and abnormal. In *Basic Problems of Ethnopsychiatry* (eds B. Gulati & G. Devereux), pp. 1–34. Chicago: University of Chicago Press.

FRANK, J. D. (1993) The views of a psychotherapist. In *Non-specific Aspects of Treatment* (eds M. Shepherd & N. Sartorius). Bern: Huber.

GARDNER, H. (1972) The structural analysis of protocols and myths: a comparison of the methods of Jean Piaget and Claude Levi-Strauss. *Semiotica*, **5**, 31–30.

GERBER, L. (1994) Psychotherapy with Southeast Asian refugees: implications for treatment of Western patients. *American Journal of Psychotherapy*, **48**, 280–293.

HAVENAAR, J. M. (1990) Psychotherapy: healing by culture. *Psychotherapy and Psychosomatics*, **53**, 8–13.

HEILMAN, S. C. & WITZTUM, E. (1994) Patients, chaperones and healers: enlarging the therapeutic encounter. *Social Science and Medicine*, **39**, 133–143.

HOCH, E. M. (1990) Experiences with psychotherapy training in India. *Psychotherapy and Psychosomatics*, **53**, 14–20.

HOWARD, G. S. (1991) Culture tales. A narrative approach to thinking, cross-cultural psychology, and psychotherapy. *American Psychologist*, **46**, 187–197.

HYDEN, L. C. (1995) The rhetoric of recovery and change. *Culture, Medicine and Psychiatry*, **19**, 73–90.

IVEY, A., IVEY, M. & SIMEK-MORGAN, L. (1993) *Counselling and Psychotherapy. A Multicultural Perspective*. 3rd edn. Boston: Allyn and Bacon.

KANG, S. H. (1990) Training and development of psychotherapy in Korea. *Psychotherapy and Psychosomatics*, **53**, 46–49.

KAREEM, J. & LITTLEWOOD, R. (1992) *Intercultural Therapy*. Oxford: Blackwell Science.

KIRMAYER, L. J. (1993) Healing and the invention of metaphor: the effectiveness of symbols revisited. *Culture, Medicine and Psychiatry*, **17**, 161–195.

KLINE, F., ACOSTA, F., AUSTIN, W., *et al* (1980) The misunderstood Spanish-speaking patient. *American Journal of Psychiatry*, **137**, 1530–1533.

KOSS, J. D. (1987) Expectations and outcome for patients given mental health care or spiritist healing in Puerto Rico. *American Journal of Psychiatry*, **144**, 56–61.

LAGO, C. & THOMPSON, J. (1996) *Race, Culture and Counselling*. Buckingham: Open University Press.

LEDERER, W. (1959) Primitive psychotherapy. *Psychiatry*, **22**, 255–265.

LITTLEWOOD, R. & LIPSEDGE, M. (1988) Psychiatric illness among British Afro-Caribbeans. *British Medical Journal*, **296**, 950–951.

———, MOORHOUSE, S. & ACHARYYA, S. (1992) The cultural specificity of psychotherapy. *British Journal of Psychiatry*, **161**, 574.

MORRIS, P., SILOVE, D., MANICAVASAGAR, V., *et al* (1993) Variations in therapeutic interventions for Cambodian and Chilean refugee survivors of torture and trauma: a pilot study. *Australian and New Zealand Journal of Psychiatry*, **27**, 429–435.

NEKI, J. (1976) An examination of the cultural relativism of dependence as a dynamic of social and therapeutic relationships. II. Therapeutic. *British Journal of Medical Psychology*, **49**, 11–22.

——, JOINET, B., HOGAN, M., *et al* (1985) The cultural perspective of therapeutic relationship – a viewpoint from Africa. *Acta Psychiatrica Scandinavica*, **71**, 543–550.

NOON, J. M. & LEWIS, J. R. (1992) Therapeutic strategies and outcomes: perspectives from different cultures. *British Journal of Medical Psychology*, **65**, 107–117.

ORLEY, J. (1970) *Culture and Mental Illness*. Nairobi: East Africa Publishing House.

PEDERSEN, P., DRAGUNS, J., LONNER, W., *et al* (1981) *Counselling across Cultures*. Hawaii: East-West Center.

PENTONY, P., DRAGUNS, J., LONNER, W., *et al* (1981) *Models of Influence in Psychotherapy*. New York: Free Press.

RODER, F. & HERSFELD, B. (1995) Group psychotherapy for Turkish patients with a translator – a report with comments of the first, constituting session. *Psychiatrische Praxis*, **22**, 135–139 (in German).

ROYCE, W. S. & MUEHLKE, C. V. (1991) Therapists' causal attributions of clients' problems and selection of intervention strategies. *Psychological Reports*, **68**, 379–386.

SANCHEZ, E. G. & MOHL, P. C. (1992) Psychotherapy with Mexican-American patients. *American Journal of Psychiatry*, **149**, 626–630.

SCHREIBER, S. (1995) Migration, traumatic bereavement and transcultural aspects of psychological healing: loss and grief of a refugee woman from Begameder county in Ethiopia. *British Journal of Medical Psychology*, **68**, 135–142.

SPECK, R. & ATTNEAVE, C. (1973) *Family Process*. New York: Pantheon.

STILES, W., SHAPIRO, D. & ELLIOTT, R. (1986) Are all psychotherapies equivalent? *American Psychologist*, **41**, 165–180.

STORR, C. (1986) Folk and fairy tales. *Children's Literature in Education*, **17**, 63–70.

SUE, D. & SUE, S. (1990) *Counseling the Culturally Different. Theory and Practice* (2nd edn). Chichester: Wiley.

SUE, S., ZANE, N. & YOUNG, K. (1994) Research on psychotherapy with culturally diverse populations. In *Handbook of Psychotherapy and Behaviour Change*. 4th edn (eds A. Bergin & S. Garfield), pp. 783–820. New York: Wiley.

TANTAM, D. (1993) Exorcism in Zanzibar: an insight into groups from another culture. *Group Analysis*, **26**, 251–260.

—— (1995) Why select? In *The Art and Science of Psychotherapy Assessment* (ed. C. Mace). London: Routledge.

VARMA, V. (1985) The Indian mind and psychopathology. *Integrative Psychiatry*, **3**, 290–296.

WEINE, S. & LAUB, D. (1995) Narrative constructions of historical realities in testimony with Bosnian survivors of "ethnic cleansing". *Psychiatry*, **58**, 246–260.

ZHANG, M., WANG, M., LI, J., *et al* (1994) Randomised-control trial of family intervention for 78 first-episode male schizophrenic patients. An 18-month study in Suzhou, Jiangsu. *British Journal of Psychiatry*, Suppl. 24, 96–102.

17 Disorders of childhood

PAUL GARFIELD and RORY NICOL

Psychological therapies, in many forms, constitute the principal form of treatment for children with mental health problems. In this chapter we will concentrate on describing those approaches which are supported by research evidence. This may be in terms of the process of therapy or attempts to assess outcome. First, however, it is necessary to consider some of the special characteristics of psychotherapy with children.

Some special features of child psychotherapy

The first point is that children and adolescents with problems do not in general present themselves asking for psychotherapy: they are brought, usually by a parent, often referred from the school or, if there has been family breakdown, by a social worker. The effect of the child's behaviour on the family may have been a major consideration or the child may have been used as an 'entry ticket' to get help for other family difficulties. For these reasons, the problem should be viewed within a broad social context which for school-age children or teenagers will include the perspectives of family, teachers and peers.

Second, because the children are so closely bound to the immediate environment, the unit of therapy will include significant others. In more traditional practice, it is usual for the parents to be seen for guidance, advice and support as well as the child who might be the recipient of therapy. In conjoint family therapy, the emphasis has shifted further. The child is seen as part of a family social system in which each family member influences all the others and the surface expression of the problem may be an expression of negative feedback mechanisms among the social interactions within the family. In a further group of approaches, originating in the mental health consultation tradition, therapy may not include the child directly at all (Caplan, 1970).

Third, therapy can be and indeed should be carried out in a range of settings besides the out-patient clinic or in-patient unit; for example the school or the child-care residential home. Assessment of psychotherapy outcome with children requires multidimensional and multisituational perspectives sensitive to the child's age and developmental stage.

Fourth, the child's stage of development is an important consideration when planning therapy and assessing outcome, and often an important aim of therapy will be to facilitate development rather than to return the child to pre-morbid functioning (Achenbach, 1986).

As with other forms of psychotherapy, the diagnosis of the child's disorder is not the only, or even the most important predictor of outcome. Qualities that the therapist is able to bring to the process have been shown to be important. This was shown by the work of Truax and his group (Truax & Carkhuff, 1967) and more recently by Kolvin *et al* (1981). There is some evidence also to suggest that children who believe that problems and solutions are dependent on what they do (contingency beliefs) and that they have some control over their problems (control beliefs) have a better symptomatic response to therapy, whether psychodynamic, cognitive or behavioural (Weisz, 1986). Because children are usually brought for treatment by others, a focus on their control and contingency beliefs may be productive (Braswell *et al*, 1985).

Finally, the question of whether psychotherapy 'works' is a sterile one. We should be asking which form of therapy works for which child with which type of problem under what conditions. Some progress has been made towards this goal, as we shall see in what follows.

We will now move on to explore some of the more promising lines of research in more detail. The presentation will be organised around a series of common problem areas. In the present state of knowledge, this provides a more helpful account than to try to keep to formal classification systems.

Affective disorders

Therapies used with depressed adults have been adapted for younger age groups, and these include cognitive–behavioural and interpersonal therapy. There is some evidence for the effectiveness of cognitive–behavioural therapy, whereas outcome research for psychodynamic therapies developed specifically for children is less extensive. There have been few studies of the effectiveness of family therapy with depressed children.

Cognitive therapy

Cognitive therapy for depression effective with adults has been adapted for children and adolescents (Stark *et al*, 1991). The rationale is that depression in children, as with adults, has the same mechanisms (see chapter 2 for full account), being associated with a maladaptive attributional style (or cognitive schema) which results in a range of negatively biased cognitive distortions applied to the self, the outside world and the future.

Cognitive therapy aims to identify the habitual and automatic negative thinking patterns, and to help the child generate more adaptive cognitions which can replace maladaptive thinking. Brief focused group format sessions may be effective at least in the short term (Butler *et al*, 1980; Stark *et al*, 1987; Kahn *et al*, 1990). Techniques used include self-monitoring and self-evaluation, and an educative component is usually incorporated, as well as group discussion and between session tasks.

Social skills training

Depressed children have difficulties with interpersonal and coping skills (Stark *et al*, 1991), and these can be addressed through social skills interventions, for example teaching communication and negotiation skills.

For example, Fine *et al* (1991) provided social skills training for groups of depressed adolescents using role play and videotape feedback aiming to improve their interpersonal skills. Target skills included recognising feelings in oneself and others, conversational skills, giving and receiving positive and negative feedback, and negotiation to resolve social conflict. A third of adolescents dropped out. Depression improved after treatment and this was maintained at nine-month follow-up. However, there were no significant changes in measures of cognitive distortions which although not specifically targeted might have been expected to improve with improvement of depression. This points to the complexity of the relationship between cognitive variables and depression. A further question is whether depressed adolescents actually have these social skills deficits, or whether they have acquired them but are not using them.

Combination of cognitive therapy with other approaches

Both a cognitive–behavioural group, and a 'self-modelling' group in which depressed children were encouraged to focus on behaviours incompatible with depression (e.g. smiling, verbalising positive self-attributions) with the help of videotape feedback were effective compared with controls (Kahn *et al*, 1990). Butler *et al* (1980) described an intervention focusing on depressed children's social skills and problem solving using role-play, and found that it was more successful than a purely cognitive approach. It may be that a combination of techniques is the most successful. However, longer follow-up studies are required. These children were recruited from school screening procedures and not from clinic referrals.

Behavioural techniques such as pleasant events scheduling may be included in treatment, on the basis that depressed children do not expose themselves to the positively reinforcing (operant conditioning) effects of pleasurable activity.

A multicomponent treatment was described by Lewinsohn *et al* (1990) who combined a cognitive intervention aiming to control irrational and negative thoughts, a behavioural approach (pleasant events scheduling), social skills training and relaxation training. There was a significant improvement in depression after treatment compared with a waiting list control group, and this was maintained at 6-month follow-up. Interestingly, the addition of a parallel parent group made no difference to self or observer ratings of depression, although parents reported fewer behaviour problems. Reynolds & Coats (1986) also showed improvement with a similar intervention (but without concurrent relaxation training) at 5-week follow-up. It is unclear which are the most important components of therapy, or whether they act synergistically.

Relaxation training

In adults relaxation training seems to increase coping skills and hence a sense of self-mastery (Goldfried & Trier, 1974). As a treatment for depression, the procedure has beneficial effects with children (Kahn *et al*, 1990) and adolescents (Reynolds & Coats, 1986) in the short term.

Interpersonal psychotherapy

Originally developed for depressed adults, with whom it is effective at least in moderate depression, interpersonal psychotherapy has been adapted for use with adolescents (Moreau *et al*, 1991). It is a brief therapy focusing on depression in the context of current interpersonal relationships and social role functioning; psychological conflicts and transference relationships are not stressed. Problem areas of particular concern are grief, interpersonal role disputes, role transitions, and interpersonal deficits (social skills). When adapted for adolescents common developmental issues include separation, relationship to authority, and peer and sexual relationships. Although promising, so far there have been no published studies attesting to its efficacy with adolescents.

Individual psychoanalytic treatment

Psychoanalytic psychotherapy for severely deprived children who have been in care is described by Boston & Szur (1983). One aim was to modify the internalised images of rejecting parental figures. These were clinic referred children, and of interest was that a number of them were not in stable placements, usually a requirement for this form of therapy. Although a preliminary assessment study was encouraging (Lush *et al*, 1991), the methodology was naturalistic and requires further development.

Smyrnios & Kirkby (1993) assessed both brief and time-unlimited individual psychodynamic treatment for children with emotional disorders. They found that only a minimal contact control group produced improvements in target problem and family functioning at 4 years, although this might have reflected the experience of the different therapists. Greater frequency of psychoanalytic treatment (four times a week) may result in improvement in flexibility of adaptation and relationships (Heinicke & Ramsey-Klee, 1986), although it is unlikely to be practical for most children.

Group approaches

Fine *et al* (1989) treated depressed adolescents in a non-focused brief therapeutic group in which mutual support, universality and expression of personal difficulties were encouraged. The therapists were initially educative and directive, fostering interaction and group boundaries, but later becoming more facilitative and reflective. Measures of depression improved and were maintained at 9-month follow-up (Fine *et al*, 1991), similar to the results of a social skills group (see above).

Preschool approaches

Attachment disorder

A treatment approach to anxious attachment in infants and toddlers which has shown some promise, termed infant–parent psychotherapy, is described by Lieberman (1992). Infants who show insecure attachment behaviours such as poverty of exploration, reckless behaviour, or 'idealised' behaviour in which assertive striving for autonomy is absent, are included in therapy sessions with their mothers. The aim is to provide a corrective attachment experience for their mothers, and in particular there is a focus on the process and interpretation of projective identification between mother and child. The therapist maintains a flexible approach with respect to which member of the dyad receives attention, and to the form of communication used. Anxiously attached children of high risk mothers receiving this form of therapy for a year showed increased adaptive behaviours by the end of therapy, similar to those shown by securely attached children, and in contrast to anxiously attached control children. The longer-term outcome of therapy is not yet reported.

Separation anxieties are common in this age group, although do not often become severe or persistent. Barnett (1984) carried out an interesting study of anxious children identified by observation and palmar sweat tests on their first day at preschool. Ratings of anxiety improved significantly after a free play situation, but improvement was not observed in those who were read a story. Anxious children engaged in more fantasy and dramatic play than non-anxious children, suggesting that the play opportunity may have been a successful attempt to cope with anxiety.

Preschool development and behaviour problems

In a large-scale community-based study of three-year-old children and their families, three treatment regimes, health visiting, mother and toddler groups, and family therapy, were compared with a control group (Nicol *et al*, 1983). The randomised trial consisted of 59 or more subjects per group. Children were followed up at 1 and 3 years. At 1-year follow-up, mother and toddler groups were beneficial to toddlers with clinically significant disorder but not to those with mild disorder. Some of the more significant individual problems also showed benefit, for example eating problems showed consistent improvement with health visiting. The mother and toddler groups were carried out by collaborative work between social workers who ran the mothers groups, and health visitors who carried out the play groups.

Not all the results of this study were beneficial; for example mother and toddler groups were also associated with increased maternal irritability, and family therapy was associated with a worrying retardation in development.

There are a number of other small-scale studies using behavioural approaches for sleep problems (e.g. Adams & Rickert, 1989) and for oppositional behaviour, but the most substantial is the cognitive problem-solving training approach of Spivack *et al* (1976). The technique here is essentially to teach the children verbal mediators of impulsive behaviour and build these into the children's response repertoire. A number of studies have shown that this treatment approach is effective, although others have failed to do so.

School-based approaches

Play therapy is a commonly used form of treatment particularly for younger children. An assessment of its effectiveness was included in a school-based study in Newcastle (Kolvin *et al*, 1981). Small play therapy groups for children aged 7 and 8 were run on principles based on the work of Axline (1947): the therapists aimed to develop a warm relationship with the child, to be alert to and accepting of the child's expression of feelings, and to respect the child's attempts to solve his or her own problems. The therapists were non-directive and provided toys to promote interactions and social role experimentation. For children with neurotic disorders, play therapy resulted in significant improvement at 18 months and three years after the baseline assessments, compared with a control group. Other evidence for the effectiveness of play therapy for children with socially withdrawn behaviour in school is provided by Furman *et al* (1979), who also noted that it was more helpful in the presence of a younger child.

Rogerian principles were adapted in group therapy with an older age group (11 to 12) with neurotic and conduct problems in the Newcastle study. This 'group discussion' was also non-directive and focused on 'here and now' interactions. Children with both types of problems improved. The fact that these treatments were provided in groups may have been a particularly important factor, although interestingly the therapist's assessment of cohesiveness and openness of discussion did not correlate with outcome, as might have been expected from a reading of Yalom's curative factors in groups (Yalom, 1975). Children's own perceptions of what is helpful may however include factors of cohesiveness, fostering hope but also guidance and feedback (Chase, 1991). Children of this age carry out many of their activities in groups and this mode of treatment may be particularly acceptable (Dwivedi, 1993).

Behaviour modification was also shown to be effective for 10–11-year-old children. Teachers were encouraged to make use of elements of a functional analysis of behaviour, and provide social reinforcement in the classroom.

The Newcastle study as a whole suggested that the children continued to improve for at least 18 months after the ending of treatment, compared with controls; structural changes in the children's personality may have occurred, or alternatively more subtle changes in behaviour and social functioning during treatment may have been amplified by positive feedback through relations with others. The therapist qualities of extroversion, treatment assertiveness and openness correlated with better outcome, whereas empathy, warmth and genuineness did not; this rather surprising result may reflect the need for more assertiveness in a school setting.

Anxiety disorders in middle childhood and adolescence

Phobias

Desensitisation consisting of graduated exposure to the feared stimulus until the anxiety response is extinguished, is effective in children (Ollendick, 1986). It can be carried out in fantasy, in reality, or in combination (Miller *et al*, 1972). Modelling of the feared situation with vicarious learning is also productive with children (Ollendick, 1986), and can be carried out in groups. A cognitive component in which children are taught coping strategies (for example reassuring self-statements) can be used in addition to behavioural practice (Graziano & Mooney, 1980). Relaxation training can also help children cope with anxiety, especially during exposure sessions. The involvement of parents in supervising the treatment at home is particularly important.

Obsessive–compulsive disorder

Treatments for obsessive–compulsive disorder are reviewed by Wolff & Wolff (1991). Behavioural therapy used with adults is often applied to adolescents and children and is probably the treatment of choice (Rapoport *et al*, 1993). The rationale is that the two age groups have similar symptoms, and that many adults have their disorder begin in adolescence. Exposure to the feared stimulus followed by response prevention may be helpful if the cooperation of the child and family can be enlisted: for example washing rituals following fears of contamination would be approached by agreeing a contract with the child in which they would be encouraged to 'contaminate' themselves (e.g. by touching a tap) and then refrain from washing for as long as the urge to do so is present; this may need to be for several hours. The aim is to encourage habituation to the anxiety. Thought stopping (distraction techniques) may be more useful for obsessional symptoms.

The secretive nature of these symptoms warrants assessments from both the child and other family members.

Bereavement

Children and adolescents, even quite young children, show a variety of emotional and behavioural reactions after the death of a parent, and in some cases these may be prolonged (Arthur & Kemme, 1964; Raphael, 1982; Van Eerdewegh *et al*, 1982, 1985). What is less clear is when spontaneous resolution is unlikely and intervention is required. Black & Urbanowicz (1985) describe a family-based bereavement intervention with 22 families compared with a control group, and showed that the intervention was associated with fewer behavioural and emotional problems in the children at 1-year follow-up: there was a better outcome where the child was able to cry and talk about the dead parent after bereavement. In the rare special case of the child witnessing a parental murder by the other parent Black *et al* (1992) recommend crisis intervention and bereavement counselling as soon as possible to minimise the development of post traumatic stress disorder, although comparative studies of different treatments have not been carried out.

Children of parental separation and divorce

Children of parents who separate may show short-term adjustment difficulties including emotional and behavioural problems, and for some these continue long-term (Wallerstein & Kelly, 1980; Wallerstein, 1987; Hetherington & Clingempeel, 1992; Garmezy & Masten (1994). Where a specific childhood disorder arises, this will need specific treatment. Grych & Fincham (1992) have reviewed the work on interventions for children of divorce: many are prevention studies. It is important to specify the age of the child at parental separation, and the age at which the intervention is provided: longer term problems may only arise at particular developmental stages, and long-term follow-up has not always been carried out.

Children whose parents have separated may improve on ratings of adjustment and anxiety after group treatment compared with controls, in the short term (Pedro-Carroll & Cowen, 1985; Stolberg & Garrison, 1985; Alpert-Gillis *et al*, 1989). The children in these studies were aged 7 to 12, having experienced a parental separation a very variable length of time previously. Interventions have included problem-solving approaches, cognitive–behavioural methods to enhance social role-taking and communication skills, and discussion of feelings including self-blame and anger. Children's attitudes and beliefs about the divorce can change positively if these are specifically targeted (Roseby &

Deutsch, 1985), although this was not associated with improved symptom ratings.

Eating disorders

These are covered in detail in chapter 9. However, it is worth noting that family therapy is more helpful than individual supportive therapy for adolescents under the age of 18 whose illness has lasted less than 3 years (Russell *et al*, 1987). The form of family therapy was derived from structural and Milan systemic interventions, but included a greater focus on the eating behaviours. A later study from the same group (Legrange *et al*, 1992) found that family counselling consisting of separate supportive sessions for the patient and counselling for the parents produced similar symptom relief as formal family therapy in 12- to 17-year-old patients; the family therapy-treated parents expressed more critical comments at follow-up, although it is not clear if this was a treatment effect.

Therapy with younger children with anorexia and other related eating disorders is described by Lask & Bryant-Waugh (1993): a multidisciplinary approach is advocated involving attention to physical, social and psychological factors, using a range of therapies including family, individual, group and art, drama and play therapies. The effectiveness of therapy with this younger age group has been little assessed.

Conduct disorders

The range of behaviours incorporated in the term 'conduct disorders' is wide, and Kazdin (1987) recommends that treatment should be focused on specific problem areas. Often there are associated academic problems, interpersonal difficulties, and major family difficulties, and these areas will need addressing in addition. Many of the therapeutic techniques which have been assessed are based on social learning theory and incorporate cognitive and behavioural approaches (described in Kendall, 1991), while some studies have shown the effectiveness of family therapy. In younger children intervention studies have been targeted mostly at parents, while as children become older, the therapies increasingly include the children and adolescents directly. Many are provided in a group format. Older adolescents with conduct disorders may be identified in terms of their offending, and interventions applied within the penal system need special consideration.

Early and middle childhood – parent management training and family approaches

Parent management training (PMT) aims to teach parents how to observe and define problem behaviours shown by their children, and then to provide contingent reinforcement of prosocial behaviours (such as sharing, or cooperative play), and avoid reinforcing 'coercive' behaviours (Patterson, 1982). The parents have an opportunity to observe and practice positive reinforcement (smiling and praise) as well as time-out techniques in preference to unsuccessful forms of punishment, in the session. Children in these families were thought to have learned to respond to aversive experiences including punishment with aggression, often modelling themselves on their parents. Observed changes in parental behaviour consist of reduced reinforcement of child aversive behaviour rather than positive reinforcement of child prosocial behaviours, although both were addressed. Evidence for the effectiveness of PMT is reviewed by Patterson & Fleischman (1979). Children with aggressive behaviours seem to respond better than those with non-aggressive behaviours such as stealing and lying. The improvements generalised to other siblings who had also shown coercive behaviours (Arnold *et al*, 1975). PMT was less successful with some high risk families suffering adverse life events such as unemployment, parental separation, and poverty, and in some cases intensive intervention involving over 100 hours of therapy were required.

Parent training has also been provided for groups of parents with some interventions including the use of videotape modelling (showing vignettes of modelled parenting skills); indeed, viewing videotapes alone produced improvements in child behaviour up to 1 year (Webster-Stratton *et al*, 1989), although only a combined intervention including therapist-led discussion led to stable changes by 3 years (Webster-Stratton, 1990). However, teachers were less likely to report improved behaviour, and child behaviour problems persisted more commonly with parents who were single or suffering from depression (Webster-Stratton & Hammond, 1990).

Single parents of conduct disordered children who improve with PMT are more likely to report greater social support; however, recruitment of an ally nominated by the parent did not result in improved outcome (Dadds & McHugh, 1992). Marital discord is predictive of poorer outcome, and providing adjunctive partner support training to decrease coercion and increase mutually supportive behaviours improved child conduct problems in this group (Dadds *et al*, 1987).

Family therapy, in which the family system rather than the individual child is a focus for change, may be a useful approach although firm conclusions from research are not available. Simpson (1990) assessed the effectiveness of a team approach derived from Milan systemic therapy with families of primary school children who had a range of disorders, most commonly conduct or mixed disorders. The therapists explored the belief systems of family members about the meaning of their relationships and behaviours, using techniques of circular questioning within a neutral stance (Palazzoli *et al*, 1980, elaborated by Cecchin, 1987). The therapy resulted in similar improvements in child symptoms after treatment and at 6-month follow-up compared to standard child psychiatry treatment (mostly non-family therapy), but there were more beneficial changes in family relationships. Families receiving Milan therapy required fewer sessions, and missed fewer appointments. Whether this was a more efficient result is unclear as more therapists were involved in each family therapy session, than were in standard treatment sessions.

Early and middle childhood – individual and group work

Parent management training may not be suitable for children where the parent does not wish to take part. Other approaches involve direct intervention with the children themselves. One approach has evolved from the view that children with conduct problems have deficits and biases in social cognitive skills (Lochman *et al*, 1991). For example angry and aggressive children may have cognitive deficiencies and distortions in the way that they perceive neutral events, attributing hostile intent to others, especially in ambiguous situations (Dodge & Frame, 1982; Feindler, 1991). These children may generate fewer alternative responses to aggression, may decide on their responses to social cues more quickly (Dodge & Newman, 1981), and be less likely to take the perspective of the other person. The aim of therapy is to modify dysfunctional thought processes, and teach a step-wise problem-solving approach using self-instructions: the therapist is active, modelling and reinforcing more appropriate cognitive processes.

Most studies have been carried out in a group format. Lochman *et al* (1984) found improvements in aggressive and disruptive behaviours for aggressive children treated with an anger coping programme, although teacher ratings were more resistant to change than those of observers or parents. Dubow *et al* (1987) found improvements in teacher ratings of aggressive and prosocial behaviour following a cognitive–behavioural intervention, but this was not maintained at 6-month follow-up, in contrast to a play group.

Kolko *et al* (1990) identified interpersonal social skills deficits among mainly conduct disordered child in-patients; a social-cognitive skills training group which included instruction and role-play resulted in greater improvements in the targeted skills compared to a social activity group. Improvements were maintained 1 year later; however, the effects on the children's conduct problems were not reported. In another study (Kazdin *et al*, 1987) child in-patients with conduct disorders were individually taught to generate alternative solutions, to think through the consequences of actions, and to take the perspectives of others. This was more effective in reducing aggressive behaviours and increasing prosocial behaviours, than an individual non-directive treatment (relationship therapy) in which the therapist provided empathy, warmth and unconditional positive regard.

Behaviour modification was used effectively in a community centre where children with antisocial behaviour aged 8 to 17 engaged in broad-based activities with non-referred children (the St Louis experiment described in Kazdin, 1987). Mixed groups of problem and non-referred children run by experienced leaders were the most successful.

Adolescents

Studies with adolescents with conduct disorder have commonly identified them via their delinquent behaviour. The adolescents may be referred from court or may be residents of penal institutions. We will not be reviewing residential and penal therapeutic treatments here. Treatment of young offenders with delinquent behaviour has been reviewed by Hollin (1993).

Functional family therapy (FFT), an intervention derived from systems theory has been used with adolescents referred from the courts. Systems theory views a child's problem behaviour as one component within the wider network of interactions within the family. Based on this idea strategic therapy (Watzlawick *et al*, 1974; Weakland *et al*, 1974) aims to identify the repetitive patterns of behaviour with which the families organise themselves around the child's difficulty: the family's attempted solution becomes the problem. The problem may also be seen to serve a function for the family (Haley, 1976). In FFT the therapist observes these interactions and patterns of communications, and brings this to the notice of the family, and encourages negotiation and contingency contracting. FFT resulted in improvements in family functioning and a lower rate of re-offending in both the index adolescent and their siblings (Klein *et al*, 1977) suggesting that changes in the system had indeed occurred. The ability of the therapist to establish a warm relationship with the family and structure sessions with self-confidence was associated with a better outcome (Alexander *et al*, 1976), perhaps not surprisingly.

Hyperkinetic disorder

Baer & Nietzel (1991) conducted a meta-analysis of 36 controlled outcome studies of cognitive–behavioural therapy for impulsivity. The children in these studies were aged mainly between 4 and 14; treatment techniques included modification of self-statements, reinforcement strategies, and problem-solving approaches in a variety of combinations. Overall, the interventions showed improvement in impulsivity in the treated children, compared with the control children. The impulsivity of treated children fell to below the mean of non-impulsive children, while that of the control children remained above the mean. There were no differences when age, sex, diagnosis, length of treatment, or group *vs* individual treatment were considered. Parents reported the least change, and the interventions did not lead to improvements in other problem behaviours.

Parent management training was assessed with 23 pre-schoolers with attention deficit disorder with hyperactivity (Pisterman *et al*, 1989). Parent groups were instructed in strategies of attending to appropriate behaviour, giving clear and appropriate commands, and use of time-out. The treatment group also received supervised practice in the clinic with the assistance of videotape feedback. Three months after treatment, there was improved parent–child interaction, compliance, and hyperactivity scores, but no generalisation to other behaviours. Bloomquist *et al* (1991) however showed few improvements with a multicomponent school-based cognitive–behavioural intervention.

Meta-analyses

The technique of meta-analysis has provided information regarding factors which influence therapy effectiveness. Meta-analysis involves pooling results from a large number of studies of psychotherapy, and undertaking a mathematical analysis with respect to factors of interest. The results of a meta-analysis are only as good as the original studies. Casey & Berman (1985) calculated that the average treated child was more improved than 71% of those untreated (effect size); however, treatment and subject variables which influence effect size were of more interest. Boys improved less than girls. Treatment of social adjustment problems was less successful than treatment of other problems (hyperactivity, phobias, somatic problems). Behavioural treatments seemed to be more effective than non-behavioural treatments, although this was mainly due to the specificity of behavioural outcome measures. There were no differences between group, individual or play therapy, nor whether child or parents were seen for treatment. Parents and observers noted greater improvements than teachers or the children themselves. Studies of family therapy were excluded. On the important question of what works for what problem the results were inconclusive. Broadly similar results were found by Weisz *et al* (1987). Therapists with less training were more effective with younger children than with adolescents, consistent with the view that adolescents' problems are more resistant to change.

To date controlled studies of family therapy for childhood disorders are restricted to a few problem areas (reviewed by Gurman *et al*, 1986), although it is a commonly used modality. Meta-analytic studies of family therapy have indicated rather variable effect sizes (Hazelrigg *et al*, 1987; Markus *et al*, 1990) based on small numbers of studies.

Conclusion

In this chapter we have concentrated on the wealth of ideas and approaches that have been applied to child disorders. It can be seen that these have been developed in abundance. In general, however, the quality of research designs that have been used to describe interventions and evaluate outcomes have not been so impressive and have lagged behind advances in adult research. There is a need for greater investment in this important area of work with children and young people.

References

ACHENBACH, T. M. (1986) The developmental study of psychopathology: Implications for psychotherapy and behavior change. In *Handbook of Psychotherapy and Behavior Change* (eds S. L. Garfield & A. E. Bergin), pp. 117–154. New York: Wiley.

ADAMS, L. S. & RICKERT, V. I. (1989) Reducing bedtime tantrums: Comparison between positive routines and graduated extinction. *Pediatrics*, **84**, 756–761.

ALEXANDER, J. F., BARTON, C., SCHIAVO, R. S., *et al* (1976) Systems behavioral intervention with families of delinquents: Therapist characteristics, family behavior, and outcome. *Journal of Consulting and Clinical Psychology*, **44**, 656–664.

ALPERT-GILLIS, L. J., PEDRO-CARROLL, J. L. & COWEN, E. L. (1989) The children of divorce intervention program: Development, implementation, and evaluation of a program for young urban children. *Journal of Consulting and Clinical Psychology*, **57**, 583–589.

ARNOLD, J. E., LEVINE, A. G. & PATTERSON, G. R. (1975) Changes in sibling behavior following family intervention. *Journal of Consulting and Clinical Psychology*, **43**, 683–688.

ARTHUR, B. & KEMME, M. L. (1964) Bereavement in childhood. *Journal of Child Psychology and Psychiatry*, **5**, 37–49.

AXLINE, V. M. (1947) *Play Therapy*. New York: Ballantine Books.

BAER, R. A. & NIETZEL, M. T. (1991) Cognitive and behavioral treatment of impulsivity in children: A meta-analytic review of the outcome literature. *Journal of Clinical Child Psychology*, **20**, 400–412.

BARNETT, L. A. (1984) Research note: Young children's resolution of distress through play. *Journal of Child Psychology and Psychiatry*, **25**, 477–483.

BLACK, D. & URBANOWICZ, M. A. (1985) Bereaved children: Family intervention. In *Recent Research in Developmental Psychopathology* (ed. J. E. Stevenson), pp. 179–187. Oxford: Pergamon Press.

———, HARRIS-HENDRICKS, J. & KAPLAN, T. (1992) Father kills mother: Post-traumatic stress disorder in the children. *Psychotherapy and Psychosomatics*, **57**, 152–157.

BLOOMQUIST, M. L., AUGUST, G. J. & OSTRANDER, R. (1991) Effects of a school-based cognitive–behavioral intervention for ADHD children. *Journal of Abnormal Child Psychology*, **19**, 591–605.

BOSTON, M. & SZUR, R. (1983) *Psychotherapy with Severely Deprived Children*. London: Routledge & Kegan Paul.

BRASWELL, L., KOEHLER, C. & KENDALL, P. C. (1985) Attributions and outcomes in child psychotherapy. *Journal of Social and Clinical Psychology*, **3**, 458–465.

BUTLER, L., MIEZITIS, S., FRIEDMAN, R., *et al* (1980) The effect of two school-based intervention programs on depressive symptoms in preadolescents. *American Educational Research Journal*, **17**, 111–119.

CAPLAN, G. (1970) *The Theory and Practice of Mental Health Consultations*. London: Tavistock.

CASEY, R. J. & BERMAN, J. S. (1985) The outcome of psychotherapy with children. *Psychological Bulletin*, **98**, 388–400.

CECCHIN, G. (1987) Hypothesizing, circularity and neutrality revisited: An invitation to curiosity. *Family Process*, **26**, 405–413.

CHASE, J. L. Inpatient adolescent and latency-age children's perspectives on the curative factors in group psychotherapy. *Group*, **15**, 95–108.

DADDS, M. R., SCHWARTZ, S. & SANDERS, M. R. (1987) Marital discord and treatment outcome in behavioural treatment of child behaviour problems. *Journal of Consulting and Clinical Psychology*, **55**, 396–403.

——— & MCHUGH, T. A. (1992) Social support and treatment outcome in behavioral family therapy for child conduct problems. *Journal of Consulting and Clinical Psychology*, **60**, 252–259.

DODGE, K. A. & NEWMAN, J. P. (1981) Biased decision-making processes in aggressive boys. *Journal of Abnormal Psychology*, **90**, 375–379.

——— & FRAME, C. L. (1982) Social cognitive biases and deficits in aggressive boys. *Child Development*, **53**, 620–635.

DUBOW, E. F., HUESMANN, L. R. & ERON, L. D. (1987) Mitigating aggression and promoting prosocial behaviour in aggressive elementary schoolboys. *Behavior Research and Therapy*, **25**, 527–531.

DWIVEDI, K. N. (1993) *Group Work with Children and Adolescents: A Handbook*. London: Jessica Kingsley.

FEINDLER, E. L. (1991) Cognitive strategies in anger control interventions for children and adolescents. In *Child and Adolescent Therapy: Cognitive Behavioral Procedures* (ed. P. C. Kendall), pp. 66–97. New York: Guilford Press.

FINE, S., GILBERT, M., SCHMIDT, L., *et al* (1989) Short-term group therapy with depressed adolescent outpatients. *Canadian Journal of Psychiatry*, **34**, 97–102.

———(1991) Group therapy for adolescent depressive disorder: A comparison of social skills and therapeutic support. *Journal of the American Academy of Child and Adolescent Psychiatry*, **30**, 79–85.

FURMAN, W., RAHE, D. F. & HARTUP, W. W. (1979) Rehabilitation of socially withdrawn preschool children through mixed-age and same-age socialization. *Child Development*, **50**, 915–922.

GARMEZY, N. & MASTEN, A. S. (1994) Chronic adversities. In *Child and Adolescent Psychiatry: Modern Approaches*, 3rd edn (eds M. Rutter, E. Taylor & L. Hersov), pp. 191–208. Oxford: Blackwell Scientific.

GOLDFRIED, M. R. & TRIER, C. S. (1974) Effectiveness of relaxation as an active coping skill. *Journal of Abnormal Psychology*, **83**, 348–355.

GRAZIANO, A. M. & MOONEY, K. C. (1980) Family self-control instruction for children's nighttime fear reduction. *Journal of Consulting and Clinical Psychology*, **48**, 206–213.

GRYCH, J. H. & FINCHAM, F. D. (1992) Interventions for children of divorce: Toward greater integration of research and action. *Psychological Bulletin*, **111**, 434–454.

GURMAN, A. S., KNISKERN, D. P. & PINSOF, W. M. (1986) Research on the process and outcome of marital and family therapy. In *Handbook of Psychotherapy and Behavior Change*, 3rd edn (eds S. L. Garfield & A. E. Bergin), pp. 565–624. New York: Wiley.

HALEY, J. (1976) *Problem-Solving Therapy*. New York: Harper and Row.

HAZELRIGG, M. D., COOPER, H. M. & BORDUIN, C. M. (1987) Evaluating the treatment effectiveness of family therapies: An integrative review and analysis. *Psychological Bulletin*, **101**, 428–442.

HEINICKE, C. M. & RAMSEY-KLEE, D. M. (1986) Outcome of child psychotherapy as a function of frequency of the session. *Journal of the American Academy of Child and Adolescent Psychiatry*, **25**, 247–253.

HETHERINGTON, E. M. & CLINGEMPEEL, W. G. (1992) Coping with marital transitions. *Monographs of the Society for Research in Child Development*, **57**, No.s 2–3.

HOLLIN, C. R. (1993) Advances in the psychological treatment of delinquent behaviour. *Criminal Behaviour and Mental Health*, **3**, 142–157.

KAHN, J. S., KEHLE, T. J., JENSEN, W. R., *et al* (1990) Comparison of cognitive behavioral, relaxation, and self-modeling interventions for depression among middle school students. *School Psychology Review*, **19**, 196–211.

KAZDIN, A. E. (1987) Treatment of antisocial behavior in children: Current status and future directions. *Psychological Bulletin*, **102**, 187–203.

———, ESVELDT-DAWSON, K., FRENCH, N. H., *et al* (1987) Problem-solving skills training and relationship therapy in the treatment of antisocial child behavior. *Journal of Consulting and Clinical Psychology*, **55**, 76–85.

KENDALL, P. C. (1991) *Child and Adolescent Therapy: Cognitive–Behavioral Procedures*. New York: Guilford Press.

KLEIN, N. C., ALEXANDER, J. F. & PARSONS, B. V. (1977) Impact of family systems intervention on recidivism and sibling delinquency: A model of primary prevention and program evaluation. *Journal of Consulting and Clinical Psychology*, **45**, 469–474.

KOLKO, D. J., LOAR, L. L. & STURNICK, D. (1990) Inpatient social-cognitive skills training groups with conduct disordered and attention deficit disordered children. *Journal of Child Psychology and Psychiatry and Allied Disciplines*, **31**, 737–748.

KOLVIN, I., GARSIDE, R. F., NICOL, A. R., *et al* (1981) *Help Starts Here. The Maladjusted Child in the Ordinary School*. London: Tavistock.

LASK, B. & BRYANT-WAUGH, R. (1993) *Childhood Onset Anorexia Nervosa and Related Eating Disorders*. Hove: Lawrence Erlbaum.

LEGRANGE, D., EISLER, I., DARE, I., *et al* (1992) Evaluation of family treatments in adolescent anorexia nervosa: A pilot study. *International Journal of Eating Disorders*, **12**, 347–357.

LEWINSOHN, P. M., CLARKE, G. N., HOPS, H., *et al* (1990) Cognitive–behavioral treatment for depressed adolescents. *Behavior Therapy*, **21**, 385–401.

LIEBERMAN, A. F. (1992) Infant–parent psychotherapy with toddlers. *Developmental Psychotherapy*, **4**, 559–574.

LOCHMAN, J. E., BURCH, P. R., CURRY, J. F., (1984) Treatment and generalization effects of cognitive–behavioural and goal-setting interventions with aggressive boys. *Journal of Consulting and Clinical Psychology*, **52**, 915–916.

———, WHITE, K. J. & WAYLAND, K. K. (1991) Cognitive–behavioral assessment and treatment with aggressive children. In *Child and Adolescent Therapy, Cognitive–Behavioral Procedures* (ed. P. C. Kendall), pp. 25–65. New York: Guilford Press.

LUSH, D., BOSTON, M. & GRAINGER, E. (1991) Evaluation of psychoanalytic psychotherapy with children: Therapists' assessments and predictions. *Psychoanalytic Psychotherapy*, **5**, 191–234.

MARKUS, E., LANGE, A. & PETTIGREW, T. F. (1990) Effectiveness of family therapy: a meta-analysis. *Journal of Family Therapy*, **2**, 205–221.

MILLER, L. C., BARRETT, C. L., HAMPE, E., *et al* (1972) Comparison of reciprocal inhibition, psychotherapy, and waiting list control for phobic children. *Journal of Abnormal Psychology*, **79**, 269–279.

MOREAU, D., MUFSON, L., WEISSMAN, M. M., *et al* (1991) Interpersonal psychotherapy for adolescent depression: Description of modification and preliminary application. *Journal of the American Academy of Child and Adolescent Psychiatry*, **30**, 642–651.

NICOL, A. R., STRETCH, D. & FUNDUDIS, T. (1983) *Preschool Children in Troubled Families. Approaches to Intervention and Support.* Chichester: Wiley.

OLLENDICK, T. H. (1986) Child and adolescent behavior therapy. In *Handbook of Psychotherapy and Behavior Change* (eds S. L. Garfield & A. E. Bergin), pp. 525–563. New York: Wiley.

PALAZZOLI, M., BOSCOLO, L., CECCHIN, G., *et al* (1980) Hypothesizing – Circularity – Neutrality: Three guidelines for the conductor of the session. *Family Process*, **19**, 3–12.

PATTERSON, G. R. (1982) *A Social Learning Approach to Family Intervention. III. Coercive Family Process.* Oregon: Castalia Publishing Company.

—— & FLEISCHMAN, M. J. (1979) Maintenance of treatment effects: some considerations concerning family systems and follow-up data. *Behaviour Therapy*, **10**, 168–185.

PEDRO-CARROLL, J. L. & COWEN, E. L. (1985) The children of divorce intervention program: An investigation of the efficacy of a school based prevention program. *Journal of Consulting and Clinical Psychology*, **53**, 603–611.

PISTERMAN, S., McGRATH, P., FIRESTONE, P., *et al* (1989) Outcome of parent-mediated treatment of preschoolers with attention deficit disorder with hyperactivity. *Journal of Consulting and Clinical Psychology*, **57**, 628–635.

RAPHAEL, B. (1982) The young child and the death of a parent. In *The Place of Attachment in Human Behaviour* (eds C. M. Parkes & J. Stevenson-Hinde), pp. 131–150. New York: Basic Books.

RAPOPORT, J. L., LEONARD, H., SWEDO, S. E., *et al* (1993) Obsessive compulsive disorder in children and adolescents: Issues in management. *Journal of Clinical Psychiatry*, **54**, 27–29.

REYNOLDS, W. M. & COATS, K. I. (1986) A comparison of cognitive-behavioral therapy and relaxation training for the treatment of depression in adolescents. *Journal of Consulting and Clinical Psychology*, **54**, 653–660.

ROSEBY, V. & DEUTSCH, R. (1985) Children of separation and divorce: Effects of a social role-taking group intervention on fourth and fifth graders. *Journal of Clinical Child Psychology*, **14**, 55–60.

RUSSELL, G. F. M., SZMUKLER, G. I., DARE, C., *et al* (1987) An evaluation of family therapy in anorexia nervosa and bulimia nervosa. *Archives of General Psychiatry*, **44**, 1047–1056.

SIMPSON, L. (1990) The comparative efficacy of Milan family therapy for disturbed children and their families. *Journal of Family Therapy*, **13**, 267–284.

SMYRNIOS, K. X. & KIRKBY, R. J. (1993) Brief therapy versus psychodynamic therapy. *Journal of Consulting and Clinical Psychology*, **61**, 1020–1027.

SPIVACK, G., PLATT, J. J. & SHURE, M. B. (1976) *The Problem Solving Approach to Adjustment.* San Francisco: Jossey-Bass.

STARK, K. D., REYNOLDS, W. M. & KASLOW, N. J. (1987) A comparison of the relative efficacy of self-control therapy and a behavioral problem-solving therapy for depression in children. *Journal of Abnormal Child Psychology*, **15**, 91–113.

——, ROUSE, L. W. & LIVINGSTON, R. (1991) Treatment of depression during childhood and adolescence: cognitive–behavioral procedures for the individual and family. In *Childhood and Adolescent Therapy: Cognitive–Behavioral Procedures* (ed. P. C. Kendall), pp. 165–206. New York: Guilford Press.

STOLBERG, A. L. & GARRISON, K. M. (1985) Evaluating a primary prevention program for children of divorce: the Divorce Adjustment Project. *American Journal of Community Psychology*, **13**, 111–124.

TRUAX, C. B. & CARKHUFF, R. R. (1967) *Towards Effective Counselling and Psychotherapy*. Chicago: Aldine.

VAN EERDEWEGH, M. M., BIERI, M. D., PARRILA, R. H., *et al* (1982) The Bereaved Child. *British Journal of Psychiatry*, **140**, 23–29.

——, CLAYTON, P. J. & EERDEWEGH, P. V. (1985) The bereaved child: Variables influencing early psychopathology. *British Journal of Psychiatry*, **147**, 188–194.

WALLERSTEIN, J. S. (1987) Children of divorce: Report of a ten year follow-up of early latency-age children. *American Journal of Orthopsychiatry*, **57**, 199–211.

—— & KELLY, J. B. (1980) *Surviving the Breakup, How Children and Parents Cope with Divorce*. London: Grant McIntyre.

WATZLAWICK, P., WEAKLAND, J. & FISCH, R. (1974) *Change: Principles of Problem Formation and Problem Resolution*. New York: WW Norton and Company.

WEAKLAND, J. H., FISCH, R., WATZLAWICK, P., *et al* (1974) Brief therapy: Focused problem resolution. *Family Process*, **3**, 141–168.

WEBSTER-STRATTON, C. (1990) Long-term follow-up of families with young conduct problem children: From preschool to grade school. *Journal of Clinical Child Psychology*, **19**, 144–149.

——, HOLLINGSWORTH, T. & KOLPACOFF, M. (1989) The long-term effectiveness and clinical significance of three cost-effective training programs for families with conduct-problem children. *Journal of Consulting and Clinical Psychology*, **57**, 550–553.

—— & HAMMOND, M. (1990) Predictors of treatment outcome in parent training for families with conduct problem children. *Behavior Therapy*, **21**, 319–337.

WEISZ, J. R. (1986) Contingency and control beliefs as predictors of psychotherapy outcomes among children and adolescents. *Journal of Consulting and Clinical Psychology*, **54**, 789–795.

——, WEISS, B., ALICKE, M. D., *et al* (1987) Effectiveness of psychotherapy with children and adolescents: A meta-analysis for clinicians. *Journal of Consulting and Clinical Psychology*, **55**, 542–549.

WOLFF, R. P. & WOLFF, L. S. (1991) Assessment and treatment of obsessive–compulsive disorder in children. *Behavior Modification*, **15**, 372–393.

YALOM, I. (1975) *The Theory and Practice of Group Psychotherapy*. 2nd edn. New York: Basic Books.

18 Psychotherapy for bipolar disorder

JAN SCOTT

It is estimated that an adult developing bipolar disorder (BD) in his/ her mid-20s effectively loses 9 years of life, 12 years of normal health and 14 years of work activity. In addition, the suicide-related mortality and the psychosocial consequences for 'significant others' identify BD as a significant public health problem (Prien & Potter, 1990). The firstline treatment for BD remains pharmacotherapy, and the advent of lithium and other drugs have undoubtedly improved the quality of life for many individuals. However, Joyce (1992) noted that, even under optimal research conditions, prophylaxis will protect fewer than 50% of people with BD against further episodes. Given the increasing interest in the use of psychotherapy in treatment-resistant depressive and schizophrenic disorders, it seems surprising that such initiatives have not been applied more systematically to individuals with BD. This paper highlights the reasons why such approaches may have been ignored, emphasises why they should now be used, and identifies potential avenues for future research.

Why have psychological approaches been overlooked?

There appear to be three reasons why clinicians have been reluctant to employ psychosocial interventions: firstly, aetiological models which highlight the strong genetic and biological correlates of BD have dominated the research agenda; secondly, it was long believed that patients with BD made a full inter-episode recovery; and thirdly, psychoanalysts have historically expressed greater ambivalence about the suitability of psychotherapy for people with manic–depressive illness compared with people with other severe disorders. The latter is

This paper was first published in the *British Journal of Psychiatry* (1995), **167**, 581–588.

probably the most important influence. Fromm-Reichmann wrote that in comparison with individuals with schizophrenia, people with bipolar illness were poor candidates for psychotherapy because they lacked introspection, were too dependent and were likely to discover and then play on the therapist's 'Achilles' heel'. Yalom suggested that the inclusion of a bipolar person in a therapy group was "one of the worst calamities" that could occur. Although others argued strongly for the importance of psychological treatments (e.g. Benson, 1975), the relative lack of empirical support for such developments (no large-scale, randomised, control trial has ever been published) meant that clinicians received little encouragement or advice on how to incorporate such approaches into treatment.

The discouraging views on psychotherapy with people with bipolar illness were mainly published in the pre-lithium era. As such, reticence about trying to cure acute mania with a talking therapy is easily understood. However, the holistic approach advocated in modern practice encourages the integration of biomedical and psychosocial models of disorder. The treatment of acute mania rightly focuses initially on pharmacotherapy, but when the mental state is stabilised then the devastating impact of the episode on the individual and his/her family clearly needs addressing. Even if the person was functioning well premorbidly, or apparently makes a full inter-episode recovery, he or she will need help in coming to terms with having a chronic and recurrent disorder. Also, Goodwin & Jamison (1990) have argued that as establishing 'control' of biological factors is essential to the effective management of BD, it is vital to understand and overcome psychological barriers to compliance with pharmacotherapy.

Psychosocial issues in BD

There are a number of problems related to BD and compliance where psychosocial therapies could have a role but have so far been underused.

Problems related to the disorder

Premorbid personality and coping skills may predict an individual's reaction to the diagnosis. Other psychosocial problems in BD may relate to actual or anticipated losses, or the nature and severity of the illness and its impact on relationships.

Adjustment problems

A comprehensive review of premorbid personality by Goodwin & Jamison (1990) suggests that individuals with BD are more similar to, than different from, 'normal' controls. Although remitted bipolar people show lower rates of personality disorder (23%) than remitted unipolar people (35%), adjustment after discharge is significantly worse, with 60% of BD cases exhibiting functional impairment (Harrow *et al*, 1990). Persistent affective symptoms account for about half the cases of poor adjustment.

The reasons why others with BD show such deficits are less certain as robust premorbid predictors of adjustment are lacking. What is clear is that calm acceptance of the diagnosis and full adherence with treatment are exceptional. Goodwin & Jamison (1990) state that on discovering that the illness is chronic, recurrent and potentially life-threatening, predictable reactions are denial, anger, ambivalence and anxiety. All these responses can have adverse effects if they become protracted. Joyce (1992) noted that readmission can be predicted by illness behaviour, with those who fail to recognise or respond to evolving symptoms or who are less accepting of drugs having a worse outcome. Resentment and frustration may impair relationships with the family, social network and professionals trying to offer treatment. People with bipolar illness with high levels of anxiety often use inappropriate strategies to try to avoid relapses, such as excessive self-monitoring and extreme restrictions on their lifestyle. The perceived stigma of the diagnosis may also adversely affect self-image and lead to social avoidance.

Kahn (1990) highlights the special problem of 'dual vulnerability' in individuals with early-onset BD. He argues that mood instability or other prodromal symptoms preceding onset of the disorder may negatively influence interactions with people at home. A vicious cycle develops where the suboptimal environment created then adversely affects the individual's personal development which further damages interpersonal interactions even before the first illness episode occurs. Goodwin & Jamison (1990) also argue that early-onset BD may arrest or interrupt the completion of 'developmental tasks' that normally lead to independence and leaving home.

Loss

Individuals with BD may experience significant distress or relapse if concrete or abstract losses are not acknowledged and addressed. Financial and employment problems are cited by 70% of people and their partners as the most frequent long-term difficulties (Targum *et al*,

1981). In the first year after a manic episode, Harrow *et al* (1990) reported that 23% of people with BD were continuously unemployed, and 36% showed a clear decline from their premorbid level of functioning at work. Loss of self-esteem may result from the loss of status. Relationships may be lost because of irrevocable damage done by aberrant behaviour during a manic episode. These losses are often accompanied by feelings of guilt. Overall, the apparent lack of control over life undermines any belief in self-efficacy and may lead to demoralisation, particularly if recurrences occur when the person is complying with medication (Kahn, 1990).

As well as real current losses, anticipated losses may also lead the person to give up hope for the future. Detection of hopelessness is important as it is a key variable in determining whether suicidal ideas are acted upon. Inquiring about the meaning of the illness often reveals that people now view themselves as defective (Rush, 1988; Goodwin & Jamison, 1990) and express anxieties about the potential loss of actual or hoped for relationships, or ambivalence about the advisability of having children. Younger people become more hopeless as they gradually realise that they may never achieve career or other goals, or attain autonomy.

Goodwin & Jamison (1990) also highlight losses related to treatment, but stipulate that realistic losses must be distinguished from unrealistic losses (where the disorder or the treatment are inappropriately blamed for all past and current difficulties). Realistic losses may include reduced energy, productivity and sexual activity. The loss of creativity associated with 'highs' has negative consequences for some individuals.

Interpersonal relationships

Unlike the extensive literature on unipolar depressive disorders, there are less data on the effect of BD on marital and family relationships, or the effects of these relationships on the prognosis of the disorder. Frank *et al* (1981) found that marital adjustment in couples where one spouse suffered from BD was similar to that in matched control couples where both spouses were mentally healthy. Other studies report less favourable outcomes, with significantly higher divorce and separation rates and expressed conflict in the marriages of bipolar people compared with unipolar people and community controls. Brodie & Leff (1971) reported that divorce in bipolar people (which occurred in 57% of their sample) was always instigated after the first manic episode.

Bipolar people are also reported to have fewer confiding relationships than control subjects. Targum *et al* (1981) noted that 53% of healthy spouses said that they would not have married their bipolar partner, and 47% said that they would not have had children had they known the disorder would occur. People tended to underestimate the impact of the disorder on their relationships. Overall, healthy spouses regard the problems associated with the disorder as more severe and the effects of treatment as more beneficial than their bipolar partners.

Bipolar individuals and their healthy spouses agree that depression is easier to cope with and accept than mania as the spouse tends to be sympathetic and perceive the disorder as beyond the patient's control (Targum *et al*, 1981). The threat of violence and poor judgement, particularly with respect to interpersonal interactions and financial extravagance, tend to dominate concerns about mania. Healthy spouses often regard the behaviour of someone with hypomania as deliberate and spiteful. Interestingly, Hooley *et al* (1987) demonstrated that marital adjustment in spouses of patients who suffer more florid manic episodes is actually better than in spouses of patients with less severe symptoms. This may be because these extreme types of behaviour are more readily accepted as uncontrollable (Goodwin & Jamison, 1990).

The literature on the parenting skills of bipolar patients is sparse. Suggestions that parent–child bonding may be disrupted by lack of consistent care, or that mothers with BD are less attentive to their children's needs, come from small, mainly descriptive studies and it is difficult to extrapolate to other samples.

The influence of interpersonal relationships on BD outcome must also be considered. In a study of 23 bipolar patients, Miklowitz *et al* (1988) found that intrafamilial levels of expressed emotion (EE) and affective style (AS) predict the likelihood of relapse over 9 months' follow-up. Social adjustment after discharge was also predicted by AS profile. The most striking finding in this study was a relapse rate of 94% if *either* EE level was high *or* AS profile was negative *regardless* of treatment regime, medication compliance, baseline symptoms, illness history or demography. If the AS profile was benign and EE level low, the relapse rate was only 17%. High relapse rates and symptom exacerbation despite adequate lithium prophylaxis have also been noted in bipolar patients reporting stress related to marital disharmony or experiencing other interpersonal events.

Problems relating to adherence

Data on medication adherence in bipolar cases relate mainly to lithium. Information on carbamazepine and other drugs is generally lacking, although non-adherence rates for carbamazepine (38%) tend to be lower than rates for lithium treatment (51%) (Goodwin & Jamison, 1990). Up to 75% of relapses in bipolar disorder may be associated with non-adherence.

Prevalence and patterns of non-adherence

Reported non-adherence rates for lithium prophylaxis vary between 20–50%, with about one in five patients failing to comply despite a good therapeutic outcome. Goodwin & Jamison (1990) make a plea for more research, commenting that, unlike non-response (which has been extensively examined), non-adherence should be reversible through good clinical management and a therapeutic relationship which facilitates the discussion of adherence problems.

Adherence is rarely all or nothing. Full adherence and total non-adherence are the most overt types of behaviour, but intermittent and late patterns are reported. The prevalence of intermittent adherence is high: 47% of people with BD discontinue lithium against medical advice on at least one occasion and 34% discontinue on two or more occasions. Some individuals describe a cyclical pattern of strict adherence immediately after an illness episode, followed by reducing adherence, leading to non-adherence if they remain symptom free. This behaviour pattern is reinforced by the fact that side-effects disappear early, often leading to the patient feeling better, while the reappearance of symptoms is delayed and not always associated with non-adherence in the patient's mind (Rush, 1988).

Late adherence (where early drug refusal is later replaced by adherence) is of interest as it highlights the critical need to identify and tackle denial. It appears that some individuals initially reject both the diagnosis and the medication. With time, evidence of disorder and the negative consequences of untreated episodes lead to the development of insight and gradual acceptance of the rationale for medication (Goodwin & Jamison, 1990).

Risk factors for non-adherence

Several studies identify that lithium adherence rates are increased in those with a stable social network, those who perceive the symptoms as severe and treatment as effective, and those with obsessional personality traits (Goodwin & Jamison, 1990). The most common factors associated with lithium non-adherence are younger age, male gender, experience of fewer illness episodes and previous history of treatment non-adherence. Non-adherence rates are particularly high during the first year of lithium treatment and in those who have persistent elevated mood, a history of grandiosity or who complain of missing 'highs'. The latter is noteworthy as patient surveys suggest that fear of depression is a stronger motivating factor for adherence than fear of mania.

Drug side-effects undoubtedly account for a significant proportion of cases of non-adherence, although psychiatrists may rate side-effects as a more important cause of non-adherence than patients (Jamison & Akiskal, 1983). Clinicians and sufferers also differ in their views of which side-effects are most problematic and which lead to non-adherence (Jamison *et al*, 1979). It is reported that 75% of side-effects regarded by psychiatrists as most important are somatic symptoms, while 80% of side-effects regarded by people with BD as most worrying are cognitive changes such as mental confusion and memory problems (Jamison & Akiskal, 1983). One explanation for this disparity is that clinicians and patients disagree about whether a particular feature is a side-effect or a symptom. However, a review of patient reports of somatic side-effects found that although certain complications (such as excessive thirst) occur more frequently, the side-effects they found least acceptable and most likely to lead to non-adherence were weight gain and tremor (Goodwin & Jamison, 1990). These findings clearly have implications for how doctors and patients communicate about treatment.

Only a small literature exists on individual attitudes towards lithium treatment (Cochran & Gitlin, 1988; Rush, 1988; Peet & Harvey, 1991). Recurring themes are a greater risk of non-adherence in individuals who dislike having their moods 'controlled' by medication and see the disorder and the need to receive long-term pharmacotherapy as a personal weakness. They often express the view that if they simply tried harder then relapses would not occur.

In a study of 48 out-patients, Cochran & Gitlin (1988) demonstrated that both individual attitudes and social influences (namely what significant others expect an individual to do) modify lithium adherence. Aetiological theories and treatment advice of relatives who suffer from mental disorder strongly influence patient beliefs, and the quality of the doctor–patient relationship also significantly affects adherence. If the patient perceived the psychiatrist as ambivalent about the treatment or the patient was not motivated to do as expected, he/she was less likely to adhere. A control trial of 60 lithium clinic attenders also demonstrated that those offered an educational programme showed improved knowledge and more favourable attitudes towards pharmacotherapy and better medication adherence than those receiving standard treatments alone (Peet & Harvey, 1991).

Outcome studies

There are a number of descriptive articles on the use of psychosocial interventions in BD, but few publications address outcome, and empirical treatment studies are rare. The available research is reviewed; none was undertaken in Britain.

Individual therapy

Anecdotal reports of the benefits of individual therapy for people with bipolar illness can be found in the psychoanalytic and cognitive–behavioural literature. The largest case series was published by Benson (1975) who described a 41-month, open, follow-up study. Twenty-four out of 31 people (21 women) who received psychotherapy in addition to lithium maintenance treatment were reported to have a good clinical outcome.

Cochran's (1984) study of the impact of six sessions of individual cognitive therapy on lithium adherence and clinical outcome in bipolar out-patients is the only one to include a control group. Twenty-eight people with BD who were newly referred to a lithium clinic were randomly assigned to cognitive therapy or 'treatment as usual'. On subjective and observer ratings (including serum lithium levels), adherence was significantly better at six-week and six-month follow-up in the intervention group. Only three subjects assigned to cognitive therapy (21%) as opposed to eight (57%) control subjects discontinued lithium against medical advice, and admission rates were significantly lower in the cognitive therapy group.

Couples and group therapy

Davenport and colleagues (1977) described the use of psychodynamic 'couples group therapy' (*n*=12) and retrospectively contrasted this approach with lithium clinic attendance (*n*=11) and community mental health centre (CMHC) follow-up (*n*=42). Individuals were not randomly allocated to the different treatments, but all those included in the study had been admitted for mania 2–10 years previously and had an intact marriage at the time of discharge. At follow-up, the 'couples group therapy' people were functioning significantly better in terms of social and family adjustment and reported no readmissions or marital failures. The CMHC group had the worst outcome (16 readmissions; 10 marital failures; three suicides), but the differences between these patients and lithium clinic attenders were non-significant. Treatment method was the only predictor of outcome identified.

No controlled trials of group therapy (combined with lithium treatment) exist, but four open studies have been published. Shakir *et al* (1979) and later Volkmar *et al* (1981) reported on a therapy group for 15 lithium-responsive, bipolar people (13 men) which ran for a number of years. Shakir and colleagues identified significant 'before and after' changes in people's functioning in the two years before and two years after the introduction of group therapy. Before therapy, 10 people had a history of poor adherence and admissions, the group spent an average of 16 weeks a year in hospital, and only five individuals were in regular employment. After about 51 weeks' attendance at a 'Yalom-style' group, only three individuals were admitted over the next two years, the average length of in-patient stay was three weeks per year, serum lithium levels and adherence rates were improved and 10 people were in continuous employment. Volkmar and colleagues wrote that the shared experience of BD and lithium treatment enhanced the therapy process, but highlighted that it was not possible to distinguish the specific effects of psychotherapy from the non-specific benefits of close follow-up.

Kripke & Robinson (1985) describe a long-term out-patient support group for 14 bipolar people (13 men), eight of whom were still attending the group 12 years later. Anecdotal evaluation suggested that problem-solving strategies were better received than dynamic analysis. Perceived benefits were reduced rates of admission and enhanced social and economic functioning.

Finally, Wulsin *et al* (1988) described a long-term group run monthly at a CMHC for 22 bipolar out-patients (12 women) over four years. Unlike the other studies, the group focused on interpersonal relationships, and the prescribing of lithium was done solely outside this setting. Reductions in admission were reported, but the drop-out rate was 55%.

Family therapy

Fitzgerald (1972) noted his clinical impressions of the benefits of family therapy for a consecutive series of 25 bipolar patients. Others describe general benefits from this approach, but more systematic data are provided by Glick and colleagues (1994). In a cross-national study of 24 in-patients with severe affective illnesses, people who received individual and family psychoeducation showed better resolution of the index episode and better global outcome 12–18 months after discharge.

A further large-scale, randomised, controlled trial using an in-patient family intervention (IFI) has been undertaken by the above research group (Spencer *et al*, 1988; Clarkin *et al*, 1990). This study looked at outcome 18 months after discharge in 169 in-patients who received six sessions of IFI during their hospital stay. The results for the 50 cases of affective disorders were reported separately (Clarkin *et al*, 1990). The data on 21 bipolar subjects (14 women) within this group represent the only randomised control study of psychological treatments undertaken in BD. Twelve subjects were allocated to IFI and nine to the control intervention (the usual in-patient treatment programme). Drop-out rates and treatment after discharge did not differ significantly between the two groups. The immediate and long-term outcome data demonstrated that, in comparison to all other groups, female bipolar IFI patients showed significantly better social, family, leisure, work and role performance and significantly improved family attitudes to treatment. Although the gains made by female bipolar IFI subjects diminished with time, the results held even when other variables were controlled for. Female bipolar subjects benefited significantly from IFI, whereas male bipolar subjects and unipolar subjects showed either no benefit or, in some cases, a negative effect.

Prien & Potter (1990) point out that there are two populations of bipolar people to be considered when providing family therapy: older bipolar people with a spouse (and children); and young adults with early-onset BD who live with their nuclear family. The latter group may benefit from an adaptation of behavioural family therapy (BFT) previously advocated in schizophrenia by Falloon. A pilot study of eight people treated with lithium and BFT suggested that the approach was well received by sufferers and their families (Miklowitz *et al*, 1988) and, over 9 months, relapse rates in this group (13%) were significantly lower than those in a similar group of 23 people who received lithium alone (70%).

Comment

Most of the studies reviewed are unsophisticated or inadequate in a number of ways: only a small number of recognised research tools or defined outcome measures were used, and only two studies (Cochran, 1984; Clarkin *et al*, 1990) randomly allocated people to either a psychosocial or control treatment. These are the most comprehensive studies available, also employing more clearly defined treatment methods (CT and IFI). However, the relatively small sample sizes render the statistical power low and make definitive statements about outcome unwise.

Some tentative conclusions can be drawn from the researchers' observations. Individual therapy clearly improved knowledge about BD and its treatment and allowed sufferers to explore beliefs about these issues in detail. Group process benefited from the homogeneous nature of the sample and, provided that individuals were engaged in the therapy, admissions did not unduly disrupt the proceedings. Sharing knowledge about the disorder helped those who denied or underestimated problems to gain insight and awareness into their difficulties. Couples group therapy was helpful in educating spouses about the disorder, allowed exploration of patients' own attitudes and reduced stress. Similar benefits accrued from family therapy in both female in-patients (IFI) and younger out-patients (BFT). Older men may do well in individual or group formats. Possible explanations are that the families of male bipolar patients may be more critical than the families of female patients, or that men with BD are hypersensitive to interpersonal stimuli and find family therapy more stressful (Clarkin *et al*, 1990).

Conclusions

For many decades, the dominant research agenda in bipolar disorder has been biological. The impact of drugs on acute symptoms and relapse rates has been emphasised so strongly that the role of other therapies has been ignored. However, there are limits to the efficacy of pharmacotherapy and, although treatment adherence is a recognised issue, little is known of the psychological barriers to adherence (Rush, 1988). The paucity of psychosocial research in BD has many parallels with the situation regarding schizophrenia about 20 years ago. Work on schizophrenia has since demonstrated an interaction between biological vulnerability and psychosocial dimensions, and the need for adjunctive psychotherapies is now accepted. Prien & Potter (1990) note that BD may disrupt the person's family environment, reduce ability to cope with stress, impair social adjustment and lead to deficits similar to the negative symptoms of defect states. Life events and intrafamilial stress have also been implicated in early relapses. On the basis of these data, there are implications for clinical practice and future research.

Clinical implications

Many clinicians employ psychosocial strategies in the management of BD. While flexibility of style and techniques is often required to cope with fluctuating moods and other psychopathology, there is some consistency in the descriptions of beneficial approaches (Rush, 1988; Goodwin & Jamison, 1990), and most clinicians reiterate the findings of the National Institute of Mental Health collaborative study on depression that systematic clinical management in combination with pharmacotherapy is a simple and effective strategy. Organising an agenda for follow-up appointments ensures coverage of all topics. Assume that adherence will become an issue for all people at some point and create an atmosphere in which ambivalence or obstacles can be anticipated, discussed and simple behavioural techniques introduced (such as 'pairing' tablet-taking with a routine activity) to facilitate adherence.

Given the importance of other people's attitudes, and research evidence that sufferers underestimate the impact of BD, then extending the psycho-educational approach is appropriate. Frank *et al* (1985) reported that after people with BD and their families attended a 1-day educational workshop, there were no reported cases of treatment non-adherence. Handouts and videos can also be used to supplement sessions (Peet & Harvey, 1991). Sufferers and their relatives may also engage in simple diary-keeping to identify early warning symptoms of relapse, or record response to medication so that decisions regarding changes can be made more objectively. Identifying 'high-risk situations' for relapse and developing a hierarchy of coping responses (including how to access mental health services) are other possible uses of such data.

Some research suggests that the first year after the onset of BD is a crucial time for people in terms of adjusting to the disorder, developing insight and adhering with treatment, systematic clinical management at this stage may be a simple strategy for improving outcome. Lastly, although clear guidelines for adjunctive psychological therapy for BD are not available, the use of cognitive, brief dynamic, interpersonal, couples or family therapy should at least be considered more often.

Research implications

There are a number of obvious areas for future research.

A greater understanding of individual and environmental vulnerability factors that influence onset or outcome of BD episodes is required. In unipolar depression there is evidence that cognitive dysfunction and problem-solving deficits influence the course of the disorder. No similar literature exists for BD. If certain dysfunctional attitudes were associated with persistence of symptoms, then it might be possible to develop non-drug strategies to modify these beliefs. The work on AS and EE also needs to be extended to larger subject samples. If the evidence confirms that drugs do not protect the individual against the adverse effects of high EE, it clearly has implications for the use of adjunctive family therapy techniques. Lastly, while many life events are unavoidable, their occurrence signals a period of increased risk of relapse in people with BD and offers an opportunity for integrated biopsychosocial research.

The problems of medication adherence need to be examined. Only 1–2% of the papers written on lithium explore this, and even less is known about adherence to other drugs. Frank *et al* (1985) suggest that researchers have a duty to identify and account for cases of non-adherence in treatment studies so that we can improve our understanding. More work on attitudes towards BD and its treatment should be undertaken. Family attitude studies were mainly undertaken in the USA some time ago and therefore need to be repeated.

Randomised control trials are required to establish the short- and long-term benefits of psychotherapy over the usual treatment regime. Evidence of which approaches will be most effective is lacking, so different psychotherapies need to be compared. It will be important to distinguish specific and non-specific benefits (Lam, 1991). Short-term structured, 'manualised' therapies adapted for use with BD, such as cognitive therapy, IFI, BFT and interpersonal therapy, should be investigated initially. Follow-up in these studies must extend beyond the acute phase to assess any longer term benefits and, as drop-out rates are likely to be high, recruitment will have to be active and extensive to ensure that the sample is sufficiently large to reliably assess outcome.

Bloch *et al* (1994) suggest that psychosocial factors contribute about 25–30% to the prognostic variance in BD. Psychosocial variables that affect adherence with medication will also share a small proportion of the variance attributed to biological factors. Given that psychosocial aspects make a significant contribution to outcome, the opportunity for empirical research and the introduction of systematic clinical interventions should not be ignored. The evidence in this review suggests that BD sufferers and their carers would both welcome and benefit from such initiatives.

References

BENSON, R. (1975) The forgotten treatment modality in bipolar illness: psychotherapy. *Diseases of the Nervous System*, **36**, 634–638.

BLOCH, S., HAFNER, J., HARARI, E., *et al* (1994) *The Family in Clinical Psychiatry*, pp. 92–108. Oxford: Oxford Medical.

BRODIE, H. & LEFF, M. (1971) Bipolar depression – a comparative study of patient characteristics. *American Journal of Psychiatry*, **127**, 1086–1090.

CLARKIN, J., GLICK, G., HAAS, G., *et al* (1990) A randomized clinical trial of in-patient family intervention. V: results for affective disorder. *Journal of Affective Disorders*, **18**, 17–28.

COCHRAN, S. (1984) Preventing medical non-compliance in the out-patient treatment of bipolar affective disorder. *Journal of Consulting and Clinical Psychology*, **52**, 873–878.

—— & GITLIN, M. (1988) Attitudinal correlates of lithium compliance in bipolar affective disorders. *Journal of Nervous and Mental Diseases*, **176**, 457–464.

DAVENPORT, Y., EBERT, M., ADLAND, M., *et al* (1977) Couples therapy as an adjunct to lithium maintenance of the manic patient. *Journal of Orthopsychiatry*, **47**, 495–502.

FITZGERALD, R. (1972) Mania as the message: treatment with family therapy and lithium carbonate. *American Journal of Psychotherapy*, **26**, 535–547.

FRANK, E., PRIEN, R., KUPFER, D., *et al* (1985) Implications of non-compliance on research in affective disorders. *Psychopharmacology Bulletin*, **21**, 37–42.

——, TARGUM, S., GERSHON, E., *et al* (1981) A comparison of non-patient with bipolar-well spouse couples. *American Journal of Psychiatry*, **138**, 764–768.

GLICK, I., BURTI, L., OKONOGI, K., *et al* (1994) Effectiveness in psychiatric care. III: psychoeducation and outcome for patients with major affective disorder and their families. *British Journal of Psychiatry*, **164**, 104–106.

GOODWIN, F. & JAMISON, K. (1990) Psychotherapy. In *Manic–Depressive Illness* (eds F. Goodwin & K. Jamison), pp. 725–745. Oxford: Oxford University Press.

HARROW, M., GOLDBERG, J., GROSSMAN, L., *et al* (1990) Outcome in manic disorders. *Archives of General Psychiatry*, **47**, 665–671.

HOOLEY, J., RICHTERS, J., WEINTRAUB, S., *et al* (1987) Psychopathology and marital distress: the positive side of positive symptoms. *Journal of Abnormal Psychology*, **96**, 27–33.

JAMISON, K. & AKISKAL, H. (1983) Medication compliance in patients with bipolar disorders. *Psychiatric Clinics of North America*, **6**, 175–192.

——, GERNER, R. & GOODWIN, F. (1979) Patient and physician attitudes towards lithium: relationship to compliance. *Archives of General Psychiatry*, **36**, 866–869.

JOYCE, P. (1992) Prediction of treatment response. In *Handbook of Affective Disorders* (ed. E. S. Paykel), pp. 453–464. London: Churchill Livingstone.

KAHN, D. (1990) The psychotherapy of mania. *Psychiatric Clinics of North America*, **13**, 229–240.

KRIPKE, D. & ROBINSON, D. (1985) Ten years with a lithium group. *McLean Hospital Journal*, **10**, 1–11.

LAM, D. (1991) Psychosocial family interventions in schizophrenia: a review of empirical studies. *Psychological Medicine*, **21**, 423–441.

MIKLOWITZ, D., GOLDSTEIN, M., NUECHTERLEIN, K., *et al* (1988) Family factors and the course of bipolar affective disorder. *Archives of General Psychiatry*, **45**, 225–231.

PEET, M. & HARVEY, N. (1991) Lithium maintenance: 1. A standard education programme for patients. *British Journal of Psychiatry*, **158**, 197–200.

PRIEN, R. & POTTER, W. (1990) NIMH workshop report on treatment of bipolar disorder. *Psychopharmacology Bulletin*, **26**, 409–427.

RUSH, A. (1988) Cognitive approaches to adherence. In *Review of Psychiatry* (vol. 8) (eds A. Frances & R. Hales), pp. 627–642. Washington, DC: American Psychiatric Association.

SHAKIR, S., VOLKMAN, F., BACON, S., *et al* (1979) Group psychotherapy as an adjunct to lithium maintenance. *American Journal of Psychiatry*, **136**, 455–456.

SPENCER, J., GLICK, I., HAAS, G., *et al* (1988) A randomized control trial of in-patient family intervention. III: effects at 6-month and 18-month follow-ups. *American Journal of Psychiatry*, **145**, 1115–1121.

TARGUM, S., DIBBLE, E., DAVENPORT, Y., *et al* (1981) The family attitude questionnaire. Patients' and spouses' views of bipolar illness. *Archives of General Psychiatry*, **38**, 562–568.

VOLKMAR, F., SHAKIR, S., BACON, S., *et al* (1981) Group therapy in the management of manic–depressive illness. *American Journal of Psychotherapy*, **42**, 263–267.

WULSIN, L., BACHOP, M. & HOFFMAN, D. (1988) Group therapy in manic–depressive illness. *American Journal of Psychotherapy*, **42**, 263–271.

Index

Compiled by LINDA ENGLISH